T0183688

Practical Hadoop Ecosystem

A Definitive Guide to Hadoop-Related
Frameworks and Tools

Deepak Vohra

Apress®

Practical Hadoop Ecosystem: A Definitive Guide to Hadoop-Related Frameworks and Tools

Deepak Vohra

ISBN-13 (pbk): 978-1-4842-2198-3   ISBN-13 (electronic): 978-1-4842-2199-0
DOI 10.1007/978-1-4842-2199-0

Library of Congress Control Number: 2016954636

Cover image designed by Freepik

Managing Director: Welmoed Spahr
Lead Editor: Steve Anglin
Technical Reviewers: John Yeary and Simon Bisson
Editorial Board: Steve Anglin, Pramila Balan, Laura Berendson, Aaron Black, Louise Corrigan, Jonathan Gennick, Robert Hutchinson, Celestin Suresh John, Nikhil Karkal, James Markham, Susan McDermott, Matthew Moodie, Natalie Pao, Gwenan Spearing
Coordinating Editor: Mark Powers
Copy Editor: Kezia Endsley
Compositor: SPi Global
Indexer: SPi Global
Artist: SPi Global

Distributed to the book trade worldwide by Springer Science+Business Media New York, 233 Spring Street, 6th Floor, New York, NY 10013. Phone 1-800-SPRINGER, fax (201) 348-4505, e-mail orders-ny@springer-sbm.com, or visit www.springeronline.com. Apress Media, LLC is a California LLC and the sole member (owner) is Springer Science + Business Media Finance Inc (SSBM Finance Inc). SSBM Finance Inc is a **Delaware** corporation.

For information on translations, please e-mail rights@apress.com, or visit www.apress.com.

Apress and friends of ED books may be purchased in bulk for academic, corporate, or promotional use. eBook versions and licenses are also available for most titles. For more information, reference our Special Bulk Sales–eBook Licensing web page at www.apress.com/bulk-sales.

Any source code or other supplementary materials referenced by the author in this text are available to readers at www.apress.com. For detailed information about how to locate your book's source code, go to www.apress.com/source-code/. Readers can also access source code at SpringerLink in the Supplementary Material section for each chapter.

Printed on acid-free paper

Contents at a Glance

Contents

About the Author

Deepak Vohra is a consultant and a principal member of the NuBean.
com software company. Vohra is a Sun-certified Java programmer and
web component developer. He has worked in the fields of XML, Java
programming, and Java EE for over seven years. Vohra is the coauthor
of *Pro XML Development with Java Technology* (Apress, 2006). He is also
the author of the *JDBC 4.0* and *Oracle JDeveloper for J2EE Development,
Processing XML Documents with Oracle JDeveloper 11g, EJB 3.0 Database
Persistence with Oracle Fusion Middleware 11g,* and *Java EE Development
in Eclipse IDE* (Packt Publishing). He also served as the technical reviewer
on *WebLogic: The Definitive Guide (O'Reilly Media, 2004)* and *Ruby
Programming for the Absolute Beginner* (Cengage Learning PTR, 2007).

About the Technical Reviewer

 **John Yeary** is a Principal Software Engineer on Epiphany CRM Marketing at Infor Global Solutions. John has been a Java evangelist and has been working with Java since 1995. Yeary is a technical blogger with a focus on Java Enterprise Edition technology, NetBeans, and GlassFish. He is currently the Founder of the Greenville Java Users Group (GreenJUG). He is as instructor, mentor, and a prolific open source contributor.

John graduated from Maine Maritime Academy with a B.Sc. Marine Engineering with a concentration in mathematics. He is a merchant marine officer and has a number of licenses and certifications. When he is not doing Java and F/OSS projects, he likes to hike, sail, travel, and spend time with his family. Yeary is also the Assistant Scoutmaster in the Boy Scouts of America (BSA) Troop 767, and Outdoor Ethics Master Trainer in the Blue Ridge Council of the BSA.

Organizations and projects:

- Java User Groups Community Leader (`Java.net`)
- Java Enterprise Community Leader (`Java.net`)
- JavaOne Technical Content Reviewer: Java Tools and Emerging Languages (Four Years)
- JavaOne Technical Content Reviewer: Java EE Platform and Frameworks (Three Years)
- JavaOne 2011, 2013 Planning Committee
- Duke's Choice Award Selection Committee (2010-2013)
- JavaOne Speaker (2009-2013)
- JCP Member
- Project Woodstock Committer and Maintainer (`http://java.net/projects/woodstock`)
- Java Boot Camp Project Owner (`http://java.net/projects/certbootcamp`)

Foreword

I want to welcome you to the world of Hadoop. If you are novice or an expert looking to expand your knowledge of the technology, then you have arrived at the right place. This book contains a wealth of knowledge that can help the former become the latter. Even most experts in a technology focus on particular aspects. This book will broaden your horizon and add valuable tools to your toolbox of knowledge.

When Deepak asked me to write the foreword, I was honored and excited. Those of you who know me usually find I have no shortage of words. This case was no exception, but I found myself thinking more about what to say, and about how to keep it simple.

Every few years, technology has a period of uncertainty. It always seems we are on the cusp of the next "great" thing. Most of the time, we find that it is a fad that is soon replaced by the next shiny bauble. There are some moments that have had an impact, and some that leave the community guessing. Let's take a look at a couple of examples to make a point.

Java appeared like manna from the heavens in 1995. Well, that is perhaps a bit dramatic. It did burst on to the scene and made development easier because you didn't need to worry about memory management or networking. It also had this marketing mantra, which was "write once, run anywhere". It turned out to be mostly true. This was the next "great" thing.

Rolling ahead to 1999 and the release of J2EE. Again, we encounter Java doing all the right things. J2EE technologies allowed, in a standard way, enterprises to focus on business value and not worry about the technology stack. Again, this was mostly true.

Next we take a quantum leap to 2006. I attended JavaOne 2005 and 2006 and listened to numerous presentations of where J2EE technology was going. I met a really passionate developer named Rod Johnson who was talking about Spring. Some of you may have heard of it. I also listened as Sun pushed Java EE 5, which was the next big change in the technology stack. I was also sold on a new component-based web UI framework called Woodstock, which was based on JavaServer Faces. I was in a unique position; I was in charge of making decisions for a variety of business systems at my employer at the time. I had to make a series of choices. On the one hand I could use Spring, or on the other, Java EE 5. I chose Java EE 5 because of the relationships I had developed at Sun, and because I wanted something based on a "standard". Woodstock, which I thought was the next "great" thing, turned out to be flash in the pan. Sun abandoned Woodstock, and well... I guess on occasion I maintain it along with some former Sun and Oracle employees. Spring, like Java EE 5, turned out to be a "great" thing.

Next was the collapse of Sun and its being acquired by the dark side. This doomsday scenario seemed to be on everyone's mind in 2009. The darkness consumed them in 2010. What would happen to Java? It turned out everyone's initial assessment was incorrect. Oracle courted the Java community initially, spent time and treasure to fix a number of issues in the Java SE stack, and worked on Java EE as well. It was a phenomenal wedding, and the first fruits of the union were fantastic—Java SE 7 and Java EE 7 were "great". They allowed a number of the best ideas to become reality. Java SE 8, the third child, was developed in conjunction with the Java community. The lambda, you would have thought, was a religious movement.

While the Java drama was unfolding, a really bright fellow named Doug Cutting came along in 2006 and created an Apache project called Hadoop. The funny name was the result of his son's toy elephant. Today it literally is the elephant in the room. This project was based on the Google File System and Map Reduce. The baby elephant began to grow. Soon other projects with cute animal names like Pig, or more even more apt, Zookeeper, came along. The little elephant that could soon was "the next great thing".

Suddenly, Hadoop was the talk of the Java community. In 2012, I handed the Cloudera team a Duke's Choice Award for Java technology at JavaOne. Later that year, version 1.0 was released. It was the culmination of hard work for all the folks who invested sweat and tears to make the foundation of what we have today.

As I sit here wondering about Java EE 8 and its apparent collapse, I am reminded that there is still innovation going on around me. The elephant in the room is there to remind me of that.

Some of you may be wondering what Hadoop can do for you. Let's imagine something fun and how we might use Hadoop to get some answers. Where I live in South Carolina, we have something called a Beer BBQ 5K. It is a 5K run that includes beer and BBQ at the end, along with music. Some folks will just do the beer and BBQ. That is fine, but in my case I need to do the run before. So we have data coming in on the registration; we have demographic data like age and gender. We have geographic data: where they call home. We have timing data from the timing chips. We have beer and BBQ data based on wristband scans. We have multiple races in a year.

Hmm... what can we do with that data? One item that comes to mind is marketing, or planning. How many women in which age groups attended and what beer did they drink? How many men? Did the level of physical activity have any effect on the consumption of BBQ and beer? Geographically, where did attendees come from? How diverse were the populations? Do changing locations and times of the year have different effects? How does this compare with the last three years? We have incomplete data for the first year, and the data formats have changed over time. We have become more sophisticated as the race and the available data have grown. Can we combine data from the race with publicly accessible information like runner tracking software data? How do we link the data from a provider site with our data?

Guess what? Hadoop can answer these questions and more. Each year, the quantity of data grows for simple things like a Beer BBQ 5K. It also grows in volumes as we become more connected online. Is there a correlation between Twitter data and disease outbreak and vector tracking? The answer is yes, using Hadoop. Can we track the relationship between terrorists, terrorist acts, and social media? Yes, using.... well, you get the point.

If you have read this far, I don't think I need to convince you that you are on the right path. I want to welcome you to our community, and if you are already a member, I ask you to consider contributing if you can. Remember "a rising tide raises all boats," and you can be a part of the sea change tide.

The best way to learn any technology is to roll up your sleeves and put your fingers to work. So stop reading my foreword and get coding!

—John Yeary
NetBeans Dream Team
Founder Greenville Java Users Group
Java Users Groups Community Leader
Java Enterprise Community Leader

PART I

Fundamentals

CHAPTER 1

■ ■ ■

Introduction

Apache Hadoop is the de facto framework for processing and storing large quantities of data, what is often referred to as "big data". The Apache Hadoop ecosystem consists of dozens of projects providing functionality ranging from storing, querying, indexing, transferring, streaming, and messaging, to list a few. This book discusses some of the more salient projects in the Hadoop ecosystem.

Chapter 1 introduces the two core components of Hadoop—HDFS and MapReduce. Hadoop Distributed Filesystem (HDFS) is a distributed, portable filesystem designed to provide high-throughput streaming data access to applications that process large datasets. HDFS's main benefits are that it is fault-tolerant and designed to be run on commodity hardware. Hadoop MapReduce is a distributed, fault-tolerant framework designed for processing large quantities of data stored in HDFS, in parallel on large clusters using commodity hardware.

Chapter 2 introduces Apache Hive, which is a data warehouse for managing large datasets stored in HDFS. Hive provides a HiveQL language, which is similar to SQL but does not follow the SQL-92 standard fully, for querying the data managed by Hive. While Hive can be used to load new data, it also supports projecting structure onto data already stored. The data could be stored in one of the several supported formats, such as Avro, ORC, RCFile, Parquet, and SequenceFile. The default is TextFile.

Chapter 3 introduces the Hadoop database called Apache HBase. HBase is a distributed, scalable NoSQL data store providing real-time access to big data; NoSQL implies that HBase is not based on the relational data model. HBase stores data in HDFS, thus providing a table abstraction for external clients. An HBase table is unlike a relational database table in that it does not follow a fixed schema. Another difference of RDBMS is the scale of data stored; an HBase table could consist of millions of rows and columns. As with the other Hadoop ecosystem projects, HBase can run on clusters of commodity software.

Chapter 4 introduces Apache Sqoop, a tool for bulk transfer of data between relational databases such as Oracle database and MySQL database and HDFS. Sqoop also supports bulk transfer of data from RDBMS to Hive and HBase.

Chapter 5 introduces Apache Flume, a distributed, fault-tolerant framework for collecting, aggregating, and streaming large datasets, which are typically log data, but could be from other data sources such as relational databases.

Chapter 6 discusses Apache Avro, a schema based data serialization system providing varied data structures. Avro provides a compact, fast, binary data format typically used to store persistent data.

Chapter 7 discusses another data format called Apache Parquet. Parquet is a columnar data storage format providing complex data structures and efficient compression and encoding on columnar data to any Hadoop ecosystem project.

Chapter 8 introduces Apache Kafka, a distributed publish-subscribe messaging system that is fast, scalable, and durable. As with the other Hadoop ecosystem projects, Kafka is designed to process large quantities of data and provide high throughput rates.

Chapter 9 discusses another distributed, scalable, and fault-tolerant framework called Apache Solr. Solr provides indexing and data integration for large datasets stored in HDFS, Hive, HBase, or relational databases. Solr is Lucene-based and one of the most commonly used search engines.

© Deepak Vohra 2016
D. Vohra, *Practical Hadoop Ecosystem*, DOI 10.1007/978-1-4842-2199-0_1

Chapter 10 introduces Apache Mahout, a framework for machine learning applications. Mahout supports several machine-learning systems, such as classification, clustering, and recommender systems.

The different Apache Hadoop ecosystem projects are correlated, as shown in Figure 1-1. MapReduce processes data stored in HDFS. HBase and Hive store data in HDFS by default. Sqoop could be used to bulk transfer data from a relational database management system (RDBMS) to HDFS, Hive, and HBase. Sqoop also supports bulk transfer of data from HDFS to a relational database. Flume, which is based on sources and sinks, supports several kinds of sources and sinks with the emphasis being on streaming data in real time in contrast to one-time bulk transferring with Sqoop. Flume is typically used to stream log data and the sink could be HDFS, Hive, HBase, or Solr, to list a few. Solr could be used to index data from HDFS, Hive, HBase, and RDBMS. HDFS stores data in a disk filesystem and is in fact an abstract filesystem on top of the disk filesystem. Solr also stores data in a disk filesystem by default, but can also store the indexed data in HDFS.

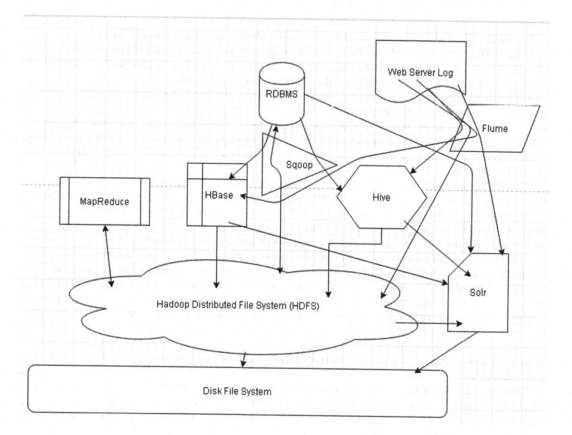

Figure 1-1. *The Apache Hadoop ecosystem*

Next, we introduce some of the concepts used by Apache Hadoop's core components HDFS and MapReduce, and discuss why Hadoop is essential for web-scale data processing and storage.

Core Components of Apache Hadoop

Hadoop has two main components: the Hadoop Distributed Filesystem (HDFS) and MapReduce. The HDFS is a data storage and data processing filesystem. HDFS is designed to store and provide parallel, streaming access to large quantities of data (up to 100s of TB). HDFS storage is spread across a cluster of nodes; a single large file could be stored across multiple nodes in the cluster. A file is broken into blocks, which is an abstraction over the underlying filesystem, with default size of 64MB. HDFS is designed to store large files and lots of them.

MapReduce is a distributed data processing framework for processing large quantities of data, distributed across a cluster of nodes, in parallel. MapReduce processes input data as key/value pairs. MapReduce is designed to process medium-to-large files. MapReduce has two phases: the map phase and the reduce phase. The map phase uses one or more mappers to process the input data and the reduce phase uses zero or more reducers to process the data output during the map phase. The input files is converted to key/value pairs before being input to the map phase. During the map phase, input data consisting of key/value pairs is mapped to output key/value pairs using a user-defined map() function. The map output data is partitioned and sorted for input to the reduce phase. The map output data is partitioned such that values associated with the same key are partitioned to the same partition and sent to the same reducer. During the reduce phase, the data output from the map phase is processed to reduce the number of values associated with a key, or using some other user-defined function. The Google implementation of the MapReduce programming model is discussed at http://static.googleusercontent.com/media/research.google.com/en//archive/mapreduce-osdi04.pdf.

Why Apache Hadoop?

Large-scale computation models have been necessitated by the increasing scale of datasets being generated and processed. Examples of big data scenarios include large-scale market data being generated for marketable products, consumer preferences data, market trends data, social media data, and search engine data.

Shortcomings in Current Computing Systems

Different distributed systems overcome the challenges to large-scale computational models differently, prioritizing some issues more than others, and in the process making trade-offs.

NFS (Network FileSystem) is the most commonly used distributed filesystem. The design of NFS is very constrained; it provides remote access to a single logical volume on a single machine. A client has access to only a portion of the NFS filesystem, which the client can mount on its local filesystem and access as if it were a local filesystem. One of the main advantages of NFS is that the filesystem is transparent to the client. NFS has the following disadvantages:

- The data on NFS is stored on a single machine. If the machine fails, the entire filesystem becomes unavailable.

- All clients access the same remote filesystem, which could overload the NFS.

- Clients must copy the data to the local filesystem before being able to use the data.

When designing a large-scale system, these basic assumptions that apply to traditional systems have to be disregarded:

- Hardware must be reliable.

- Machines have identities with explicit communication between them.

- A dataset can be stored on a single machine.

- All data is structured data.

The scale of data involved in big data scenarios is many orders of magnitude larger than in traditional computational models. Whereas traditional computational models process data in the range of a few MB to 100s of MB, large-scale computational models process data in the range of 100s of GB to 100s of TB and even several PB. At such a large scale, the input data won't fit into a single machine's memory or disk drive. Individual machines have limited resources in terms of CPU processor time, RAM, hard disk space, and network bandwidth. An individual dataset won't fit into a single machine and won't be able to be processed on a single machine. A single disk drive won't be able to store even the temporary output from processing large quantities of data, much less store the input data. With multi-gigabyte datasets being transmitted, network switches will become saturated and the available network bandwidth won't be sufficient for the large datasets. With machines on different racks, the network bandwidth between machines on different racks would be less than the network bandwidth between nodes on the same rack. A large-scale computational model must be able to manage the resources efficiently. Additional resources may be required to implement features designed for a large-scale model. For example, if data is to be replicated for durability, additional disk space becomes a requirement. Synchronizing between multiple machines is an issue unique to large-scale computational models. Efficient network communication protocols have to be used to communicate between the different nodes on a large-scale cluster.

Failure recovery has to be implemented to recover from partial failures. For example, if a machine fails, the processing of a section of dataset fails. The computation has to be restarted on a different machine, thus incurring some computation time loss. The computation capacity, proportional to the number of machines lost, is lost. Failure in some of the components changes the network topology and starting recomputation in the event of a failure may not be trivial. Some of the related computation previously completed successfully but not yet used may also be lost in the event of a machine failure.

Data durability is an issue in a large-scale computational model. If a machine is lost, the data stored on the machine is also lost. If replicas of the lost data are available, the data is recoverable, but if no replicas are available, the data is not durable.

With large datasets, the probability of some sections of datasets getting corrupted increases. Data corruption detection has to be implemented to provide data reliability and data availability. If data corruption is not detected, computation could be erroneous. If data corruption is not addressed, some data may be lost and not available for computation.

Large-scale computation requires that the input data be distributed across multiple machines and processed in parallel on different machines. One of the results of using multiple machines is that the probability of failure increases; the more machines there are in the cluster, the more likely one of those machines will fail. Failures could get cascaded. Machine failure and program recovery is an issue in large-scale models only, as with a single-machine model recovery of the program is not an option; if the machine fails, the program fails.

Failure of some of the components in a large-scale system is inevitable and the failure is also likely to happen more often. Examples of partial failures include failure of network switches and routers, high network traffic, hard drive failure on individual machines, running out of memory and disk space, and data corruption. In a large-scale computational model, the rest of the components are expected to continue to function.

Scalability of a large-scale computation model is another issue. If more and more computational units are added, as in a distributed system, the computational model should scale well.

How Is Hadoop Better than Other Distributed Computing Systems?

A distributed system in the context of data computation is a system in which computation is distributed across a set of machines instead of using a single machine. Why are distributed systems required? If the scale of data has increased, why can't the capacities of individual machines also increase proportionally? New processors with multi-CPU cores (dual-core, quad-core, or more) provide multiple threads to process more data in parallel, but the processor speed diminishes slightly, due to thermal requirements, with an increase in the number of CPU cores per processor. For example, a dual-core processor may have a speed of 3.5GHz, while a quad-core processor has 3.0GHz. Even if a single-machine with thousands of CPU cores is built, it would not be feasible for individual hard drives to read data fast enough to be processed in parallel on the multi-CPU core processors. An individual hard disk drive has a limited read speed in the range of 60-100MB/sec. For example, if a 12-core processor is used on a single machine with multiple I/O channels, data is input to the machine at the rate of 1200MB/sec (assuming an upper range rate). A 10TB dataset would take 2.3 hours to read the data. If 100 similar machines are used, the 10TB is read in 1.38 minutes. This demonstrates the advantage of using multiple machines in a distributed system.

Grid computing is not new. Other distributed grid systems such as MPI, PVM, and Condor have been used in the past. The grid emphasis is to distribute the workload. Data stored in NetApp filer or SAN drives used in conjunction with several compute nodes. Sharing is slow on most of the single-storage based distributed systems. In contrast, Hadoop distributes the data on several nodes instead of storing it in a single file.

Some reliability demands on distributed systems that support large-scale computational models are:

- *Support partial failure.* Must support graceful decline in application performance rather than a full halt.

- *Data recoverability.* If components fail, their workload must be taken up by the functioning machines.

- *Individual recoverability.* A full restart should not be required. If a node fails, it should be able to restart and rejoin the cluster.

- *Consistency.* Concurrent operations or partial failures should not cause externally visible nondeterminism.

- *Scalability.* The distributed system should be able to take an increased load without performance degradation or complete failure. A graceful decline in performance is still preferred over complete failure. An increase in the number of machines should provide a proportionate increase in the capacity.

Hadoop is a large-scale distributed processing system designed for a cluster consisting of hundreds or thousands of nodes, each with multi-processor CPU cores. Hadoop is designed to distribute and process large quantities of data across the nodes in the cluster. Hadoop does not require any special hardware and is designed for commodity hardware. Hadoop may be used with any type of data, structured or unstructured. Hadoop is not a database, nor does Hadoop replace traditional database systems. Hadoop is designed to cover the scenario of storing and processing large-scale data, which most traditional systems do not support or do not support efficiently. Hadoop can join and aggregate data from many different sources and deliver results to other enterprise systems for further analysis.

Hadoop is designed to process web-scale data in the order of hundreds of GB to 100s of TB, even to several PB. Hadoop provides a distributed filesystem that breaks up the input data and distributes the data across several nodes in a cluster. Hadoop processes the distributed data in parallel using all the machines (nodes) in the cluster. Data is processed on the same node as the data is stored if feasible, as a result providing data locality. Not having to move large amounts of data for computation reduces the network bandwidth usage. Hadoop is designed for commodity hardware in which component failure is expected rather than an exception, and Hadoop provides automatic detection and recovery of failure and other design implementations such as replicating data across the cluster for durability. If one machine fails, a data replica on another machine can be used.

Considering the differences in the network bandwidth between nodes on the same rack and nodes on different racks, Hadoop uses a rack-aware placement policy when creating a new file, reading from a file, or processing input data.

To make data durable, Hadoop replicates stored data. If a machine fails and the data on the machine is lost, a replica of the data is used, and the data is re-replicated to its replication level. Making redundant copies of data adds to the disk space requirements, and as a result only a fraction of disk space is actually being used to store a single copy of the data. For data reliability, Hadoop uses checksum verification on the data stored in its filesystem. If corrupt data is found, it is not used and a replica of the data is used instead. Corrupt data replicas are replaced with non-corrupt data and the corrupt data is removed from the filesystem. A data scanner runs periodically and automatically to scan for corrupt data.

Hadoop provides recovery in the event of computation failure. A failed computation is performed again, sometimes even having to re-compute related computation. If some of the disk drives fail, computation may be able to continue with the other disk drives.

Other distributed systems such as HTCondor (formerly Condor) also provide a high-throughput, parallel computational model. Hadoop is unique in its simplified programming model (MapReduce), which allows quick development and running of distributed applications. Hadoop is also unique in its ability to efficiently and automatically distribute data and computation code across the multiple machines in the cluster, as a result utilizing the parallelism provided by multi-CPU cores effectively. HTCondor does not distribute data automatically and a separate SAN (Storage Area Network) is required for the purpose. While the programming model in Hadoop does not require communication between independent processes running in parallel on a subset of the dataset, in HTCondor communication between multiple commute nodes must be managed with a communication system such as MPI (Message Passing Interface). Individual nodes in Hadoop also communicate with each other, but the communication is implicit in contrast to the more traditional distributed systems in which data has to be marshaled explicitly over sockets or through MPI buffers using application code. In Hadoop, explicit communication between nodes is not permitted. In Hadoop, partitioning of data is implemented using a built-in partitioner and shuffling of data between different phases of data processing is also implemented implicitly without user-defined application code.

Individual machines in Hadoop are more independent of each other than in other distributed systems, which makes failure recovery more favorable, since a failure of a single machine does not affect other machines in the distributed system. Multiple user programs do not need to communicate with each other and failure of a process does not affect other processes running in parallel on other machines (in machine failure) or even the same machine (in process failure).

Hadoop provides a linear scalability as the scale of data stored and processed increases and as additional resources are added. A Hadoop application developed for a 12-machine cluster can be scaled nearly linearly to hundreds and thousands of machines without much modification. The performance of the Hadoop platform does not degrade with an increase in the scale of data or an increase in the number of machines.

Other distributed programming systems, such as HTCondor, MPI, and PVM, may perform better or comparably at a small scale, but do not scale well with an increased dataset load or increased number of machines. For example, MPI performs better than Hadoop with a small number of machines up to 12, but if the number of machines is increased to several tens or hundreds and the data processed is increased, a lot of refactoring such as modifying the application program is required. The performance of other distributed systems such as MPI degrades (or does not increase linearly) at a large scale. Other distributed systems may also have some design limitations at a large scale, which makes their scaling limited.

While MapReduce MRv1 is designed to run only MapReduce applications, YARN (Yet Another Resource Negotiator) or MRv2 supports running other applications besides MapReduce. Motivations for MapReduce are data processing of large datasets (> 1TB), massively parallel (hundreds or thousands of CPUs), and easy to use without having to code communication between nodes. The reduce phase does not start until the map phase has completed, which could put a limit on the job progress rate if a few of the map processes are slow. If some slow map phase processes are slowing down, the whole job the master daemon runs redundant copies of slow moving processes and uses the results from the redundant process that completes first. In MapReduce, data processing is divided into two phases: the map phase and the reduce phase. The only communication between different processes is copying the output from the map phase to the reduce phase. The master daemon assigns tasks based on location of data; the map phase tasks run on the same machine (or the same rack) as the machine with the data. Map task input is divided into input splits, which are sized based on the block size. Individual input splits are processed by separate processes in parallel. Processes are independent of each other. The master daemon detects failure in a process and reruns failed processes. Restarting processes does not require communication with other processes. MapReduce is functional programming with distributed computing. MR factors out reliability concerns from application logic. With MapReduce, a user or developer does not have to implement system level details of synchronization, concurrency, hardware failure, inter-node communication, process failure, and failure recovery.

What Kind of Computations Is Hadoop Suitable For?

Hadoop is suitable for iterative jobs such as graph algorithms. Each iteration must read or write data to disk. I/O and latency cost of an iteration is high.

What Kind of Computations Is Hadoop Not Suitable For?

Hadoop is not suitable for:

- Applications that need shared state or coordination. MapReduce tasks are independent and are shared-nothing. Shared state requires scalable state store.
- Low-latency applications.
- Small datasets.
- Finding individual records.

HDFS Daemons

The HDFS daemons are the NameNode, Secondary NameNode, and DataNode.

NameNode

The NameNode is the master daemon in the HDFS. NameNode's function is to maintain the HDFS namespace metadata, which includes the filenames, directory names, file permissions, directory permissions, file-to-block mapping, block IDs, and block locations in RAM. The metadata is kept in RAM for fast access. NameNode stores the metadata information in a fsimage file in the NameNode's local filesystem. The stored namespace state does not include the block locations. The block locations are kept only in memory and when the NameNode starts, the block locations are constructed from the block lists sent by DataNodes when they join the NameNode and also in periodic reports. NameNode does not directly read or write to the HDFS. When a client requests a file to read, the NameNode provides the client with the block locations of the file and the client reads the file directly. When a client creates a new file, the NameNode provides the client with a list of block locations ordered by distance from the client and the client writes to the blocks directly.

NameNode also keeps an edit log of all the transactions made in the HDFS namespace that would alter the namespace, such as creating a file, deleting a file, and creating block replicas. The edits log is also stored by the NameNode local filesystem as EditLog file. The modifications information in NameNode RAM is flushed to the edit log on the NameNode disk periodically. When the NameNode starts, it starts in Safe mode, during which the edit log is applied to the image file fsimage to create a new fsimage file, which is stored. The NameNode exits the safe mode and starts with an empty edits file. The edit log is also check-pointed periodically by the Secondary NameNode.

In CDH5, the NameNode namespace URI is configured in the configuration property fs.defaultFS in core-default.xml.

```
<property>
 <name>fs.defaultFS</name>
 <value> hdfs://<namenode host>:<namenode port>/</value>
</property>
```

Another important property that must be configured is dfs.permissions.superusergroup in hdfs-site.xml. It sets the UNIX group whose users are to be the superusers for HDFS.

```
<property>
 <name>dfs.permissions.superusergroup</name>
 <value>hadoop</value>
</property>
```

The NameNode stores the namespace metadata fsimage file and the edit log file in directories configured using the dfs.namenode.name.dir property in hdfs-site.xml. At least two directories are recommended to be configured for the NameNode, preferably one on the NFS mount.

```
<property>
 <name>dfs.namenode.name.dir</name>
 <value>/data/1/dfs/nn,/nfsmount/dfs/nn</value>
</property>
```

The dfs.namenode.http-address on the NameNode specifies the HTTP address for the NameNode web UI to listen on.

```
<property>
  <name>dfs.http.address</name>
  <value>0.0.0.0:50070</value>
</property>
```

If HDFS high availability is not used, the NameNode is a single point of failure (SPOF) in the HDFS. The failure of the NameNode causes the HDFS become unavailable until the NameNode is restored. If HDFS high availability is not used, a Secondary NameNode is typically used.

Secondary NameNode

Since all the file modifications that alter the HDFS namespace are kept in the edits log, which is check-pointed by the NameNode only once at startup, the edits file could get very large during the operation of NameNode and take up extra disk space. Another disadvantage of a large edits log file is that when the NameNode starts and checkpoints the edits log to the fsimage file, the check-pointing could take a long time, resulting in delay in the NameNode starting in functional mode.

The Secondary NameNode's function is to make periodic checkpoints of the edits log to the fsimage file while the NameNode is running. When an edits log file has been check-pointed, it is cleared and as result occupies less disk space on the NameNode. With periodic check-pointing of the edits log, the edits log does not grow in size as much. When NameNode starts, it does not take as much time to checkpoint the edits log to the fsimage image, as the edits log is relatively smaller. As a result, the NameNode startup is faster.

The Secondary NameNode makes a new checkpoint using an interval configured in the hdfs-default. xml property dfs.namenode.checkpoint.period, which has a default setting of 3600 secs (1 hour). Another checkpoint setting that overrides dfs.namenode.checkpoint.period is dfs.namenode.checkpoint.txns, which specifies the number of transactions (the default value is 1,000,000 transactions) after which a checkpoint must be made regardless of whether the dfs.namenode.checkpoint.period interval has been exceeded or not. Secondary NameNode polls the NameNode periodically to find the number of uncheck-pointed transactions, as configured in dfs.namenode.checkpoint.check.period; the default is every 60 seconds. When a checkpoint is to be made, Secondary NameNode downloads the fsimage file and the edits log from the NameNode and stores the temporary copies of the two in two sets of directories configured by the dfs.namenode.checkpoint.dir property and the dfs.namenode.checkpoint.edits.dir property respectively in hdfs-default.xml.

The default value of both of these configuration properties is file://${hadoop.tmp.dir}/dfs/ namesecondary. The number of copies of the fsimage file and the edits log the Secondary NameNode keeps is configured in the dfs.namenode.num.checkpoints.retained property; the default is two copies. The maximum network bandwidth for image transfer between the NameNode and the Secondary NameNode may be limited using the dfs.image.transfer.bandwidthPerSec property in hdfs-default.xml. A value of 0 (the default) implies that throttling is disabled. The image transfer bandwidth is limited so that the NameNode can carry out its normal operation. The image transfer may be timed out using the dfs.image. transfer.timeout property with a default value of 600000ms (10 minutes). Secondary NameNode applies the checkpoint and uploads the fsimage file back to the NameNode, as shown in Figure 1-2.

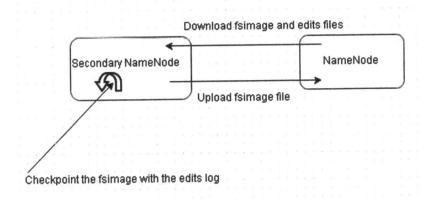

Figure 1-2. *Check-pointing by secondary NameNode*

As mentioned, a NameNode applies a checkpoint of the edits log to the fsimage file on NameNode startup. The checkpoint on NameNode startup is based on the number of transactions stored in the edits log. The number of transactions stored in the edits log are not exactly those that represent previously uncheck-pointed transactions. Some extra transactions are stored as configured in the dfs.namenode.num.extra. edits.retained property, the default extra transactions being 1000000. Another configuration property that affects extra edit logs stored is the dfs.namenode.max.extra.edits.segments.retained, which specifies the number of extra edit log segments stored. The default is 10000. If the number of extra transactions as set in dfs.namenode.num.extra.edits.retained makes the extra edit segments exceed the setting in dfs. namenode.max.extra.edits.segments.retained, the value set in the latter is used to limit the number of extra transactions stored.

Secondary NameNode check-pointing could fail when loading the fsimage file or when applying the edits log. If the Secondary NameNode checkpoint fails, it retries *x* number of times as configured in dfs.namenode.checkpoint.max-retries. The default is three retries.

A cluster can have only one NameNode and one Secondary NameNode. On a production cluster, the Secondary NameNode should be located on a different node than the NameNode for two reasons:

- The Secondary NameNode on a separate node does not take up the much-needed RAM required by the NameNode.

- The Secondary NameNode on a separate node makes the HDFS more fault-tolerant because if the NameNode fails, the fsimage file can be re-created from the copy stored on the Secondary NameNode node.

To configure the Secondary NameNode, add the name of the Secondary NameNode host to the conf/slaves file and set a NameNode address for the Secondary NameNode to connect to for check-pointing. Use the following setting for dfs.namenode.http-address on the Secondary NameNode node.

```
<property>
  <name>dfs.namenode.http-address</name>
  <value><namenode.host.address>:50070</value>
</property>
```

If the NameNode loses all copies of the fsimage file and edits log, it may import the latest checkpoint stored in the dfs.namenode.checkpoint.dir directory using the following command.

```
hadoop namenode  -importCheckpoint
```

An empty dfs.namenode.name.dir directory is required to import the checkpoint prior to running the preceding command.

DataNodes

The DataNode is a slave daemon for storing the HDFS data. Data is broken into blocks and stored on the DataNodes. The blocks are replicated using a replication factor, as configured in the dfs.replication property in hdfs-default.xml; the default replication is 3. The block size is configured in the dfs.blocksize property in hdfs-default.xml, with the default value being 128MB. The HDFS blocks are an abstraction over the underlying filesystem of the DataNode. The directories in which the DataNode stores the blocks are configured in the dfs.datanode.data.dir property in hdfs-default.xml.

```
<property>
 <name>dfs.datanode.data.dir</name>
 <value>/data/1/dfs/dn,/data/2/dfs/dn,/data/3/dfs/dn</value>
</property>
```

By default, if any of the data volumes (directories) fails, the DataNode shuts down, but a certain number of failed volumes may be tolerated using the dfs.datanode.failed.volumes.tolerated property, which has a default value of 0.

```
<property>
    <name>dfs.datanode.failed.volumes.tolerated</name>
    <value>1</value>
    <final>true</final>
  </property>
```

A DataNode communicates with the NameNode periodically (every three seconds by default) and also block reports to the NameNode periodically. In the block reports, a DataNode reports which block replicas it has and if any block replicas are corrupted. The NameNode also creates block replicas for under-replicated blocks and removes block replicas for over-replicated blocks. If any block replicas are corrupted, another replica of the block is created from an uncorrupted replica and the corrupted replica is removed. The NameNode updates the namespace metadata if it is required. DataNode also runs a block scanner periodically to determine if any blocks have been corrupted. When the NameNode starts up, it first starts in safe mode, during which no new files may be created, deleted, or modified and only reads are allowed. While in the safe mode, the DataNode block reports are evaluated to ascertain if a sufficient number of block replicas are available to transition to a fully functional state. If a sufficient number of block replicas are not available on DataNodes, the NameNode creates the required replicas. When data is read or written by a client, the NameNode obtains the block locations in which data to be read is available, or in which new data may be added, and sends the block locations to the client. The client reads from or writes directly to the DataNode. Clients are the RPC protocol used to communicate with the DataNodes. The DataNode Web UI HTTP address is configured in dfs.datanode.http.address.

```
<property>
 <name>dfs.datanode.http.address</name>
 <value>0.0.0.0:50070</value>
</property>
```

The DataNode server address for data transfer is configured in dfs.datanode.address. If the port is 0, the server starts on a free node.

```
<property>
 <name> dfs.datanode.address </name>
 <value> 0.0.0.0:50010 </value>
</property>
```

Not all the space on a DataNode has to be used up for HDFS and for system stability it is recommended to reserve some disk space on DataNodes for non-dfs use. The dfs.datanode.du.reserved configuration property (default value of 0) in hdfs-default.xml sets the disk space to be reserved.

```
<property>
    <name>dfs.datanode.du.reserved</name>
    <value>1073741824</value>
    <final>true</final>
  </property>
```

DataNode uses multiple threads to transfer data in and out of the DataNode, as configured in dfs.datanode.max.transfer.threads. The default is 4096.

DataNodes that do not communicate with the NameNode for a certain period of time, as configured in dfs.namenode.stale.datanode.interval, are marked as stale by the NameNode. The default interval for being marked stale is 30000msec (30sec). If stale DataNodes are to be avoided for reads, set dfs.namenode.avoid.read.stale.datanode to true (the default value is false), which adds the stale DataNodes to the end of the read list supplied to the client. Similarly, if stale DataNodes are to be avoided for write, set dfs.namenode.avoid.write.stale.datanode to true (the default value is false). If the number of stale DataNodes becomes too great such that if stale DataNodes are avoided for write, very few DataNodes would be available for write, so set dfs.namenode.write.stale.datanode.ratio to indicate a ratio of stale to total DataNodes after which stale DataNodes are to be avoided for a write. The default value for dfs.namenode.write.stale.datanode.ratio is 0.5f.

By default, NameNode continues to provide clients with block locations from stale DataNodes (DataNodes that do not communicate with the NameNode at the preconfigured interval of 30 seconds).

When new block locations for adding blocks to a new file are requested from NameNode, the policy is to select DataNodes for new blocks in order to balance the disk space usage across the DataNodes. If all the DataNodes in the cluster are balanced in terms of disk space utilization, block assignments are done on a round-robin basis. The HDFS architecture is shown in Figure 1-3.

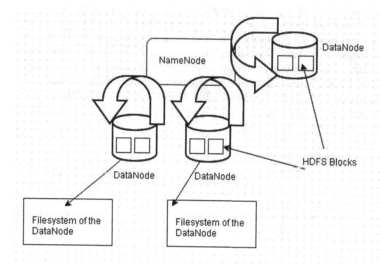

Figure 1-3. *HDFS architecture*

MapReduce Daemons

Two versions of the MapReduce processing frameworks are provided: *MapReduce 1* (MR1) for Apache Hadoop 1 and *YARN* (MR2) for Apache Hadoop 2. The default MapReduce framework in CDH5 is MR2 or YARN. MR1 is also supported in Apache Hadoop 2. The daemons in MR1 are JobTracker and TaskTracker.

JobTracker

JobTracker is the master daemon in the MapReduce and its function is to coordinate running the MapReduce jobs, including providing the job client with a job ID for a MapReduce job, accepting job submissions from the client, initiating a job, scheduling job tasks on the TaskTracker, monitoring the tasks, and relaunching a task if it fails within the constraints of maximum allowable attempts for a task. TaskTrackers communicate with the JobTracker periodically. The MapReduce architecture is shown in Figure 1-4.

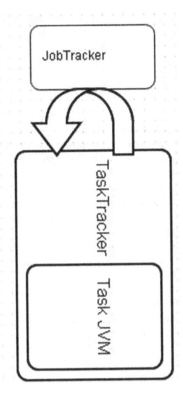

Figure 1-4. *MapReduce architecture*

In the MRv1 architecture, which is made of a JobTracker and one or more TaskTrackers, the JobTracker performs the following functions.

1. Client applications submit MapReduce jobs to the JobTracker.

2. JobTracker finds the location of data from the NameNode.

3. JobTracker finds TaskTrackers with available slots suited to the type of the task (map or reduce) at or close to the data.

4. JobTracker submits the job to the TaskTrackers. TaskTrackers launch the tasks.

5. JobTracker monitors the TaskTrackers.

6. JobTracker resubmits failed jobs if required.

7. JobTracker tracks job completion status and provides information about the same to client applications.

JobTracker does it all—the resource management, task scheduling, and task monitoring. The job task logs may be viewed on the JobTracker web UI. JobTracker provides fault-tolerance in MapReduce by restarting failed tasks. TaskTrackers communicate with the JobTracker periodically and if a JobTracker does not receive communication from a TaskTracker for a configured interval (mapreduce.jobtracker.expire. trackers.interval), which is 10 minutes by default, the TaskTracker is considered lost and the JobTracker reruns the tasks. If the job is in the map phase, the JobTracker will rerun all the map tasks. If the job is in the reduce phase, the JobTracker will rerun only the failed reduce tasks.

JobTracker also schedules extra tasks in parallel for slow-running tasks, called *speculative execution*. The Reporter object passed to the map() and reduce() functions in the old API may be used to increment counters with the incrCounter() method. The counters incremented by the mappers and reducers are collected and aggregated by the JobTracker for later retrieval.

TaskTracker

TaskTracker is a slave daemon in MapReduce. A cluster may consist of several TaskTrackers. A TaskTracker has map slots to run map tasks and reduce slots to run reduce tasks. The TaskTracker's function is to run a MapReduce job's tasks in the map/reduce slots. The JobTracker requests the TaskTracker to launch a new task. TaskTracker launches map/reduce tasks in child JVMs and monitors the task's progress. TaskTracker communicates with the JobTracker periodically about the status of the tasks and availability of map/reduce slots for running new tasks. TaskTracker has the provision to run multiple tasks in sequence on the same JVM.

In MR1, the JobTracker is required to handle both resource management and task scheduling. The CDH4 introduced several new features, including MapReduce v2 (YARN) and high-availability NameNode. In YARN, MapReduce v2 replaces JobTracker with ResourceManager to handle resource management and accept job submission, and a per-application ApplicationMaster obtains the resources from the ResourceManager and launches and monitors tasks. NodeManager is used in MRv2 to manage node user processes such as launch and monitor resource containers. NodeManager replaces the TaskTracker. A MapReduce JobHistory server was added in MRv2 to aggregate job and task information and logs. YARN (MRv2) provides a more generic distributed framework to develop applications of any kind, not just MapReduce applications. An application in MRv2 is a classical MR job or a directed acyclic graph (DAG) of jobs. For MRv2, the following configuration property must be set in mapred-site.xml to use YARN.

```
<property>
 <name>mapreduce.framework.name</name>
 <value>yarn</value>
</property>
```

MRv2 has the following daemons with the JobTracker equivalent daemons being ResourceManager, ApplicationMaster, and JobHistoryServer, and the TaskTracker equivalent daemon being NodeManager.

ResourceManager

ResourceManager is the master MapReduce daemon in MRv2. The ResourceManager manages the global allocation of compute resources to MapReduce applications and starts per application ApplicationMasters. ResourceManager does not initiate tasks to be launched nor does it handle monitoring tasks and re-launching failed tasks. The tasks management is assigned to the ApplicationMasters. ResourceManager has two main components: Scheduler and ApplicationsManager. The Scheduler's function is the allocate resource containers to applications. ApplicationsManager's function is to accept job submissions and launch and monitor ApplicationMaster containers, one per application. ApplicationMasters handle an application's tasks, launching, monitoring, and re-launching tasks if required.

NodeManager

NodeManager is a per-cluster node daemon that manages the user processes on the node in coordination with the ApplicationMasters. The ResourceManager and the NodeManager constitute the data computation framework. NodeManager's role is to manage resource containers including starting containers, monitoring their status (resource usage) and reporting the same to the ResourceManager/Scheduler. A resource container is an abstraction of a resource (CPU and memory). Cluster resources are allocated in terms of the number of containers; NodeManager's role includes ensuring that an application is not using more resources than it has been allocated.

A script, configured in `yarn-default.xml`, may be run on a NodeManager periodically to check the NodeManager's state, such as the state of all the local disks.

Application-specific services, called the auxiliary services, may be plugged into the NodeManager. The auxiliary services are loaded by the NodeManager on startup. For MRv2 applications shuffle is a typical service loaded by NodeManager.

ApplicationMaster

ApplicationMaster is a per application slave daemon in MapReduce. ApplicationMaster handles an application's lifecycle including scheduling tasks, launching tasks, monitoring tasks, re-launching tasks if a task fails, and handling speculative execution.

The ApplicationMaster's function includes negotiating resources (resource containers) from the ResourceManager/Scheduler and coordinating with the NodeManager to run and monitor tasks on the containers. Each map/reduce task runs in a container, which can run either of the two kinds of tasks. The containers are not tasks specific and the same container can run either a map task or a reduce task.

The ApplicationManager, in coordination with the NodeManager, starts, monitors, and restarts an application's individual tasks. Each map/reduce task runs within a container instead of a map/reduce slot in MR1's TaskTracker. The resource containers are not specific to a map/reduce task as the TaskTracker's slots are. Either of map or a reduce task can run on a resource container, which provides greater flexibility and availability in comparison to the map/reduce slots of TaskTracker. The containers are optimized for cluster utilization in comparison to the map/reduce slots.

The `ContainerManagerProtocol` is used by the ApplicationMaster to communicate with the NodeManager to start and stop containers and get status updates on containers.

JobHistory Server

Job history in MRv1 is archived by the JobTracker. In MRv2, the JobHistory Server is used to archive job history. JobHistory Server's role is to archive job and task information and logs. Job and task logs may be viewed on the JobHistory Server at `http://localhost:19888/jobhistory`.

Resource Allocations with YARN

YARN (Yet Another Resource Negotiator) is a dedicated component in MRv2 for the cluster resource manager. The JobTracker functions have been delegated to the JobHistory Server (job completion status), a ResourceManager (cluster resource management), and one or more ApplicationMasters (MapReduce processing). The YARN architecture is shown in Figure 1-5.

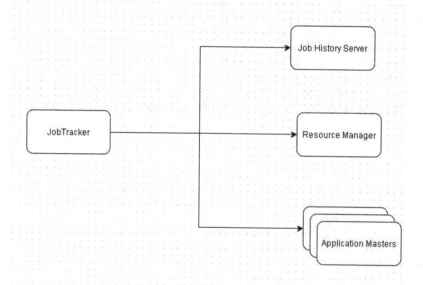

Figure 1-5. *YARN architecture*

The basic unit of a resource has changed in MRv2. In MRv1 the basic unit of a resource is a TaskTracker slot, which is specific to a map task or a reduce task. A map slot is used for a map task and a reduce slot is used for a reduce task. A map slot is not usable with a reduce slot and a reduce slot is not usable with a map task. The MRv1 resource allocation has some drawbacks:

- Resources, the slots, are task-specific and can be used with a task of a different type, which makes the total pool of available resources to map and reduce tasks inflexible.

- Under-utilization of clusters when more map or reduce tasks are running. The slots for the other type of tasks are not being used.

- Cluster resources cannot be shared with non-MR applications such as Impala and Giraph.

- Scalability is limited by one JobTracker per cluster and about 4,000 nodes per cluster.

YARN overcomes these limitations as follows.

- No slots are used. Instead resource containers are used to allocate resources. Dynamic resource allocation means the same container may be used with map and reduce tasks.

- A container is not specific to a particular type of task (map or reduce). As a result, the cluster is utilized fully.

- Supports MR and non-MR applications running on the same cluster. Impala or Giraph could be running alongside MR applications.

- The JobTracker's MapReduce processing function has been moved to ApplicationMasters and a cluster may have several ApplicationMasters.

The TaskTracker in MRv1 has been replaced with NodeManagers in MRv2. The YARN components that participate in resource allocation are the ResourceManager and the per-node NodeManager. The ResourceManager runs on the master node, is the global resource scheduler, and it allocates cluster resources among the different applications, not just the MapReduce applications. NodeManagers run on the slave nodes and communicate with the ResourceManager.

The basic unit of a resource is not a slot, but an abstraction called a *container*. Resources are allocated to a container in terms of memory (MB) and CPU (virtual cores). The amount of resources available on each node is configured in terms of memory and virtual cores, which are allocated to a node with the yarn.nodemanager.resource.memory-mb and yarn.nodemanager.resource.cpu-vcores properties in yarn-site.xml. The default memory allocated to all the containers on a node is 8192MB and the default number of CPU cores that are allocated to all containers on a node is eight. The node capacity is available to both map and reduce tasks. The virtual cores are provided for multi-threading and the number of virtual cores are limited by the number of physical cores on a node machine. The memory and virtual core resources are allocated to containers in discrete chunks, not by any arbitrary value. The minimum memory that is allocated to a container is configured with the yarn.scheduler.minimum-allocation-mb setting in yarn-site.xml and has the default value of 1024MB. The amount by which memory may be incremented is set with the yarn.scheduler.increment-allocation-mb property, with a default value of 1MB. The minimum number of virtual cores that may be allocated to a container are configured with the yarn.scheduler.minimum-allocation-vcores setting in yarn-site.xml, with the default value of 1. The number of cores may be incremented only in multiple of the value set in the yarn.scheduler.increment-allocation-vcores property, which defaults to 1. The maximum memory that is allocated to a container is configured with the yarn.scheduler.maximum-allocation-mb setting in yarn-site.xml and has the default value of 8192MB. The maximum number of virtual cores that may be allocated to a task are configured with the yarn.scheduler.maximum-allocation-vcores setting in yarn-site.xml, with the default value of 32. The number of cores may be incremented only in multiple of the value set in the yarn.scheduler.increment-allocation-vcores property, which defaults to 1.

The map and reduce tasks run in containers and so do ApplicationMasters. The amount of memory the ApplicationManager needs may be configured with the yarn.app.mapreduce.am.resource.mb property in yarn-site.xml, with the default being 1536. The number of CPU virtual cores the ApplicationManager needs is configured with the yarn.app.mapreduce.am.resource.cpu-vcores property in yarn-site.xml with the default being 1. The number of virtual cores required for each map task may be configured with the mapreduce.map.cpu.vcores property in mapred-site.xml with the default value of 1. Similarly, the number of virtual cores required for each reduce task may be configured with the mapreduce.reduce.cpu.vcores property in mapred-site.xml with the default value of 1. A NodeManager could have multiple containers based on the available resources on the node and the resources allocated per container. The containers within a node do not have to have the same amount of resources allocated to them. For example, a NodeManager could have three containers, as shown in Figure 1-6.

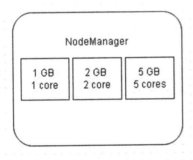

Figure 1-6. *NodeManager with three containers*

The different nodes do not need the same resource distribution. Another node running an ApplicationMaster in a separate container and another container could have the resource allocation shown in Figure 1-7.

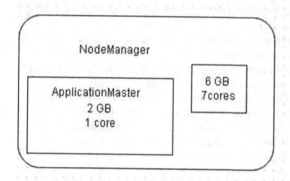

Figure 1-7. *Resource allocation on another node*

Containers are created by the ResourceManager on request from applications. The sum of resources in all containers on a node must not exceed the node resource capacity. Each container can run a task (map or reduce) at a time. The same container may be used to run a task of a different type after one task completes.

One ApplicationMaster per application is created. As map/reduce is not the only supported framework the ApplicationMaster is framework/application specific. The ApplicationMaster runs in a container. ApplicationMaster may request more containers to run map/reduce tasks as required. An ApplicationMaster could be running map or reduce or both types of tasks simultaneously on different containers, which could be on different nodes, as shown in Figure 1-8.

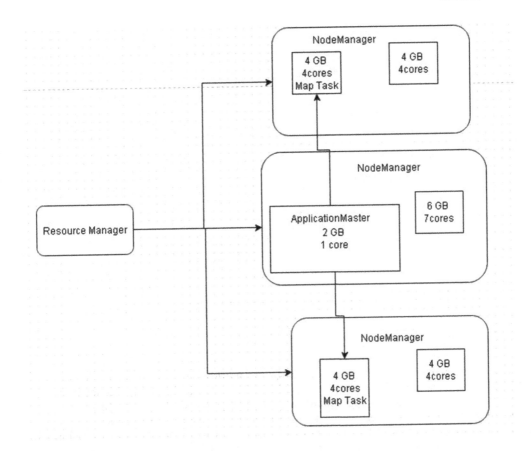

Figure 1-8. *Running tasks on multiple containers*

When a ResourceManager receives a client request to run an application, it creates a container for the ApplicationMaster to run in and launches the ApplicationMaster via the NodeManager. Subsequently, the RM handles AM requests for additional resources, as required to run the application's tasks. The RM provides the AM the containers (container IDs) and the NodeManager launches tasks on the containers, as shown in Figure 1-9. When an application completes, the RM deallocates the containers running the application. The same containers could subsequently be allocated to a different AM running another application. As the containers are not task type specific, the same container can run map and reduce tasks in subsequent runs.

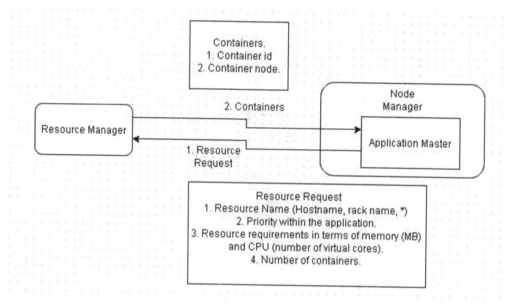

Figure 1-9. *Resource allocation*

The NodeManagers register with the ResourceManager and provide info about the node resources to the RM. It is the NodeManagers that manage the container processes including the ApplicationMaster containers. The NodeManagers launch ApplicationMasters on request from the ResourceManager. The NodeManagers launch processes (map/reduce tasks for MR framework) on the ApplicationMasters on ResourceManager's request. The NodeManagers provide logging services to applications by aggregating logs in the HDFS. NodeManagers run auxiliary services and also manage which users may submit applications via the ACLs.

After an ApplicationMaster has launched, the ApplicationMaster requests resources from the ResourceManager with a resource request, and the ResourceManager allocates resources as containers.

Next, we discuss memory allocation on a node with an example. Consider a node with 90GB of RAM and 4-hex core (24 cores) CPUs. With about one-two containers per core, that would provide about 40 containers per node. With 90GB on the node and reserving 10GB for the OS, there would be 80GB available for the YARN.

```
<?xml version="1.0" encoding="UTF-8"?>
<configuration>
  <property>
    <name>yarn.nodemanager.resource.memory-mb</name>
<value>81920</value>
  </property>
```

For 40 containers with 80GB of RAM, there would be a minimum RAM per container of 2GB.

```
<property>
    <name>yarn.scheduler.minimum-allocation-mb</name>
<value>2048</value>
  </property>
```

In configuring memory allocation for tasks, the following factors should be considered.

- Physical RAM limit for each map/reduce task

- JVM heap size limit per task

- Virtual memory per task

Configure 4GB for map tasks and 4GB for reduce tasks in `mapred-site.xml`.

```
<property>
<name>mapreduce.map.memory.mb</name>
<value>4096</value>
</property>
<property>
<name>mapreduce.reduce.memory.mb</name>
<value>4096</value>
</property>
```

Each container runs a JVM for a map/reduce task. Set the JVM heap size to be lower than the memory limits for map/reduce tasks. For example, set the JVM heap size to 3GB.

```
<property>
<name>mapreduce.map.java.opts</name>
<value>-Xmx3072m</value>
</property>
<property>
<name>mapreduce.reduce.java.opts</name>
<value>-Xmx3072m </value>
</property>
```

The JVM heap size limits the physical memory available to map/reduce tasks. The virtual memory (physical and paging) available to map/reduce tasks may be configured using the `yarn.nodemanager.vmem-pmem-ratio` property in `yarn-site.xml`, which has a default value of 2.1. The `yarn.nodemanager.vmem-pmem-ratio` property sets the ratio between the virtual and physical memory available to containers.

```
<property>
<name>yarn.nodemanager.vmem-pmem-ratio</name>
<value>2.1</value>
</property>
```

YARN supports the fair scheduler and the FIFO scheduler with the Fair scheduler being the default. Capacity scheduler from MRv1 is also supported. The MRv2 Fair Scheduler supports hierarchical queues with which queues may contain subqueues, which share the resources allocated to a queue. As the node capacities have been redefined from number of map/reduce tasks to memory and number of virtual cores the `minMaps`, `maxMaps`, `minReduces`, and `maxReduces` properties in the fair scheduler allocation file have been replaced with resources limiting properties. The per-queue properties that may be configured in the fair scheduler allocation file are listed in Table 1-1.

Table 1-1. *Fair Scheduler Per-Queue Properties*

Property	Description
minResources	Specifies the minimum resources for a queue in terms of memory and number of virtual cores. An example setting could be "512MB, 1 vcores".
maxResources	Specifies the maximum resources for a queue in terms of memory and number of virtual cores. An example setting could be "2048MB, 6 vcores".
maxRunningApps	Specifies the maximum number of apps from a queue to run simultaneously.
weight	Specifies the weight for the queue in sharing the cluster with other queues. The default value is 1.
schedulingPolicy	Specifies the scheduling policy used. The following values may be set: "fifo"/"fair"/"drf". The default is "fair".
aclSubmitApps	Specifies the users who may submit applications to the queue.
minSharePreemptionTimeout	Specifies the number of seconds after which a queue that is under its minimum share preempts containers to take resources from other queues.

The other elements that may be set in the fair scheduler allocation file are discussed in Table 1-2.

Table 1-2. *Fair Scheduler Allocation File Properties*

Element	Description
<user/>	The maximum number of apps may be set with the maxRunningApps property.
<userMaxAppsDefault/>	Specifies the default number of maximum apps per user.
<fairSharePreemptionTimeout/>	Specifies the number of seconds after which a queue that is under its fair share will try to preempt containers to take resources from other queues.
<defaultQueueSchedulingPolicy/>	Specifies the scheduling policy used. The per-user schedulingPolicy setting overrides the global setting.

An example fair scheduler allocation file is the following.

```
<?xml version="1.0"?>
<allocations>
  <queue name="user1">
    <minResources>1024 mb,1vcores</minResources>
    <maxResources>4096 mb,3vcores</maxResources>
    <maxRunningApps>20</maxRunningApps>
    <aclSubmitApps>hdfs,admin</aclSubmitApps>
    <weight>1.0</weight>
    <schedulingPolicy>fair</schedulingPolicy>
```

```
    <queue name="user1-sub">
        <aclSubmitApps>root</aclSubmitApps>
        <minResources>512 mb,1vcores</minResources>
    </queue>
  </queue>
  <user name="root">
    <maxRunningApps>20</maxRunningApps>
  </user>
  <user name="hdfs">
    <maxRunningApps>10</maxRunningApps>
  </user>
  <user name="admin">
    <maxRunningApps>5</maxRunningApps>
  </user>
  <userMaxAppsDefault>5</userMaxAppsDefault>
  <fairSharePreemptionTimeout>60</fairSharePreemptionTimeout>
</allocations>
```

The Workflow of the MapReduce Job

The workflow of the MapReduce job running on YARN is as follows. It is also illustrated in Figure 1-10.

1. Client gets the application ID from the ResourceManager.

2. Client submits the application to the ResourceManager.

3. The ResourceManager launches an ApplicationMaster in coordination with a NodeManager to run the application.

4. The ApplicationMaster registers with the ResourceManager.

5. The ApplicationMaster requests container resources from the ResourceManager.

6. The ResourceManager sends container resources to the ApplicationMaster.

7. The ApplicationMaster sends a request to NodeManager to start an allocated container.

8. The NodeManager launches the container and starts the task assigned to the container.

9. The NodeManager sends a status report about the containers and the task running in a container to ApplicationMaster.

10. When a container has completed running a task, the ApplicationMaster requests the NodeManager to stop the container.

11. The NodeManager stops the container.

12. The ApplicationMaster notifies the ResourceManager about its completion (success or failure).

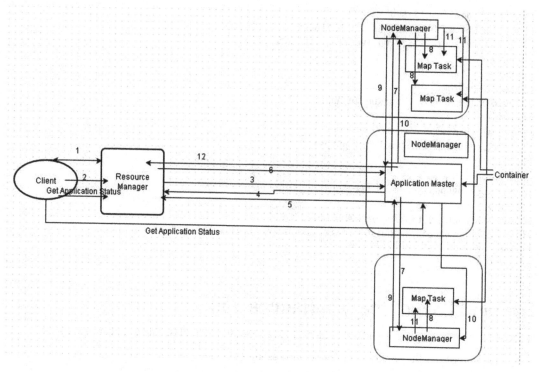

Figure 1-10. *Workflow of the YARN (MapReduce) job*

In addition to the process discussed in running an application, the client may get application statuses from the ResourceManager or the ApplicationMaster directly. The NodeManager sends the node status to the ResourceManager periodically.

Some additional discussion about each of the phases of an application are as follows.

- The client gets the application ID from the ResourceManager using the `ApplicationClientProtocol` protocol with the `ApplicationClientProtocol#` `getNewApplication(GetNewApplicationRequest request)` method. The ResourceManager sends a monotonically increasing globally unique application id. Client runs in its own JVM.

- Client submits the application to ResourceManager with `ApplicationClientProtocol# submitApplication(SubmitApplicationRequest request)`. In the SubmitApplicationRequest the client includes the queue information and the resources requirement in terms of memory (MB) and CPU (virtual cores). The resources information is submitted with the `org.apache.hadoop.yarn.api.records.Resource` class. The ResourceManager returns a `org.apache.hadoop.yarn.api.protocolrecords.SubmitApplicationResponse`, which is empty and does not include information about whether the application was submitted successfully and started. The client needs subsequently to get the application report with the `getApplicationReport(GetApplicationReportRequest request)` method. The ResourceManager returns `GetApplicationReportResponse`, which includes a ApplicationReport with the information about the application, including application name, host on which ApplicationMaster is running, RPC port of the ApplicationMaster, start time of the application, tracking URL, and application status. The RM does not keep the application info beyond a failover or a restart. Before submitting the application, the client copies the resources (jars and binaries) to the HDFS.

- The ResourceManager launches an ApplicationMaster to run the application on a node with available resources. The ApplicationManager component of the ResourceManager requests the NodeManager to launch the first container to run ApplicationMaster and the NodeManager starts the ApplicationMaster container. The ApplicationManager also restarts the ApplicationMaster if the ApplicationMaster fails. The ApplicationMasters are framework/application-specific and for a MapReduce application, a MRAppMaster is launched.

- ApplicationMaster registers with the ResourceManager using the `ApplicationMasterProtocol.registerApplicationMaster(RegisterApplicationMasterRequest request)` method. The ResourceManager responds with `RegisterApplicationMasterResponse`, which includes information about maximum capability of allocated resources in the cluster.

- ApplicationMaster requests container resources from ResourceManager with AllocateRequest using the `ApplicationMasterProtocol.allocate(AllocateRequest request)` method. The `AllocateRequest` includes the progress information, a list of ResourceRequests about the application's resource requirements, and a list of unused containers being returned. A ResourceRequest includes the priority of the request, the name of the machine or rack on which the resource is required, with the asterisk (*) value indicating any host/rack. The resource is required. A resource specification includes the memory (MB) and/or the CPU (number of virtual cores).

- ResourceManager sends container resources to ApplicationMaster with AllocateResponse. AllocateResponse includes a list of newly allocated containers, a list of completed containers' statuses, a list of nodes whose status has been updated, the number of available nodes in the cluster, a description of resources requested by the cluster, and an `AMCommand` to let the ApplicationMaster to take some action such as `resync` or `shutdown`. A container represents a resource allocated on a cluster and includes information such as `ContainerId`, `NodeId`, and `Resource` allocated to the container.

- ApplicationMaster sends a request to NodeManager to start an allocated container using the ContainerManagementProtocol protocol and the ContainerManagementProtocol.startContainers(StartContainersRequest request) method. The request includes the allocated resource capability, environment settings for the task to run in the container, the resources (binaries and jars) to copy to the container, and the commands to run on the container. The NodeManager returns a StartContainersResponse response from which a list of successfully started containers may be obtained with the getSuccessfullyStartedContainers method.

- NodeManager starts the container and the task assigned to the container in a task JVM. The task JVM gets the application resources from the HDFS. Containers send MapReduce statuses about the task running in a container to NodeManager.

- NodeManager sends status reports about containers and task running in a container to ApplicationMaster when the ApplicationMaster requests them using the ContainerManagementProtocol.getContainerStatuses (GetContainerStatusesRequest request). The NodeManager responds with a GetContainerStatusesResponse, which has a method called getContainerStatuses() to get container statuses as List<ContainerStatus>.

- When a container has completed running a task, the ApplicationMaster requests NodeManager to stop the container using the ContainerManagementProtocol.st opContainers(StopContainersRequest request) method. The NodeManager responds with a StopContainersResponse from which a list of successfully stopped containers may be obtained using the getSuccessfullyStoppedContainers() method.

- NodeManager stops the container and notifies the ApplicationMaster in a status report as in Step 9.

- ApplicationMaster notifies the ApplicationManager component of ResourceManager about its completion (success or failure) with the ApplicationMasterProtocol.fini shApplicationMaster(FinishApplicationMasterRequest request) method and it unregisters with the ResourceManager.

HDFS High-Availability Daemons

Earlier sections mentioned several limitations, including the NameNode being a single point of failure (SPOF) in the cluster. HDFS high-availability daemons provide a Standby NameNode that takes over if the active NameNode fails. The secondary NameNode is not used with HDFS high-availability NameNode. As a result the HDFS daemons determine whether HDFS HA is enabled. HDFS high-availability NameNodes require configuration and are not enabled by default in CDH5. The HDFS high-availability daemons are Active NameNode, Standby NameNode, JournalNodes, ZooKeeper, and DataNodes.

Active NameNode

With HDFS HA, two NameNodes run in the cluster simultaneously in active/passive configuration. The NameNode that is active at a given instance is called the *active NameNode*. The active NameNode's function in a HA is the same as a NameNode's function in non-HA HDFS. The active NameNode's hardware is the same as a non-HA NameNode and also the same as the standby NameNode.

Standby NameNode

With HDFS HA, the NameNode that is passive at a given instance is called the *standby NameNode*. The standby NameNode is a hot standby and if the active NameNode fails or crashes, the active NameNode fails over to the standby NameNode automatically (fast failover). Fast failover has to be configured by setting the `dfs.ha.automatic-failover.enabled` property to `true` in `hdfs-default.xml` if the active NameNode is to fail over to the standby NameNode in the event of failure of the active NameNode. Fast failover implies that the standby NameNode automatically becomes the active NameNode. Administrator-mediated failover can also be used for planned maintenance.

The standby NameNode preserves enough state to provide a fast failover if required. This implies that the active NameNode's namespace state must be synchronized with the standby NameNode's state. Two methods are available to synchronize the namespace state between the active and standby NameNodes:

- Quorum-based storage
- Shared storage using NFS

With quorum-based storage, the active NameNode and standby NameNode both communicate with a quorum (group) of JournalNodes, which keep a journal of edits (modifications) logged by the active NameNode. The active NameNode logs edits as they are made and the standby NameNode reads the edits as they are logged to the JournalNodes and applies the edits to its namespace state. The active NameNode logs the edits to the majority of the JournalNodes in the quorum. With shared storage using NFS, a shared directory, configurable in `hdfs-default.xml` using configuration property `dfs.namenode.shared.edits.dir`, is used to synchronize the state between the active NameNode and the standby NameNode. The active NameNode logs edits in the namespace state to the shared directory and the standby NameNode reads the edits from the shared directory and updates its namespace state. A fencing method transitions the standby NameNode to the active NameNode state so that only one NameNode is active and is logging to the shared edits directory at a time.

Since the standby NameNode applies a checkpoint of the edits received from the shared storage (Quorum based or shared directory based) to the namespace state in its `fsimage` file, a `Secondary NameNode` is not required with HDFS HA.

JournalNodes

JournalNodes daemons are used with Quorum-based storage to synchronize state between the active NameNode and the standby NameNode. The active and standby NameNodes communicate with a quorum of JournalNodes. When any namespace modification is made on the active NameNode the edits are sent to the majority of JournalNodes. A quorum has multiple JournalNodes, usually an odd number, with at least three JournalNodes. With N JournalNodes, the system can tolerate $(N-1)/2$ failures, which is why an odd number of JournalNodes should be used. The standby NameNode reads the edits from one of the JournalNodes and applies them to its namespace state to keep its namespace state up to date. JournalNodes allow only one of the NameNodes to be in active state at any time. The active/standby NameNode architecture is shown in Figure 1-11.

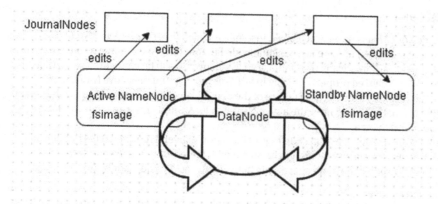

Figure 1-11. *Active/standby NameNode*

JournalNode daemons are lightweight and may be collocated on nodes with other daemons such as the MRv1 JobTracker, NameNode, or MRv2 ResourceManager.

ZooKeeper

ZooKeeper is a coordination daemon used to coordinate fast failover of the active NameNode to the standby NameNode. ZooKeeper has two functions in a HA HDFS cluster:

- Detect failure of the active NameNode. Each of the active NameNodes and the standby NameNodes maintains an active session in the ZooKeeper. When the active NameNode fails, the ZooKeeper detects the failure as a result of the failed NameNode's session in the ZooKeeper ending.

- The ZooKeeper initiates a failover to the standby NameNode and provides a mechanism for active NameNode election.

DataNodes

The function of the DataNode in HDFS HA is the same as in HDFS non-HA. With HA, the DataNode communicates with both the NameNodes periodically and sends block reports to the active and standby NameNodes so that the namespace state in the standby NameNode is up to date to facilitate fast failover if required.

Benefits and Challenges of HDFS

Hadoop Distributed Filesystem (HDFS) is a distributed, scalable, fault-tolerant filesystem to store, process, and provide parallel streaming access to large quantities of data on commodity hardware.

The benefits of HDFS over a traditional filesystem are as follows.

HDFS Is Distributed

HDFS is a distributed filesystem in which a file (or other input data) is broken into blocks and stored across several (hundreds or thousands) nodes in a cluster. A single file can have blocks on multiple nodes (machines). The blocks are replicated. The blocks being distributed and replicated provide fault tolerance to data, as the failure of a single node does not cause data loss. The file being distributed also provides availability of data on multiple nodes for data locality.

Block Abstraction

The file blocks are replicated and stored on the underlying filesystem. The HDFS blocks are an abstraction over the DataNodes' filesystem. Block abstraction makes it feasible to store large files. A file in the HDFS can be larger than any single disk on the underlying filesystem of a DataNode, as a file's blocks can be stored over multiple disks in the cluster.

Scalable

HDFS is designed for fast, concurrent access from multiple clients. HDFS provides high aggregate data bandwidth and scales linearly to hundreds or thousands of nodes in the cluster. The performance of the cluster does not degrade due to addition of new nodes. Elasticity is a goal. The number of nodes in a cluster is never constant.

Fault-Tolerant

HDFS is designed to store data reliably. As HDFS is distributed over multiple nodes, failure of some of the nodes is inevitable and failure of a single node should not cause the data to become unavailable. Block replication is used to provide durability to data. Each file block is replicated three times by default. If a block is lost due to failure of a node, another replica of the block is used and the block is re-replicated from another replica.

Data Locality

HDFS is a storage and data-processing filesystem. Data locations are exposed and HDFS provides data locality by moving the computation to the data rather than the data to the computation, as is done in traditional filesystems. As HDFS is designed for data-intensive (involving large quantities of data) computation, it is much more efficient to move the computation to the data as moving the relatively small computation code to the data utilizes less network bandwidth and increases the overall throughput of the system. HDFS is designed to integrate well with MapReduce.

Data Coherency

HDFS is a write-once-read-many paradigm filesystem. HDFS does not support updates or modifications to the stored data. Sections of stored data cannot be modified/deleted. Data append is supported. The write-once-read-many model provides data coherency. A MapReduce application or a web search application is compatible with the write-once-read-many model, which also enables high throughput data access.

Parallel Streaming Access to Data

HDFS provides parallel streaming access to multiple (tens of thousands) clients. HDFS is designed for batch processing rather than interactive user access. HDFS is designed for high throughput of data rather than low latency. Some of the POSIX requirements have been disregarded to enable high throughput streaming access to data. HDFS is designed for large streaming, sequential reads of data and is not optimized for random seeks to arbitrary positions in files.

Large Quantities of Data

HDFS stores and processes large quantities of data in the order of several PB. A single file can be 100s of GB to 100s of TB. HDFS is optimized for large datasets, much larger than what is supported by traditional filesystems such as EXT and NTFS. HDFS supports medium-to-large files and tens of millions of files.

Unstructured Data

Data stored in HDFS is not required to conform to some schema. HDFS is designed to support unstructured data.

Commodity Hardware

No special hardware is required for HDFS. HDFS is designed to be used on commodity hardware. HDFS is portable across heterogeneous hardware platforms.

Portability

No special hardware is required for HDFS. HDFS is designed to be used on commodity hardware. HDFS is portable across heterogeneous hardware platforms. HDFS's software components are built using Java, which is a portable language with multi-platform support.

TCP/IP Protocol

HDFS communication protocols are built over TCP/IP, the most common protocol.

Accessible

HDFS is accessible with several interfaces: Java API, a C language wrapper for the Java API, HTTP browser, and command-line FS Shell. Several frameworks are available to make HDFS mountable on UNIX as a standard filesystem.

HDFS High Availability

Prior to HDFS high availability, HDFS was a single point of failure (SPOF). With the addition of the active NameNode/standby NameNode configuration in the high-availability HDFS, the NameNode is not a SPOF. High availability of the HDFS is a goal when the HDFS is used in HA mode.

HDFS architecture is designed for a particular type of applications, mainly MapReduce applications. HDFS does have some challenges or limitations, which are as follows.

Single Point of Failure

NameNode, the master daemon in HDFS, is a single point of failure in the HDFS. If the NameNode fails, the HDFS becomes unavailable until the NameNode is restored. HDFS high availability provides the option to fail over to a hot standby NameNode.

Write-Once Model

The write-once-read-many model does have its advantages for which HDFS is designed but as a result HDFS does not support updates or modifications to the stored data. Sections of stored data cannot be modified/deleted. Data append is supported.

Not Optimized for Random Seek

HDFS is designed for large streaming, sequential reads of data and is not optimized for random seeks to arbitrary positions in files.

Local Caching Not Supported

As the files are large and designed for sequential reads, local caching of data is not supported.

Commodity Hardware Failure

HDFS is designed for commodity hardware in which failure of some components is a norm rather than an exception. Automatic detection of faults and recovery is a goal in HDFS.

Detection of Hardware Failure and Recovery

HDFS is a distributed filesystem and consists of hundreds or thousands of nodes. Data is broken, replicated, and distributed across the different nodes in the cluster. HDFS is designed for commodity hardware, which is not very reliable. With such a large number of machines in the cluster and the fact that HDFS is designed for commodity hardware, the probability of some component or other failing is non-trivial. Failure of some components or machines is a norm rather than an exception. A failure of 2-10 nodes a day per 1000 nodes is to be expected. Failure rates could be about 1% per month. Automatic detection of faults and recovery is a goal in HDFS.

File Sizes, Block Sizes, and Block Abstraction in HDFS

High throughput is one of main goals of HDFS. HDFS can be scaled to hundreds and even thousands of nodes and provides high aggregate data bandwidth.

Block Sizes

A file is not stored as a complete artifact in HDFS. A file is broken into blocks and stored in HDFS, as shown in Figure 1-12. The division of a file into blocks is transparent to the client. Blocks of the same file can reside on different machines in the cluster. HDFS does not support storing multiple files in a block.

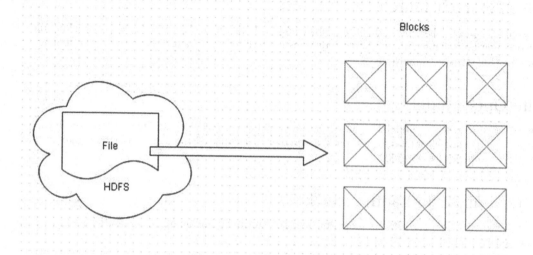

Figure 1-12. *File blocks*

The default block size is 128MB in CDH5 and is configured in the configuration property dfs.blocksize in hdfs-default.xml. The dfs.blocksize value may be set in bytes or case-insensitive suffixes k (kilo), m (mega), g (giga), t (tera), p (peta), and e (exa). For example, a block size of 128MB may configured as follows using bytes size.

```
<property>
  <name>dfs.blocksize</name>
  <value>134217728</value>
</property>
```

Or, the 128MB block size may be configured as follows using a suffix.

```
<property>
  <name>dfs.blocksize</name>
  <value>128m</value>
</property>
```

For durability, each block is replicated across the cluster with a default replication value of 3. Replication is discussed in detail in a later section.

Block size is user selectable on a per-file basis. Too small a block size is discouraged as it would result in a large number of blocks for a file, even for a relatively small file. A new configuration property has been introduced in hdfs-default.xml. The dfs.namenode.fs-limits.min-block-size property sets a limit on the minimum block size to 1MB by default. The minimum block size could be limited to 16MB, for example, as follows.

```
<property>
  <name> dfs.namenode.fs-limits.min-block-size </name>
  <value>16m</value>
</property>
```

Why is too small a block size an issue? For several reasons:

- Because the NameNode has to keep the metadata on all the blocks in the namespace and a very small block size would result in too many blocks to manage in the NameNode namespace. The NameNode maintains the namespace state in RAM and having to manage too many blocks could make the NameNode run out of memory. Every block and file occupies 150 bytes in memory. Approximately 1.5GB of NameNode memory is used for every 10 million blocks stored in the filesystem. The NameNode namespace could get utilized to 95% of its capacity while the disk is underutilized to only a fraction of its capacity.

- The difference in namespace utilization is pronounced by the fact that blocks are replicated. Consider a file of 512MB stored in HDFS with default block size of 512MB, as shown in Figure 1-13. Even with a replication factor of three, the NameNode namespace is manageable.

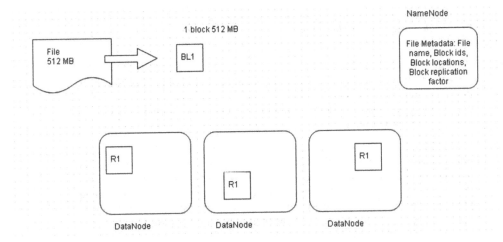

Figure 1-13. A file stored in a single block

- If the block size is decreased to 128MB, the number of blocks including the replicas to store the same 512MB file increases by four, as shown in Figure 1-14.

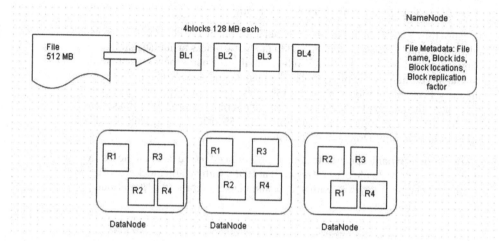

Figure 1-14. *A single file stored in multiple blocks*

- During the map phase an input file is broken into input splits and each input split is assigned to a separate map task. The FileSystem block size is an upper bound for input splits. Having a very small block size would generate several input splits and launch several map tasks. A task incurs a setup and teardown overhead of map JVMs and also incurs a scheduling overhead, all of which could slow down the job.

- For a small block size the number of map tasks would be relatively more and, if the number of nodes in the cluster does not support as many map tasks in parallel, the job would take longer as some of the map tasks would need to wait for other map tasks to complete. Also, more map tasks generate more map outputs and more map segments are required to be merged before and during the reduce phase. If map output size is proportional to the HDFS block size, bigger blocks would require more Spill buffer memory and more storage for map-side spills.

Too large a block size is also discouraged. Too large a block size has the following disadvantages:

- The cluster may be underutilized as fewer map tasks are launched with an input split created based on a larger block size, with the file size comparable to the larger block size. With very few map tasks, not all the nodes on the cluster may be utilized, which would slow down the job. A block size that would generate enough number of maps to run in parallel and utilize the whole cluster would reduce the job runtime.

- Putting all or most of a file data in a single block or very few blocks increases the probability of data corruption, as a single block corruption would corrupt the data for a whole file.

- Large block sizes decrease the parallelism that can be achieved, as the number of blocks per file decreases, resulting in fewer nodes having a block for a file to be made available to a MapReduce job.

An optimal block size is based on several factors: cluster size, map task complexity, map task capacity of cluster, and average size of input files.

Block Abstraction

An HDFS block is an abstraction over filesystem blocks. Each block is stored in a separate file in the local filesystem of the DataNode. With the DataNode abstraction that's independent of local storage HDFS supports the physical filesystem heterogeneity. Block abstraction keeps the design simple. Replication is at the block level rather than the file level. Block size does not refer to file on disk. A file that is smaller than a block does not occupy a full block equivalent storage on the underlying storage. For a block size of 64MB, a 1MB file will not take 64MB on disk. The block in HDFS is logically built over the physical blocks of underlying filesystem (e.g., ext3/fat). The HDFS filesystem is not physically divided into blocks (such as 64MB or 128MB). HDFS does not make block boundaries between records.

The default block size and the recommended block size in HDFS is made large in comparison to the disk block size to make file data transfer time from the disk significantly larger than the seek latency. The seek latency is the time delay taken to seek the start of a disk block. As a result, the time to transfer a large file made of multiple blocks is based on the disk transfer rate and is not affected by the seek latency. For example, if the seek time is 10ms and the data transfer rate from the disk is 100MB/sec for a negligible seek time of 1% of transfer time, the block size should be 100MB. To further the example, if the block size is made 100KB, and the seek time is 10ms, the file transfer time at 100MB/sec would be 1ms, which is less than the seek time, and as a result the seek time incurs an overhead.

Block abstraction has the following benefits:

- Large files can be stored. A file in the HDFS can be larger than any single disk in the network. Blocks from a file can be stored across the different disks in the cluster.

- Blocks provide fault-tolerance and availability by virtue of their being replicated across the cluster. If a block becomes available, another replica of the block can be accessed transparent to the client.

- Block as a unit of abstraction rather than a file simplifies the storage subsystem.

File Sizes

HDFS supports large files and large number of files. A typical HDFS cluster has tens of millions of files and a typical file in HDFS is several (hundreds) of MB to GB each, with some in the range of a few TB, in size. A typical file is 100MB or larger. The NameNode maintains the namespace metadata of the files such as the filename, directory name, user, group, permissions, file-to-block mapping, block IDs, block generation timestamp, block locations, block replication.

Extremely small files are discouraged, as too many small files could degrade performance. A file is considered small if its size is much less than the block size. For example, if the block size is 128MB and the file size is in the range of 1MB to 50MB, the file is considered a small file. Log files are typically small files. With several small files the number of files and blocks (name objects) in the namespace for the NameNode to manage increases. Approximately 1.5GB of NameNode memory is used for every 10 million blocks or 10 million files stored in the filesystem. For every 10 million files in the filesystem the NameNode requires 3GB of memory with block size being comparable to file size.

The HDFS is not designed for small files. The HDFS is designed with the goal of providing efficient streaming access to large files. Small files require a lot of seeks from multiple DataNodes.

Block capacity is underutilized. As the NameNode keeps the namespace in the RAM, the memory could run out or be completely utilized while the disk storage is underutilized. For example, storing 10 million small files, each of which is less than 15MB (much less than the default block size of 64MB), could cause the NameNode namespace RAM be utilized to capacity while the disk storage is only 25% utilized.

Extremely large files are also discouraged as too large a file or files could degrade performance. The `dfs.namenode.fs-limits.max-blocks-per-file` property limits the number of blocks created per file. The default value of `dfs.namenode.fs-limits.max-blocks-per-file` is 1 million. The main purpose of the property is to discourage a very small block size and as a result too many small blocks for a small/medium sized file. The limit is high enough that a large file can still be stored. For example, with a block size of 128MB and 1 million blocks per file, a file with maximum size of 128TB can be created. A very large number of blocks, either due many small files, or the block size being too small as compared to the file size puts a load on the NameNode namespace. The maximum blocks per file and minimum block size limits are implemented by the NameNode.

HDFS Quotas

The HDFS has the provision to set quotas on the number of names used and the amount of space used for individual directories. The `dfsadmin -setQuota` command may be used to set name quota and the `dfsadmin -setSpaceQuota` command may be used to set space quota. The following command sets a limit on the number of name objects to 1000 in some DataNode data directories.

```
dfsadmin -setQuota 1000  /data/1/dfs/dn /data/2/dfs/dn /data/3/dfs/dn /data/4/dfs/dn
```

The name objects are the files, the blocks, and the directories. The space quota indirectly affects an allowable block size and an allowable file size. For example, a small block size could generate too many blocks and the name quota for a directory could get exceeded. Similarly, many small files could exceed the name quota. The following command sets the space quota to 2TB for some DataNode data directories.

```
dfsadmin -setSpaceQuota 2t /data/1/dfs/dn /data/2/dfs/dn /data/3/dfs/dn /data/4/dfs/dn
```

With the space quota set to 2t a file larger than 2TB cannot be stored in the HDFS. Corresponding `clr` commands `dfsadmin -clrQuota` and `dfsadmin -clrSpaceQuota` are also provided to clear quotas. Quotas apply to directories, not to users or groups. No default quotas are set.

Hadoop Archive

Hadoop Archive (HAR) provides an alternative to storing a large number of small files. HAR packs a number of small files into large files. The original files in the HAR can be accessed in parallel without expanding the HAR file. HAR decreases the namespace usage and as a result NameNode memory usage as a single HAR file replaces several small files in the NameNode namespace. HAR files don't support compression and are immutable.

Data Replication

Files stored in the HDFS are broken into blocks and the blocks replicated across the cluster for fault-tolerance, redundancy, and availability. The default block replication is three. The block replication may be set on a per-file basis. The maximum block replication is 512 by default and configured with the `dfs.replication.max` property in `hdfs-default.xml`. The minimal block replication is 1 and set with the `dfs.namenode.replication.min` property. Blocks are replicated for the following reasons:

- *Data durability.* If one block replica is lost due to machine failure or block corruption, data is not lost as other block replicas are available.

- *Fault-tolerance.* If a block replica is lost, another block can be used and a client can access another copy of the block or MapReduce application accessing the file is still able to access the file. Fault-tolerance provides data reliability.

- *Data locality.* Data locality is the closeness of the map input data to the map task. With more block replicas, data is local to more nodes.

- *Speculative execution.* If a task is slow, redundant copies of the task are launched and the task that completes first is used. With block replicas speculative execution becomes feasible.

Configuring Replication

The default block replication is configured using the configuration property dfs.replication in hdfs-site. xml or hdfs-default.xml.

```
<configuration>
    <property>
        <name>dfs.replication</name>
        <value>3</value>
    </property>
</configuration>
```

The replication factor may also be configured when creating a file using the FileSystem API.

```
public static final String input = "input.txt";
public static final String message = "Input Message\n";
Configuration conf = new Configuration();
    FileSystem fs = FileSystem.get(conf);
    Path path = new Path(input);
    try {
      if (fs.exists(path)) {
        fs.delete(path);
      }
      FSDataOutputStream out = fs.create(path, (short)3);
    out.writeUTF(message);
      out.close();
```

For a file that's already in the HDFS, the replication may be set using the setReplication(Path src,short replication) method.

```
fs.setReplication(path,(short)3)
```

With the default replication value of 3, each file block is replicated three times. For a single DataNode cluster, for example if a file is broken into five blocks, each block is replicated three times, as shown in Figure 1-15.

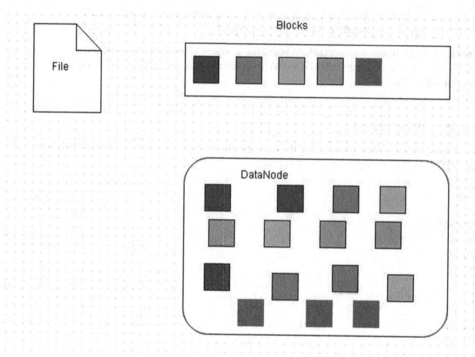

Figure 1-15. *Block replication example*

The NameNode keeps the block locations for each file in the RAM for easy access so that if a block requires replication the replication is performed quickly without having to access disk to retrieve block locations. In the following example (Figure 1-16), file1 is stored in blocks 1, 2, and 5. File file2 is stored in blocks 3, 4, and 6. Each block is replicated three times across the DataNodes on the cluster.

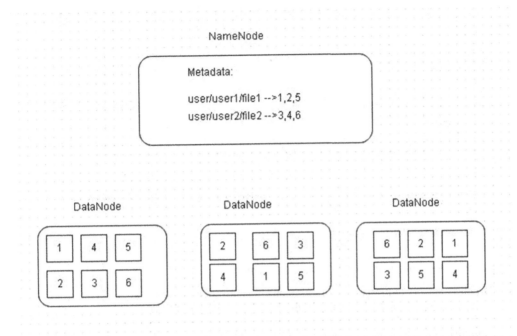

Figure 1-16. *NameNode keeps the block locations*

Data Flow in Replication

Creating a file is initiated by the client and the file is written to the DataNodes directly by the client. Client makes a request to the NameNode to create a file. The NameNode assigns blocks for the file on the DataNodes and sends a list of DataNodes and block locations ordered according to proximity to the client, back to the client. The client sends file data to the first DataNode in the list. For example, if a file is broken into two blocks, the client sends the two blocks R1 and R2 to the first DataNode. DataNodes form a pipeline and data is transferred from one DataNode to the next in the pipeline, as shown in Figure 1-17. For example, the two blocks R1 and R2 are replicated three times across the cluster.

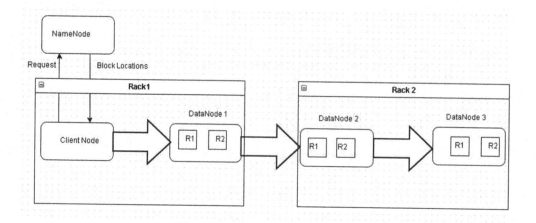

Figure 1-17. *Three replicas of blocks R1 and R2*

The sequence followed in replicating file blocks is as follows:

1. The client sends a request to create a file using the FileSystem API. First, a temporary internal buffer is created for the file. The client sends file data to the internal buffer. A client-side buffer is used to improve network throughput. Without client-side buffering network speed and congestion reduces the throughput.

2. When the internal buffer has data equivalent to fill one block, the client request is forwarded to the NameNode.

3. The NameNode assigns blocks and DataNodes for the configured number of replicas for the block and sends the block locations and DataNodes hosting the blocks to the client. The DataNodes and block locations are ordered according to their proximity from the client. The DataNodes assigned to receive the block replicas form a pipeline. The ordering of DataNodes in a pipeline according to proximity to the client minimizes the network distance from the client to the last DataNode and as a result minimizes the inter-rack and inter-node write traffic, thus improving write performance. A shorter distance between two nodes implies greater bandwidth to transfer data. HDFS I/O is designed and optimized for batch processing that requires high throughput, such as a MapReduce job.

4. The block of data in the internal buffer is sent to the first DataNode in the pipeline in a sequence of packets. The packet size is configured with the `dfs.client-write-packet-size` property in `hdfs-site.xml` with a default value of 64KB.

5. When the first DataNode has received a packet of data and written the packet to its repository it forwards the packet of data to the second DataNode in the pipeline.

6. Similarly, the second DataNode receives block data a packet at a time and fills a block replica. The second DataNode forwards block data, a packet at a time, to the third DataNode in the pipeline. The DataNodes send acknowledgement message to the NameNode to indicate that they have received blocks. The data pipeline is shown in Figure 1-18.

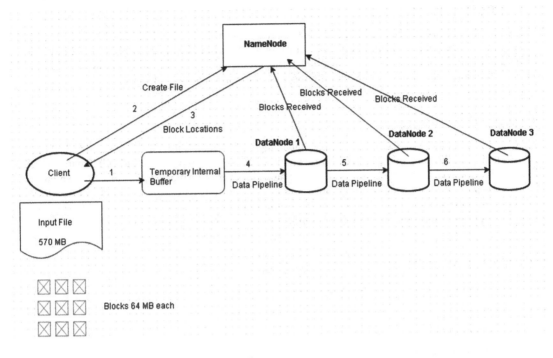

Figure 1-18. *Data pipeline in creating block replicas*

When a client opens a file to read from the client fetches the blocks and block locations list from the NameNode. The block locations are ordered by their proximity to the client and the client tries the closest replica first. The read attempt from the first replica could fail due to several reasons such as the DataNode being unavailable, the replica not being hosted on the DataNode, or the replica being corrupt based on checksums verification. The second replica is tried if the read from the first replica fails.

Under Replication

The NameNode keeps the replication level of the block to the configured or default value. DataNodes send block reports to the NameNode periodically and if the NameNode detects that a block has become under or over replicated the NameNode corrects the replication level. A block could get under replicated because some of the replicas have become corrupted or the replication level has been increased, for example. In response to the periodic communication the NameNode receives from a DataNode a NameNode could instruct a DataNode to create replicas of blocks. The NameNode provides the list of the target nodes and the block locations for the replicas. The target nodes are organized into a pipeline in the order of their proximity from the block replica to be re-replicated. Similarly to when creating a file, data is pushed from the block to be replicated to the closest node in the target nodes pipeline. Subsequently, data is transferred from one DataNode to the next in the pipeline until the required number of replicas are created. When a block becomes under-replicated it is not replicated immediately on detecting an under-replication, but placed in a replication priority queue. A block with only one replica has the highest priority and a block with number of replicas greater than two-thirds of its configured replication level has the lowest priority. A background thread scans the replication priority queue and creates replicas using the same replica placement policy as when creating replicas for a new file. If the number of replicas for the under-replicated block is one the new replica is placed on a different rack. For an under-replicated block with two replicas on the same rack, the new replica is placed on a different rack. For an under-replicated block with two replicas on different racks, the new replica is placed on a node on one of the racks.

Over Replication

When a block becomes over replicated, the NameNode removes a replica. The replica chosen to be removed is in keeping with the goal of maximizing storage utilization while not reducing the block's availability. The NameNode will prefer not to remove a replica so that the number of racks is reduced. The NameNode will prefer to remove a replica from a DataNode with the least amount of available disk space.

Misplaced Replicas

For fault-tolerance, the NameNode also ensures that all replicas of a block are not on the same rack. If the NameNode detects that all replicas for a block are on the same rack, the block is treated as being misplaced and the NameNode replicates the block to a different rack using the same block replica placement policy. After a new replica of a misplaced block has been created on a new rack, the NameNode gets the notification in a block report that a block is over-replicated. The NameNode removes an old replica from the rack that had all the replicas to bring the total number of replicas to the configured replication level.

Storage Requirements in Replication

The storage requirements are based on the following factors.

- File size

- Block size

- Replication factor

- Non-DFS storage including for intermediate map outputs

- Compression ratio

Because each file is replicated three times by default, the DataNode capacity planning should be computed keeping in consideration the storage requirements for replication. About 25% of disk space should be kept for intermediate map outputs, which implies that effectively only 25% of disk space is available for file storage. To demonstrate with an example, if a file is 1000MB and a default replication factor of 3 is used, the storage requirement for the file is 3000MB. Adding 25% for intermediate map outputs the disk capacity for a DataNode at 4000MB.

Also keep in mind that a file most likely won't completely fill the blocks. For example, if the block size is 512MB and the file size is 10000MB, the number of blocks required is computed to be 10000/512, which is 19.53. As the block size is fixed as configured in the dfs.blocksize property, the required number of blocks would be 20. With a replication factor of 3, 60 blocks of 512MB each would require a storage of 30, 720MB. An exact storage requirement calculation would suggest a storage requirement of 10000x3=30,000MB.

Another factor to consider in capacity planning is whether compression is used to store files in the HDFS. Based on file content and the compression algorithm, compression of text files would result in a compression ratio of about 10-20. For example, if the file size is 10,000MB and the block size is 512MB, 60 blocks would result in a storage requirement of 30, 720MB. Keeping 25% for intermediate map outputs storage requirement becomes 40,960MB. If the compression ratio is 10, the storage requirement becomes 4096MB. For a file of 10,000MB with compression ratio of 10 and 25% extra space for map outputs, the required storage with block replication of 3 is only 4,096MB, about 40% of the file size.

NameNode Federation

HDFS stores file data in blocks, which are an abstraction over the underlying filesystem of the DataNode. The NameNode stores the metadata for the data stored in HDFS namespace. One NameNode can manage one namespace in the HDFS. HDFS is designed on an architecture in which namespace is decoupled from the stored data. The main reason for decoupling the namespace from the data is that metadata operations are fast while data transfer is slow. With decoupling, multiple clients can by served concurrently and each client can transfer data by using the throughput of the entire cluster. NameNode stores the metadata of HDFS namespace in RAM to make the metadata operations fast. Therefore, the size of the namespace is limited by the size of the NameNode RAM. HDFS federation adds support for multiple namespaces/NameNodes.

The metadata includes file and directory hierarchy, file-to-block mapping on DataNodes, DataNode-to-blocks mapping, block IDs, block locations, file owner, file permissions, file modification time, file generation stamp, and number of block replicas, as shown in Figure 1-19.

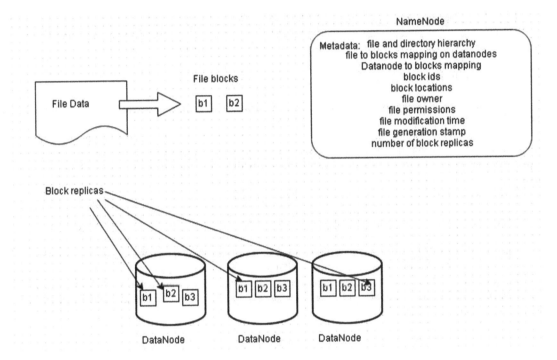

Figure 1-19. NameNode metadata

The metadata objects are blocks, files (file inodes), and directories. Each metadata object occupies about 150-200 bytes in the NameNode's RAM. With a block size of 128MB (default) each file is stored in 1.5 blocks on average. As a block does not store data from multiple files, the number of HDFS blocks allocated per file rounds up to 2. The NameNode's RAM memory requirements for 100 million files with a block replication level of 3 is computed as follows.

```
100 million files=200 million blocks
```

With each block requiring 200 byte in memory, RAM requirements for blocks are as follows:

```
200x1000000x200=40 GB
```

Memory requirement for files metadata are as follows:

```
100x1000000x200=20 GB
```

Total NameNode memory requirements for 100 million files is 60GB.

The number of files per directory on an average in a cluster is about 30. Total number of directories for 100 million files is 333333. The NameNode memory requirements for directories are as follows.

```
333333x200=.0666 GB
```

The NameNode RAM requirement for directories is negligible as compared to the RAM requirement for files and blocks.

The storage on the underlying filesystem is based on the actual file data, not on the number of HDFS blocks. With each file using equivalent of 1.5 HDFS blocks with HDFS block size as 128MB the HDFS capacity in the preceding example to store 100 million files with a replication factor of 3 is as follows.

```
100x1000000x1.5x3x128x1024x1024=6.03x10^16 bytes=60 PB
```

1PB of disk storage requires about 1GB of NameNode RAM. The ratio may vary based on number of blocks per file and block size.

The NameNode's RAM capacity puts a limit on the storage capacity of the HDFS. NameNode's RAM capacity is a limiting factor on the scalability of the HDFS. Most hardware has a limit of about 128GB, which would imply a limit of 128PB on the storage capacity of a HDFS cluster support with a single NameNode. The prior HDFS architecture supports only one namespace per HDFS cluster. The single namespace HDFS architecture is shown in Figure 1-20.

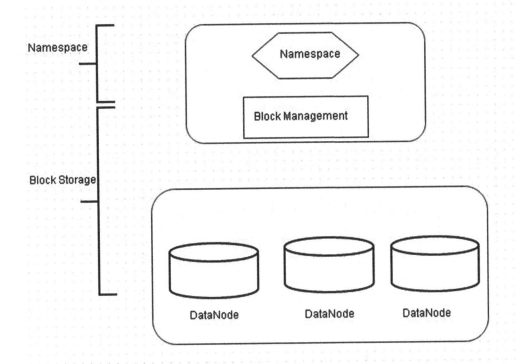

Figure 1-20. *Single namespace HDFS architecture*

If the HDFS is to be scaled to store more data, more than one NameNode is required to store the corresponding metadata for the data. HDFS Federation provides support for multiple namespaces/ NameNodes in a HDFS cluster. The set of blocks associated with a namespace is called a block pool. Each block pool is managed independently of the other block pools and the block pools from all the namespaces are associated with the a common set of DataNodes. Each NameNode manages its associated namespace and block pool independent of other NameNodes. If a NameNode fails the DataNodes continue to serve the other NameNodes. A block pool and a namespace associated with a Namespace together is called a *namespace volume* and constitutes a self-contained unit of management. The HDFS federation architecture is shown in Figure 1-21.

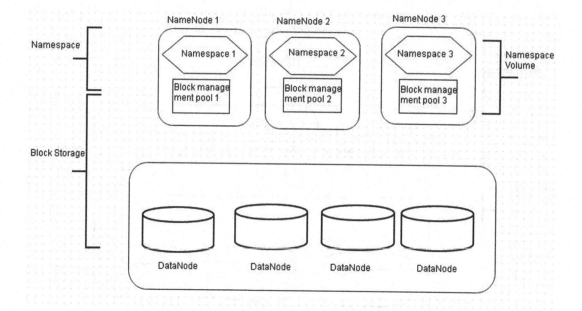

Figure 1-21. *HDFS federation architecture*

With multiple namespaces associated with a cluster, the storage capacity that can be served by the HDFS federation increases. With the preceding example, if each NameNode has a RAM of 128GB the storage capacity that can be supported with three NameNodes in a HDFS Federation becomes 128x3=384PB.

Use Cases for HDFS Federation

HDFS federation is suitable for the following use cases:

- Large deployments. Large deployments use a lot of disk storage could benefit from HDFS federation. As discussed in the example, by using three NameNodes in a HDFS federation, the disk storage capacity increases to 384PB. If 10 NameNodes are used, the disk storage capacity would increase 10-fold.

- A lot of small files. If a lot of small files are stored in the HDFS cluster, the associated namespace objects (files and blocks) increase and the NameNode RAM required to store the metadata for the namespace also increases.

- Small block size. If a very small block size is used, the number of namespace objects increases and the associated NameNode RAM requirement also increases. The minimum block size is configured using the `dfs.namenode.fs-limits.min-block-size` property in `hdfs-default.xml` as 1MB by default. If the block size is set as 1MB or less with the `dfs.blocksize` property the number of namespace objects would increase and the NameNode RAM required to store the metadata also increases. The maximum number of blocks per file is limited by the `dfs.namenode.fs-limits.max-blocks-per-file` property to 1 million.

- Performance. The filesystem operations throughput is limited by a single node in the architecture prior to 60K. Increasing the number of NameNodes increases the read/write operations throughput.

- Isolation of applications and users. Production-critical applications that require a guaranteed NameNode RAM can be isolated to a separate namespace.

- Generic storage service. The block pool abstraction makes it feasible to develop new applications built on the block storage layer without the need to use a filesystem interface. For example, a block pool that caches data to make the distributed cache more efficient. Another example is a block pool for MapReduce temp storage with a different garbage collection scheme.

In the prior architecture, the namespace is tightly coupled with the block management, making direct usage of the storage not feasible.

Data Locality

Moving large quantities of data across a network to a relatively much smaller computation code is not very efficient and data is processed on the same node as the data is stored if feasible, as a result providing data locality. Not having to move large amounts of data for computation reduces the network bandwidth usage. Data locality is defined as how close the computation and input data are in terms of the rack level, node level, core-switch level, and higher network topology levels. We are most interested in the node-level data locality, which implies computation and input data are collocated on the same node. Data locality is only used in the context of input data to a map task, not map output intermediate data, not reduce task input data. The intermediate map output data is stored on a local disk regardless. The reduce input data is the map output data shuffled to the reducers and cannot use data locality as it is processed data from the map phase. Data locality involves using data local to a node for map phase computation on the same node. Files are spread across the cluster and a compute process running on a node operates on a subset of the file data. The data a compute process operates on is the data on the node itself. Most data is read from the local disk to the CPU without having to move data from across the cluster for computation. Data locality is accomplished as computation is moved to the data rather than moving data to the computation. Data locality improves computation and cluster performance.

Node-level data locality may not always be feasible. Node-level data locality uses the fact that the TaskTracker, the daemon that runs a task, is usually collocated on the same node as the DataNode, the daemon that stores data blocks. The following procedure is used to implement data locality.

1. The TaskTracker notifies the JobTracker about available map slots.

2. The JobTracker tries to find a map task that has input data stored local on the TaskTracker node.

3. If such a map task is found, the JobTracker schedules a map task on the TaskTracker node, as a result using data locality. If multiple map tasks with input data on the same node are found, only one of the tasks is scheduled and can use data locality. The other map tasks that have node-local input data cannot use data locality in the assignment of the particular map slot.

4. If a map task with input data on the TaskTracker-same node is not found, the JobTracker tries to find a map task with input data on the same rack as the TaskTracker. If such a map task is found, the JobTracker schedules the map task, thus implementing rack-level data locality.

5. If a map task with input data is not found on the same rack as the TaskTracker node, a random map task is scheduled, as a result can't use data locality.

Data locality is particularly suited to Hadoop for the following reasons:

- Hadoop involves processing large quantities of data. In comparison, the computation code (the map/reduce functions) is negligible. In a data-intensive computing framework, it is much more efficient to move the computation to the data, as shown in Figure 1-22, than the data to the computation. For a CPU-intensive framework, data locality isn't as important.

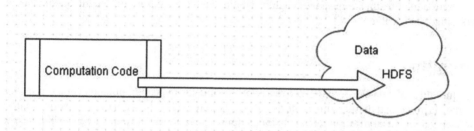

Figure 1-22. *Moving computation code to the data*

- Hadoop is a distributed framework scalable to a large number (up to thousands) of nodes grouped in racks, which are connected by network switches, distributed across the cluster. Moving the data around the cluster would involve high network bandwidth usage. In comparison, moving the computation code to the data reduces network traffic and facilitates high throughput of data processed.

- Hadoop is designed for commodity hardware with component failure as an expected feature. Moving large quantities of data would put load on the network, increasing the chance of network component failure. With having to move a large quantities of data a component failure, such as a switch failure, would degrade performance. In contrast, with data locality even if some switch fails, computation can be restarted on some other node/rack.

Data locality is implemented using the following strategies:

- Rack-aware network topology.

- Multiple replicas of a block placed using the rack-aware topology. The more replicas there are for a block, the more the block data is available locally to more nodes. Sometimes it's better to use more than the default number of three replicas to achieve greater data locality.

- Multiple map tasks scheduled on data-local nodes.

As a result of computation being moved to the data rather than the data to the computation, a lot of client reads handled by HDFS are local reads. Typically, when a client requests to read a file, the DataNode reads the file and sends data to the client over TCP. An optimization introduced to use data locality is a short-circuit local read in which the DataNode is bypassed and a client reads a file from a local disk directly. Short-circuit local reads improve the performance of reads and are feasible only if data is available to a client on a local node.

Rack-Aware Placement Policy

Data is stored in blocks on the HDFS filesystem. Data blocks are replicated, three times by default, for data durability and high availability. Block replicas are distributed across the cluster's racks and nodes using a rack placement policy. NameNode uses a rack-aware replica placement policy to improve data reliability, durability, and network bandwidth utilization. Using the rack-aware replica placement policy replicas of a block are placed on different DataNodes in the cluster on different racks so that failure of a single DataNode or rack does not make all replicas of a block unavailable. Block replicas on other DataNodes/racks are used in the event of failure of a DataNode or a rack. The rack-aware replica placement policy is implemented by the NameNode. Using the default rack-aware replica placement policy, replicas of a block are placed as follows.

1. The first block replica is placed on the same node as the client. If the client request to create a file originates outside the cluster, the first replica is placed on a random node on the cluster.

2. The second replica is placed on a random node on another rack.

3. The third replica is placed on different node on the same rack as the second replica. With three replicas, one rack has two-thirds of the replicas. The reason the second replica is not placed on the same rack as the first and the third replica on a different rack, which would also make two-thirds of the replicas on the same rack, is that if replication is set to 2, all the replicas would be on the same rack. With all replicas on the same rack if the rack fails all replicas are lost without a replica to replicate from.

4. The fourth and subsequent replicas are placed randomly across the cluster with a bias against nodes/racks already having replicas. If it's feasible, no more than two replicas are placed on the same rack and no more than one replica is placed on the same node. The objective is to spread out the replicas across the cluster, consideration the probability of a rack failure is much less than the probability of node failure. For example, with two racks, the fourth replica is placed on the first rack. The replica placement is illustrated in Figure 1-23.

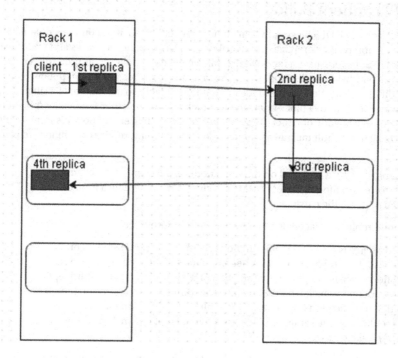

Figure 1-23. *Replica placement on two racks*

The replica placement policy is not strictly adhered to in that it is also ascertained if a target node chosen for replica placement is a suitable target node in terms of network traffic on the node, available space on the node.

It is because of data locality that it is not recommended to use Storage Area Networks (SANs) or Network Attached Storage (NAS) because of the network overhead involved.

Network Topology, Network Bandwidth, and Rack Placement Policy

HDFS runs on a cluster of machines arranged in a network topology that is configured in the configuration property net.topology.impl in core-default.xml. The default implementation of the HDFS network topology is a three-layer one as shown in Figure 1-24. A cluster may consist of many data centers consisting of racks of machines.

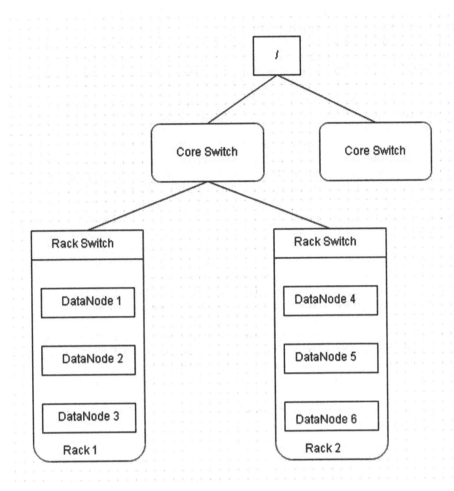

Figure 1-24. *HDFS network topology*

Nodes on a rack share a switch, the rack switch, and rack switches are connected by one or more core switches. DNSToSwitchMapping maps a DataNode's DNS address to a rack switch and a default implementation of DNSToSwitchMapping is configured in core-default.xml using configuration property net.topology.node.switch.mapping.impl as org.apache.hadoop.net.ScriptBasedMapping. The default implementation of DNSToSwitchMapping is based on a using a script that may be configured using net.topology.script.file.name in core-site.xml. The network topology script receives as arguments a list of IP addresses/hostnames of nodes in the cluster and returns the rack name/rack ID for each of the nodes. The maximum number of IP address arguments that a network topology script may be invoked with is set in the configuration property net.topology.script.number.args in core-default.xml; the default value being 100. If a value for net.topology.script.file.name is not set, all nodes are assumed to belong to the same rack, the DEFAULT_RACK. Rack IDs are hierarchical in naming structure and are similar to path names. The default rack ID for every node is /default-rack, and rack IDs are configurable using a pathname pattern such that elements of the path further on the left are higher up on the hierarchical tree.

For example, a node could have a rack ID /core-switch-name/rack-switch-name/rack-name. With a rack-aware replica placement policy NameNode uses a topology script to determine the rack location of nodes. At DataNode startup each DataNode determines to which rack it belongs to using a topology script and notifies the NameNode of the rack ID on registration. The NameNode keeps a rackid-datanode map and tries to place replicas across racks. The number of levels of caches in the network topology is set with the configuration property mapreduce.jobtracker.taskcache.levels in mapred-default.xml. The default value of 2 for mapreduce.jobtracker.taskcache.levels implies that tasks are cached in the network topology at two levels—host level (host ➤ task mapping) and rack level (rack ➤ task mapping). It is recommended that you test the topology script before deploying it. The routing of data packets is directed using network topology discovered by or set in switches and routers, and the rack IDs are used to find near and far nodes based on network latency. Two nodes on the same rack have a lower latency and higher bandwidth than two nodes on different racks. In-rack latency is lower than cross-rack latency. Rack switch uplink bandwidth is usually less than its downlink bandwidth. Rack-awareness and rack IDs are used for block replica placement and MapReduce map task placement. The ApplicationMaster in MRv2 provides hostnames to the ResourceManager when requesting resource containers so that the Scheduler can provide data-local containers for data locality.

Data flow between nodes on different racks has to go through multiple switches. Usually, network bandwidth between nodes in the same rack is greater than network bandwidth between nodes on different racks. Network bandwidth is based on distance between two nodes The block replica placement policy provides a tradeoff between minimizing the write overhead and maximizing reliability, availability, and aggregate read bandwidth. The aggregate read bandwidth is compromised to some extent as the three replicas are placed on two racks instead of three replicas on three different racks. Pluggable topology scripts are used to determine rack location of nodes, information which is used when replicating blocks to nodes.

For a small cluster in which all nodes are connected by a single switch, only two levels of locality are defined: on-machine and off-machine. When data is loaded from the DataNode's local disk to HDFS, one copy is loaded to the local node and two copies are loaded to two other nodes in the cluster chosen at random.

The org.apache.hadoop.fs.BlockLocation class provides methods in Table 1-3 to implement rack-aware replica and task placement.

Table 1-3. *BlockLocation Class Methods*

Method	Description
public String[] getHosts()	Returns the array of hosts hosting a block.
public String[] getNames()	Returns an array of hostname:port hosting a block.
public String[] getTopologyPaths()	Returns an array of topology paths for nodes hosting a block, the last component of the path being the host.
public void setHosts(String[] hosts)	Sets an array of hosts hosting a block.
public void setNames(String[] names)	Sets an array of hostname:port hosting a block.
public void setTopologyPaths(String[] topologyPaths)	Sets an array of topology paths hosting a block.

How Does HDFS Store, Read, and Write Files?

The data storage component HDFS has been discussed earlier in some detail. HDFS is a distributed, fault-tolerant, storage filesystem designed to store large quantities of data (100s of TB) on a cluster of nodes using commodity hardware.

HDFS breaks a large file into blocks, transparent to the client, and stores blocks, replicated for data durability, reliability, and locality on DataNode filesystems. Blocks are stored on independent machines and provide parallel access for read. The block size is set in the configuration property dfs.blocksize in hdfs-default.xml with a default value of 128MB.

```
<property>
    <name>dfs.blocksize</name>
    <value>128m</value>
</property>
```

HDFS is designed for large files written once and read several times, thus simplifying data coherency issues. HDFS is optimized for sequential streaming reads of large files. The org.apache.hadoop. fs.FileSystem class represents a generic filesystem including the HDFS. Reading and writing to a file in HDFS requires the configuration files hdfs-default.xml and hdfs-site.xml in the classpath.

File data is read and written in a streaming mode. High sustained throughput, which scales about linearly, is prioritized over low latency. Data is buffered during read and write operations and the size of the buffer is determined by the configuration properties file.stream-buffer-size and io.file.buffer. size (for sequence files) in core-default.xml, with the default buffer size being 4KB. HDFS manages checksumming, replication, and compression.

Reading a File

To read a file from the HDFS, first obtain a FileSystem object. Create a Configuration object using the default configuration parameters. If hdfs-site.xml and hdfs-default.xml are not in the classpath, add them to the classpath.

```
Configuration conf = new Configuration();
conf.addResource(new Path("HADOOP_CONF/conf/hdfs-site.xml"));
conf.addResource(new Path("HADOOP_CONF/conf./hdfs-default.xml"));
```

The static methods get(Configuration conf), get(URI uri, Configuration conf), or get(URI uri, Configuration conf, String user) in the FileSystem class may be used to obtain a filesystem.

```
FileSystem fs = FileSystem.get(conf);
```

A file or a directory in the HDFS filesystem is represented with the org.apache.hadoop.fs.Path class. Create a Path object to the file to be read. A relative path starts with / and is relative to the base directory on the HDFS. The base directory for a user is /usr/$USER.

```
Path inFile = new Path("input.txt");
```

A Path object may also be constructed using the HDFS filesystem URL.

```
Path inFile = new Path("hdfs://host:port/input.txt");
```

Obtain a FSDataInputStream object using the filesystem's open(Path) method.

```
FSDataInputStream in = fs.open(inFile);
```

The FSDataInputStream class implements the PositionedReadable interface, which adds the provision for positional reading; read from a given position within a file. FSDataInputStream also implements the Seekable interface, which adds the provision to seek within a file. Seekable's seek(long pos) method seeks to the specified position from the start of the file with the next read being from the position.

Read the file from the FSDataInputStream object using the read(byte[]) method, which reads some number of bytes and stores them in a buffer array. The read(byte[]) method returns the number of bytes read. First, create a byte[] buffer to write the file read. Invoke the read(byte[]) method to read the FS data input stream into the buffer and use a while loop to output the buffer using a UTF8 character set.

```
byte[] buffer = new byte[BUFFER_SIZE];
int bytesRead = 0;
ByteArrayOutputStream bufferOutput = new ByteArrayOutputStream();
        while ((bytesRead = in.read(buffer)) > 0) {
bufferOutput.write(bytesRead);
}
```

The FSDataInputStream class wraps the FSInputStream in a DataInputStream and buffers input through BufferedInputStream. FSDataInputStream provides several read methods to read the buffered data.

For example, a UTF8 encoded string may be generated from the file read from the HDFS as follows.

```
String msg=in.readUTF(buffer);
```

When the read is complete, close the input stream using the close() method.

```
in.close();
```

The client reads directly from the DataNodes using a FSDataInputStream. The NameNode is only involved in providing the block locations to the client. The HDFS read path is shown in Figure 1-25.

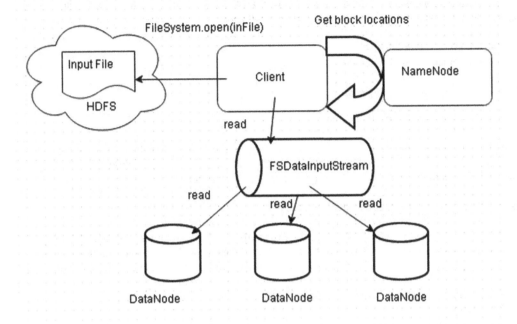

Figure 1-25. *HDFS read path*

DataNodes support read-ahead of block data into the operating system buffer cache using Hadoop-native libraries with the dfs.datanode.readahead.bytes property in hdfs-default.xml. Read-ahead improves performance especially if disk read is contended. By default 4MB are cached.

```
<property>
    <name>dfs.datanode.readahead.bytes</name>
    <value>4193404</value>
</property>
```

For workloads that read only small sections of a block, the data is cached behind read. When data is read from a DataNode disk and delivered to a client, it may be advantageous to cache that data in the OS buffer cache behind read, especially for workloads that read only a small section of a block. If the workload is too large to benefit from the caching in OS buffer cache, the cache may be purged by setting the dfs.datanode.drop.cache.behind.reads property to true; the default is false.

```
<property>
    <name>dfs.datanode.drop.cache.behind.reads</name>
    <value>true</value>
</property>
```

Writing a File

The procedure to write a file to the HDFS is similar to reading a file. First, obtain a FileSystem object using a Configuration object created with the default configuration parameters.

```
Configuration conf = new Configuration();
 FileSystem fs = FileSystem.get(conf);
```

Specify the Path on HDFS to write to.

```
Path outFile = new Path("output.txt");
```

The FileSystem class provides the overloaded create() method to open a FSDataOutputStream to the path on HDFS to be written to. The create(Path f, boolean overwrite) method opens an FSDataOutputStream to the specified path with the provision to overwrite.

```
FSDataOutputStream out=fs.create(outFile,true);
```

The FSDataOutputStream class implements the Flushable and Syncable interfaces to flush and sync the data output stream, respectively. The FSDataOutputStream class provides several methods to write to HDFS. For example, write a String message to output.txt using the writeUTF(String str) method.

```
String msg="Test to create a file on HDFS";
out.writeUTF(msg);
```

Close FSDataOutputStream using the close() method.

```
out.close();
```

As another example, read from an input file and write the file to the HDFS.

```
byte[] buffer = new byte[BUFFER_SIZE];
Path inFile = new Path("input.txt");
Path outFile = new Path("output.txt");
FSDataInputStream in = fs.open(inFile);
FSDataOutputStream out=fs.create(outFile);

int bytesRead = 0;
        while ((bytesRead = in.read(buffer)) > 0) {
            out.write(buffer, 0, bytesRead);
}

in.close();
out.close();
```

The input, output paths may be specified as command-line arguments.

```
Path inFile = new Path(argv[0]);
Path outFile = new Path(argv[1]);
```

In addition to the create(Path) method, the FileSystem class provides several other create methods to obtain a FSDataOutputStream to a path on the HDFS.

An example application to read and write to the HDFS is as follows.

```java
import java.io.IOException;
import org.apache.hadoop.conf.Configuration;
import org.apache.hadoop.fs.FileSystem;
import org.apache.hadoop.fs.FSDataInputStream;
import org.apache.hadoop.fs.FSDataOutputStream;
import org.apache.hadoop.fs.Path;

public class HDFSReadWriteFile {

  public static void main (String[] argv) throws IOException {
    Configuration conf = new Configuration();
    FileSystem fs = FileSystem.get(conf);

    Path inFile = new Path("input.txt");
    Path outFile = new Path("output.txt");

    FSDataInputStream in = fs.open(inFile);
    FSDataOutputStream out = fs.create(outFile);
    byte buffer[] = new byte[512];
    try {
      int bytesRead = 0;
      while ((bytesRead = in.read(buffer)) > 0) {
       out.write(buffer, 0, bytesRead);
      }
    } catch (IOException e) {
      System.err.println("Error while reading or writing file");
    } finally {
     in.close();
      out.close();
    }
  }
}
```

During the file write to HDFS, the file is written directly to the DataNodes using a FSDataOutputStream. The NameNode provides a list of block locations to the client. A DataNode pipeline is created ordered by distance from the client. Data is not written to each DataNode directly, but written to the closest DataNode to client. From the first DataNode data is written to the other DataNodes in the pipeline until the required number of block replicas have been created. The data is written using the data queue. An acknowledgment message is sent back along the DataNode pipeline in the ack queue. The HDFS write path is shown in Figure 1-26.

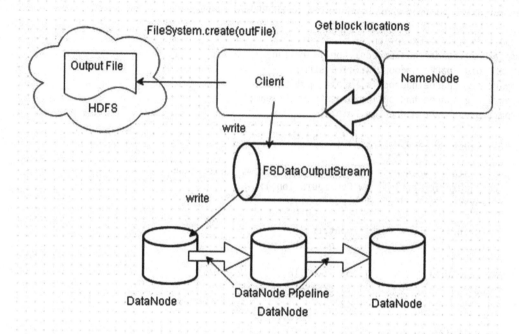

Figure 1-26. *DataNode pipeline in writing a file*

If while writing to the DataNode pipeline, a DataNode/network failure in the DataNodes pipeline occurs, the DataNode is replaced with another DataNode. The feature to replace a failed DataNode is enabled with the property dfs.client.block.write.replace-datanode-on-failure.enable, which has a default value of true. The policy to replace failed DataNodes is configured in the dfs.client.block.write. replace-datanode-on-failure.policy property. The DEFAULT policy to replace DataNodes does take into account the availability of DataNodes and the required replication level, but for a small cluster of three or fewer nodes in which a replacement DataNode is most likely not available, it may be suitable to set dfs. client.block.write.replace-datanode-on-failure.enable to false or set dfs.client.block.write. replace-datanode-on-failure.policy to NEVER.

```
<property>
    <name>dfs.client.block.write.replace-datanode-on-failure.enable</name>
    <value>false</value>
</property>
```

If dfs.client.block.write.replace-datanode-on-failure.policy is set to NEVER or dfs.client. block.write.replace-datanode-on-failure.enable is set to false the failed DataNode is removed from the pipeline and a new pipeline is constructed from the remaining DataNodes. Another option for the dfs.client.block.write.replace-datanode-on-failure.policy is ALWAYS, which replaces the failed DataNode regardless of other factors.

After a file is written and closed, bytes written cannot be altered or removed. New data may be added using append. While a client has opened a file for writing no other client can write to the file. Only when a client closes the file other clients may open the file for writing. The client has a renewable time limit to have exclusive access to a file for write. When the time limit expires, another client may preempt the exclusive access to the file. After a hard limit of one hour, if a client has neither renewed the time limit nor closed the file, HDFS closes the file and makes the file accessible to other clients for write. The configuration property dfs.namenode.accesstime.precision sets the default precision up to which the last access time to a file is kept. By default the last access time to file is kept precisely to the hour. A file open for write by one client may be accessed by other clients for concurrent reads. If a file is open for writing, the new data added is not guaranteed to be available to a client until the file is closed. A file open for writing may be flushed using the FSDataOutputStream's hflush() method to make the data available to other clients for read. The data in the client's user buffer is flushed with hflush() method.

When data is written to a DataNode disk, it may be advantageous to cache data in the OS buffer cache behind write, especially for workloads that write only a small section of a block. If the workload is too large to benefit from the caching in the OS buffer cache, the cache may be purged by setting the dfs.datanode.drop.cache.behind.reads property to true; the default is false.

```
<property>
    <name> dfs.datanode.drop.cache.behind.writes</name>
    <value>true</value>
  </property>
```

By default, the OS does not immediately enqueue data written to a DataNode disk. Some workloads can benefit in terms of performance by enqueuing data immediately after being written to disk. The default OS policy is to wait 30 seconds. Setting the dfs.datanode.sync.behind.writes property to true syncs data immediately after being written to disk.

```
<property>
    <name>dfs.datanode.sync.behind.writes</name>
    <value>true</value>
  </property>
```

FileSystem supports other file operations such as copying, moving, deleting, renaming files, and making directories. In addition to the provision to set replication level and file permissions in create() methods, separate methods to set replication and permissions are also provided. Validation methods to find if a file already exists or if a path is a file or a directory are also provided. For example, isFile can be used to determine if a file already exists and that it indeed is a file as follows.

```
if(fs.exists(inFile))
if(fs.isFile(inFile))
```

HDFS provides the provision to append to a file using the append(Path f), append(Path f,int bufferSize), and append(Path f,int bufferSize,Progressable progress) methods in FileSystem. The provision to append files is enabled with the dfs.support.append property, with a default value set to true.

```
<property>
 <name>dfs.support.append</name>
 <value>true</value>
 </property>
```

The append() methods return a FSDataOutputStream.

```
FSDataOutputStream out=fs.append(outFile);
int bytesRead = 0;
        while ((bytesRead = in.read(buffer)) > 0) {
            out.write(buffer, 0, bytesRead);
}
```

Storing a File

HDFS stores files on DataNodes local filesystem. A file is broken into blocks and the blocks are replicated, three times by default and configurable with the dfs.replication configuration property. The HDFS blocks are an abstraction over the underlying filesystem. Each block is stored as a data file and a corresponding checksum file. The data files and the checksum files are stored in the DataNode's data directories, which are configured in hdfs-default.xml.

```
<property>
 <name>dfs.datanode.data.dir</name>
 <value>/data/1/dfs/dn,/data/2/dfs/dn,/data/3/dfs/dn</value>
</property>
```

As blocks are written to, the distribution of blocks across the cluster may become uneven. Some DataNodes could have more blocks than others due to several reasons, including the following:

- There is a replica placement policy to keep one replica of the block on the same rack as the node on which a client is creating a file. The second replica is on another rack and the third replica is on a different node on the other rack. Blocks are spread to different nodes on a rack and different racks across the cluster for data durability.

- A new DataNode added to a cluster does not have any blocks stored on it.

For optimized use of the HDFS, storage should be evenly balanced across the cluster. A balancer tool is provided to balance the data across the cluster evenly as specified by a threshold value. The balancer tool moves blocks from a relatively over-utilized node to a less utilized node without reducing the number of replicas on a rack, changing the number of replicas a block has, or causing block loss. The replica placement policy should be adhered to in rebalancing the blocks across the cluster. The balancer tool can be run on a HDFS cluster while a files are being read and written and deleted. The following command may be run by an administrator.

```
bin/start-balancer.sh [-threshold ]
```

The threshold parameter specifies a percentage defined as follows.

```
|Utilization of the node-Utilization of the cluster|<= threshold
```

Utilization is defined as follows.

```
Utilization =Used capacity/Total capacity
```

For example, the following command starts the balancer and balances the block storage across a DataNode to within 5% of the cluster utilization. The default threshold is 10%.

```
bin/start-balancer.sh -threshold 5
```

Balancing a cluster should not saturate the network bandwidth such that not enough bandwidth is available for other file operations. The configuration property dfs.datanode.balance.bandwidthPerSec specifies the maximum bandwidth each DataNode can utilize to balance as bytes/sec, with a default value of 1MB/sec.

```
<property>
 <name>dfs.datanode.balance.bandwidthPerSec</name>
 <value>1048576</value>
</property>
```

As rebalancing moves blocks around the associated namespace (such as block locations and block replicas), the NameNode has to be updated. Rebalancing should not cause the NameNode to become too busy to serve other requests.

Checksum Verification

HDFS also provides a mechanism to detect block corruption using CRC32 checksum verification during reading and writing. The blocks stored on HDFS could become corrupted, which would result in data loss. Block replication does provide data durability and the provision to re-replicate blocks from a uncorrupted replica. But, if all replicas of a block become corrupted, the block is lost.

To prevent block corruption and early detection of block corruption checksum verification is used for blocks read and written to HDFS. The client computes the checksum for a file, and the file data and checksum data are bundled in a HDFS packet to be written to the HDFS. The packet size is configured with the file.client-write-packet-size property and has a default value of 64KB. File data is sent to the DataNode pipeline one packet at a time. As a file is created and written on the HDFS, a checksum block is also created for each file data block and stored along with the data block. Data is stored in blk_<id> files and checksums are stored in blk_<id>.meta files.

On the underlying filesystem of the DataNode, a block checksum file is stored along with the data file. The number of bytes per checksum is configured with file.bytes-per-checksum configuration and the io.bytes.per.checksum (for sequence files) in core-default.xml with default value being 512 bytes. The file.bytes-per-checksum and io.bytes.per.checksum value must not be larger than file.stream-buffer-size and io.file.buffer.size respectively. When a file is read, the checksum for a file data block is sent along with each data block to the client. The client recomputes the data block checksum and validates it with the checksum sent along with the data block. If the newly computed checksum is different than the checksum stored in the checksum file and sent to the client, the block is deemed to have become corrupted. Another replica of the block is sent to the client and the block is replicated to bring the replication level to the configured replication. The checksum verification may be turned off using the filesystem's SetVerifyChecksum(boolean verifyChecksum) method.

DataNode periodically validates the checksums using a block scanner and reports any block corruption, if detected, to the NameNode in the periodic block reports. If a block is found to be corrupted, the NameNode creates another replica of the block from a non-corrupted replica and removes the corrupted block replica.

File is served to the client using TCP socket, not Hadoop RPC. During read, the client receives a list of block locations from the NameNode, ordered according to the distance from the client. The client reads from the closest block location first and reads from the farther block locations only if required; for example, if a nearer block location is corrupted. For the write path client keeps two queues ; the data queue and the ack queue. The data queue sends the file data and the ack queue receives acknowledgements when data is written successfully.

The org.apache.hadoop.fs.FileUtil class provides a collection of file processing util methods, including for copying files between filesystems.

Hadoop Cluster in Data Storage and in Data Processing

The cluster operation in storage involves the following.

1. Input data is broken into HDFS blocks, which is just an abstraction.

2. Blocks are replicated and stored on the DataNode's underlying filesystem, the data directories configured with `dfs.datanode.data.dir`.

3. The metadata for the blocks is kept by the NameNode. The metadata includes the filename, file permissions, block IDs, block locations, and number of replicas. The HDFS namespace metadata is kept in the NameNode's RAM, and also on the NameNode's storage as `fsimage`.

4. The DataNode communicates with the NameNode periodically, every three seconds by default.

5. The DataNode also periodically (every hour) sends block reports to the NameNode about block replicas it is storing, including any corrupt blocks.

6. The NameNode may request, in response to a communication from DataNode, the DataNode to create additional replicas of a block, or reduce block replicas, or remove block replicas.

7. Any modifications made to the HDFS namespace are logged in an edits log.

8. Periodically, the secondary NameNode downloads the `fsimage` and the edits log from the NameNode and applies a checkpoint on the `fsimage`, which implies the edits log is merged with the `fsimage`. The check-pointed `fsimage` is uploaded back to the `NameNode`. The Hadoop cluster in data storage is shown in Figure 1-27.

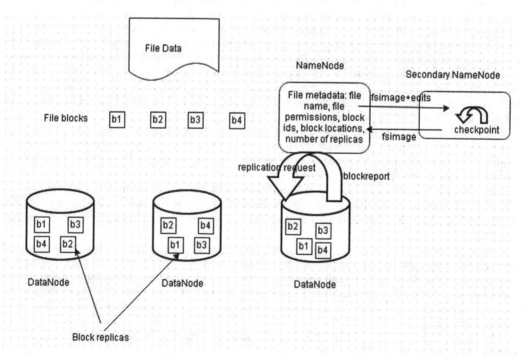

Figure 1-27. *Hadoop cluster in data storage*

As introduced, MapReduce is a data processing framework in which input data from HDFS is processed as a job in two phases: the map phase and reduce phase. The map phase consists of a user-defined map() function. During the map phase, data is input to a mapper as key/value pairs and the mapper emits intermediate key/value pairs. The map() function in the mapper is invoked for each key/value pair in the input data. The map outputs are partitioned and sorted. The reduce phase consists of shuffling the map outputs, merge-sorting the map outputs and reducing the map outputs using a reduce() function. The data input to the reduce() function consists of key/value pairs and the value is actually a list of values. The user-defined reduce() function reduces the input key/<list of values> pairs into a key/value pair. The output from the reducer is the job output and is stored back in the HDFS.

The MapReduce (MR1) cluster operates as follows during data processing.

1. The client copies the job resources, which include the input splits meta-information, job configuration, and job mapper and reducer classes, and the job driver class, to the HDFS DataNodes. The job resources are replicated 10 times by default.

2. A client submits a job (consisting of map and reduce tasks) to the JobTracker.

3. JobTracker schedules a map task on a TaskTracker in response to periodic communication from TaskTracker. TaskTracker periodically notifies the JobTracker about the status of tasks and the availability of map/reduce slots. JobTracker includes the meta-information for data input split to be processed. Data locality is used, if feasible, to launch a map task on the same machine where its input data is stored.

4. The TaskTracker retrieves input records from the DataNodes using the input split meta-info.

5. TaskTracker launches a JVM for the task and launches a map task. One map task is launched for each input split. The map tasks are launched in parallel on TaskTrackers by the JobTracker. The maximum number of map tasks that may launched on the same TaskTracker simultaneously is determined by the mapreduce.tasktracker.map.tasks.maximum configuration property and is 2 by default.

6. The map outputs are partitioned, sorted, and shuffled to the reducer machine's TaskTracker for the reduce phase.

7. The copying of the map outputs to the reducer is the only inter-node communication in MapReduce data processing. The reduce tasks shuffle map segments assigned to them from the map tasks. The shuffle is a parallel copy operation in which the map outputs on the map task are not deleted. The number of parallel copies involved in the shuffle is determined by mapreduce.reduce.shuffle.parallelcopies, with default value of 5. The number of concurrent threads involved in the shuffle is determined by the mapreduce.tasktracker.http.threads configuration property, with the default of 40 threads. Shuffle is an all-map-to-all-reduce operation in which map segments from all the map tasks are copied to all the reduce tasks. The map segments are fetched using HTTP into the Shuffle buffer. The shuffle is an across the tasks network operation and could involve a delay due to various reasons including network issues, and map tasks not having been completed.

8. The map segments in the shuffle buffer are merge-sorted. The JobTracker schedules the reduce tasks when a fraction of the map tasks, as determined by the `mapreduce.job.reduce.slowstart.completedmaps` configuration property, have completed successfully. The number of reduce tasks that may be launched simultaneously on a TaskTracker is configured using the `mapreduce.tasktracker.reduce.tasks.maximum` property and defaults to 2.

9. TaskTracker launches a JVM for a reduce task and launches the reduce task. The number of reduce tasks is configured in the job configuration and is 1 by default as configured in the `mapreduce.job.reduces` property in `mapred-default.xml`.

10. When the job completes the reduce tasks output files in the job output directory, which are committed to the job's final output location, which is typically HDFS. The reduce task output files are not merged in the job's final output location.

The cluster operation for all the daemons in data storage and processing in MRv1 is shown in Figure 1-28.

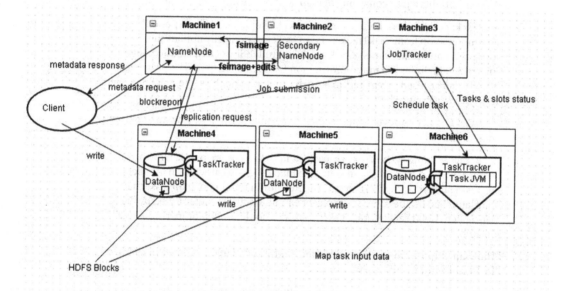

Figure 1-28. *Hadoop cluster in data storage and processing*

JVM Reusage

By default, a new JVM is launched for each task. Launching a new JVM incurs an overhead and if a job is small it may be advantageous to do some of the *ubertasking*, a feature that enables running multiple tasks in the same JVM, one after the other. Ubertasking has to be enabled by setting `mapreduce.job.ubertask.enable` to `true` in `mapred-default.xml`. The number of tasks that may run sequentially in the same JVM is configured in `mapreduce.job.jvm.numtasks`, default is 1. If `mapreduce.job.jvm.numtasks` is set to `-1`, any number of tasks may be run in the same JVM. The number of tasks per JVM may also be set using the `setNumTasksToExecutePerJvm(int numTasks)` method in JobConf. The maximum number of maps a job may have to be eligible for ubertasking is nine and is set in the `mapreduce.job.ubertask.maxmaps` property. The value may be overridden downward, for example a value of 3 may be set but a value of 10 may not be set.

A job cannot have more than one reduces to be eligible for ubertasking, the threshold for the reduces is configured in `mapreduce.job.ubertask.maxreduces`, with a default value of 1. The `mapreduce.job.ubertask.maxreduces` default value may be overridden only downward, implying that 0 is the only other valid value. Another factor that is considered in ubertasking is `mapreduce.job.ubertask.maxbytes`, the maximum number of allowable bytes in the input for a job to be eligible for ubertasking. The default value of `mapreduce.job.ubertask.maxbytes` is the block size as set in `dfs.block.size` or `dfs.blocksize`. JVM reuse is not supported in MRv2, which is discussed next.

The MRv2 daemons are ResourceManager, ApplicationMaster, and NodeManager. The role of the JobTracker is divided into a global ResourceManager and a per-application ApplicationMaster. The ResourceManager consists of a Scheduler and an ApplicationsManager. A MapReduce job is submitted to the ApplicationsManager. The ResourceManager provides two main services.

- Scheduler. A pluggable component that manages the resource scheduling policy. The schedulers supported are FifoScheduler (default for MapReduce1), CapacityScheduler, and FairScheduler (default for YARN). Cloudera recommends FairScheduler for both MapReduce1 and YARN. Scheduler's role is to allocate resources to the applications running in the cluster keeping into consideration the constraints of capacities and queues. The Scheduler does not monitor or track the status of an application, nor does it restart failed tasks. Scheduler assigns resources using the abstraction of resource containers, which encapsulate resources as memory, CPU, disk, and network.

- ApplicationsManager. ApplicationsManager's role is to manage running ApplicationMasters in the cluster including starting, monitoring, and restarting AMs in the event of a failure. ApplicationsManager accepts job submissions and starts the first ApplicationMaster container.

The protocol used by a client to communicate with the ResourceManager, to launch an application for example, is ApplicationClientProtocol. The protocol used by an ApplicationMaster registers/de-registers with the ResourceManager and request for resource containers from the Scheduler is ApplicationMasterProtocol.

The ApplicationMaster's role is to negotiate resources (resource containers) from the ResourceManager/Scheduler and coordinate with the NodeManager to execute and monitor tasks on the containers. The ApplicationMaster, in coordination with the NodeManager, starts, monitors, and restarts an application's individual tasks. Each map/reduce task runs in a container instead of a map/reduce slot in MR1's TaskTracker. The resource containers are not specific to a map/reduce task as the TaskTracker's slots are either map or reduce slots. Either of map or a reduce task can run on a resource container, which provides greater flexibility and availability in comparison to the map/reduce slots of TaskTracker. The containers are optimized for cluster utilization in comparison to the map/reduce slots.

The protocol used by the ApplicationMaster to communicate with the NodeManager to start/stop containers and get status updates on containers is ApplicationClientProtocol.

NodeManager's role is to manage resource containers including starting containers, monitoring their status (resource usage), and reporting the same to the ResourceManager/Scheduler. A resource container is an abstraction of a resource (CPU, memory, disk, and network). Cluster resources are allocated in terms of number of containers and NodeManager's role includes monitoring that an application is not using more resources than it has been allocated.

The MRv2 (YARN) cluster operates as follows during data processing.

1. A client obtains an application ID from the ResourceManager/ApplicationsManager. The response from the ResourceManager includes information about the cluster such as minimum/maximum resource capabilities.

2. A client submits an application (a MapReduce job or a directed application graph) to the ResourceManager/ApplicationsManager and includes the following information:

    a. Application ID

    b. Application name

    c. Application queue

    d. Application priority

    e. User submitting the application

    f. Information defining the container in which the ApplicationMaster is to be launched and run. The information defining the container, includes local resources (binaries, jars, and classpath).

3. ResourceManager allocates a container with the required specification and starts an ApplicationMaster for the application on the container.

4. After the ApplicationMaster has initialized, it registers with the ResourceManager/Scheduler. ApplicationMaster communicates with the ResourceManager periodically.

5. An ApplicationMaster may request for resource containers based on task requirements. The container specification includes the following information:

    Hostname: The asterisk (*) implies any host.

    Resource capability: Memory in MB, as multiples of minimum capacity and less than maximum capacity.

    Priority: When certain containers are required with higher priority. As map tasks are run before the reduce tasks, the map task containers would usually be assigned higher priority.

    The container request includes the following information:

    Number and specification of requested containers.

    Any containers to be deallocated.

    Response id.

    Progress update as a value in the range of 0 to 1.

6. ResourceManager allocates containers based on cluster capacity, application priorities, and scheduling policy. The response from the ResourceManager includes the following information:

    a. Reboot flag indicating if the ApplicationMaster needs to be rebooted as it might have got out of sync.

    b. Number and specification of allocated containers.

    c.   Status of resources in the cluster, information which may be used to re-prioritize tasks if resource capacity is limited.

    d.   Completed containers, information which an ApplicationMaster may use to re-launch failed tasks.

    e.   Number of nodes (machines) in the cluster.

7.   After a container has been allocated, the ApplicationMaster coordinates with the NodeManager to start the containers, launch tasks on the containers, and monitor the status of the tasks. NodeManager also communicates with the ResourceManager about resource usage by the application, such as if an application is using more than the allocated resources.

8.   The container retrieves input records from the DataNodes for a map task to process. Input to reduce tasks is shuffled from map tasks.

9.   When a MapReduce job completes the job, output is committed to HDFS.

The different daemons in MRv2 and the communication protocols (`AMRMProtocol`, `ClientRMProtocol`, and `ContainerManager`) between them is shown in Figure 1-29.

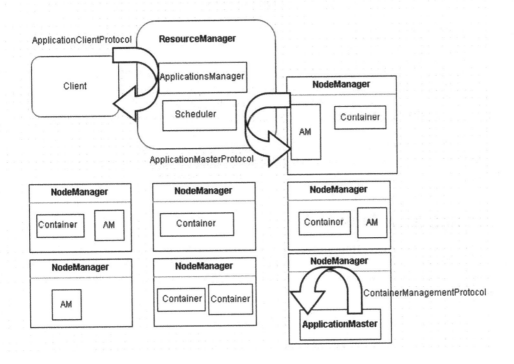

Figure 1-29. *MRv2 daemons*

The cluster operation for all the daemons in data storage and processing in MRv2 are shown in Figure 1-30.

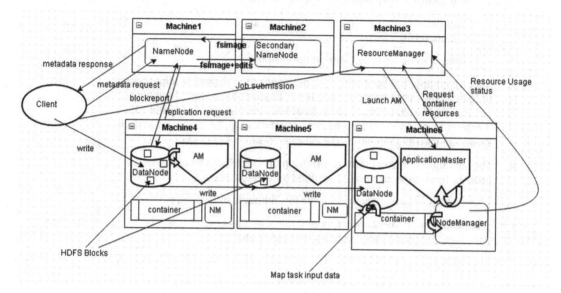

Figure 1-30. *MRv2 cluster operation*

As Hadoop clusters grow in size, it becomes increasingly difficult to manage a cluster. Because ResourceManager has only the function of scheduling it manages the cluster more easily. ResourceManager, a pure scheduler, optimizes cluster utilization using criteria such as capacity guarantees, fairness and SLAs. As map/reduce slots, which could only be used to run either map or reduce tasks, have been replaced with resource containers, which may be used for either map or reduce tasks, the resources are utilized more efficiently. YARN supports not only MapReduce, but also any other programming model such as graph processing and iterative modeling. MRv1 and MRv2 daemons should not be run simultaneously on a cluster, as it is not supported and they will degrade performance if they run together.

The Old and New APIs

Hadoop API (classes and interfaces) provides access to the HDFS and MapReduce frameworks. Version 0.20.x introduced a new MapReduce API. The new API is independent of the MR version. MRv1 and MRv2 may be used with either the old API or the new API. The main differences between the old API and the new API are listed in Table 1-4.

Table 1-4. *Differences Between the Old and New APIs*

Feature	Old API	New API
MapReduce package	org.apache.hadoop.mapred	org.apache.hadoop.mapreduce
Mapper class/interface	interface Mapper<K1,V1,K2,V2>	class Mapper<KEYIN,VALUEIN, KEYOUT,VALUEOUT>
Reducer class/interface	interface Reducer<K2,V2,K3,V3>	Reducer<KEYIN,VALUEIN, KEYOUT,VALUEOUT>
Collect map output	OutputCollector<K,V>.collect (K key,V value)	Mapper. Context.write(KEYOUT key,VALUEOUT value)
Customized mapper execution	MapRunnable<K1,V1,K2,V2>.run (RecordReader<K1,V1> input,OutputCollector<K2,V2> output, Reporter reporter)	Mapper.run(org.apache.hadoop. mapreduce.Mapper.Context context)
Job configuration	Class JobConf	Class Job
Job submission	JobClient.runJob(JobConf) JobClient.submitJob(JobConf)	Job.submit() Job.waitForCompletion(boolean verbose)
Map output filename	part-nnnnn	part-m-nnnnn
Reduce output filename	part-nnnnn	part-r-nnnnn
Mapper's map() method	Mapper.map(K1 key, V1 value, OutputCollector<K2,V2> output, Reporter reporter)	Mapper.map(KEYIN key,VALUEIN value,org.apache.hadoop. mapreduce.Mapper.Context context)
Reducer's reduce() method	Reducer.reduce(K2 key,Iterator<V2> values,OutputCollector<K3,V3> output,Reporter reporter)	Reducer.reduce(KEYIN key,Iterable<VALUEIN> values,org.apache.hadoop. mapreduce.Reducer.Context context)
Set up mapper/reducer	configure(JobConf job)	setup(Context context)
Close mapper/reducer	close()	cleanup(Context context)
Set Job class	new JobConf(Configuration, Class) new JobConf(Class)	Job.setJarByClass(Class<?> cls)
Get InputSplits from InputFormat	InputSplit[] getSplits(JobConf job,int numSplits)	List<InputSplit> getSplits(JobContext context)
Create RecordReader from InputFormat	RecordReader<K,V> getRecordReader(InputSplit split,JobConf job,Reporter reporter)	RecordReader<K,V> createRecordReader(InputSplit split, TaskAttemptContext context)
InputFormat for multiple files	MultiFileInputFormat<K,V>	CombineFileInputFormat<K,V>

(continued)

Table 1-4. (*continued*)

Feature	Old API	New API
Create key object	RecordReader.createKey()	RecordReader.getCurrentKey()
Create value object	RecordReader.createValue()	RecordReader.getCurrentValue()
Get next record	RecordReader.next(K key,V value)	RecordReader.nextKeyValue()
Create RecordWriter from OutputFormat	OutputFormat.getRecordWriter (FileSystem ignored,JobConf job,String name,Progressable progress)	OutputFormat.getRecordWriter (TaskAttemptContext context)
Check output specification	OutputFormat.checkOutputSpecs (FileSystem ignored,JobConf job)	OutputFormat. checkOutputSpecs(JobContext context)
Cluster state	Class ClusterStatus	Class ClusterMetrics
Job status	interface RunningJob	Class JobStatus

Data Serialization Options

Data serialization is the process of converting data in memory to bytes that are transmitted over the network or written to disk. Data serialization is performed at three phases of a MapReduce application.

- Serialization to the wire (network) for interprocess communication (IPC) using RPC
- Serialization of intermediate map outputs locally to disk
- Serialization at the reducers, which is also the MapReduce application output, to HDFS

The intermediate map outputs are serialized to the network and the disk. The MapReduce job output is serialized to HDFS. Different serialization frameworks such Avro, Thrift, and Protocol Buffers offer advantages based on the scenario.

Writables

The default serialization interface in Hadoop is org.apache.hadoop.io.Writable, which any key or value type in Hadoop Map Reduce framework should implement. Any key or value type in the hadoop MapReduce framework implements Writable. A Writable is a serializable object that implements simple, efficient, serialization protocol based on DataInput and DataOutput. The DataInput interface is used to read bytes from a binary stream and convert to any of the Java primitive types such as short, int, double. DataInput may also be used to read a string from data in a slightly modified UTF8 format. The DataOutput interface is used to convert from any Java primitive types and outputting bytes to a binary stream. DataOutput also outputs a string to a slightly modified UTF8 format. An example of using Writables is the mapper used in the MapReduce program.

```
public class WordCountMapper implements Mapper<LongWritable, Text, Text, IntWritable> {}
```

Each of the input key, input value, output key and output value types LongWritable, Text, and IntWritable implement the Writable interface. The main advantage of Writables is efficiency resulting from their compactness. The compact representation of Writables results from not storing the types in the serialized representation.

But Writables have disadvantages too, one being their inefficiency in storing the different binary storage formats for MapReduce input and output. Starting with Hadoop 0.17, any Serialization framework may be used in a MapReduce program with the org.apache.hadoop.io.serializer. Serialization<T> interface, which encapsulates a Serializer/Deserializer pair. Using a Serializer<T> objects of type <T> may be serialized to an java.io.OutputStream with the serialize(T t) method. Using the Deserializer<T> interface objects from an input stream may be deserialized to type <T> with the deserialize(T t) method. Serialization for Writables is provided using the org.apache.hadoop. io.serializer.WritableSerialization class, which implements the org.apache.hadoop.io.serializer. Serialization<Writable> interface. WritableSerialization delegates to Writable.write(java. io.DataOutput) and Writable.readFields(java.io.DataInput). With the support for the Serialization framework Thrift types, which were otherwise inefficient to use may be used in a MapReduce program.

The requirement for key and value is as follows:

- Implement the Writable interface

- Be accepted by a serialization registered with SerializationFactory

The default output format from a MapReduce job is TextOutputFormat, which generates plain text files. For generating binary output, configure the output format as SequenceFileOutputFormat, which generates sequence files as output. A SequenceFile is a flat file consisting of binary key/value pairs. Sequence files provide serialization/deserialization of arbitrary data types not just text files. Sequence files are suitable for intermediate map outputs. Sequence files can be read quickly into the mapper, which makes Sequence files especially suitable as a MapReduce job output in which the job output is to be read in another MapReduce job.

Avro

Avro has replaced Hadoop Record I/O, which was used, but is presently deprecated, for simplifying serialization and deserialization of records in a language-neutral method. Avro is a schema-based serialization framework, which stores data using Avro data files. The schema is serialized with the data file, which has the advantage of not having to store the type information in the data file. Avro's main advantages are as follows:

- Flexible schema

- Generic data handling without code generation

- Compact, smaller size binary untagged data files

The schemas are defined in JSON. The advantage of using Avro is that a different schema may be used in serialization and deserialization and Avro handles the missing/extraneous/updated fields. For example, use the following JSON schema for serialization.

```
{
    "type": "record",
    "name": "Catalog",
    "fields": [
        {"name": "name", "type": "string"},
        {"name": "id", "type": "int"},
        {"name": "journal", "type": "string"},
        {"name": "editions", "type": {"type": "array", "items": "string"}}
    ]
}
```

Subsequently modify the schema to the following:

```
{
    "type": "record",
    "name": "Catalog",
    "fields": [
        {"name": "name", "type": "string"},
        {"name": "id", "type": "string"},
        {"name": "publisher", "type": "string"},
        {"name": "editions", "type": {"type": "array", "items": "string"}}
    ]
}
```

The modified schema may be used for deserialization of the binary data.

Avro offers two choices for encoding data when serializing: binary and JSON. In the binary format the schema is included at the beginning of the file and the binary data is serialized untagged resulting in a smaller data file. Using a schema, the binary data may be encoded/decoded in JSON. The flexibility of converting between binary and JSON formats makes Avro a suitable serialization framework in a scenario in which the priorities/requirements are schema flexibility and serialization performance resulting from a compact binary file. Avro supports generic data handling with the `GenericData.Record` key abstraction, which is a set of key/value pairs in which the name is the field name and the value is one of the Avro supported data types. Instantiating a generic record involves providing a JSON-encoded schema definition and fields are accessed using put/get methods. The "generic" approach to data handling simplifies the code base in contrast to the "static" code generation. Avro's dynamic typing provides serialization and deserialization without code generation.

Serialization for Avro types is provided using the `org.apache.hadoop.io.serializer.avro.AvroSerialization<T>` class, which implements the `org.apache.hadoop.io.serializer.Serialization<Writable>` interface. `AvroSerialization` delegates to `Writable.write(java.io.DataOutput)` and `Writable.readFields(java.io.DataInput)`. The `org.apache.avro.hadoop.io.AvroSequenceFile` class is a wrapper around `SequenceFile` that supports serializing Avro data. `AvroSequenceFile` is implemented as follows:

- Avro key data is wrapped in the `AvroKey` object.

- Avro value data is wrapped in the `AvroValue` object.

- AvroSerialization is configured and registered with SerializationFactory to accept only objects that are instances of `AvroKey` or `AvroValue`.

Comparing Sequence Files and Avro

Both SequenceFile and Avro are binary formats and have native support in Hadoop. Neither require code generation.

Avro data files are smaller size and compact in comparison to SequenceFiles. Avro supports complex data structures such as records, arrays, maps, enums, and unions, while SequenceFile doesn't. Avro provides greater interoperability with applications in other programming languages such as C, C++, PHP, and Ruby. Avro supports versioning using which different data version data files may be processed using a Avro MapReduce application that has been modified such as to add/remove fields, or rename a class. A `Writable` class may be explicitly made to manage versioning and backward compatibility using a version number, but forward compatibility (old application to process new data files) would still not be supported. Avro is more suitable to be used with other frameworks in the Hadoop ecosystem such as Flume, Sqoop, Pig, and Hive.

Unlike Writables in sequence files, Avro does not require generated code to be in the classpath to process data imported from Flume and Sqoop, which simplifies the data processing of Flume and Sqoop imported files. Pig and Hive cannot process custom Writables in sequence files. Reverting to text has the disadvantage of losing the ability to split compressed data, which is required to efficiently process data in parallel.

Thrift

Thrift is a software library and a code-generation toolset developed with the goal to enable reliable and efficient communication across programming languages by providing a common library for the data types and service interfaces. All the data types and interfaces may be defined in a single language-neutral Thrift file to create RPC clients and servers efficiently. Thrift's architecture consists of two layers in the runtime library: protocol layer and transport layer. The protocol layer provides the serialization and deserialization and the transport layer provides the reading and writing to the network. As the protocol and transport layers are included with the runtime library the service may be defined independent of the protocol and transport layers. The protocol and transport may be modified without having to recompile the service. Thrift supports versioning.

Protocol Buffers

Protocol buffers are a language-neutral and platform-neutral mechanism for serializing structured data and for interprocess communication (IPC). Language-neutral implies implementations for protocol buffers are available in all the commonly used languages such as Java, C++, PHP, and JavaScript. Serialization using protocol buffers involves the following:

1. Define message formats in a .proto file using the Interface Definition Language (IDL). Message formats include the file- and wire- formats.

2. Generate source code using the protocol buffer compiler.

3. Use a language-specific protocol buffer API to read and write messages.

The main advantages of protocol buffers are the following:

- Simple (not object-oriented) remote procedure calls

- Efficient binary data serialization

- Efficient in terms of network bandwidth

- Support for forward versioning; a remote service can support older versions of a client

- Support for backward versioning; a remote service can support newer versions of a client

The Hadoop RPC was based on Writables serialization earlier. Writables made it difficult to evolve the protocol while keeping wire compatibility. Writables based RPC also did not distinguish between on-wire data types and client data types, which made it difficult to add new features to the common data types and keep the compatibility. With Hadoop 2.x, the serialization mechanism for on-wire formatting is pluggable and separate from the data types in the client code. The default serialization for on-wire data types is protocol buffers.

Comparing Thrift and Protocol Buffers

With the Thrift and protocol buffers being similar in suitability and both being designed for serialization to the wire, the choice between these is based on other factors. Use protocol buffers over Thrift in the following scenarios:

- Language support is not as important. Protocol buffers support fewer languages than Thrift.

- An RPC implementation is already available. Protocol buffers, unlike Thrift, do not include an RPC implementation.

- On the wire data size is a high priority. Serialized objects in protocol buffers are slightly smaller than Thrift.

- Speed is a high priority. When using optimize_for=SPEED, protocol buffers are slightly faster than Thrift.

Use Thrift over protocol buffers in the following scenarios:

- For a wider language support, especially for languages not supported by protocol buffers

- Support for additional data structures such as Map and Set

- Full client/server implementation built-in

Choosing a Serialization Mechanism

The most suitable serialization mechanisms (other factors may make a different serialization mechanism more suitable) for the different serialization scenarios are as follows:

- Serialization to the wire. Protocol buffers or Thrift, protocol buffers being the default.

- Serialization of intermediate map outputs locally to disk. Avro or SequenceFiles because intermediate map outputs are compressed for storage and transport and most compression algorithms such as Snappy and LZO are not natively splittable. Splittability is important in a parallel model MapReduce framework for parallel processing. SequenceFiles are splittable and Avro data files are splittable regardless of the compression codec used. An Avro file may be read without knowing whether it is compressed. In contrast, plain text files are not splittable.

- Serialization of output from reducers, which is also the MapReduce application output, to HDFS. Writables or Avro are suitable based on other factors.

Avro, Thrift, and protocol buffers are more suitable than Writables for complex data structures such as arrays, maps, and nested records. They are also more suitable as they support flexible schemas with schema evolution.

Other factors to consider when choosing a serialization mechanism are the following.

- Serialization/deserialization time

- Serialized file size

Thrift and protocol buffers are equally fast and faster than Avro. But, the serialized file size is smaller in Avro due to the data being untagged.

Filesystem Shell Commands for HDFS

Hadoop filesystem commands are run using the bin/hdfs script as follows.

```
hdfs dfs [COMMAND [COMMAND_OPTIONS]]
```

The filesystem (FS) refers not only to the HDFS but also other filesystems Hadoop supports such as Local FS and HFTP FS. HDFS filesystems use the HDFS scheme. An HDFS directory path may be specified using the hdfs://namenodehost prefix or the relative path starting with the root directory in HDFS /. The following subsections discuss some of commonly used Hadoop filesystem commands for HDFS.

Making a Directory

The mkdir command is used to create one or more directories in the HDFS. The mkdir command is used as follows.

```
hdfs dfs -mkdir [-p] <paths>
```

If the -p option is used, all the preceding directories in the directory path are created.

For example, the following command creates the /user/hadoop/dir1 directory and the /dir2/dir3 directories, including all the directories in the directory path.

```
hdfs dfs -mkdir -p /user/hadoop/dir1 hdfs://localhost:8020/dir2/dir3
```

It returns 0 on success and -1 on error.

Listing Files and Directories

The ls command lists the stats for a given file or directory. For a given directory, the command lists the files and subdirectories. Its usage is as follows.

```
hdfs dfs -ls <args>
```

The ls command with a dir arg lists the following stats.

```
permissions userid groupid modification_date modification_time dirname
```

For a file as arg, the ls command lists the following stats.

```
permissions number_of_replicas userid groupid filesize modification_date modification_time
filename
```

For example, the following command lists the files and directories in the /user/hadoop/dir1 directory.

```
hdfs dfs -ls /user/hadoop/dir1
```

The recursive version of the command is lsr with the following use.

```
hdfs dfs -lsr <args>
```

The following command lists all the subdirectories and the files in them for the /dir1 directory.

```
hdfs dfs -lsr hdfs://localhost:8020/dir1
```

The ls command returns 0 on success and -1 on error.

Putting Files in the HDFS

The put command is used to put files from the local filesystem, or stdin in the HDFS. The put command is as follows.

```
hdfs dfs -put <localsrc> ... <dst>
```

<localsrc> specifies the local files to put in HDFS and <dfs> specifies the destination in the HDFS.

For example, the following command puts localfile1 and localfile2 in the HDFS directory /user/hadoop/dir1.

```
hdfs dfs -put localfile1 localfile2 hdfs://localhost:8020/user/hadoop/dir1
```

A synonymous command is copyFromLocal, which restricts the source to the local filesystem. The -f option of copyFromLocal overwrites the destination. The moveFromLocal command is also similar to the put command, with the difference that the local source directory is deleted after copying.

The put command returns 0 on success and -1 on error.

Creating a File

The touchz command is used to create a file of zero length and has the following syntax.

```
hdfs dfs -touchz URI [URI ...
```

For example, the following command creates two files—file1 in /user/hadoop/dir1 and file2 in /user/hadoop/dir2. The directory path must already be created.

```
hdfs dfs -touchz /user/hadoop/dir1/file1 hdfs://localhost:8020/user/hadoop/dir2/file2
```

The touchz command returns 0 on success and -1 on error. The command fails if the file already exists and is not zero length.

Changing Group Associations for Files and Directories

The chgrp command is used to change group association for files and directories. The usage of chgrp is as follows.

```
hdfs dfs -chgrp [-R] GROUP URI [URI ...]
```

The -R option makes the changes recursively throughout the filesystem. Recursively implies subdirectories and files in the subdirectories. The user running the command must either be a superuser or the owner of the file/directory.

For example, the following command sets the group of the /user/hadoop/dir1 directory and subdirectories and files in the directory and subdirectories to hadoop. The group of /user/hadoop/dir2/ file1 is also set to hadoop.

```
hdfs dfs -chgrp -R hadoop /user/hadoop/dir1 hdfs://localhost:8020/user/hadoop/dir2/file1
```

Changing Permissions of Files

The chmod command is used to change the permissions of files and its usage is as follows.

```
hdfs dfs -chmod [-R] <MODE[,MODE]... | OCTALMODE> URI [URI ...]
```

The -R option makes the changes recursively throughout the filesystem. Recursively implies subdirectories and files in the subdirectories. The user running the command must either be a superuser or the owner of the file/directory.

For example, the following command changes the permissions of the /file1 file and the /user/ hadoop/dir2 directory to 700.

```
hdfs dfs -chmod -R 700 hdfs://localhost:8020/file1 /user/hadoop/dir2
```

Changing Owner of Files and Directories

The chown command is used to change the owner of files and directories. The use of chown is as follows.

```
hdfs dfs -chown [-R] [OWNER][:[GROUP]] URI [URI ]
```

The owner group may also be specified with OWNER:GROUP. The -R option makes the changes recursively throughout the filesystem. Recursively implies subdirectories and files in the subdirectories. The user running the command must either be a superuser or the owner of the file/directory.

For example, the following command sets the owner of the /user/hadoop/dir1 directory and subdirectories and files in the directory and subdirectories to hadoop:hadoop. The owner of /user/hadoop/ dir2/file1 is also set to hadoop:hadoop.

```
hdfs dfs -chown -R hadoop:hadoop  /user/hadoop/dir1 hdfs://localhost:8020/user/hadoop/dir2/
file1
```

Copying Files to the Local Filesystem

The get command is used to copy files from the HDFS to the local filesystem. The command syntax is as follows.

```
hdfs dfs -get [-ignorecrc] [-crc] <src> <localdst>
```

A .crc file is created in the local filesystem for checksum verification. By default, files that fail the CRC checksum verification are not copied. To copy the files that fail the checksum verification, include the – ignorecrc option. The –crc option also copies the .crc files.

For example, the following command copies /user/hadoop/file1 from HDFS to the /user/local/ file1 local filesystem.

hdfs dfs -get /user/hadoop/file1 /user/local/file1

A synonymous command is copyToLocal, which restricts the destination to the local file reference. The get command may also be used to copy from HDFS to HDFS, although it is not designed for the purpose. The get command returns 0 on success and -1 on error.

Appending to a File

The appendToFile command is used to append one or more files from the local filesystem or stdin to a HDFS file and its usage is as follows.

```
hdfs dfs -appendToFile <localsrc> ... <dst>
```

For example, the following command appends the local files localfile1 and localfile2 to the HDFS / user/hadoop/dir1/hadoopfile1 file.

```
hdfs dfs -appendToFile localfile1 localfile2 /user/hadoop/dir1/hadoopfile1
```

The appendToFile command returns 0 on success and -1 on error.

Copying HDFS Files to STDOUT

The cat command is used to copy local or/and HDFS files to stdout and its usage is as follows.

```
hdfs dfs -cat URI [URI ...]
```

For example, the following command copies the local file file:///file1 and HDFS file hdfs:// localhost:8029/file2 to stdout.

```
hdfs dfs -cat file:///file1 hdfs://localhost:8029/file2
```

The tail command outputs the last KB of a file to stdout. The command use is as follows.

```
hdfs dfs -tail [-f] URI
```

The -f option outputs appended data as the file grows, as in UNIX. For example, the following command outputs the last KB from file1 in the HDFS root directory.

```
hdfs dfs -tail hdfs://localhost:8020/file1
```

The tail command returns 0 on success and -1 on error.

Testing a File

The test command is used to test a file's existence, if the file is zero length, and if the file is a directory. Its use is as follows.

```
hdfs dfs -test -[ezd] URI
```

The command options are discussed in Table 1-5.

Table 1-5. *The Test Command Options*

Option	Description
-e	Tests if the file exists. Returns 1 if true and 0 if false.
-z	Tests if the file is zero length. Returns 1 if true and 0 if false.
-d	Tests if the file is a directory. Returns 1 if true and 0 if false.

For example, the following command verifies if the file1 exists in HDFS.

```
hdfs dfs -test -e hdfs://localhost:8020/file1
```

Counting Files and Directories

The count command is used to count the number of files and directories for one or more HDFS paths and its use is as follows.

```
hdfs dfs -count [-q] <paths>
```

The default output columns are DIR_COUNT, FILE_COUNT, CONTENT_SIZE, and FILE_NAME. If the –q option is used, the output columns are QUOTA, REMAINING_QUOTA, SPACE_QUOTA, REMAINING_SPACE_QUOTA, DIR_COUNT, FILE_COUNT, CONTENT_SIZE, and FILE_NAME.

For example, the following command outputs the CONTENT_SIZE and FILE_NAME columns for /file1 in HDFS and the DIR_COUNT, FILE_COUNT, CONTENT_SIZE, and FILE_NAME columns for /dir1 in HDFS.

```
hdfs dfs -count hdfs://localhost:8020/file1 hdfs://localhost:8020/dir1
```

The stat command lists the stats on a file path; its usage is as follows.

```
hdfs dfs -stat path
```

The stat command returns 0 on success and -1 on error.

Copying Files in HDFS

The cp command is used to copy files from one or more sources to a destination in HDFS. If multiple files are copied, the destination must be a directory. The –f option overwrites the destination if it already exists. The –p option preserves topax; the timestamps, ownership, permission, ACL, XAttr. If -p is specified with no arg, it preserves timestamps, ownership, permission. The -pa parameter, which is the -p option and the arg 'a', also preserves ACL.

```
hdfs dfs -cp [-f] [-p | -p[topax]] URI [URI ...] <dest>
```

For example, the following command copies the files /user/hadoop/file1 and /user/hadoop/file2 to the /user/hadoop/dir1 directory.

```
hdfs dfs -cp hdfs://localhost:8020/user/hadoop/file1 /user/hadoop/file2 hdfs://
localhost:8020/user/hadoop/dir1
```

The cp command returns 0 on success and -1 on error.

Moving Files Within the HDFS

The mv command is used to move files within HDFS and its usage is as follows.

```
hdfs dfs -mv URI [URI ...] <dest>
```

If multiple files are copied, the destination must be a directory.

For example, the following command moves file1, file2, and file3 from the HDFS root directory to the dir1 directory.

```
hdfs dfs -mv hdfs://localhost:8020/file1 hdfs://ocalhost:8020/file2 hdfs://ocalhost:8020/
file3 hdfs://ocalhost:8020/dir1
```

The source files are deleted after moving to the destination. The mv command returns 0 on success and -1 on error.

Displaying File and Directory Sizes

The du command is used to display the disk usage (sizes) of files and directories in a given directory or the size of a given file. Its usage is as follows.

```
hdfs dfs -du [-s] [-h] URI [URI ...]
```

The -s option aggregates the file sizes rather than listing individual file sizes. The -h option formats the sizes in a readable format such as 128M instead of 134217730.

For example, the following command lists the file size for the /user/hadoop/file1 file and the file and directory sizes for the /user/hadoop/dir1 directory.

```
hdfs dfs -du /user/hadoop/file1 hdfs://localhost:8020/user/hadoop/dir1
```

The du command returns 0 on success and -1 on error.

An alternative to using the du command with the -s option is the dus command (deprecated) with the following usage.

```
hdfs dfs -dus <args>
```

Outputting a File in Text Format

The text command outputs a file (ZIP or TextRecordInputStream) in text format; its usage is as follows.

```
hdfs dfs -text <src>
```

Removing Files and Directories

The rm command is used to remove files and empty directories and its usage is as follows.

```
hdfs dfs -rm [-skipTrash] URI [URI ...]
```

The rm command returns 0 on success and -1 on error.

The [-skipTrash] option skips the trash and deletes the files immediately, which could be useful when deleting files from an over-quota directory.

For example, the following command deletes /user/hadoop/dir1 in HDFS and file1 in /user/hadoop/dir2.

```
hdfs dfs -rm hdfs://localhost:8020/user/hadoop/dir1 /user/hadoop/dir2/file1
```

If the directory to remove is not empty, add the -f option. The -f option does not display a diagnostic message or modify the exit status to indicate an error if the file does not exist. For example, you can remove the non-empty directory /user/hadoop/dir1 with the following command.

```
hdfs dfs -rm -f hdfs://localhost:8020/user/hadoop/dir1
```

To delete subdirectories recursively, use the -rm -r or -rm -R command, which has the following syntax.

```
hdfs dfs -rm -r [-skipTrash] URI [URI ...]
```

For example, you can remove the non-empty hdfs://localhost:8020/user/hadoop/dir1 directory and all subdirectories (non-empty) with the following command.

```
hdfs dfs -rm -r  hdfs://localhost:8020/user/hadoop/dir1
```

The command to empty the trash is expunge and its usage is as follows.

```
hdfs dfs -expunge
```

Choosing Key and Value Types for MapReduce Jobs

A functional MapReduce job consists of a map phase and an optional reduce phase, as shown in Figure 1-31. In the map phase input data is divided into input splits and processed by one or more map tasks running in parallel on the Hadoop cluster. By default the input data is in the HDFS. If the reduce phase is used, the output from the map tasks is sorted and input to one or more reduce tasks also running in parallel. The reduce phase may begin after at least one map task has completed. The output from the reduce phase is the final result of the MR job. A MR job takes input data as a set of key/value pairs, processes the data using map and reduce functions and outputs a set of key/value pairs. The map phase produces a set of intermediate key/value pairs, which are partitioned, sorted, merged, and input to the reduce phase.

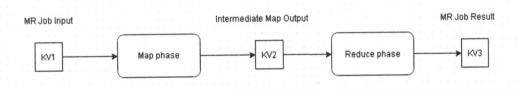

Figure 1-31. Key/values in MapReduce

The key and value types are significant as follows.

- Each set of key/value pairs is homogeneous, which implies that all key/value pairs are the same type in terms of key type and value type. For example, all the key/value pairs in the KV1 set must be of the same type such as (string, string).

- The key/value pairs are not homogeneous across the different sets/phases; the key/value pairs need not be the same type across the different phases. For example, the key/value types in the MR Job input could be (string,string), and intermediate map output could be (integer, string) and MR job output could be (string, integer).

The requirement for the uniqueness of the keys is as follows.

- The MR Job input keys must be unique.

- The intermediate keys are not required to be unique.

- The MR job output keys are also not required to be unique.

After the map phase, the key/value pairs are sorted and merged into a (key/value-list) pairs in which each value could actually be a list of values. The (key/value-list) pairs are input to the reduce phase.

The interfaces to use in map and reduce functions are determined by the key and value types in each phase. Before developing a MapReduce job, determine the data types required in each phase using the following guidelines.

- Choose the map input key and value type based on the input data. For example, in a word count Map Reduce job in which the input is a document with text on each line, the suitable types for the input key/value pairs would be (integer, string) to represent the line number and text on each line.

- Choose the map phase intermediate output key/value types based on the final result of the MR job. For example for a word count MR job the final result represents the number of times a word occurs in the input. The map phase generates a key/value pair for each word in the input with the key as the word and value as 1, which in effect is including each word in the count. The map phase output key/value types are (string, integer). The output from the map phase could include multiple key/value pairs with the same key.

- The map phase output key/value types must match the reduce phase input key/value types.

- The reduce phase output key/value types represent the required outcome of the MR job. For example, for a word count MR job the reduce phase output is the occurrence frequency for each word. The key/value pairs types for the reduce phase would be (string, integer).

The key/value pair types are specified in the job configuration, which is discussed in another section.

The Lifecycle of a Mapper and a Reducer in a MapReduce Job

The `org.apache.hadoop.mapred.Mapper<K1,V1,K2,V2>` interface in the old API and the `org.apache.hadoop.mapreduce.Mapper<KEYIN,VALUEIN,KEYOUT,VALUEOUT>` class in the new API are used to create map tasks in a MR job. Map tasks map input key/value pairs to intermediate key/value pairs. The `org.apache.hadoop.mapred.Reducer<K2,V2,K3,V3>` interface in the old API and the `org.apache.hadoop.mapreduce.Reducer<KEYIN,VALUEIN,KEYOUT,VALUEOUT>` class in the new API are used to create reduce tasks in a MR job. A reduce tasks takes as input keys and a set of values associated with each key and produce as output keys and a smaller set of values associated with each key.

A MR job may consist of one or more mappers and zero or more reducers. We discuss a job with at least one mapper and one reducer. When a job is launched the InputFormat generates InputSplits from the input. For example, for file input the InputFormat generates FileSplits. The MR framework launches one map task for each InputSplit.

In the old API, a mapper would typically extend the MapReduceBase and implement the mapper interface. The mapper input key must be a `WritableComparable` and the mapper input value must be a `Writable`. The `configure(JobConf)` method from the `MapReduceBase` class may be overridden to access the job configuration. The map method signature is `map(K key, V val, OutputCollector<K, V> output, Reporter reporter)` and is typically overridden to process the input key/value pair, report progress using the `Reporter` object argument and collect the output from the `map()` function using the `OutputCollector.collect()` method. An example of a mapper implementation in the old API is as follows.

```
import WritableComparable;
import Writable;
import MapReduceBase;
import Mapper;
import JobConf;
import OutputCollector;
import Reporter;

public class SampleMapper<K extends WritableComparable, V extends Writable>
     extends MapReduceBase implements Mapper<K, V, K, V> {
//Access the JobConf for the Job using configure(JobConf) method.
     public void configure(JobConf job) {

     }

     public void map(K key, V val, OutputCollector<K, V> output, Reporter reporter)
     throws IOException {
       // Process the <key, value> pair

       // Report progress with reporter.progress();
       // Output the result
       output.collect(key, val);
     }
}
```

The lifecycle of a mapper in the old API (shown in Figure 1-32) involves the following:

1. The InputFormat generates the InputSplits from the input. The InputFormat also generates the RecordReader to convert the InputSplits to records (key/value pairs)

2. The MR framework launches a map task for each InputSplit in the input.

3. The RecordReader parses the InputSplit and generates key/value pairs (records) to be input to the Mapper's `map()` function.

4. The MR framework invokes the `map()` method for each key/value pair generated by the RecordReader from the InputSplit.

5. The `map()` method processes the input key/value pair.

6. The map() method may optionally use the Reporter object to report progress.

7. An OutputCollector collects the output key/value pairs. The map() function may generate no key/value pair at all.

8. The output key/value pairs are first written to the task's temporary output directory.

9. The map() method is invoked again until all key/value pairs generated by the RecordReader from the InputSplit have been processed.

10. If the map task completes successfully, the OutputCommitter commits the map task's output to the Spill buffer. The map output file has the name part-nnnn.

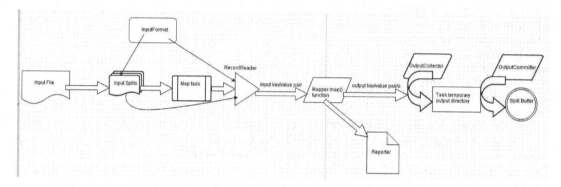

Figure 1-32. *The lifecycle of a mapper in the old API*

In the new API, a mapper implementation would typically extend the Mapper class. The mapper input key must be a WritableComparable and the Mapper input value must be a Writable. The map() method signature is map(KEYIN key, VALUEIN value, Mapper.Context context) and is typically overridden to process the input key/value pair, and write the output from the map() function using the Context.write() method. In addition to the map() method, the new API Mapper also includes a setup() method to run any preliminary setup, and a cleanup() method to run any post-map cleanup. The MR framework invokes the mapper's run() method to start the map task. An example of a mapper implementation in the new API is as follows.

```
import Mapper;
import LongWritable;
import Text;
import IntWritable;
public class SampleMapper extends Mapper<LongWritable, Text, Text, IntWritable>{

    private final static IntWritable one = new IntWritable(1);
    private Text word = new Text();
```

```
public void run(Context context) throws IOException, InterruptedException {
    setup(context);
    while (context.nextKeyValue()) {
      map(context.getCurrentKey(), context.getCurrentValue(), context);
    }
    cleanup(context);
}

        @Override
        protected void setup(Context context) throws IOException,
                        InterruptedException {

        }

        @Override
        protected void map(LongWritable key, Text value, Context context)
                        throws IOException, InterruptedException {

                StringTokenizer tokenizer = new StringTokenizer(value.toString());
                while (tokenizer.hasMoreTokens()) {
                        word.set(tokenizer.nextToken());
                        context.write(word, one);
                }
        }

        @Override
        protected void cleanup(Context context) throws IOException,
                        InterruptedException {

        }

}
```

The lifecycle of a mapper in the new API (shown in Figure 1-33) involves the following:

1. The InputFormat generates the InputSplits from the input. The InputFormat also generates the RecordReader to convert the InputSplits to records (key/value pairs)

2. The MR framework launches a map task for each InputSplit in the input.

3. The RecordReader parses the InputSplit and generates key/value pairs (records) to be input to the mapper's map() function.

4. The MR framework invokes the mapper's run() method to run the map task.

5. The MR framework invokes the mapper's setup() method.

6. The MR framework invokes the map() method for each key/value pair generated by the RecordReader from the InputSplit.

7. The map() method processes the input key/value pair.

8. The map() method may optionally use the StatusReporter object using the Context object to report progress.

9.   The map() method invokes the Context.write() method to generate the output key/value pairs. The map() function may generate no key/value pair at all.

10.   The output key/value pairs are first written to the task's temporary output directory.

11.   The map() method is invoked again until all key/value pairs generated by the RecordReader from the InputSplit have been processed.

12.   If the map task completes successfully the OutputCommitter commits the map task's output to the Spill buffer. The map output file has the name part-m-nnnn, in which m indicates a map task output.

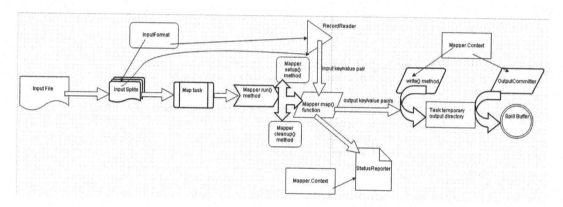

Figure 1-33. *The lifecycle of a mapper in the new API*

A MR job has as many reducers (reduce tasks) as the number of partitions in the map task. In the old API, a reducer would typically extend the MapReduceBase class and implement the reducer interface. The reducer input key must be a WritableComparable and the reducer input value must be a Writable. The configure(JobConf) method from the MapReduceBase class may be overridden to access the job configuration, as in the mapper. The map method signature is reduce(K2 key, Iterator<V2> values, OutputCollector<K3,V3> output, Reporter reporter) and is typically overridden to process the input key/values, report progress using the Reporter object argument and collect the output from the reduce() function using the OutputCollector.collect() method. An example of a reducer implementation in the old API is as follows.

```
import WritableComparable;
import Writable;
import MapReduceBase;
import Reducer;
public class SampleReducer<K extends WritableComparable, V extends Writable>
     extends MapReduceBase implements Reducer<K, V, K, V> {
    public void configure(JobConf job) {

    }
```

```
public void reduce(K key, Iterator<V> values,
                   OutputCollector<K, V> output,
                   Reporter reporter)
throws IOException {

  while (values.hasNext()) {
    V value = values.next();

    // Process the <key, value> pair

      reporter.progress();
    // Output the <key, value>
    output.collect(key, value);
  }

 }
}
```

The lifecycle of a reducer in the old API (Figure 1-34) involves the following:

1. The map outputs assigned to the Reduce task are shuffled (copied) from the mappers (map tasks) nodes, across the network using HTTP, to the Shuffle buffer on the reducer node. The map segments are shuffled both from the Spill buffer and the disk on the mapper nodes.

2. When the Shuffle buffer becomes full or the threshold for shuffled map outputs is exceeded, the map segments are spilled to disk.

3. The map segments are merged using both in-memory merge and on-disk merge. The merged spill files may be merged repeatedly to create larger intermediate spill files.

4. All the map segments are merged and sorted using a sorter, and optionally a secondary sorter. A single input file to be processed by the reduce() function is generated from the merge-sorted map segments.

5. The MR framework launches a reduce task for the merge-sorted reduce input file.

6. The MR framework invokes the reduce() method for each key/values group (<key, (list of values)> pair) in the reduce input file. A grouping Comparator may be used to group key/values.

7. The reduce() method processes the input <key, (list of values)> pair.

8. The reduce() method may optionally use the Reporter object to report progress.

9. An OutputCollector collects the output key/values group (<key, (list of values)> pair). The reduce() function may generate no key/value pair at all. The OutputCollector is created by the OutputFormat.

10. The output key/values groups (<key, (list of values)> pairs) are first written to the reduce task's temporary output directory using a RecordWriter. The RecordWriter is created by the OutputFormat.

11. The reduce() method is invoked again until all key/values groups (<key, (list of values)> pairs) in the reduce input file have been processed.

89

12. If the reduce task completes successfully the OutputCommitter commits the reduce task's output to the job's output directory.

13. When all the reduce tasks for a job have completed successfully the OutputCommitter commits the job. The reduce task output files are committed to the job's output location, typically HDFS. The reduce task output files have the format part-nnnn. The number of reduce output files generated is the same as the number of reduce tasks/partitions in the job. The reduce output files (part-nnnn) are not merged by the MR framework and output as separate files in the job's output.

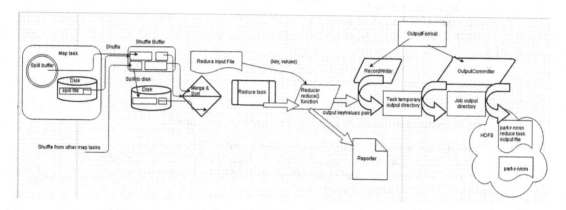

Figure 1-34. *The lifecycle of a reducer in the old API*

In the new API, a reducer implementation would typically extend the Reducer class. The reducer input key must be a WritableComparable and the reducer input value must be a Writable. The reduce method signature reduce(KEYIN key, Iterable<VALUEIN> values, Reducer.Context context) and is typically overridden to process the input key/values pair, and write the output from the reduce() function using the Context.write() method. In addition to the reduce() method, the new API Reducer also includes a setup() method to run any preliminary setup, and a cleanup() method to run any post-reduce cleanup. The MR framework invokes the reducer's run() method to start the reduce task. An example of a reducer implementation in the new API is as follows.

```
import WritableComparable;
import Writable;
import Reducer;
import IntWritable;
public class IntSumReducer extends Reducer<K extends WritableComparable, V extends
Writable> {
   private IntWritable result = new IntWritable();

public void run(Context context) throws IOException, InterruptedException {
    setup(context);
    while (context.nextKey()) {
      reduce(context.getCurrentKey(), context.getValues(), context);
    }
    cleanup(context);
  }
```

```
@Override
        protected void setup(Context context) throws IOException,
                            InterruptedException {

        }

@Override
    public void reduce(Key key, Iterable values,
                            Context context) throws IOException {
        int sum = 0;
        for (IntWritable val : values) {
            sum += val.get();
        }
        result.set(sum);
        context.write(key, result);
    }

@Override
protected void cleanup(Context context) throws IOException,
                            InterruptedException {

        }

}
```

The lifecycle of a reducer in the new API (see Figure 1-35) involves the following:

1. The map outputs assigned to the Reduce task are shuffled (copied) from the mappers (map tasks), across the network using HTTP, to the Shuffle buffer on the reducer. The map segments are shuffled both from the Spill buffer and the disk on the map tasks or nodes.

2. When the Shuffle buffer becomes full or the threshold for shuffled map outputs is exceeded, the map segments are spilled to disk.

3. The map segments are merged using both in-memory merge and on-disk merge. The merged spill files may be merged repeatedly to create larger intermediate spill files.

4. All the map segments are merged and sorted using a sorter, and optionally a secondary sorter. A single input file to be processed by the reduce() function is generated from the merge-sorted map segments.

5. The MR framework launches a reduce task for the merge-sorted reduce input file.

6. The MR framework invokes the reducer's run() method to run the reduce task.

7. The MR framework invokes the reducer's setup() method.

8. The MR framework invokes the reduce() method for each key/values pair in the reduce input file.

9. The reduce() method processes the input key/values pair.

10. The reduce() method may optionally use the StatusReporter object using the Context object to report progress.

11. The reduce() method invokes the Context.write() method to generate the output key/values pair. The reduce() function may generate no key/values pair at all.

12. The output key/values pair are first written to the reduce task's temporary output directory by the RecordWriter.

13. The reduce() method is invoked again till all key/values pairs in the reduce input file have until processed.

14. If the reduce task completes successfully the OutputCommitter commits the reduce task's output to the job output directory.

15. If the job completes successfully, when all the reduce tasks for a job have completed successfully, the OutputCommitter commits the job. The reduce task output files are committed to the job's output location, typically HDFS. The reduce task output files have the format part-r-nnnn, in which r indicates a reduce task. The number of reduce output files generated is the same as the number of reduce tasks/partitions in the job. The reduce output files (part-r-nnnn) are not merged by the MR framework and output as separate files in the job's output.

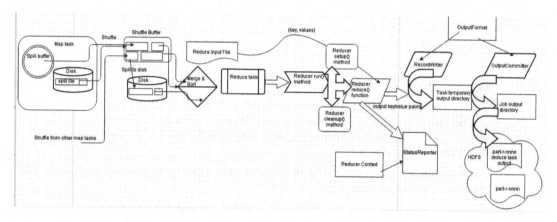

Figure 1-35. *The lifecycle of a reducer in the new API*

The Relationship of Input Keys to Output Keys

MapReduce provides two phases of data processing, the map phase and the reduce phase. In a typical MapReduce job the map phase runs before the reduce phase. The reduce phase can begin only after at least one map task has completed. A MR job could be configured to be map-only in which the number of reducers is set to 0. This section considers a MR job with both a map phase and a reduce phase.

During the map phase, the mapper's map() method is invoked for each key/value pair (record) in the input data. The algorithm used by the map() function is as follows.

```
map(k,v) → <k',v'>*
```

(k,v) constitutes an input key/value pair, also called a record. Only one key/value pair can be input to a single call to the map() function.

k is the input key. Only one key is input in each call to the map() function. The input key type must implement the WritableComparable interface. The input key must be unique for a mapper.

v is the input value. Only one value is input in each call to the map() function. The input value type must implement the Writable interface.

<k'v'> constitutes an output key/value pair. A call to the map() function may emit 0, 1, or more key/value pairs as indicated by the *.

k' is the output key. The output key type must implement the WritableComparable interface. The output key type may be the same or different than the input key type. The output key is not required to be unique.

v' is the output value. The output value type must implement the Writable interface. The output value type may be the same or different than the input value type.

The map phase's output is copied to the reduce phase to be processed by the reduce() function. During the reduce phase the reducer's reduce() method is invoked for each key/<list of values> pair in the map phase's outputs. The algorithm used by the reduce() function is as follows.

```
reduce(k',<v'>*)  →  <k'',v''>*
```

(k',<v'>*) constitutes an input key/<list of value> pair. Only one key/<list of value> pair can be input to a single call to the reduce() function. The list of values may consist of 0, 1, or more values.

k' is the input key to the reduce() function. Only one key is input in each call to the reduce() function. The input key type must implement the WritableComparable interface. The type of k' must be the same as the map() function's output key type.

v' is the input value to the reduce() function. A list of values associated with the same key is input in each call to the reduce() function. The input value type must implement the Writable interface. The type of v' must be the same as the map() function's output value type.

<k''v''> constitutes an output key/value pair from the reduce() function. A call to the reduce() function may emit 0, 1, or more key/value pairs as indicated by the *.

k'' is the output key. The output key type must implement the WritableComparable interface. The output key type may be the same or different than the reduce() function's input key type.

v'' is the output value. The output value type must implement the Writable interface. The output value type may be the same or different than the reduce() function's input value type.

Mapper Input/Output Types

In the new API, a mapper is defined using the Mapper class as follows.

```
public class Mapper<KEYIN,VALUEIN,KEYOUT,VALUEOUT>
```

Mapper is a generic class and its type parameters are listed in Table 1-6.

Table 1-6. *Mapper Class Generic Parameters*

Type Parameter	Description
KEYIN	The input key type
VALUEIN	The input value type
KEYOUT	The output key type
VALUEOUT	The output value type

In the old API, a mapper is defined using the mapper interface as follows.

```
org.apache.hadoop.mapred.Mapper<K1,V1,K2,V2>
```

When a map task is launched, the InputFormat validates the task's input. The mapper's map() function's input key/value types are the key/value types associated with the InputFormat as most InputFormats have corresponding key/value types. The RecordReader created by the InputFormat to convert the InputSplits to key/value pairs is compatible with the key/value types for the InputFormat. For example, for TextInputFormat, a LineRecordReader is created to generate key/value pairs of type LongWritable/Text. TextInputFormat is the default InputFormat, implying that if no InputFormat is configured the InputFormat is TextInputFormat. The key/value types associated with some of the InputFormats are listed in Table 1-7.

Table 1-7. *Key/Value Types*

InputFormat	Key Type	Value Type
TextInputFormat	LongWritable	Text
KeyValueTextInputFormat	Text	Text
SequenceFileInputFormat	User defined	User defined
SequenceFileAsBinaryInputFormat	BytesWritable	BytesWritable
SequenceFileAsTextInputFormat	Text	Text
SequenceFileInputFilter	User defined	User defined
NLineInputFormat	LongWritable	Text
CombineFileInputFormat	User defined	User defined
DBInputFormat	LongWritable	User defined
DelegatingInputFormat	User defined	User defined

The old API defines some additional InputFormats as listed in Table 1-8.

Table 1-8. *InputFormats in the Old API*

InputFormat	Key Type	Value Type
CompositeInputFormat	User defined	TupleWritable
LineDocInputFormat	DocumentID	LineDocTextAndOp
StreamInputFormat	Text	Text
TeraInputFormat	Text	Text

Mapper's map() function's input key/value types, if not specified using JobConf (old API) or Job (new API), are the input key/value types associated with the InputFormat. For example, if InputFormat is TextInputFormat, the key/value types associated with TextInputFormat are LongWritable/Text, which makes the mapper's map() function's input key/value types as LongWritable/Text. If the mapper's map() function's output key/value types are not set using the JobConf or Job API, the map() function's output key/value types are the same as input types, which are LongWritable/Text. This makes the input key/value types reduce() as LongWritable/Text, and output key/value types for job as LongWritable/Text also. The output from reduce() is the output for the job.

The default OutputFormat for a job is TextOutputFormat, which does not have any key/value types associated with it by default and which either defaults to the same as the reducer's input key/value types or may be user defined. InputFormat/OutputFormat other than the default may be configured as follows.

```
JobConf conf = new JobConf(new Configuration(), SampleJob.class);
conf.setInputFormat(KeyValueTextInputFormat.class);
conf.setOutputFormat(SequenceFileOutputFormat.class);
```

Map output key/value types other than the default may be configured as follows.

```
conf.setMapOutputKeyClass(LongWritable.class);
conf.setMapOutputValueClass(Text.class);
```

Mapper Input/Output Number of Keys/Values

Only one key/value pair is input to a call to mapper's map() function. The number of output key/value pairs may be 0, 1, or more. Each call to OutputCollector.collect() method in the same call to the map() function adds one key/value pair to the map() function's output. For example, in the following Mapper class the map() function emits a key/value pair for each call to the OutputCollector.collect() method. As many invocations to the OutputCollector.collect() method are made as the number of tokens in a line of input. As a result, the number of key/value pairs emitted from a call to the map() function is the number of tokens in the line input to the map() function.

```
import LongWritable;
import Text;
import IntWritable;
public class WordCountMapper extends
Mapper<LongWritable, Text, Text, IntWritable> {
    private final static IntWritable one = new IntWritable(1);
    private Text word = new Text();

    public void map(LongWritable key, Text value, OutputCollector<Text,IntWritable> output,
Reporter reporter)
    throws IOException, InterruptedException {

    String line = value.toString();
    StringTokenizer tokenizer = new StringTokenizer(line);
    while (tokenizer.hasMoreTokens()) {
        word.set(tokenizer.nextToken());
        output.collect(word, one);
        }
    }
}
```

In the new API, the number of key/value pairs emitted is the number of invocations to the Context. write() method, which is equal to the number of tokens in the input line.

```
import LongWritable;
import Text;
import IntWritable;
```

```
public class WordCountMapper extends
Mapper<LongWritable, Text, Text, IntWritable> {
    private final static IntWritable one = new IntWritable(1);
    private Text word = new Text();

    public void map(LongWritable key, Text value, Context context)
    throws IOException, InterruptedException {

    String line = value.toString();
    StringTokenizer tokenizer = new StringTokenizer(line);
    while (tokenizer.hasMoreTokens()) {
        word.set(tokenizer.nextToken());
        context.write(word, one);
        }
    }
}
```

If no call to the OutputCollector.collect() or Context.write() method is made in the map() function, the number of key/value pairs emitted from the mapper is zero. Similarly, if one call to OutputCollector. collect() or Context.write() method is made, the number of key/value pairs emitted is one.

Reducer Input/Output Types

A reduce() function's input key/value types expected are the same as the job's output key/value types. The reduce() input key/value types *received* are the map() function's output key/value types produced. The reduce input types received must match the reduce input types expected. The map output key/value types are the same as the map input key/value types if not configured explicitly. Most InputFormats have default types for input key/value types as listed earlier. For example, if the InputFormat is not defined or is set to the default TextInputFormat, the map input key type is LongWritable and the map() input value type is Text which makes the default output key/value types for the map() as also LongWritable/Text.

This makes the key/value types received by the reduce() function as LongWritable/Text. If a job output key/value types are not defined explicitly, the reduce() output key/value types becomes the reduce() input key/value types, which are LongWritable/Text. If a job output key/value types are defined explicitly, the reduce() function's key/value output types are the same as job's output key/value types, and the reduce() function's input key/value types are the same as reduce()'s output key/value types.

If a job output key/value types are defined explicitly, and the map() output key/value types are not defined explicitly, explicit job output key/value types must match the default map() output key/value types. The map output types are required to be the same as the job's output types, because the map's output key/value types are the received input key/value types for the reduce() and the job's explicit output key/value types are the expected input key/value types for the reduce() function. As mentioned, the expected and received input key/value types for the reduce() function must be the same. If the job output key/value types are different than the map output key/value types produced, an exception is thrown during task attempt. For example, if the job output key/value type are set as follows.

```
job.setOutputKeyClass(Text.class);
 job.setOutputValueClass(IntWritable.class);
```

And if the InputFormat is TextInputFormat and no map() output key/value types are set explicitly, the map output key/value types are the default LongWritable/Text, which become the received input key/value types for reduce(). But, the expected reduce input types are Text/IntWritable as configured in Job configuration. The expected and the received input key/value types being different for reduce(), the following exception gets generated during task attempt when the InputFormat/OutputFormat are validated.

java.io.IOException: Type mismatch in key from map: expected org.apache.hadoop.io.Text, received org.apache.hadoop.io.LongWritable

The exception is generated regardless of how the mapper or reducer are defined. For example, the mapper could be defined to indicate that the map output key/value types match the reduce input/key value types and also produce key/value types expected by the reduce() function. The mapper could be defined as follows.

```
import LongWritable;
import Text;
import IntWritable; public class WordCountMapper extends
Mapper<LongWritable, Text, Text, IntWritable> {
    private final static IntWritable one = new IntWritable(1);
    private Text word = new Text();

    public void map(LongWritable key, Text value, OutputCollector<Text,IntWritable> output,
Reporter reporter)
    throws IOException, InterruptedException {

    String line = value.toString();
    StringTokenizer tokenizer = new StringTokenizer(line);
    while (tokenizer.hasMoreTokens()) {
        word.set(tokenizer.nextToken());
        output.collect(word, one);
        }
    }
}
```

The reducer can be defined as follows.

```
import LongWritable;
import Text;
import IntWritable;
import Reducer;
public class WordCountReducer extends Reducer<Text, IntWritable, Text, IntWritable> {
public void reduce(Text key, Iterator<IntWritable> values,
    OutputCollector<Text,IntWritable> output, Reporter reporter) throws IOException,
InterruptedException {
int sum = 0;
while (values.hasNext()) {
    sum += values.next().get();
}
output.collect(key, new IntWritable(sum));
 }
}
```

But, the input/output specification validation by the InputFormat/OutputFormat (TextInputFormat/ TextOutputFormat) finds a mismatch in the expected and received key/value types for the reduce() function and generates an exception when the map task is attempted.

The map() output key/value types produced, as indicated by the InputFormat, must match the key/value types expected by the reduce() input.

```
job.setMapOutputKeyClass(Text.class);
job.setMapOutputValueClass(IntWritable.class);
```

The default input key/value types for most InputFormats are defined. Some InputFormat key/value types must be user defined.

Reducer Input/Output Number of Keys/Values

Only one key/<list of values> pair is input to a call to reducer's reduce() function. The number of output key/value pairs may be 0, 1, or more. Each call to the OutputCollector.collect() method in the same call to the reduce() function adds one key/value pair to the reduce() function's output. For example, in the following Reducer class, the reduce() function emits a key/value pair for each call to the OutputCollector.collect() method. Only one invocation to the OutputCollector.collect() method is made in the reduce() method. As a result, the number of key/value pairs emitted from a call to the reduce() function is one.

```
public class WordCountReducer extends Reducer<Text, IntWritable, Text, IntWritable> {
public void reduce(Text key, Iterator<IntWritable> values,
    OutputCollector<Text,IntWritable> output, Reporter reporter) throws IOException,
InterruptedException {
int sum = 0;
while (values.hasNext()) {
    sum += values.next().get();
}
output.collect(key, new IntWritable(sum));
 }
}
```

In the new API, the number of key/value pairs emitted is the number of invocations to the Context.write() method, which is equal to one.

```
public class WordCountReducer extends Reducer<Text, IntWritable, Text, IntWritable> {
public void reduce(Text key, Iterable<IntWritable> values, Context context) throws
IOException, InterruptedException {
int sum = 0;
while (values.hasNext()) {
    sum += values.next().get();
}
                context.write(key, new IntWritable(sum));
 }
}
```

If no call to the OutputCollector.collect() or Context.write() method is made in the reduce() function, the number of key/value pairs emitted from the reducer is zero. Similarly, if one call to OutputCollector.collect() or Context.write() method is made, the number of key/value pairs emitted is one.

Sorting Keys and Values

Map outputs are continuously sorted and merged until they are merged into a single reduce file for the reducer. Map outputs in the Spill buffer are partitioned. The following partition function is used.

```
partition(k', total partitions) àpartition for k
```

Within a partition the keys are sorted in-memory. Within each partition, the key/value pairs are ordered in increasing key order.

```
(k', v') →  ascending(k')
```

For example, if a partition has the following key/value pairs:

```
(k1, v1)
(k1, v2)
(k3, v3)
(k1, v4)
(k2, v5)
```

The sorting of keys gives the following order:

```
(k1, v1)
(k1, v2)
(k1, v4)
(k2, v5)
(k3, v3)
```

The org.apache.hadoop.util.QuickSort class is used for sorting keys. The quickSort is implemented by comparing the keys and sorting the keys in ascending order.

```
void quickSort(int arr[], int left, int right) {
      int index = partition(arr, left, right);
      if (left < index - 1)
            quickSort(arr, left, index - 1);
      if (index < right)
            quickSort(arr, index, right);
}

int partition(int arr[], int left, int right)
{
      int i = left, j = right;
      int tmp;
      int pivot = arr[(left + right) / 2];
```

```
        while (i <= j) {
            while (arr[i] < pivot)
                i++;
            while (arr[j] > pivot)
                j--;
            if (i <= j) {
                tmp = arr[i];
                arr[i] = arr[j];
                arr[j] = tmp;
                i++;
                j--;
            }
    };

    return i;
}
```

When the map outputs exceed the Spill buffer memory, the map outputs are spilled to disk as spill files. The spill files are merged and sorted to larger spill files. After the spill files are shuffled to the reducer, the map segments from the different mappers are merge-sorted. The map segments are spilled to disk and further merge-sorted on the disk. If the Shuffle memory is not enough for merge-sorting map outputs, an external sort is applied on the spill files to create a merge-sorted reduce input file. The keys in the map outputs, later merged into reduce input files, are sorted to give an ordered collection.

The automatic sorting of keys gives an ascending order. As many different key spaces could have been partitioned to the same reducer, all instances of the same key need to grouped together so that they are sent together in a single call to the reduce() function. A secondary sort of values is required if a reducer receives keys from more than one key space.

As discussed, a composite key comparator is used for secondary sorting. A composite key is made up of a natural key and a secondary key. For example, the following map() function takes a URL and document as input and outputs a composite key and URL as output. The composite key has the document checksum as the natural key and the pagerank as the secondary key.

```
(url, document) →  (document checksum & url pagerank, url)
```

A composite key comparator may be used to secondary sort the key/value pairs. The natural key checksum is sorted in increasing order and the secondary key pagerank is ordered in decreasing order. The secondary sort function is as follows.

```
(checksum & pagerank, url) →  (ascending(checksum) & descending(pagerank), url)
```

As values associated with a key must be input to same call or reduce() function, a sorting of values is required to group values associated with the same key together. A grouping comparator is used to group values associated with the same key. For example, if the map outputs are as follows.

```
(c2, 1, url1)
(c1, 5, url3)
(c3, 4, url2)
(c1, 3, url5)
(c2, 2, url4)
```

The secondary sort using a composite key produces the following ordered collection. The checksums are sorted in increasing order and the pageranks are ordered in decreasing order.

100

```
(c1, 5, url3)
(c1, 3, url5)
(c2, 2, url4)
(c2, 1, url1)
(c3, 4, url2)
```

Using grouping of values produces the following groups of values.

```
(c1, 5, url3)
(c1, 3, url5)

(c2, 2, url4)
(c2, 1, url1)

(c3, 4, url2)
```

Partitioners and combiners are used to partition and combine data respectively and the need for partitioner and combiner functions is based on data distribution.

Partitioners

Partitioner is used to partition map outputs (key/value pairs) among one or more reducers of a MapReduce job. Each key in a partition constitutes a key space and has an associated list of values. Partitioning data is based on some property to create smaller groups for analysis. For example, log entries may be partitioned by date for analysis. Map outputs are partitioned into partitions from which the reducers subsequently fetch the map outputs for processing on the reducers. The number of partitions is the same as the number of reducers (reduce tasks). Map outputs (key, value pairs) in the same partition are sent to the same reducer. Mappers of a MapReduce job emit intermediate (key, value) pairs and the partitioner must determine to which reducer each of the (key, value) pair goes to. Regardless of which mapper has emitted a (key,value) pair, all the (key, value) pairs with the same key are partitioned into the same partition and shuffled to the same reducer. A MapReduce job could have several mappers, and map() intermediate outputs for a particular mapper are partitioned independently of other map() outputs for other mappers. Partitions are identified by partition numbers.

Partitioner in the MapReduce framework is implemented using the org.apache.hadoop. mapred.Partitioner<K2,V2> interface in the old API and the org.apache.hadoop.mapreduce. Partitioner<KEY,VALUE> class in the new API. The Partitioner<K2,V2> interface in the old API extends the org.apache.hadoop.mapred.JobConfigurable interface. A partitioner partitions the key space of the intermediate map outputs. The key or a subset of the key is used to derive the partition number, typically using a hash function. The partitioner interface/class provides a getPartition() method that returns the partition number (as an int) to which a key, and therefore the (key,value) record is to be sent to.

```
public abstract int getPartition(KEY key,
                                 VALUE value,
                                 int numPartitions)
```

The numPartitions in the getPartition method is the number of reduce tasks in the MapReduce job. The getPartition() method receives the key/value records and the total number of partitions and returns the partition number. The partition number returned is in the range of 0 to numPartitions −1. All the records (key/value pairs) with the same key are assigned the same partition, which implies the same reducer. For any two keys k1 and k2, k1.equals(k2) implies get(k1, *, n)== get(k2, *, n) for all values indicated by *. If the number of reduce tasks is 0, the keys are not partitioned.

With multiple mappers running in parallel map outputs from each mapper are partitioned and sorted locally. A common partition for map outputs from all mappers is not created. Only a common partition number is created.

The default partitioner implementation is org.apache.hadoop.mapred.lib.HashPartitioner<K2,V2> and partitions the keys by their Object.hashCode(). The HashPartitioner uses the following algorithm to determine the partition number.

```
key.hashcode() % numPartitions
```

Therefore, the Partition function is in effect a partition(key). The number of partitions is the same as the number of reduce tasks and the number of reduce tasks is configured using the setNumReduceTasks(int n) method in org.apache.hadoop.mapred.JobConf class in the old API.

```
JobConf conf = new JobConf(new Configuration(), SampleJob.class);
conf.setNumReduceTasks(3);
```

The number of partitions is configured using the setNumReduceTasks(int n) method in the org. apache.hadoop.mapreduce.Job class in the new API. In the preceding example with the old API and following example, the number of reduce tasks and therefore the number of partitions is configured to be 3.

```
Job job=new Job(new Configuration(), "SampleJob");
job.setNumReduceTasks(3);
```

If the number of reduce tasks is three, the number of partitions is also three. Mapper output from a mapper is partitioned into three partitions and shuffled to three reducers, as in Figure 1-36. All the records (key/value pairs) with the same key are partitioned and shuffled to the same reducer.

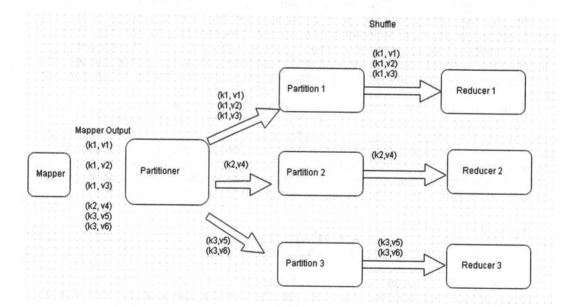

Figure 1-36. *A MapReduce example using three partitions*

Each key space does not necessarily have to be partitioned into its own partition; the number of partitions does not necessarily have to be the same as the number of key spaces. If you use two reducers instead of three in the same example, the three key spaces are partitioned into two partitions instead of three. In Figure 1-37, two of the key spaces (k1, *) and (k3, *) are partitioned into the same partition and therefore shuffled to the same reducer. One key space (k2, *) is partitioned into a separate partition and shuffled to a different reducer.

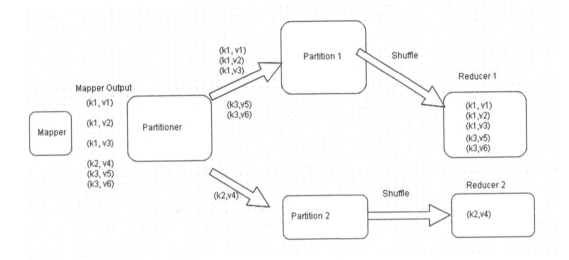

Figure 1-37. *A MapReduce example with two key spaces partitioned into the same partition*

With multiple map functions generating map outputs assigned to the same partition, MapReduce does not impose any order on the key/value pairs that are grouped together in the default partition. With two reducers the key spaces are not necessarily ordered across the reducers. In the preceding example, key spaces (k1, *) and (k3, *) are on one reducer and key space (k2, *) is on a different reducer. A more preferred partitioning is where the keys and key spaces are ordered across the reducers, as shown in Figure 1-38.

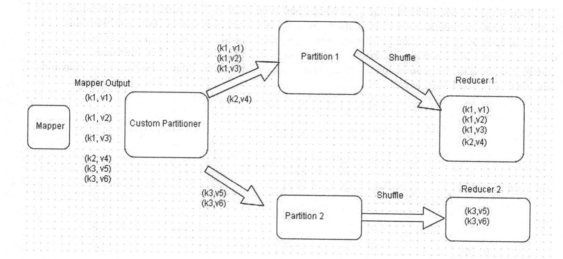

Figure 1-38. *A partitioning with the keys and key spaces ordered across the reducers*

Total ordering of keys and other custom partitioning requires a custom partitioner. A custom partitioner may be created by implementing the partitioner interface and overriding the getPartition method.

```
import Partitioner;
public class TotalOrderPartitioner implements Partitioner {

public int getPartition(KEY key,VALUE value, int numPartitions){

//custom implementation
}
```

In the new API, a custom partitioner is created by extending the Partitioner class.

```
public class TotalOrderPartitioner extends Partitioner {

public int getPartition(KEY key,VALUE value, int numPartitions){

//custom implementation
}
}
```

A custom partitioner is configured on a Job configuration using the setPartitionerClass(Class<? extends Partitioner> cls) class in the JobConf interface in the old API and the Job class in the new API.

```
conf.setPartitionerClass(TotalOrderPartitioner.class);
```

For randomly distributed data, the default partitioner results in approximately even sized partitions. But, if the data is skewed, the partitions won't be evenly sized. For example, if the map outputs have an inordinate number of records with a particular key k1 and very few records with other keys, the partition for the k1 key space will be disproportionately larger than the other partitions. A large number of key/value pairs are shuffled to one reducer in comparison to other reducers. An uneven distribution of reducer load could result in one reducer taking an inordinate amount of time to complete while other reducers have completed, as a result delaying the job. A custom partitioner would be suitable to correct a data skew.

In addition to the default `HashPartitioner`, some other built-in partitioners are provided by the MR framework, as discussed in Table 1-9.

Table 1-9. *Other Built-In Partitioners*

Partitioner	Description
BinaryPartitioner	Partitions keys using a configurable part of the bytes array returned by `BinaryComparable.getBytes()`.
IndexUpdatePartitioner	Partitions keys such that values in the same shard are in the same partition. Only available in the old API.
TotalOrderPartitioner	Partitions keys implementing a total order using split points from external source.
KeyFieldBasedPartitioner	Partitions keys based on certain key fields.
SecondarySort. FirstPartitioner	Partitions keys based on the first part of the key. Only available in the new API. Typically a hash function on the key or the subset of the key is used.

It may not always be obvious which partitioning algorithm to use. The MR framework provides the `InputSampler<K,V>` class to determine in advance which partitioning function to use based on a sample. The InputSampler class is used with the `TotalOrderPartitioner` and provides the built-in sampling functions listed in Table 1-10 as nested classes/interfaces.

Table 1-10. *InputSampler Class Sampling Functions*

Sampling Function	Description
InputSampler.IntervalSampler<K,V>	Samples from s splits at regular intervals. Useful for sorted data.
InputSampler.RandomSampler<K,V>	General-purpose sampler that samples from random points in the input.
InputSampler.Sampler<K,V>	Samples using an InputFormat.
InputSampler.SplitSampler<K,V>	Samples the first n records from s splits. Inexpensive sampling function for random data.

Some partitioners are more suitable than other partitioners for a certain type of MR job. For example, in a PageRank MR job, a RangePartitioner would be particularly suitable as web pages are processed in ranges.

Combiners

Combiners are used to perform mapper-side initial partial aggregation before the data arrives at the reducer. A combiner function is a combine(k2; list(v2)) function. Combiner is in effect a local reduce before the global reduce. Combiner is used in-memory to aggregate intermediate map outputs after they are partitioned and sorted. The objective of using a combiner is to optimize bandwidth usage and disk storage by the MR job. After being partitioned and sorted, the map outputs are spilled to disk and subsequently shuffled to the reducer nodes. Using a combiner has two benefits:

- As the map outputs are aggregated, the disk storage space for the intermediate map outputs is reduced.

- With less data to shuffle across to the reducers, the network bandwidth usage is reduced.

A Combiner class may be configured using the setCombinerClass(Class<? extends Reducer> cls) method in the JobConf class in the old API and the Job class in the new API.

```
JobConf conf = new JobConf(new Configuration(), SampleJob.class);
conf.setCombinerClass(SampleCombiner.class);
Job job=new Job(new Configuration(), "SampleJob");
job.setCombinerClass(SampleCombiner.class);
```

If a reduce() function is both commutative and associative, the reduce function may be used as the combiner. A binary operator * on a set S is said to be commutative if x*y=y*x for all x, y, in S. A binary function f is said to commutative if f(x,y)=f(y,x). An example of a commutative function is addition.

1+4=4+1

A binary operation * is said to be associative on a set S if all x, y, and z in S the following applies.

x*(y*z)=(x*y)*z

In functional notation, for a function to be associative, the following should apply.

f(x, f(y,z))=f(f(x,y),z)

An example of an associative function is addition.

1+(4+5)=(1+4)+5

A reduce function for a word count MapReduce job is both associative and commutative and therefore it may be used as a combiner.

```
JobConf conf = new JobConf(new Configuration(), WordCountJob.class);
conf.setCombinerClass(WordCountReducer.class);
conf.setReducerClass(WordCountReducer.class);
```

For example, if a WordCount map task emits multiple records with the same (key,value), a reducer may be used as a combiner on the mapper-side node for initial aggregation. To elaborate on the example, if the word "the" has four occurrences in the mapper input, the intermediate map output will have four (the, 1) records, all of which will be partitioned to the same partition. Similarly, the word "of" with two instances is partitioned to a different partition and the word "and" is partitioned to a third partition. Using a combiner, the records with the same key may be combined into a single record. Instead of having to shuffle four instances of (the, 1) only one record (the, 4) is required to be shuffled to the reducer, as a result reducing the network bandwidth usage, as shown in Figure 1-39.

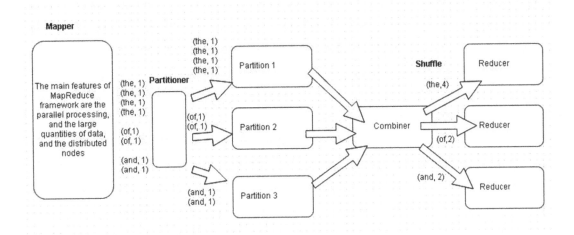

Figure 1-39. *An example of using a combiner to reduce the number of records shuffled to the reducer*

In the preceding example with the combiner, one reducer could be used instead of three as the value list for each key has already been combined. Without a combiner, more records would have to be shuffled across the network to the reducers, as a result increasing network bandwidth usage, as shown in Figure 1-40. A combiner makes the shuffle faster by reducing the amount of data to be shuffled.

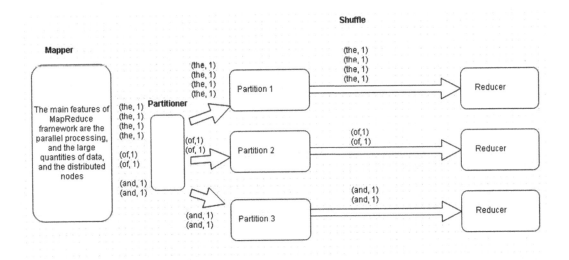

Figure 1-40. *The number of records shuffled to the reducer increases if combiner is not used*

A reducer may not always be suitable as a combiner. For example, a reduce function to compute the average distance from a set of distance key/value pairs cannot be used as a combiner. For example, if a combiner function runs on the map outputs to aggregate records by computing average distance from a subset of the records, the reducer does get fewer records, only two instead of six in the initial map outputs, in the example. But, the Job output of (d, 22.5) is not the same as if a combiner were not used. If a combiner is used, the output is shown in Figure 1-41.

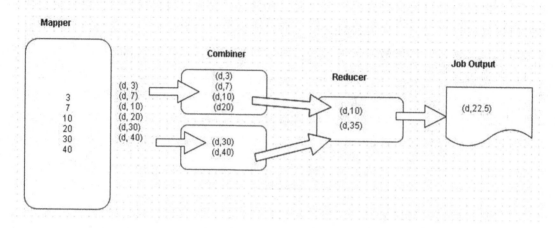

Figure 1-41. *MapReduce job output if combiner is reduced*

If a combiner is not used, all the map outputs are shuffled directly to the reducer and the Job output is (d, 18.33), as shown in Figure 1-42. The difference in result when using the reduce function as the combiner function is because the reduce function to compute average distance from a set of records is not associative and commutative.

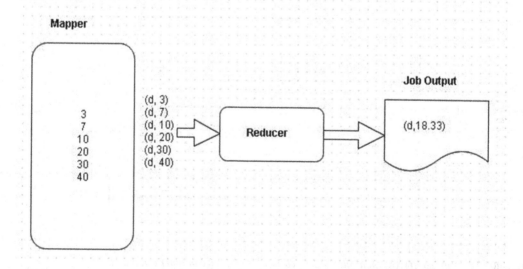

Figure 1-42. *MapReduce output when using the reduce function as the combiner function*

108

The reduce function to compute addition in the WordCount MR job is both associative and commutative and therefore may be used as a combiner. But, not the reduce function to compute the average. A custom Combiner class may be suitable if the reduce function is not suitable. For example, in the example to compute average distance, a combiner function that computes the sum of distances may be used in conjunction with a reduce function that computes the average, taking into account the number of additions involved.

The following are some of the use-cases in which a combiner would be suitable.

- A job to perform aggregation and the Reduce input groups counter is much less than the Reduce input records counter. A Reduce input groups counter is for the number key spaces input to Reduce phase, while a Reduce input records counter is for the number of records input to the Reduce phase. A much larger input records counter indicates that one or a few of the key spaces have a disproportionately large number of records. Using a combiner on the map side to pre-aggregate the records would reduce the number of records by combining records in the key spaces with a large number of records. Using a combiner equalizes the data associated with each key and as a result lessens the skew in the reduce phase.

- Map outputs bytes are multiple gigabytes per node and as a result the shuffle size is also large. A combiner would reduce the shuffle size by aggregating map outputs on the mapper side before they are shuffled to the reducers.

- Much of the intermediate map output is being spilled to disk as indicated by the number of spilled records being much larger than the number of map output records. A combiner would be suitable to reduce the number of spilled records by aggregating the map outputs. A fewer number of spilled records implies less disk storage usage.

A combiner may also be used on a reducer to combine the map outputs shuffled across from the mappers, although the only benefit from combining one the reducers is to reduce the disk storage requirements for records spilled to disk.

In local aggregation, if combiners are used to perform all feasible local aggregation, at the most m x V intermediate key/value pairs would result, m being the number of mappers and V being the number of unique terms in the map outputs. It is likely that not all mappers will have all the unique terms, though. An associative array would be suitable to be used to sum the term counts in a WordCount MR job.

A combiner is not suitable if very few to no subsets of key/value pairs have common key.

As the combiner is run in-memory, sufficient memory is a requirement to store the intermediate results for combining. With a combiner running in conjunction with other map-side processes, multiple resources could be competing for the same resources.

The usage of combiner is optional and a combiner is not guaranteed to run in a MR job. As a combiner runs an indeterminate number of times, it should not have any side-effects. If the MR job deems a combiner to be suitable, instances of the combiner are run on each of the nodes that produce intermediate map output. The MR framework may chose to invoke the combiner function more than once on a subset of map outputs. A combiner is not invoked on every tuple of map output. For example, a combiner won't be invoked on a key with a single value associated. The combiner is last user-defined function that runs on map outputs before they are sent to the reducers. In certain MR jobs, combine input records and combine output records may be 0 even though a combiner is set.

Partitioners and combiners are in-memory functions and are run in the Spill buffer, which receives the map outputs. An in-memory partitions index is also kept for the in-memory partitions. Map outputs are first partitioned, subsequently sorted, and if a combiner is defined and found to be suitable the combiner is run. The partitioned, sorted, combined records are merged and spilled to disk as spill files when the Spill buffer memory becomes full or the threshold is reached. An in-memory spill index is kept for spill files. The combiner is invoked during the merge phase and may reduce buffer memory usage by combining tuples such that records that would otherwise would have been only-merged and spilled to disk do not require a spill to disk. Each spill file may have one or more partitions merged. If compression is enabled the Spill buffer records are compressed before being spilled to disk. The io.sort.spill.percent configuration property in mapred-site.xml defines the limit in the Spill buffer. When the map outputs exceed io.sort. mb* io.sort.spill.percent, map outputs are spilled to disk. An index file corresponding to each spill file is also generated. An index file specifies the partition offset for the partitions in the spill file. A record in a spill file is called a SpillRecord. A spill file and an index file are shown in Figure 1-43.

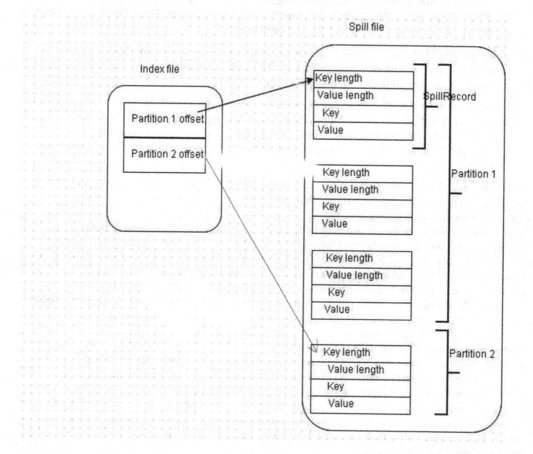

Figure 1-43. *A spill file and a index file*

The spill files are merged on-disk to generate a map output file and a corresponding index file, as shown in Figure 1-44. Some intermediate merged files may also be generated. The combiner may again be invoked during the merge of the spill files and intermediate files. During shuffle, the reducer fetches map outputs, based on partitions assigned to each reducer, from the merged and partitioned map output files on the disk and also from the partitioned, sorted and combined map outputs in the Spill buffer RAM. A partition in a map output file or the Spill buffer is called a map segment. In Shuffle, relevant map segments are copied to the reducers.

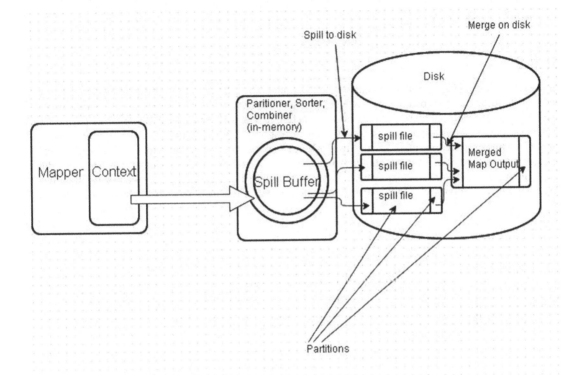

Figure 1-44. *Merging spill files*

Combiners may also be used in a streaming job with the –combiner option.

```
bin/hadoop jar /path/to/hadoop-version-streaming.jar  -mapper mapperProgram -combiner
reducerProgram  -reducer reducerProgram –input  /input/dfs/path –output  /output/dfs/path
```

Sort and Shuffle Process

The reducer implements a reduce() function to process a set of intermediate values associated with a key to a smaller set of values. The reducer has three functions:

- Shuffle

- Sort

- Reduce

Next, we discuss shuffle and sort.

Shuffle

In the shuffle phase (Figure 1-45), the reducer fetches map outputs from mappers to be processed on the reducer. Reducers fetch map outputs via HTTP. The intermediate map outputs are copied to the reducers, not transferred and erased on the mapper nodes. The intermediate map outputs in mappers are partitioned using a partitioner and assigned a partition number corresponding to the reducer the map output is to be processed during the reduce phase of the MR job. Within a partition the map outputs are sorted. Spill files on disk are re-sorted when merged. Shuffle is an all-map-to-all-reduce input data fetching phase in a reduce task. In the shuffle phase of a MR job, intermediate map outputs from all mappers are fetched by all reducers to which the map outputs are assigned using partitioning. Only one partition can be assigned to one reducer.

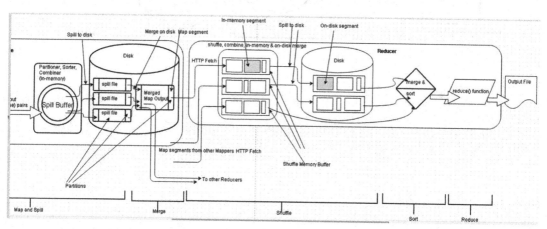

Figure 1-45. *Shuffle phase in MapReduce*

Shuffle is initiated by the reducer and involves copying intermediate map outputs from all map tasks using HTTP fetch. If compression is applied to map outputs, the shuffled map output files are decompressed into Shuffle buffer memory. As mapper and reducer tasks could be running on separate nodes shuffle involves internode communication and could be a delaying factor in job completion.

The shuffle phase fetches all map outputs associated with a reduce task from multiple nodes and merges them into one reduce input. The map outputs fetched from mappers are called map segments. The map segments are partitioned on disk and in memory on the map task according to the reduce task the map segments are assigned to. The map outputs assigned to a reduce task are first fetched into memory, a Shuffle memory buffer. The combine and merge of the map outputs from the various map tasks is initiated in memory. If the memory buffer fills up or a threshold is reached, the shuffled map outputs are spilled to disk and the merge of map segments is applied on disk. Therefore, the merge is a combination of an in-memory and on-disk process.

Before a reducer can process a key and its associated values, the merged map segments have to be presented to the reducer as a single merged and sorted input file. The map segments, both in-memory and on-disk, are merged and sorted by the reduce task. The merged and sorted map segments are input to the reduce phase of the reducer.

As map outputs on a single map task could be partitioned and assigned to different reduce tasks, not all map segments from a single map task are shuffled to the same reduce task. By the same logic, a reduce task shuffles map segments from one or more map tasks that have map segments partitioned and assigned to it.

The maximum number of transfers, assuming all reducers fetch from all maps, is maps*reduces. The intermediate map outputs on the mapper side are not deleted immediately after being copied to the reducers, as a reducer may fail and the map outputs may need to be reshuffled. The intermediate map outputs are deleted only after the job is completed.

The Shuffle handler performance can be improved by enabling shuffle read-ahead, which causes TaskTracker or NodeManager to prefetch map outputs from the mapper before sending over the socket to the reducer. Prefetch is enabled in YARN by setting mapreduce.shuffle.manage.os.cache to true (the default). Also set the mapreduce.shuffle.readahead.bytes to the number of bytes to read-ahead, the default value being 4MB. In MR1, set mapred.tasktracker.shuffle.fadvise to true (default) and set mapred.tasktracker.shuffle.readahead.bytes (4MB is the default). Ifile read-ahead, which improves merge performance, may be enabled with the mapreduce.ifile.readahead configuration property in MR2 and the Ifile read-ahead bytes may be set with mapreduce.ifile.readahead.bytes (4MB is the default).

In MR2, shuffle is handled by the NodeManagers. Configure the following properties in yarn-default.xml/yarn-site.xml for the NodeManager to provide the auxiliary services of MR2 shuffle using the Shuffle class org.apache.hadoop.mapred.ShuffleHandler.

```
<property>
    <name>yarn.nodemanager.aux-services</name>
    <value>mapreduce.shuffle</value>
  </property>
  <property>
    <name>yarn.nodemanager.aux-service.mapreduce.shuffle.class</name>
    <value>org.apache.hadoop.mapred.ShuffleHandler</value>
  </property>
```

AuxServices is a framework that NodeManager provides to configure auxiliary services.

MapReduce Job counters such as the following may be output, including shuffle counters.

```
org.apache.hadoop.mapreduce.TaskCounter
MAP_INPUT_RECORDS=5
MAP_OUTPUT_RECORDS=5
MAP_OUTPUT_BYTES=56
MAP_OUTPUT_MATERIALIZED_BYTES=72
SPLIT_RAW_BYTES=108
COMBINE_INPUT_RECORDS=5
COMBINE_OUTPUT_RECORDS=5
REDUCE_INPUT_GROUPS=5
REDUCE_SHUFFLE_BYTES=72
REDUCE_INPUT_RECORDS=5
REDUCE_OUTPUT_RECORDS=5
SPILLED_RECORDS=10
SHUFFLED_MAPS=1
FAILED_SHUFFLE=0
```

Sort

The MR framework guarantees that input to the reducer is merge-sorted to a single input file. A reduce phase is started only after all its input is available. After the shuffled map segments have been merged on the reducer, the map segments are sorted. The MR framework merge-sorts by keys as different mappers may have output the same key. The shuffle and sort phase proceed simultaneously; while the map outputs are fetched, they are merged and sorted. An external merge-sort algorithm is used when the map outputs are too large to fit into memory. The default sort class is org.apache.hadoop.util.QuickSort and is configured in the map.sort.class configuration property in mapred-default.xml.

If the natural key emitted by a map function is not significant in sorting keys and another parameter such as a timestamp is to be used in sorting keys, a composite key made from the natural key and the sort parameter of interest, such as timestamp, should be used for sorting. The natural key should be used for grouping the keys, as you still want the keys input to a reduce function call to be based on the natural key. The process of sorting keys based on a secondary key rather than the natural key is called secondary sorting.

The JobConf.setOutputKeyComparatorClass(Class<? extends RawComparator> theClass) method in the old API and the Job.setSortComparatorClass(Class<? extends RawComparator> cls) method in the new API can be used to configure the sort RawComparator to be used to sort the input to a reducer. A org.apache.hadoop.io.RawComparator<T> comparator implementation must be used for sorting keys. A Comparator is a function that applies total ordering on some collection of objects.

In addition to sorting keys using a secondary sort, a grouping of keys may be applied to group the keys to be sent to a single call of a reduce() function. The RawComparator that groups keys together for a single call to a reduce() function is set using the JobConf.setOutputValueGroupingComparator(Class<? extends RawComparator> theClass) method in the old API and the Job.setGroupingComparatorClass(Class<? extends RawComparator> cls) method in the new API. For the purpose of secondary sorting, a key is extended with a secondary key to create a composite key. Therefore, two RawComparators are used, one to sort the keys using the entire key for comparing keys, and the other to group the keys to be sent to the same call of the reduce() function using a secondary key, which is t for the parameter of interest in sorting the input. The secondary key could be a timestamp. The grouping comparator is recommended only if the equivalent algorithm for keys for sorting the intermediate keys using a secondary sort RawComparator is different than the equivalent algorithm for grouping keys in a single call to the Reducer.reduce(K2 key, Iterator<V2> values, OutputCollector<K3,V3> output, Reporter reporter) method in the old API or the Reducer.reduce(KEYIN key, Iterable<VALUEIN> values, Reducer.Context context) method in the new API. An example secondary sort class is org.apache.hadoop.examples.SecondarySort, which reads text input files that must contain two integers per line. The SecondarySort class sorts based on the first and second integer and groups based on the first integer.

As the order of the map outputs shuffled to the reduce task is non-deterministic, sort and secondary sort do not guarantee a stable reduce sort.

The RawComparator interface has only one method called compare(), which compares the byte representations of objects.

```
int compare(byte[] b1,
            int s1,
            int l1,
            byte[] b2,
            int s2,
            int l2)
```

The method compares two binary objects based on their byte representations, as listed in Table 1-11.

Table 1-11. *Parameters in Compare Methods*

Parameter	Description
b1	The first byte array
s1	The starting index in b1
l1	The length of the object in b1
b2	The second byte array
s2	The starting index in b2
l2	The length of the object in b2

Some of the built-in implementations provided for RawComparator are listed in Table 1-12.

Table 1-12. *Parameters in Compare Methods*

RawComparator Class	Description
KeyFieldBasedComparator	Compares based on a subset of fields in a key and a subset of characters within fields.
WritableComparator	Compares WritableComparable using natural ordering.
RecordComparator	Compares records.
BooleanWritable.Comparator	Comparator optimized for BooleanWritable keys.
BytesWritable.Comparator	Comparator optimized for BytesWritable keys.
ByteWritable.Comparator	Comparator optimized for ByteWritable keys.
DoubleWritable.Comparator	Comparator optimized for DoubleWritable keys.
FloatWritable.Comparator	Comparator optimized for FloatWritable keys.
IntWritable.Comparator	Comparator optimized for IntWritable keys.
LongWritable.Comparator	Comparator optimized for LongWritable keys.
LongWritable.DecreasingComparator	A decreasing comparator optimized for LongWritable keys.
NullWritable.Comparator	Comparator optimized for NullWritable keys.
SecondarySort.FirstGroupingComparator	A grouping comparator that compares only the first component in a pair.
Text.Comparator	Comparator optimized for text keys.
UTF8.Comparator	A WritableComparator optimized for UTF8 keys.

The next example demonstrates sort and secondary sort with an example. The example is of sorting web pages by their checksums and decreasing pagerank and grouping by checksum. The map() function takes as input the web page URL as key and document as value and outputs a composite key made from document checksum and URL pagerank and the URL as value. The pagerank is the secondary key and the parameter of interest in sorting. The natural key, which is the checksum, is not of interest in sorting. The mapper maps the input to the output as follows.

```
(url, document) → (document checksum & url pagerank, url)
```

The input/output for the map are as follows.

```
Map Input Value: document
Map Output Key: document checksum, url pagerank
Map Output Value: url
Partitioner: by checksum
OutputKeyComparator: by checksum and then decreasing pagerank
OutputValueGroupingComparator: by checksum
```

The sort is based on the composite key and the grouping of the keys input to the reduce() function is based on the document checksum, which is the natural key.

The key type for the MR application, WebPageCompositeKey, is a composite key made from the document checksum and pagerank. The sorting is based on the composite key with increasing order in natural key, which is checksum, and decreasing order in secondary key, which is pagerank. The grouping is based on the natural key (document checksum). The grouping comparator groups the web page URLs with the same checksum for a call to the reduce() function. The composite key is defined as follows.

```java
import java.io.DataInput;
import java.io.DataOutput;
import java.io.IOFxception;

import org.apache.hadoop.io.WritableComparable;
import org.apache.hadoop.io.WritableComparator;

/**
 *
 * WebPageCompositeKey
 *
 * The key type for this Map Reduce application.
 *
 * This particular key has two parts, the long DocumentChecksum and long PageRank.
 *
 * We do a primary grouping pass on the DocumentChecksum field to get all of the data of
 * one type together, and then our "secondary sort" during the shuffle phase
 * uses the PageRank long member to sort  urls so that they
 * arrive at the reducer partitioned and in sorted order.
 *
 * @author jpatterson
 *
 */
public class WebPageCompositeKey implements WritableComparable<WebPageCompositeKey> {

        private long DocumentChecksum= 0;
        private long PageRank = 0;

        public void set(long checksum, long pageRank) {

                this.DocumentChecksum = checksum;
                this.PageRank = pageRank;

        }
```

```java
public String getDocumentChecksum() {
        return this.DocumentChecksum;
}

public long getPageRank() {
        return this.PageRank;
}

@Override
public void readFields(DataInput in) throws IOException {

        this.DocumentChecksum = in.readUTF();
        this.PageRank = in.readLong();

}

@Override
public void write(DataOutput out) throws IOException {

        out.writeLong(DocumentChecksum);
        out.writeLong(this.PageRank);
}

@Override
public int compareTo(WebPageCompositeKey other) {

        if (this.DocumentChecksum.compareTo(other.DocumentChecksum) != 0) {
                return this.DocumentChecksum.compareTo(other.DocumentChecksum);
        } else if (this.PageRank != other.PageRank) {
                return this.PageRank < other.PageRank ? -1 : 1;

        } else {
                return 0;
        }

}

public static class WebPageCompositeKeyComparator extends WritableComparator {
        public WebPageCompositeKeyComparator() {
                super(WebPageCompositeKey.class);
        }

        public int compare(byte[] b1, int s1, int l1, byte[] b2, int s2, int l2) {
                return compareBytes(b1, s1, l1, b2, s2, l2);
        }
}

static { // register this comparator
        WritableComparator.define(WebPageCompositeKey.class,
                        new WebPageCompositeKeyComparator());
}
```

}

Next, create a composite key Comparator to be used in secondary sorting. The WebPageCompositeKeyComparator class sorts based on the pagerank in descending order and checksum in ascending order. WebPageCompositeKeyComparator implements the secondary sort.

```
import org.apache.hadoop.io.WritableComparable;
import org.apache.hadoop.io.WritableComparator;

/**
 * WebPageCompositeKeyComparator
 *
 * Purpose: Compares two WriteableComparables
 *
 * When we are sorting keys, in this case we only want to sort by checksums in
 * that we want all of the same group ids grouped together regardless of the
 * pagerank portion of their key. This functionality is provided by the
 * ChecksumGroupingComparator class
 *
 * Inside the set of k/v pairs in this group, in this secondary sort example we
 * want to sort on the second half of the key (WebPageCompositeKey) which is the
 * purpose of this class.
 *
 *
 *
 *
 */
public class WebPageCompositeKeyComparator extends WritableComparator {

        protected WebPageCompositeKeyComparator() {
                super(WebPageCompositeKey.class, true);
        }

        @Override
        public int compare(WritableComparable w1, WritableComparable w2) {

                WebPageCompositeKey k1 = (WebPageCompositeKey) w1;
                WebPageCompositeKey k2 = (WebPageCompositeKey) w2;

                int cmp = k1.getDocumentChecksum().compareTo(k2.getDocumentChecksum());
                if (cmp != 0) {
                        return cmp;
                }

                return k1.getPageRank() == k2.getPageRank() ? 0 : (k1
                                .getPageRank() < k2.getPageRank() ? -1 : 1);

        };

}
```

Next, create the natural key grouping Comparator, ChecksumGroupingComparator, based on the checksum.

```
import org.apache.hadoop.io.WritableComparable;
import org.apache.hadoop.io.WritableComparator;
```

```
/**
 *
 * ChecksumGroupingComparator
 *
 * This class is used during Hadoop's shuffle phase to group composite Key's by
 * the natural key.
 *
 *
 *
 * @author jpatterson
 *
 */
public class ChecksumGroupingComparator extends WritableComparator {

        protected ChecksumGroupingComparator() {
                super(WebPageCompositeKey.class, true);
        }

        @Override
        public int compare(WritableComparable o1, WritableComparable o2) {

                WebPageCompositeKey k1 = (WebPageCompositeKey) o1;
                WebPageCompositeKey k2 = (WebPageCompositeKey) o2;

                return k1.getDocumentChecksum().compareTo(k2.getDocumentChecksum());

        }

}
```

Create a Partitioner based on the natural key to partition the map outputs to the reducers.

```
import org.apache.hadoop.mapred.JobConf;
import org.apache.hadoop.mapred.Partitioner;

/**
 * ChecksumPartitioner
 *
 * Purpose: partitions the data output from the map phase
 * before it is sent through the shuffle phase.
 *
 * getPartition() determines how we group the data; In the case of this
 * secondary sort example this function partitions the data by only the first
 * half of the key, the Text group (key.getDocumentChecksum().hashcode()).
 */
public class ChecksumPartitioner implements
                Partitioner<WebPageCompositeKey, TimeseriesDataPoint> {

        @Override
        public int getPartition(WebPageCompositeKey key, String url,
                        int numPartitions) {
                return Math.abs(key.getDocumentChecksum().hashCode() * 127) % numPartitions;
        }
```

```
        @Override
        public void configure(JobConf arg0) {

        }
}
```

In the MR job class, the sort comparator, the grouping comparator, and the partitioner are set as follows.

```
conf.setPartitionerClass(ChecksumPartitioner.class);
conf.setOutputKeyComparatorClass(WebPageCompositeKeyComparator.class);
conf.setOutputValueGroupingComparator(ChecksumGroupingComparator.class);
```

The MR job class is defined as follows.

```
import java.util.ArrayList;
import java.util.List;

import org.apache.hadoop.conf.Configuration;
import org.apache.hadoop.conf.Configured;
import org.apache.hadoop.fs.Path;
import org.apache.hadoop.mapred.FileInputFormat;
import org.apache.hadoop.mapred.FileOutputFormat;
import org.apache.hadoop.mapred.JobClient;
import org.apache.hadoop.mapred.JobConf;
import org.apache.hadoop.mapred.TextInputFormat;
import org.apache.hadoop.mapred.TextOutputFormat;
import org.apache.hadoop.util.Tool;
import org.apache.hadoop.util.ToolRunner;

public class WebPageJob extends Configured implements Tool {

        @Override
        public int run(String[] args) throws Exception {

                JobConf conf = new JobConf(getConf(), WebPageJob.class);
                conf.setJobName("WebPageJob");

                conf.setMapOutputKeyClass(WebPageCompositeKey.class);
                conf.setMapOutputValueClass(Text.class);

                conf.setMapperClass(WebPageMapper.class);
                conf.setReducerClass(WebPageReducer.class);

                conf.setPartitionerClass(ChecksumPartitioner.class);
                conf.setOutputKeyComparatorClass(WebPageCompositeKeyComparator.class);
                conf.setOutputValueGroupingComparator(ChecksumGroupingComparator.class);

                  conf.setOutputKeyClass(LongWritable.class);
                  conf.setOutputValueClass(Text.class);
```

```
        conf.setInputFormat(TextInputFormat.class);

        conf.setOutputFormat(TextOutputFormat.class);

        FileInputFormat.setInputPaths(conf, args[0]);
        FileOutputFormat.setOutputPath(conf, args[1]);

        JobClient.runJob(conf);

        return 0;
    }

    public static void main(String[] args) throws Exception {

        int res = ToolRunner.run(new Configuration(), new WebPageJob(),
                        args);
        System.exit(res);

    }

}
```

The mapred-default.xml/mapred-site.xml defines some configuration properties (see Table 1-13) that may be used to tune the sort and shuffle process.

Table 1-13. *Configuration Properties to Tune the Sort and Shuffle Process*

Configuration Property	Description
mapreduce.task.io.sort.factor	Number of streams to merge at once when sorting files. Determines the number of open file handles. Also applies to mapper-side sorting. For the reducer the merge refers to the merge of the map output files, the spill files generated from map outputs. The default value is 10. The reducer merges together the spill files (or map output files) from the same mapper between themselves first and merges the map outputs from a mapper with the map outputs of other mappers only after a Map task has committed. The map outputs are not merged with other mappers' map tasks before a map has completed because a mapper could fail, and if a mapper fails, its map outputs from the failed mapper are discarded. Large job requiring large maps and a large number of spills to disk value should be increased to minimize disk accesses. An increased value has another benefit that as the last batch of streams is sent to the reduce() function without merging, time in merging is saved.
mapreduce.task.io.sort.mb	Buffer memory to use when sorting files, in MB. Default value is 100MB. By default, gives each merge stream 1MB. Also applies to mapper-side Spill buffer. More memory for sorting reduces spills to disk.

(continued)

Table 1-13. (*continued*)

Configuration Property	Description
mapreduce.reduce.shuffle.parallelcopies	The number of parallel copies during shuffle. The default value is 5. Value should be increased for large jobs since CPU usage also increases proportionally.
mapreduce.reduce.shuffle.retry-delay.max.ms	The maximum number of ms the reducer will delay before trying to fetch the map outputs again.
mapreduce.reduce.shuffle.connect.timeout	The maximum number of ms a reduce task spends in trying to connect to a TaskTracker to fetch map outputs. Default value is 180000 ms, which is three minutes.
mapreduce.reduce.shuffle.read.timeout	After obtaining connection with the TaskTracker the maximum number of ms a reduce task waits for map outputs to be available for fetching.
mapreduce.reduce.shuffle.input.buffer.percent	The fraction of the memory from the total heap size to be allocated for the map outputs during the shuffle. The default value is .70. If the threshold is exceeded, map outputs are spilled to disk. Ideally, the number of bytes read/written to disk should be close to 0 if they can fit the RAM. The spilled records should be ideally close to 0. If spilled records are significantly more than input records a multi-pass merge is being applied, which incurs an overhead. Reducing disk spills on reducer could increase the shuffle speed. Increasing heap size on reducer enhances performance.
mapreduce.reduce.shuffle.merge.percent	The fraction of the memory allocated for map outputs during shuffle, as configured in mapreduce.reduce.shuffle.input.buffer.percent to be used as a threshold to initiate in-memory merge of map outputs. The default value is 0.66, which implies 0.66x0.70 of the maximum heap size as the threshold.
mapreduce.reduce.input.buffer.percent	The fraction of the maximum JVM heap size that may be used to retain map outputs during reduce. When the fraction of memory used by map outputs exceeds the specified value the reduce phase begins. The default value is 0.0, which implies that the reduce phase begins only after all the map outputs have been spilled to disk and/or merge-sorted. MR assumes reducer code needs the full heap of RAM and spills all RAM segments to disk before running reduce phase. For simple reducers such as sort or aggregation, the complete heap RAM may not be required and the value may be higher to keep some map outputs in RAM if required.
mapreduce.reduce.shuffle.memory.limit.percent	Maximum fraction of the in-memory limit for the Shuffle buffer that a single shuffle may consume. The default value is 0.25, implying that a single shuffle cannot consume more than 25% of the Shuffle buffer memory.

(*continued*)

Table 1-13. (*continued*)

Configuration Property	Description
`mapreduce.shuffle.ssl.enabled`	Whether to use SSL for the HTTP fetch during shuffle. The default setting is `false`.
`mapreduce.shuffle.ssl.file.buffer.size`	Buffer size when using SSL for reading spill files. The default value is 65536.
`mapreduce.shuffle.port`	Port that the ShuffleHandler runs at the NodeManager. The default value is 8080.
`mapreduce.job.reduce.shuffle.consumer.plugin.class`	The class to be used to send shuffle requests from reduce task. The default class is `org.apache.hadoop.mapreduce.task.reduce.Shuffle`.
`mapreduce.tasktracker.http.threads`	Number of threads used for map output fetching. Default value is 40.
`mapreduce.job.reduce.slowstart.completedmaps`	The fraction of the number of maps in the job that should complete before reduces are scheduled. The default value is 0.05. After the threshold number of maps have completed and while the other maps are still running, reducers are scheduled and they start shuffling map outputs. The reduce phase is not invoked until all maps have completed as some maps may generate map outputs to be used by a reducer.
`mapreduce.task.files.preserve.failedtasks`	Should the files for failed tasks be kept? The default value is `false`. Should be enabled for failing jobs. Prevents the map outputs from being deleted from the reducer as they are consumed.

Sorting is also applied to the map outputs after being partitioned. After the partitioned, sorted, combined, and compressed map outputs are spilled to disk, map outputs are re-sorted when the spill files are merged. The output of the reducer is not re-sorted.

The efficiency of the reducers is driven mainly by the shuffle. Some of the best practices for better shuffle and sort performance are as follows.

- Compression of the intermediate map outputs enhances shuffle performance as the amount of data shuffled is reduced and as a result less network bandwidth is used during shuffling. Snappy and LZO are suitable for map outputs compression. Snappy is fast and provides reasonable compression ratio. LZO has comparable performance to Snappy during compression and provides high CPU efficiencies.

- Fewer maps should be used such that all map outputs can be sorted in one pass by keeping them in the sort buffer. Fewer maps also reduce the number of seeks required to shuffle the map outputs to the reducers. Assuming each map produces output for each reduce, the number of seeks is m x r, m being the number of maps and r being the number of reduces. Fewer maps yield larger shuffle segments, as a result of which the overhead of establishing a connection is reduced as compared to the actual transfer of map output data. Fewer maps result in fewer sorted map segment to merge on the reduce-side merge, and as a result the reduce-side merge of map outputs is more efficient as fewer merges are needed.

- Using a combiner on the partitioned and sorted map outputs before being spilled to disk reduces the data to be shuffled across to the reducers.

- Each reduce should process at least 1-2GB of data and at most 5-10GB of data. Too few reducers cause overload on the reducers and the parallel shuffling, merging, sorting, and reducing is no longer beneficial. Too many reducers also affect the shuffle adversely as too many map-to-reduce shuffles are applied.

- Network issues such as the Network Interface Card (NIC) set to auto-negotiate to 100MB. Each NIC should be running at gigabit speed and should use a dedicated network instead of a shared network. If maps are completed and reducers have not started to fetch, refer to the logs. Nagios alerts when NIC slows down. Use benchmarks such as Netperf to find if network bandwidth across all nodes is acceptable.

The sequence used to generate input splits from input files in HDFS to reduce outputs is shown in Figure 1-46.

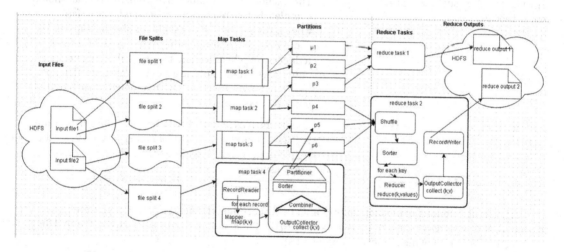

Figure 1-46. *MapReduce with shuffle and sort*

The map and reduce phases across the different MapReduce daemons with sort and shuffle included is shown in Figure 1-47.

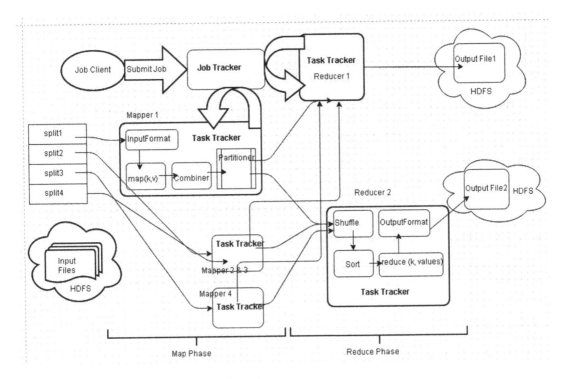

Figure 1-47. *Sort and shuffle with MapReduce phases*

MapReduce Job Configuration and Submission

A MapReduce job is an execution of a mapper and reducer across a dataset. A task is an execution of a mapper or reducer on a section of data. The configuration parameters for a job are set differently in the old API and the new API. The old API uses the org.apache.hadoop.mapred.JobConf class to set configuration parameters. For example, the following sets the InputFormat and OutputFormat for the job.

```
JobConf job = new JobConf(new Configuration(), SampleJob.class);
job.setInputFormat(SequenceFileInputFormat.class);
 job.setOutputFormat(SequenceFileOutputFormat.class);
```

JobConf objects hold (key, value) components mapping string → value, for example mapreduce. job.maps → 20. JobConf is serialized and distributed before running the job. Objects implementing the JobConfigurable interface, for example instances of org.apache.hadoop.mapred.MapReduceBase, org.apache.hadoop.mapred.TextInputFormat, org.apache.hadoop.mapred.liborg.apache. hadoop.mapred.lib.IdentityMapper<K,V>.HashPartitioner<K2,V2>, org.apache.hadoop.mapred. lib.IdentityReducer<K,V>, and org.apache.hadoop.mapred.KeyValueTextInputFormat, can retrieve the JobConf elements in the void configure(JobConf job) method. Mapper<K1,V1,K2,V2>, MapRunnable<K1,V1,K2,V2>, Partitioner<K2,V2>, Reducer<K2,V2,K3,V3> are subinterfaces of JobConfigurable, and their instances may also retrieve the JobConf in the configure() method.

The new API uses the org.apache.hadoop.mapreduce.Job class to set configuration parameters.

```
Job job = new Job(new Configuration(), "SampleJob");
job.setInputFormatClass(SequenceFileInputFormat.class);
 job.setOutputFormatClass(SequenceFileOutputFormat.class);
```

Configuration parameters may also be set using the -Dproperty=value command-line option.

Command-line properties override the properties set by other methods. For example, the map output compression is enabled and the map output compression class is set using -D as follows.

```
hadoop jar <jarname> <class> -Dmapreduce.map.output.compress=true  -Dmapreduce.map.output.
compress.codec=org.apache.hadoop.io.SnappyCodec
```

For a streaming job, the -jobconf option adds or overrides the configuration in the JobConf or Job.

```
hadoop jar  streaming/hadoop-streaming.jar -jobconf <n>=<v>
```

Configuration parameters may be also be set in the mapred-site.xml or hadoop-site.xml configuration file. For example, the number of reducers and the maximum number of map attempts is configured in hadoop-site.xml or mapred-site.xml, as follows.

```
<configuration>
<property>
    <name>mapreduce.job.reduces</name>
    <value>5</value>
    <final>false</final>
  </property>
<property>
    <name>mapreduce.map.maxattempts</name>
    <value>10</value>
    <final>true</final>
  </property>
</configuration>
```

If the parameter is set as <final>true</final>, the value cannot be overridden. If it's not set to final, the configuration specified with JobConf or Job overrides the configuration specified in hadoop-site.xml or mapred-site.xml.

A MapReduce job requires several configuration parameters to be set before a job is submitted and run. Table 1-14 shows the main configuration parameters that may be set in JobConf.

Table 1-14. Some Configuration Parameters for a MapReduce Job

Configuration Parameter	Description	Job Class Method	JobConf Class Method
Combiner class	The combiner class to combine the map outputs before shuffling the map outputs to the reducers.	`SetCombinerClass(Class<? extends Reducer> cls)`	`setCombinerClass(Class <? extends Reducer> theClass)`
Grouping comparator class	The comparator class that controls which keys are grouped together for a single call to the `Reducer.reduce()` method.	`SetGroupingComparatorClass (Class<? extends RawComparator> cls)`	`SetOutputValueGrouping Comparator(Class<? extends RawComparator> theClass)`
InputFormat class	The InputFormat class for the mapper.	`SetInputFormatClass(Class<? extends InputFormat> cls)`	`setInputFormat(Class<? extends InputFormat> theClass)`
Job jar	The Job jar file to run a MapReduce job.	`setJarByClass(Class<?> cls)`	`setJarByClass(Class cls)` `setJar(String jar)`
Job name	The name of the job to run.	`setJobName(String name)`	`setJobName(String name)`
Map output key class	The key class for the map output data.	`SetMapOutputKeyClass (Class<?> theClass)`	`setMapOutputKeyClass( Class<?> theClass)`
Map output value class	The value class for the map output data.	`SetMapOutputValueClass (Class<?> theClass)`	`setMapOutputValueClass( Class<?> theClass)`
Mapper class	The Mapper class for the job.	`setMapperClass(Class<? extends Mapper> cls)`	`SetMapperClass (Class<? extends Mapper> theClass)`
Map Speculative Execution	Whether speculative execution is to be used for map tasks.	`SetMapSpeculativeExecution (boolean speculativeExecution)`	`SetMapSpeculativeExecution (boolean speculativeExecution)`
Max map attempts	The maximum number of attempts that will be made to run a map task.		`setMaxMapAttempts(int n)`
Failed map tasks	Sets the maximum percentage of failed map tasks before the job is aborted		`SetMaxMapTaskFailuresPercent (int percent)`
Number of map tasks	Sets the number of map tasks for the job. Only provides a hint to the framework.		`setNumMapTasks(int n)`

(continued)

Table 1-14. (*continued*)

Configuration Parameter	Description	Job Class Method	JobConf Class Method
Max Reduce Attempts	The maximum number of attempts that will be made to run a reduce task.		`setMaxReduceAttempts(int n)`
Failed reduce tasks	Sets the maximum percentage of failed reduce tasks before the job is aborted.		`SetMaxReduceTaskFailures Percent(int percent)`
Number of reduce tasks	The number of reduce tasks for the job.	`SetNumReduceTasks (int tasks)`	`setNumReduceTasks(int n)`
TaskTracker failures	Sets the maximum number of failures of a job for a TaskTracker, which if exceeded, the TaskTracker is blacklisted.		`setMaxTaskFailuresPerTracker (int noFailures)`
Memory for map tasks	Sets the memory for a map task.		`setMemoryForMapTask(long mem)`
Memory for reduce tasks	Sets the memory for a reduce task.		`setMemoryForReduceTask(long mem)`
JVM	Sets the number of tasks to run per JVM.		`setNumTasksToExecutePerJvm(int numTasks)`
OutputFormat class	The OutputFormat class for the job.	`SetOutputFormatClass (Class<? extends OutputFormat> cls)`	`setOutputFormat(Class<? extends OutputFormat> theClass)`
Output key class	The key class for the job output data.	`SetOutputKeyClass (Class<?> theClass)`	`setOutputKeyClass(Class<?> theClass)`
Output value class	The value class for the job outputs.	`SetOutputValueClass (Class<?> theClass)`	`setOutputValueClass(Class<?> theClass)`
Partitioner class	The partitioner for the job.	`SetPartitionerClass (Class<? extends Partitioner> cls)`	`setPartitionerClass(Class<? extends Partitioner> theClass)`
Job priority	The job priority.		`SetJobPriority (JobPriority prio)`
Profile enabled	Whether the system should collect profiler information for some of the tasks in the job.		`setProfileEnabled(boolean newValue)`

Profile params	Profiler configuration parameters.		setProfileParams(String value)
Profile task range	Ranges of maps or reduces to profile.		setProfileTaskRange(boolean isMap, String newValue)
Reducer class	The reducer for the job.	setReducerClass(Class<? extends Reducer> cls)	setReducerClass(Class<? extends Reducer> theClass)
Reduce speculative execution	Whether speculative execution is to be used for the reduce tasks of the job.	setReduceSpeculativeExecution(boolean speculativeExecution)	setReduceSpeculativeExecution(boolean speculativeExecution)
Sort comparator class	Defines the comparator that controls how keys are sorted before they are passed to the reducer.	setSortComparatorClass(Class<? extends RawComparator> cls)	setOutputKeyComparatorClass(Class<? extends RawComparator> theClass)
Speculative execution	Whether speculative execution is to be used for the job.	setSpeculativeExecution(boolean speculativeExecution)	setSpeculativeExecution(boolean speculativeExecution)
Task output filter	The task output filter.		
Current working directory	The current working directory for the default filesystem.	setWorkingDirectory(Path dir)	setWorkingDirectory(Path dir)
Job ID	The job ID.		
Compress map output	Should the map outputs be compressed; uses the SequenceFile compression.		SetCompressMapOutput(boolean compress)
CompressionCodec	Sets the CompressionCodec class used to compress map outputs.		setMapOutputCompressorClass(Class<? extends CompressionCodec> codecClass)
Job end notification URI	The URI to send notification to after the job has ended.		SetJobEndNotificationURI(String uri)
Keep failed tasks	Should the intermediate map outputs for failed tasks be kept.		SetKeepFailedTaskFiles(boolean keep)
KeyField BasedComparator	Sets the options used to compare keys with KeyFieldBasedComparator.		SetKeyFieldComparatorOptions(String keySpec)
KeyFieldBasedPartitioner	Sets the options used to partition keys with KeyFieldBasedComparator.		setKeyFieldPartitionerOptions(String keySpec)

(continued)

Table 1-14. (*continued*)

Configuration Parameter	Description	Job Class Method	JobConf Class Method
OutputCommitter	Sets the OutputCommitter class.		`setOutputCommitter(Class<? extends OutputCommitter> theClass)`
Queue name	Sets the queue name to which the job is to be submitted. By default the "default" queue is used.		`setQueueName(String queueName)`
New Mapper API	Specifies if the new API should be used with the mapper.		`setUseNewMapper(boolean flag)`
New Reducer API	Specifies if the new API should be used with the reducer.		`setUseNewMapper(boolean flag)`
Username	Sets the username for the job.		`setUser(String user)`
Map debug script	Sets the debug script to be used when the map task fails.		`setMapDebugScript(String mDbgScript)`
Reduce debug script	Sets the debug script to be used when the reduce task fails.		`setReduceDebugScript(String rDbgScript)`

The org.apache.hadoop.conf.Configuration class, which the JobConf class extends, provides several methods (shown in Table 1-15) to set configuration parameters. It is especially useful in the new API, because the Job class does not provide equivalent configuration parameter setting methods for all of the methods in the JobConf class.

Table 1-15. *Some Configuration Class Methods in the New API*

Method	Description
public void set(String name, String value)	Sets the value of the name property
public void setBoolean(String name,boolean value)	Sets the Boolean value of the name property
public void setInt(String name,int value)	Sets the name property to an int
public void setLong(String name,long value)	Sets the name property to a long
public void setFloat(String name,float value)	Sets the name property to a float
public <T extends Enum<T>> void setEnum(String name,T value)	Sets an enum property
public void setClass(String name,Class<?> theClass,Class<?> xface)	Sets the name property to the specified class that implements the specified interface
setStrings(String name, String... values)	Sets the array of String values for a property

In the old API, the map output compression is enabled and the map output class is set as follows.

```
JobConf job = new JobConf(new Configuration(), SampleJob.class);
job.setCompressMapOutput(true);
 job.setMapOutputCompressorClass(SnappyCodec.class) ;
```

In the new API, which does not provide setter methods for compression in the Job class, compression may be enabled and the compression class set using the setBoolean and setClass methods from the Configuration class, as follows.

```
Configuration conf=new Configuration();
conf. setBoolean("mapreduce.map.output.compress", true);
conf.setClass("mapreduce.map.output.compress.codec",
            SnappyCodec.class, CompressionCodec.class);
Job job = new Job(conf, "SampleJob");
```

For an already constructed job, a Configuration instance may be obtained from the Job instance and configuration properties may be set as follows.

```
public static void enableMapOutputCompress(Job job) {
    job.getConfiguration().setBoolean("mapred.compress.map.output", true);
    job.getConfiguration().setClass("mapred.map.output.compression.codec",
            SnappyCodec.class, CompressionCodec.class);
}
```

Instead of the org.apache.hadoop.io.compress.SnappyCodec class, you can use other compression classes, for example org.apache.hadoop.io.compress.GzipCodec and org.apache.hadoop.io.compress. LzoCodec.

Some of the job configuration parameters that may be set in mapred-site.xml are listed in Table 1-16.

131

Table 1-16. *Configuration Parameters in the mapred-site.xml File*

Parameter	Description
mapreduce.task.io.sort.factor	The number of file streams to merge while sorting files
mapreduce.task.io.sort.mb	Buffer memory to use while sorting files
mapreduce.map.sort.spill.percent	Threshold as a fraction of the serialization buffer capacity at which the map outputs are spilled to disk
mapreduce.job.maps	Default number of map tasks per job
mapreduce.job.reduces	Default number of reduce tasks per job
mapreduce.jobtracker.restart.recover	Enables job recovery on restart if set to true
mapreduce.jobtracker.taskscheduler.maxrunningtasks.perjob	Maximum number of running tasks for a job before it gets preempted
mapreduce.map.maxattempts	Maximum number of attempts per map task
mapreduce.reduce.maxattempts	Maximum number of attempts per reduce task
mapreduce.reduce.shuffle.parallelcopies	Default number of parallel transfers by reduce during shuffle phase
mapreduce.task.timeout	Number of milliseconds after which a task times out if it neither inputs, outputs, or updates status
mapreduce.tasktracker.map.tasks.maximum	Maximum number of map tasks that will be run simultaneously by a TaskTracker
mapreduce.tasktracker.reduce.tasks.maximum	Maximum number of reduce tasks that will be run simultaneously by a TaskTracker
mapred.child.java.opts	Java options for the TaskTracker child processes
mapreduce.map.log.level	Logging level for the map tasks
mapreduce.reduce.log.level	Logging level for the reduce tasks
mapreduce.map.speculative	Enables speculative execution for the map tasks
mapreduce.reduce.speculative	Enables speculative execution for the reduce tasks
mapreduce.job.map.output.collector.class	MapOutputCollector implementation to use
mapreduce.job.jvm.numtasks	Number of tasks to run per JVM
mapreduce.job.ubertask.enable	Enables small-job ubertask optimization, which runs small jobs sequentially within a JVM
mapreduce.job.ubertask.maxmaps	Maximum number of maps for a job to considered suitable for ubertask optimization
mapreduce.job.ubertask.maxreduces	Maximum number of reduces for a job to considered suitable for ubertask optimization
mapreduce.input.fileinputformat.split.minsize	Minimum size chunk that a map input should be split into
mapreduce.jobtracker.maxtasks.perjob	Maximum number of tasks per job
mapreduce.output.fileoutputformat.compress	Enables job output compression if set to true

(continued)

Table 1-16. (*continued*)

Parameter	Description
mapreduce.output.fileoutputformat.compress.type	For SequenceFiles, compression type should be BLOCK, RECORD, or NONE
mapreduce.output.fileoutputformat.compress.codec	The compression class to use to compress job outputs
map.sort.class	The sort class for sorting keys
mapreduce.job.maxtaskfailures.per.tracker	Maximum number of task failures for a TaskTracker after which tasks are not assigned
mapreduce.task.profile	Should profiler information be collected for some tasks of the job
mapreduce.task.profile.maps	Sets the ranges of map tasks to be profiled
mapreduce.task.profile.reduces	Sets the ranges of reduce tasks to be profiled
mapreduce.job.queuename	Queue name
mapreduce.job.reduce.slowstart.completedmaps	Fraction of the maps for a job that should complete before reduces are scheduled
mapreduce.job.counters.limit	Maximum number of counters for a job
mapreduce.framework.name	Runtime framework for a MapReduce job
mapreduce.job.end-notification.url	URL to invoke to notify of job ending
mapreduce.job.classloader	Whether to use separate classloader for user classes in the JVM
mapreduce.am.max-attempts	Maximum number of application attempts
yarn.app.mapreduce.am.command-opts	Java options for MR ApplicationMaster processes
yarn.app.mapreduce.am.resource.mb	The amount of memory the ApplicationMaster requires
mapreduce.application.classpath	Classpath for MR applications

The org.apache.hadoop.mapred.FileInputFormat<K,V> class provides several static methods in which the JobConf is used to set the input paths for a MapReduce job, as discussed in Table 1-17.

Table 1-17. *FileInputFormat<K,V> Class Static Methods Using JobConf*

Method	Description
addInputPath(JobConf conf, Path path)	Adds an input path to the Job configuration
addInputPaths(JobConf conf, String commaSeparatedPaths)	Adds multiple input paths
setInputPaths(JobConf conf, Path... inputPaths)	Sets multiple input paths
setInputPaths(JobConf conf, String commaSeparatedPaths)	Sets multiple input paths

The org.apache.hadoop.mapred.FileOutputFormat<K,V> class provides the static method setOutputPath(JobConf conf, Path outputDir) to set the path of the output directory of the MapReduce job. For example, the input/output path may be set as follows.

```
JobConf conf = new JobConf(new Configuration(), SampleJob.class);
FileInputFormat.addInputPath(conf, new Path("input"));
FileOutputFormat.setOutputPath(conf, new Path("output"));
```

The org.apache.hadoop.filecache.DistributedCache class uses Configuration to specify files/ archives to add to the distributed cache using the addArchiveToClassPath(Path archive, Configuration conf, FileSystem fs), addCacheArchive(URI uri, Configuration conf), addCacheFile(URI uri, Configuration conf), setCacheArchives(URI[] archives, Configuration conf), and setCacheFiles(URI[] files, Configuration conf) methods.

Performance-Optimized Configuration Parameters

In the following subsections we shall discuss some performance optimized configuration parameters.

Number of Maps

The number of map tasks is based on the total size of the input, which is the total number of blocks of input files. For example, if input is 10TB (10496000) and block size is 128MB, the number of maps is about 82000. The optimum level of parallelism is about 10-100 maps per node. For CPU-light map tasks, up to 300 map tasks per node may be fine. Task setup and teardown incurs an overhead, which means a task should run for at least 60 seconds.

It is more efficient to process large datasets per map and increasing the block size to 512MB or more is one way to process more data per map. Having too many maps or too many maps with short runtimes is not efficient. Unless the maps are CPU bounded, the number of maps per application should be limited to 60,000-70,000.

Fewer maps reduce the scheduling overhead, this making task scheduling easier and availability of free slots higher.

The optimizing factors from having too few maps are that too few maps are not suitable for failure recovery. This decreases the parallelism in the map phase, which can affect data locality. Too few maps may not utilize the whole cluster effectively.

Number of Reduces

The reduces are generally less than the number of maps. An appropriate number of reduces is 0.95 or 1.75 times the number of nodes*mapreduce.tasktracker.reduce.tasks.maximum. The scaling factors are less than the whole numbers 1 and 2, which reserves some slots for speculative execution.

With 0.95, all reduces can launch immediately and begin shuffling map outputs as the maps complete. With 1.75, the reduces run in waves. The faster nodes complete the first round of reduces and start a second wave of reduces. Increasing the number of reduces increases load balancing and improves failure recovery, but also increases the framework's overhead.

The number of reduces should not be too many or too few. Too few reduces cause undue load. Also, using too few reduces is not favorable for failure recovery. Using too many reduces increases the number of shuffle transfers. Also, using too may reduces generates too many relatively small files in the output. The subsequent MapReduce job has to process a lot of files. Also the NameNode namespace has to add the many output files to the namespace, increasing the memory load on the NameNode.

Optimally, each reduce should process at least 1-2GB of data and at most 5-10GB.

Compression

Compression improves read-write performance. Compression of intermediate map outputs is recommended as it can make a job run faster. Compression decreases the network bandwidth used to shuffle map outputs to the reduces. Compression also decreases the disk space used for the spill files of map outputs. Compression rate and compression ratio are the two main factors when selecting a compression codec. Snappy or indexed LZO are the most suitable codecs for compression as they are fast (Snappy being the fastest) and provide reasonable compression ratios. If job outputs are to be processed by subsequent MR applications, use a compression codec that is splittable. The zlib/gzip/unindexed LZO are not splittable and therefore not suitable if the job outputs are to be used as input to other MR jobs. A subsequent job has to process the entire output file in a single map task, which could cause load imbalance and unfavorable failure recovery. The requirements of the subsequent job have to be considered for ascertaining the suitability of zlib/gzip/LZO as a compression codec. Bzip2 is a relatively slower codec.

Spill/Sort Buffer

Map outputs are partitioned and serialized into a Spill buffer and sorted within the partitions. If the map outputs exceed a threshold, specified by `mapreduce.map.sort.spill.percent`, in the Spill buffer the map outputs are merged and spilled to disk as spill files. A high setting may reduce or eliminate merges, but increases the probability of the map task getting blocked. If the threshold is exceeded while a spill is in progress, the collection does not block, and the subsequent spill may be larger than the threshold when the threshold is less than 0.5. For example, if the threshold is 0.3 and a spill is initiated when the threshold is reached, while the spill is in progress the remainder of the buffer fills up. The next spill's size will be 0.7 of the buffer. Minimizing the number of spills decreases map time, but a larger buffer is required to avoid multiple spills and a larger buffer decreases the memory available to the mapper. The Spill buffer memory should be optimized by taking into account the map output's size and the memory requirements for the map task. For less memory-intensive map tasks, more memory may be allocated to the Spill buffer to avoid multiple spills.

To make the map outputs sort faster, you need to provide sufficient memory for the spill/sort buffer, as configured in `mapreduce.task.io.sort.mb`. The performance of a job would increase many-folds if all the map outputs can be held in the spill/sort buffer without spilling to disk. Increasing the spill/sort buffer memory requires larger JVM heap sizes.

The `mapreduce.reduce.shuffle.memory.limit.percent` property limits how much of the shuffle memory a single map output can take up. If it's exceeded, the map output is written directly to disk without first staging in memory. The default value is 0.25.

Merges

Merges are performed on the mapper when spill files are merged on disk to generate larger spill files or a single map output file. Merges are performed on the reducer for map segments spilled to disk. The `mapreduce.task.io.sort.factor` property specifies the number of spill files that can be merged at the same time. If the number of map segments (spill files) exceed the limit, merges are made in multiple passes. The value of `mapreduce.task.io.sort.factor` should be high enough that multiple passes are not required. But, if multiple passes are required, intermediate merges are performed on the spill files on disk. If the in-memory map segments require a merge and spill to disk and the disk already has enough spill files (more than or equal to `mapreduce.task.io.sort.factor`) to make an intermediate merge essential, the in-memory map segments are included in the intermediate merge.

The `mapreduce.reduce.shuffle.merge.percent` property configures the threshold to initiate an in-memory merge. If the value is set high enough, all the map outputs fetched by a reducer may fit into memory and won't require a merge.

Another property that configures merge of in-memory map segments is `mapreduce.reduce.merge.inmem.threshold`, which sets a threshold in terms of number of files in-memory to initiate an in-memory merge and spill to disk. The default value of `mapreduce.reduce.merge.inmem.threshold` is 1000. The value should be set high as in-memory merges are less expensive than on disk merges.

Shuffle Buffer

The map outputs are fetched into the Shuffle buffer by the reducer. The mapreduce.reduce.shuffle.input. buffer.percent property configures the Shuffle buffer memory as a fraction of the total JVM heap. The value should be high enough to store large and numerous map outputs.

By default, all map outputs are merged to disk before the reduce begins to make sufficient memory available for the reduce task. The mapreduce.reduce.input.buffer.percent property configures the fraction of the total JVM heap size that map outputs may occupy while the reduce runs. The default value of 0.0 makes all the memory available to the reduce task, but the reduce task has to make more disk seeks to get the input to the reduce phase as all the map outputs have been spilled to disk. For a less memory-intensive reduce phase, it may be advantageous to set the value of mapreduce.reduce.input.buffer. percent to a non-zero fraction to reduce the number of disk seeks the reduce phase has to make.

Combiner on Reducer

Using a combiner on the reducer to merge map outputs before spilling to disk makes disk spills smaller and parallelizes spilling and fetching, which may make reduce times smaller. A combiner may be more effective than increasing buffer sizes. A combiner does not have to be configured for the reducer separately. A combiner also reduces the network traffic during the shuffle phase. A combiner does incur an overhead of serialization/de-serialization and should be used if a combiner provides 20-30% of aggregation. A combiner is configured using the setCombinerClass() method in the JobConf and Job classes.

Ubertasking

By default, a new JVM is launched for each task. Launching a new JVM incurs an overhead. If a job is small, it may be advantageous to use ubertasking, a feature that enables running multiple tasks in the same JVM, one after the other. Ubertasking has to be enabled by setting mapreduce.job.ubertask.enable to true in mapred-default.xml. The number of tasks that may run sequentially in the same JVM is configured in mapreduce.job.jvm.numtasks; the default is 1. If mapreduce.job.jvm.numtasks is set to -1, any number of tasks may be run in the same JVM.

The number of tasks per JVM may also be set using the setNumTasksToExecutePerJvm(int numTasks) method in JobConf. The maximum number of maps a job may have to be eligible for ubertasking is nine and is set in the mapreduce.job.ubertask.maxmaps property. The value may be overridden downward, for example a value of 3 may be set, but a value of 10 may not. A job cannot have more than one reduces to be eligible for ubertasking; the threshold for the reduces is configured in mapreduce.job.ubertask.maxreduces with a default value of 1. The mapreduce.job.ubertask.maxreduces default value may be overridden only downward, which implies that 0 is the only other valid value. Another factor that is considered in ubertasking is mapreduce.job.ubertask.maxbytes, the maximum number of allowable bytes in the input for a job to be eligible for ubertasking. The default value of mapreduce.job.ubertask.maxbytes is the block size as set in dfs.block.size or dfs.blocksize.

Number of Shuffle Transfers

The more transfers there are between the map phase and the reduce phase in a job, the less the throughput and the more delay due to shuffle. This means the job takes more time to complete. The number of transfers is calculated by maps*reduces, assuming an all-map-to-all-reduce shuffle in which map outputs from each map are shuffled to each reduce. Minimizing the number of shuffle transfers is important for the performance of the job. Increasing the default block size increases the default map size and as a result decreases the number of map tasks. The number of maps therefore decreases and the shuffle throughput increases. The job completion time decreases. A larger map size implies a larger shuffle map segment, which increases the throughput per connection. Larger maps also mean fewer map segments to merge on the reducer, which further implies fewer merges.

Input Datasets

MapReduce is optimized to process large amounts of data. The maps process input data in a parallel manner, typically one HDFS block of data per map, which is 128MB per map. A 128MB dataset is not large enough to benefit fully from the MapReduce's optimization for large datasets. CombineFileInputFormat<K,V> is recommended to generate input splits from multiple files especially for small files. Even with large files processing multiple input files is more efficient. Increasing the HDFS block size is another method to increase the input dataset size.

Speculative Execution

Speculative execution is running multiple attempts for a task simultaneously and using the output from the task that completes first. Speculative execution is used if a job has a slow response time due to a few slow running tasks. In a large job, if a task is taking too much time due to complex and large calculations and high throughput is required, speculative execution should be set to false, as it could increase the job response time instead of reducing it.

You can submit a job on the command line using the hadoop jar command.

```
hadoop jar <job_jar> JobDriverClass [GENERIC_OPTIONS] args
```

The [GENERIC_OPTIONS] that can be used with the hadoop jar command are listed in Table 1-18.

Table 1-18. *GENERIC_OPTIONS for the Hadoop Jar Command*

Option	Description
-conf configurationfile	Specifies an application configuration file.
-D property=value	Specifies configuration property/properties.
-fs	Specifies NameNode <local|namenode:port>.
-jt <local|jobtracker:port>	Specifies a JobTracker.
-files	Files to be copied to the cluster, to the distributed cache of each node.
-archives	Archives to be unarchived to the cluster, to the distributed cache of each node.
-libjars	Jars to be added to the classpath of the job.

An example of submitting a job using the command line is as follows.

```
bin/hadoop jar hadoop-examples.jar JobDriverClass -files cachefile.txt -libjars samplelib.
jar -archives samplearchive.zip input output
```

The input and output args are arguments to the JobDriverClass class, which is the main program of the MapReduce job.

The org.apache.hadoop.util.Tool interface is the standard tool interface for a MapReduce tool/application. The Tool interface supports handling of command-line arguments. JobClient implements the Tool interface. A typical MapReduce application implements the Tool interface and the handling of command-line options is delegated to the static method org.apache.hadoop.util.ToolRunner.run(Tool tool, String[] args) or ToolRunner.run(Configuration conf, Tool tool, String[] args). ToolRunner is a utility that runs Tools by using GenericOptionsParser to parse command-line arguments. In the following MapReduce application, org.apache.hadoop.examples.terasort.TeraSort, which implements the Tool interface, is used as an argument to the ToolRunner.run(Configuration conf, Tool tool, String[] args) method.

```java
import Configured;
import Tool;
import MapReduceBase;
import Mapper;
import LongWritable;
import Text;
import IntWritable;
public class MapReduceClass extends Configured implements Tool {
public static class SampleMapper extends MapReduceBase implements Mapper<LongWritable, Text,
Text, IntWritable> {}
public static class SampleReducer extends MapReduceBase implements Reducer<Text,
IntWritable, Text, IntWritable> {}
        public int run(String[] args) throws Exception {
           // Create a JobConf
          JobConf job = new JobConf(getConf(), MapReduceClass.class);

          // Set input/output path using command-line options

          job.setInputPath(new Path(args[1]));
          job.setOutputPath(new Path(args[2]));

          // Specify various job-specific configuration parameters  such as Mapper, Reducer

          job.setMapperClass(MapReduceClass.SampleMapper.class);
          job.setReducerClass(MapReduceClass.SampleReducer.class);

          // Submit the job
          JobClient.runJob(job);
       }

      public static void main(String[] args) throws Exception {
         // Handle generic command-line options  with ToolRunner
         int res = ToolRunner.run(new Configuration(), new TeraSort(), args);

         System.exit(res);
      }
   }
}
```

The ToolRunner.run(Configuration conf, Tool tool, String[] args) method invokes the method Tool.run(String[]) with the command-line String[] as the arg to the method.

The hadoop job command may also be used to submit a job. The syntax of the command to submit a job is as follows.

```
hadoop job [GENERIC_OPTIONS] -submit <job-file>
```

[GENERIC_OPTIONS] is the same as for hadoop jar command. An example of submitting a job using the hadoop job command is as follows.

```
hadoop job -jt host:50020 -submit job.xml
```

Input and Output Data Paths in a MapReduce Job

A MR job consists of mappers and reducers. We discuss these using an example of the how data moves through a job.

1. The input file is in the HDFS to start with, the starting location of the data.

2. InputFormat generates FileSplits from the input file, but the file splits are logical splits and do not involve data flow. A map task is launched for each file split. The InputFormat creates a RecordReader for the map task.

3. The RecordReader parses the FileSplits and converts them to key/value pairs (records). Unlike FileSplits, key/value pairs are physical chunks of data and record boundaries are kept even if InputSplit boundaries have to be crossed for a record that traverses two contiguous InputSplits.

4. The RecordReader inputs the key/value pairs to the mapper. The mapper's map() function is invoked once for each key/value pair.

5. An OutputCollector collects the key/value pairs output from the map() function into a temporary task output directory. In the new API, the context's write() method is used to output the key/value pairs from the map() method.

6. When the task completes successfully, the OutputCommitter commits the task's output from the temporary directory to the Spill memory buffer.

7. The key/value pairs are partitioned in-memory using a partitioner; the default is the HashPartitioner. Each partition has a partition number and is assigned to a reducer with the same reducer number.

8. The partitioned data is sorted within each partition.

9. The partitioned and sorted data is merged into larger map output segments.

10. If a combiner is configured, the partitioned and sorted data is combined during the merge.

11. The Spill buffer memory to be used for sorting and merging is configured using the mapreduce.task.io.sort.mb configuration property, and if the value is exceeded the map output segments are spilled to disk as spill files. If compression is enabled, the map outputs are compressed before spilling to disk.

12. The on-disk spill files are merged to generate larger intermediate spill files.

13. After a certain fraction of map tasks have completed as configured in the mapreduce.job.reduce.slowstart.completedmaps configuration property, the reduce tasks are scheduled. The reduce tasks do not start the reduce phase until all maps have completed, but begin the shuffle and merge-sort of the intermediate map outputs.

14. Using parallel copies (the number of parallel copies is configured in the `mapreduce.reduce.shuffle.parallelcopies`), map output segments are shuffled across the network using HTTP to the `reduce` task's node. The shuffle is the only communication between tasks in a MR job. Other than the shuffle, the map tasks do not communicate and the `reduce` tasks do not communicate. The shuffle is an all-map-to-all-reduce process in which partitioned (according to the reducer number) map output segments from all maps are shuffled to all the reduces to which they are assigned. The shuffle is between the Spill buffer or on-disk spill files on the map task to the Shuffle buffer on the reduce task. The number of threads used to fetch map outputs is configured in `mapreduce.tasktracker.http.threads` (it's 40 by default). The shuffle involves a copying of data and the map output segments are not deleted on the map task immediately. The map outputs are not deleted immediately because a reduce task could fail and the map outputs could be required to be reshuffled to a restarted reduce task. The map outputs are deleted only after the job has completed successfully. The map phase is shown in Figure 1-48.

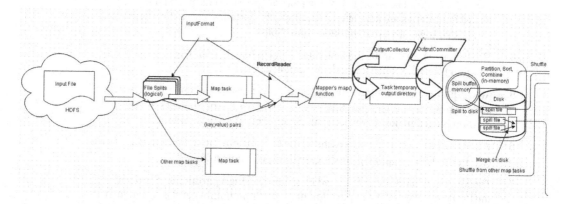

Figure 1-48. *Data movement in a MapReduce job in the map phase*

15. On the reduce task node, the Shuffle buffer receives map output segments from all the map tasks that have partitioned map outputs assigned to the reduce task. The Shuffle buffer memory is configured using `mapreduce.reduce.shuffle.input.buffer.percent`, which is the fraction of JVM's heap size to be allocated to the Shuffle buffer, and defaults to 0.70 of the maximum JVM heap size.

16. Map outputs segments in the Shuffle buffer from the different map tasks are merged and sorted. The merge is initiated when `mapreduce.reduce.shuffle.merge.percent`, which is the fraction of the Shuffle buffer memory at which to initiate merge, is exceeded. The default value of `mapreduce.reduce.shuffle.merge.percent` is 0.66, which implies that merge of map segments is initiated when the map segments occupy more than 0.66*0.70 of the maximum heap size.

17. When the map segments exceed the Shuffle buffer memory, the merge-sorted map segments are spilled to disk.

18. The spilled map segments are merged on-disk to create larger spill files.

19. If the in-memory Shuffle buffer is not sufficient to merge-sort the map output segments, an external sort is used to sort the spill files. A reduce task could be assigned key/value pairs from a single key space or key/value pairs from multiple key spaces. If a reduce task is assigned key/value pairs from a single key space, only merge-sort of the values associated with the key space is required. If reduce task is assigned multiple key spaces, all the key/value pairs in the same key space are grouped together.

20. A single reduce input file is generated for the reduce phase of the reduce task.

21. The reducer's reduce() function is invoked for each key/<list of values> pair.

22. The reduce() function processes the input and generates a key/<list of values> pair with a smaller set of values.

23. The RecordWriter outputs the key/<list of values> pairs generated by the reduce() function to the task's temporary output directory.

24. When the reduce task has completed successfully, the OutputCommitter commits the task's output to the job output directory. The reduce task's output is a part-nnnn file or a part-r-nnnn (in the new API) file. Reduce task outputs from all the reduce tasks of the job are committed to the job output directory when the reduce tasks completes successfully.

25. When the job completes successfully, the reduce task outputs in the job output directory are committed to the job's final output location, typically on the HDFS. The reduce task output files part-r-nnnn are not merged in the job's output, but are output as such to the HDFS. The job output files are replicated using the configured HDFS replication factor. A job's output files could be used as input to another job. The reduce phase is shown in Figure 1-49.

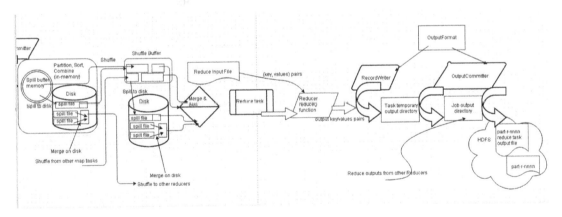

Figure 1-49. *Data movement in a MapReduce job in the reduce phase*

Selecting InputFormat and OutputFormat in a MapReduce Job

The InputFormat specifies the input specification for a job and the OutputFormat describes the output specification for a job. Given a sample job, certain InputFormat and OutputFormat are the most suitable for the job. For example, for plain text files based input, TextInputFormat<K,V>, is the most suitable as the input format

141

and to write plain text files TextOutputFormat<K,V> is the most suitable output format. TextInputFormat<K,V> and TextOutputFormat<K,V> are also the default input and output formats, respectively.

Input Formats

InputFormat classes are used to read data from the local disk or from HDFS. The root class for all input formats is org.apache.hadoop.mapreduce.InputFormat<K,V> in the new API and org.apache.hadoop.mapred.InputFormat<K,V> in the old API.

The InputFormat has the following functionality:

- Validates the input specification of the job.

- Creates InputSplits from the input files using the getSplits(JobContext context) method in the new API and the getSplits(JobConf job, int numSplits) method in the old API. InputSplits are logical splits of input files. Each InputSplit is assigned to a separate mapper. As InputSplits are logical, the data itself is not accessed.

- Creates a RecordReader to generate key/value pairs from InputSplits using the getRecordReader(InputSplit split, JobConf job, Reporter reporter) method in the old API and the createRecordReader(InputSplit split,TaskAttemptContext context) method in the new API. The key/value pairs are input to the map() function of the mapper.

The data flow provided by the InputFormat is shown in Figure 1-50. The input file in the HDFS is split into InputSplits, from which RecordReaders create key/value pairs to input to the mappers.

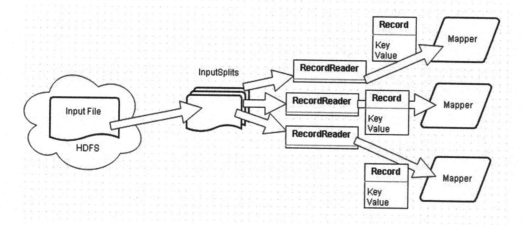

Figure 1-50. Data flow provided by the InputFormat

The org.apache.hadoop.mapreduce.lib.input.FileInputFormat<K,V> class in the new API and the org.apache.hadoop.mapred.FileInputFormat<K,V> class in the old API is the base class for file-based InputFormats. File input paths may be set using the static methods FileInputFormat.setInputPaths(JobConf conf, Path... inputPaths) and FileInputFormat.setInputPaths(JobConf conf, String commaSeparatedPaths). FileInputFormat reads all files in the specified input directories. The different types of job inputs and the most suitable InputFormats for file-based input formats are discussed in Table 1-19.

Table 1-19. InputFormats for File-Based Input Formats

Job Input	Old API Class	New API Class
Plain text files. Files are broken into lines and input one line at a time into the map() function of the mapper with line position (byte offset) in the file as the key and line text as the value. A new line is indicated with \n. A line is an input record. LineRecordReader is used to read a line of text. Performs no parsing and is useful for unformatted data or line-based records like log files. Automatically decompresses .gz files using an appropriate CompressionCodec. Compressed .gz files cannot be split and are input as each file to a single mapper. (k,v) is (LongWritable, Text).	org.apache.hadoop.mapred.TextInputFormat	org.apache.hadoop.mapreduce.lib.input.TextInputFormat
File-based input in which N lines of a file form an input split. Files are broken into splits, N lines per split, and input to the map() function of the mapper one line at a time, with line position (byte offset) of each split in the file as the key and line of text as the value. (k,v) is (LongWritable, Text).	org.apache.hadoop.mapred.lib.NLineInputFormat	org.apache.hadoop.mapreduce.lib.input.NLineInputFormat
Plain text files. Files are broken into lines and each line is divided into a key and a value separated by a separator byte (the tab character), k SEP v. If each line does not have a separator byte, the key is the line and the value is empty. New line is indicated with \n character. KeyValueLineRecordReader is used to read a line of text. Useful for reading the output of one MapReduce job as input to another MapReduce job. (k,v) is (Text, Text).	org.apache.hadoop.mapred.KeyValueTextInputFormat	org.apache.hadoop.mapreduce.lib.input.KeyValueTextInputFormat
SequenceFiles, which are special binary files specific to Hadoop. SequenceFiles allow data to read rapidly into Hadoop mappers. SequenceFiles are block compressed and provide serialization/deserialization of several arbitrary data types including text files. SequenceFiles can be generated as output of other MapReduce jobs and are an efficient intermediary data between MapReduce jobs. SequenceFiles include some metadata. (k,v) is user defined (K, V).	org.apache.hadoop.mapred.SequenceFileInputFormat<K,V>	org.apache.hadoop.mapreduce.lib.input.SequenceFileInputFormat<K,V>

(continued)

Table 1-19. (*continued*)

Job Input	Old API Class	New API Class
SequenceFiles with keys/values in String format. (k,v) is (Text, Text).	org.apache.hadoop.mapred.SequenceFileAsTextInputFormat	org.apache.hadoop.mapreduce.lib.input.SequenceFileAsTextInputFormat
SequenceFiles with keys/values in raw binary format. (k,v) is (BytesWritable, BytesWritable).	org.apache.hadoop.mapred.SequenceFileAsBinaryInputFormat	org.apache.hadoop.mapreduce.lib.input.SequenceFileAsBinaryInputFormat
Sample of SequenceFiles. (k,v) is (K, V).	org.apache.hadoop.mapred.SequenceFileInputFilter<K,V>	org.apache.hadoop.mapreduce.lib.input.SequenceFileInputFilter<K,V>
Multiple input files in which input splits are constructed from files in the input paths. Each split may contain blocks from different files. (k,v) is (K, V).	org.apache.hadoop.mapred.lib.CombineFileInputFormat<K,V>	org.apache.hadoop.mapreduce.lib.input.CombineFileInputFormat<K,V>
Multiple input files in which input splits are constructed from text files in the input paths. Each split may contain blocks from different text files. (k,v) is <LongWritable,Text>.	org.apache.hadoop.mapred.lib.input.CombineTextInputFormat	org.apache.hadoop.mapreduce.lib.input.CombineTextInputFormat
Multiple input files in which input splits are constructed from SequenceFiles in the input paths. Each split may contain blocks from different SequenceFiles. (k,v) is <K,V>.	org.apache.hadoop.mapred.lib.CombineSequenceFileInputFormat<K,V>	org.apache.hadoop.mapreduce.lib.input.CombineSequenceFileInputFormat<K,V>
Multiple input files in which input splits are constructed from files in the input paths. Each split is a subset of input files. (k,v) is <K,V>.	org.apache.hadoop.mapred.MultiFileInputFormat<K,V>	

For input from a SQL table, the InputFormat is org.apache.hadoop.mapreduce.lib. db.DBInputFormat<T> in the new API and org.apache.hadoop.mapred.lib.db.DBInputFormat<T> in the old API. The key is the LongWritable containing the record number and the value is the DBWritables. The (k,v) is of type <LongWritable,T>. The new API also provides another SQL table-based InputFormat org. apache.hadoop.mapreduce.lib.db.DataDrivenDBInputFormat<T> in which WHERE clauses separate the data into approximately equivalent shards.

An InputFormat with which joins may be performed over a set of data sources is the org.apache. hadoop.mapreduce.lib.join.CompositeInputFormat<K> in the new API and org.apache.hadoop.mapred. join.CompositeInputFormat<K> in the old API. The <k,v> is <K,TupleWritable>.

The new API provides a composable input format called org.apache.hadoop.mapreduce.lib.join. ComposableInputFormat<K,V> and requiring a user to provide a composable RecordReader.

As an example of TextInputFormat using a LineRecordReader, consider the following input.

```
MapReduce framework is a parallel
Processing, distributed
Framework
Suitable for processing large
Quantities of data
```

The following (key,value) pairs are generated.

```
(0, MapReduce framework is a parallel)
(33, Processing, distributed)
(56, Framework)
(65, Suitable for processing large)
(94, Quantities of data)
```

Custom InputFormats may be defined by extending a base class such as FileInputFormat<K,V>. For example, if a file with multi-line records separated by pipes (|) or if a CSV file is to be used as input, a custom FileInputFormat could be defined to generate records from the file. Custom RecordReaders for custom InputFormats maybe defined by extending the RecordReader<KEYIN,VALUEIN> class in the new API or by implementing the org.apache.hadoop.mapred.RecordReader<K,V> interface in the old API.

Output Formats

OutputFormat classes are used to write output to the local disk or HDFS. The root class for all output formats is org.apache.hadoop.mapred.OutputFormat<K,V> in the old API and org.apache.hadoop.mapreduce. OutputFormat<K,V> in the new API.

The OutputFormat has the following functionality:

- Validate that the output specification of the job, such as as verifying that the output directory does not already exist, using the checkOutputSpecs(JobContext context) method in the new API and the checkOutputSpecs(FileSystem ignored, JobConf job) method in the old API.

- Create a RecordWriter to output key/value pairs to an output file using the getRecordWriter(FileSystem ignored, JobConf job, String name, Progressable progress) method in the old API and the getRecordWriter(TaskAtt emptContext context) method in the new API.

- Get an output committer for the job using the getOutputCommitter(TaskAttemptCon text context) method in the new API. The output committer is used to commit the job output.

145

The data flow provided by the OutputFormat is shown in Figure 1-51. The OutputCommitter creates the temporary task output directories for the reducer tasks. The RecordWriters output key/value pairs to the temporary task output directories. The OutputCommitter commits the task outputs for successful tasks to the job output directory and commits a successful job to HDFS. Each reducer outputs a separate file in the job output directory; these files are typically named using the format part-r-nnn, in which r indicates a reduce task and nnn indicates a partition ID.

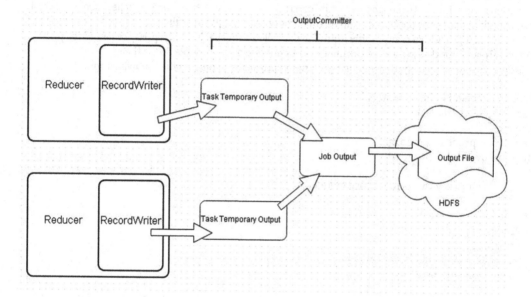

Figure 1-51. *Data flow provided by the OutputFormat*

The org.apache.hadoop.mapreduce.lib.output.FileOutputFormat<K,V> class in the new API and the org.apache.hadoop.mapred.FileOutputFormat<K,V> class in the old API is the base class for file-based OutputFormats. File output paths may be set using the static methods FileOutputFormat.setOutputName(JobContext job, String name) and FileOutputFormat.setOutputPath(Job job, Path outputDir). The different types of job outputs and the most suitable OutputFormats for file-based output formats are discussed in Table 1-20.

Table 1-20. *InputFormats for File-Based Input Formats*

Job Output	Old API	New API
Plain text files as key\tvalue on individual lines. New line is indicated with \n. Output is user readable and also suitable to be input as KeyValueTextInputFormat to another MR job. Output could also be gzipped text files. (k,v) is (K, V)	`org.apache.hadoop.mapred.TextOutputFormat<K,V>`	`org.apache.hadoop.mapreduce.lib.output.TextOutputFormat<K,V>`
SequenceFiles that are Hadoop-specific binary files suitable for inputting to another MapReduce job as SequenceFileInputFormat. Rapidly serializes arbitrary data types to a file. (k,v) is (K, V)	`org.apache.hadoop.mapred.SequenceFileOutputFormat<K,V>`	`org.apache.hadoop.mapreduce.lib.output.SequenceFileOutputFormat<K,V>`
SequenceFiles in binary(raw) format. (k,v) is <BytesWritable, BytesWritable>	`org.apache.hadoop.mapred.SequenceFileAsBinaryOutputFormat`	`org.apache.hadoop.mapreduce.lib.output.SequenceFileAsBinaryOutputFormat`
MapFiles.	`org.apache.hadoop.mapred.MapFileOutputFormat`	`org.apache.hadoop.mapreduce.lib.output.MapFileOutputFormat`
Multiple output files. Example 1: MapReduce job with at least one reducer in which the reducer outputs to different files based on the actual keys. Example 2: Map only job in which the output filename is based on an input filename. Example 3: Map only job in which the output filename is based on the keys and the input filename.	`org.apache.hadoop.mapred.lib.MultipleOutputFormat<K,V>`	
Multiple output text files.	`org.apache.hadoop.mapred.lib.MultipleTextOutputFormat<K,V>`	
Multiple output SequenceFiles.	`org.apache.hadoop.mapred.lib.MultipleSequenceFileOutputFormat<K,V>`	
SQL table. (k,v) is <K extends DBWritable,V>	`org.apache.hadoop.mapred.lib.db.DBOutputFormat<K,V>`	`org.apache.hadoop.mapreduce.lib.db.DBOutputFormat<K,V>`

(continued)

Table 1-20. (*continued*)

Job Output	Old API	New API
Null output. Consumes all output and puts them in /dev/null. Equivalent to disregarding all input. Produces no output files. Suitable if custom output files are to be generated in the reduce() function and the MR framework generated files are to be ignored.	`org.apache.hadoop.mapred.lib.NullOutputFormat<K,V>`	`org.apache.hadoop.mapreduce.lib.output.NullOutputFormat<K,V>`
Filtered output.	`org.apache.hadoop.mapred.lib.FilterOutputFormat<K,V>`	`org.apache.hadoop.mapreduce.lib.output.FilterOutputFormat<K,V>`
Lazy output.	`org.apache.hadoop.mapred.lib.LazyOutputFormat<K,V>`	`org.apache.hadoop.mapreduce.lib.output.LazyOutputFormat<K,V>`

A custom OutputFormat may be defined by extending a base class such as the abstract class `FileOutputFormat<K,V>`. A custom RecordWriter for a custom OutputFormat may be defined by extending the abstract class `RecordWriter<K,V>` in the new API or by implementing the `org.apache.hadoop.mapred.RecordWriter<K,V>` interface in the old API. For example, a custom output format and record writer to output an XML file may be developed.

The Order of Operations in a MapReduce Job

A job consists of mappers (map tasks) and reducers (reducers) running in sequence. First the map tasks run. When all the map tasks have completed and map outputs shuffled to the reduce tasks, the reduce tasks run. The reduce phase of the reduce tasks does not start until all the map tasks have completed and their outputs have been copied to the reducers. The order of operations in a MapReduce job is as follows.

1. The InputFormat validates the input specification for the job when a job is submitted.

2. The OutputFormat validates the output specification for the job. For example, it validates that the job output directory does not already exist.

3. The InputFormat splits up the input files into InputSplits, which are logical and do not involve physical splitting of the input files.

4. The OutputCommitter sets up the job during initialization, such as creating the temporary output directory for the job.

5. Each InputSplit is assigned to a map task. The OutputCommitter creates a task's temporary output directory during a task initialization.

6. The map tasks are launched in parallel on TaskTrackers by the JobTracker. The maximum number of map tasks that may launched on a TaskTracker is simultaneously determined by the `mapreduce.tasktracker.map.tasks.maximum` configuration property and is 2 by default.

7. The InputFormat provides a RecordReader implementation to convert the logical InputSplits to physical chunks of key/value pairs (records).

8. On each map task, the mapper's map() function is invoked for each key/value pair generated by the RecordReader.

9. The OutputCollector collects the map() function's output key/value pairs to a map task's temporary output directory. In the new API, the Context.write() method is used to output key/value pairs.

10. The OutputCommitter determines if a map task needs a commit. If a map task fails, the JobTracker relaunches the task.

11. If a map task completes successfully, the OutputCommitter commits the map task during which the temporary task output is promoted to the task's final output location, which is the Spill buffer.

12. The map outputs are partitioned into partitions using a partitioner; the default is the HashPartitioner. Each partition is assigned a reducer/reduce task. The partitioner is an in-memory operation.

13. Within a partition, the map outputs are sorted in-memory.

14. The map outputs are merged in-memory and, during the merge, the map outputs are combined if a combiner is configured.

15. If compression of map outputs is configured, the map outputs are compressed.

16. When the map outputs exceed the Spill buffer memory capacity, which is configured using the mapreduce.task.io.sort.mb property, the partitioned, sorted, merged, combined, and compressed map output segments are spilled to disk as spill files. An in-memory index of spill files is kept. Each spill file consists of a data file and an index file.

17. The spill files are merge-sorted on disk to create larger intermediate spill files, which are further merge-sorted to create a single partitioned, sorted map output file. The number of spill files to merge together in a single merge is determined by the mapreduce.task.io.sort.factor configuration property, which has default value of 10. An index file and a data file comprise the single map output file.

18. The reduce tasks get started when a fraction of the map tasks, as determined by the mapreduce.job.reduce.slowstart.completedmaps configuration property, have completed successfully. A reduce task is launched on a TaskTracker by the JobTracker. The number of reduce tasks that may be launched simultaneously on a TaskTracker is configured using the mapreduce.tasktracker.reduce.tasks.maximum property and defaults to 2. During reduce task initialization, the OutputCommitter creates the temporary task output directory.

19. The reduce tasks shuffle map segments assigned to them from the map tasks. The shuffle is a parallel copy operation in which the map outputs on the map task are not deleted. The number of parallel copies involved in the shuffle is determined by mapreduce.reduce.shuffle.parallelcopies, with default value of 5. The number of concurrent threads involved in the shuffle is determined by the mapreduce.tasktracker.http.threads configuration property, with the default of 40 threads. Shuffle is an all-map-to-all-reduce operation in which map segments from all the map tasks are copied to all the reduce tasks. The map segments are fetched using HTTP into the Shuffle buffer.

20. The Shuffle is an across-the-tasks network operation and could involve a delay due to various reasons including network issues and map tasks not having been completed.

21. The map segments in the Shuffle buffer are merge-sorted. The in-memory merge is initiated after the `mapreduce.reduce.shuffle.merge.percent` threshold is exceeded.

22. The map segments in the Shuffle buffer are spilled to disk when `mapreduce.reduce.shuffle.input.buffer.percent` is exceeded. The map segments are spilled as spill files.

23. The map segments on-disk are merged to create larger intermediate spill files. The number of spill files merged together in a single merge is determined by `mapreduce.task.io.sort.factor`.

24. The spill files from disk and the map segments in-memory are merged and sorted using an external sort in which a merged and sorted file is created from several spill files on disk and map output segments in-memory. Secondary sort is applied if it's configured.

25. A single sorted reduce input file is generated.

26. After the shuffle and sort phases of the reduce task are completed, the reduce phase is started. In the reduce phase, the `reduce()` function of the reducer is invoked for each (key, <list of values>) pair in the reduce input file.

27. The `reduce()` function processes the input.

28. A RecordWriter, provided by the OutputFormat, outputs (key, value) pairs generated by the `reduce()` function to the task's temporary output directory.

29. When the task completes successfully, an OutputCommitter generated by the OutputFormat commits the reduce task's output to the job output directory. Reduce task outputs from other reduce tasks are committed to the job output directory as the other reduce tasks get completed. Each reduce task output is a `part-nnnn` file (old API) or a `part-r-nnnn` file (new API).

30. The reduce output files are not merged in the job output directory.

31. When the job completes successfully, the OutputCommitter commits the job output. The reduce tasks output files in the job output directory are committed to the job's final output directory, which is typically HDFS. The reduce task output files are still not merged in the job's final output location. An external command may be used to merge the reduce task output files if required.

Refer back to Figures 49 and 50 for the order of operations in a MapReduce job.

RecordReader, Sequence Files, and Compression

In the following subsections we shall discuss RecordReader, Sequence Files and Compression.

RecordReader

The RecordReader (Figure 1-52) is used to read and parse input data. The RecordReader generates key/value pairs from input splits to input to a mapper. Input split boundaries may not necessarily correspond with record boundaries. A key/value pair is called a record and the map() function of the mapper is invoked for each record. The RecordReader takes as input the logical InputSplits generated from the job input by the InputFormat and presents a record-oriented view of input data to the mapper. A RecordReader is invoked on the TaskTracker in MR1 and the ApplicationMaster in MR2.

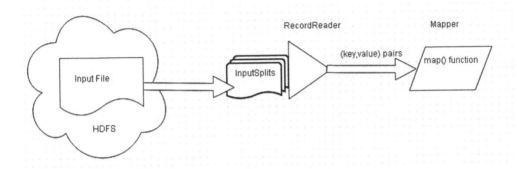

Figure 1-52. *RecordReader*

The RecordReader is an interface in the old API (`org.apache.hadoop.mapred.RecordReader<K,V>`) and a class in the new API (`org.apache.hadoop.mapreduce.RecordReader<KEYIN,VALUEIN>`). The InputFormat creates a RecordReader from an InputSplit using the method `createRecordReader(InputSplit split,TaskAttemptContext context)` in the new API and the `getRecordReader(InputSplit split,JobConf job,Reporter reporter)` method in the old API. If a file is to be parsed in a particular way, the `getRecordReader()` method must be overridden. The RecordReader takes into account the record boundaries when breaking an InputSplit into records (key/value pairs).

Different kinds of InputFormats have different RecordReaders associated with them. For example, the `TextInputFormat` class has the `LineRecordReader` associated with it.

```
public class LineRecordReader extends RecordReader<LongWritable,Text>
```

The `LineRecordReader` creates key/value pairs from a file split by using the file offset for a line as the key and the line as the value. The key generated by a `LineRecordReader` is of type `LongWritable` and the value is of type Text. The `LineRecordReader` reads each line in a FileSplit and generates key/value pairs to be input to the mapper's `map()` function, as shown in Figure 1-53.

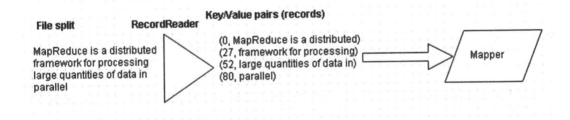

Figure 1-53. *LineRecordReader example*

If a record spans an InputSplit boundary, the RecordReader has the logic to create a complete record from multiple InputSplits, if required. A RecordReader does not break a record. For example, if the input split in the preceding example was made two file splits as indicated by |, the RecordReader will read past the file split boundary until the end of the record, which is the end of the line. The RecordReader associated with the next file split will read and parse the first full line in the split. A RecordReader with a FileSplit example is shown in Figure 1-54.

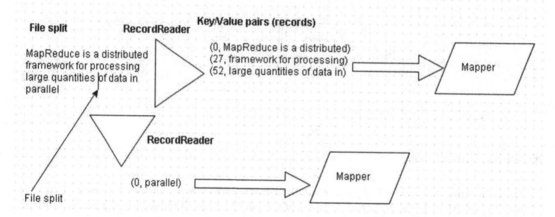

Figure 1-54. *RecordReader with FileSplit*

KeyValueLineRecordReader reads and parses the key/value records stored in the following format.

keySEPvalue

The SEP is the separator between the key and the value and is the tab character \t by default. Another separator may be configured with the property mapreduce.input.keyvaluelinerecordreader.key.value. separator in mapred-site.xml. For example, a , may be used as a separator as follows.

```
Configuration conf = new Configuration();
conf.set("mapreduce.input.keyvaluelinerecordreader.key.value.separator", ",");
Job job = new Job(conf);
job.setInputFormatClass(KeyValueTextInputFormat.class);
```

Consider the following file split to be used with a KeyValueLineRecordReader.

```
framework mapreduce
filesystem Hadoop Distributed File System
cluster 100 nodes
```

The KeyValueLineRecordReader generates the key/value pairs shown in Figure 1-55. The first separator character is used as the separator between the key and the value.

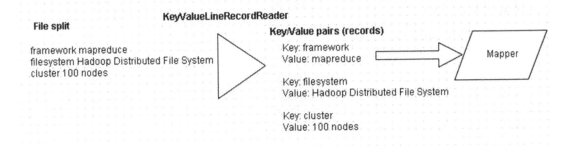

Figure 1-55. *KeyValueLineRecordReader example*

With the KeyValueLineRecordReader, both the key and value are of type TEXT.

```
public class KeyValueLineRecordReader extends RecordReader<Text,Text>
```

Some of the other built-in RecordReaders are explained in Table 1-21.

Table 1-21. *Built-In RecordReaders*

RecordReader	Description
SequenceFileRecordReader<K,V>	RecordReader for SequenceFiles. Extends RecordReader<K,V>.
SequenceFileAsTextRecordReader	Converts SequenceFile key/value to string. Extends RecordReader<Text,Text>.
SequenceFileAsBinaryInputFormat. SequenceFileAsBinaryRecordReader	RecordReader to read SequenceFiles as raw (binary) bytes. Extends RecordReader<BytesWritable,BytesWritable>.
DBRecordReader<T>	Reads records from SQL table. Extends RecordReader<LongWritable,T>.
CombineFileRecordReader<K,V>	A generic RecordReader for CombineFileSplit, which is an input split from multiple files. Different RecordReaders may be used with different data chunks from different files. Extends RecordReader<K,V>.

A custom RecordReader may be created by implementing the RecordReader interface in the old API and the RecordReader class in the new API. Reuse objects to avoid creating unnecessary objects, which could increase the GC runtime, especially with a limited heap size. In the following custom RecordReader, the getCurrentKey() and the getCurrentValue() methods reuse the key and value objects, respectively.

```
import RecordReader;
import LongWritable;
import Text;
public class CustomLineRecordReader
    extends RecordReader<LongWritable, Text> {

    private LongWritable key = new LongWritable();
    private Text value = new Text();
```

```
@Override
public void initialize(
        InputSplit genericSplit,
        TaskAttemptContext context)
        throws IOException {

}

@Override
public boolean nextKeyValue() throws IOException {

}

@Override
public LongWritable getCurrentKey() throws IOException,
        InterruptedException {
    return key;
}

@Override
public Text getCurrentValue() throws IOException, InterruptedException {
    return value;
}

@Override
public float getProgress() throws IOException, InterruptedException {

}

@Override
public void close() throws IOException {

}

}
```

Sequence Files

Sequence files are flat files consisting of key/value pairs in binary format. Sequence files provide the following benefits:

- Splittable. Suitable as input to map tasks.

- Compressible. Block compression compresses both keys and values. Benefits of compression are faster read and write and less disk space usage.

- Compact. Map outputs are sequence files by default. Sequence files provide an alternative to a large number of small files. The filename can be used as key and file content as value to compact several small files into a sequence file.

- Direct serialization and deserialization of several arbitrary data types (not just text).

Sequence files are appending only; they cannot seek to a specified key. SequenceFile provides three different formats, differing in the compression type.

- Uncompressed SequenceFile format

- Record-compressed SequenceFile format

- Block-compressed SequenceFile format

Sequence files, being in binary format, are not readable as text. Sequence files may be compressed or uncompressed. The compression type used by sequence files is represented by the enum org.apache.hadoop.io.SequenceFile.CompressionType, which has the constants listed in Table 1-22.

Table 1-22. Enum CompressionType Constants

Constant	Description
BLOCK	Compresses sequences of records together in blocks. Keys and values are collected in blocks separately and compressed. Block compression is more compressive than record compression. Uses org.apache.hadoop.io.SequenceFile.BlockCompressWriter.
NONE	Does not compress records. Uses org.apache.hadoop.io.SequenceFile.Writer.
RECORD	Compresses values only, each value separately. Uses org.apache.hadoop.io.SequenceFile.RecordCompressWriter.

The sequence files may be used as input and output in a MapReduce job. The InputFormat for sequence file is SequenceFileInputFormat and the output format for sequence file is SequenceFileOutputFormat. The SequenceFileInputFormat class provides the subclasses listed in Table 1-23.

Table 1-23. SequenceFileInputFormat Class Subclasses

SequenceFileInputFormat	Description
SequenceFileAsBinaryInputFormat	Input format for Sequence files as key/value pairs in binary format. Uses SequenceFileAsTextRecordReader to generate String representations of the binary/key value pairs.
SequenceFileAsTextInputFormat	Input format for Sequence files as key/value pairs converted to text. Uses SequenceFileAsTextRecordReader to generate string representations of the binary/key value pairs.
SequenceFileInputFilter	Input format to generate input from a sample of Sequence files.

The SequenceFileOutputFormat<K,V> class provides only one subclass, the SequenceFileAsBinaryOutputFormat, which is used to output sequence files in binary format from a MR job.

Sequence files provide automatic serialization and deserialization to the mapper and the reducer. For example, the input format is set to SequenceFileAsTextInputFormat and the output format is set to SequenceFileAsBinaryOutputFormat, as follows.

```
Job job = new Job(new Configuration());
job.setInputFormatClass(SequenceFileAsTextInputFormat.class);
job.setOutputFormatClass(SequenceFileAsBinaryOutputFormat.class);
```

A sequence file may be created and stored in the HDFS filesystem using the FileSystem API.

```
private static void createSequenceFile(byte[][] data, int numRecords) throws Exception {

Configuration conf = new Configuration();
JobConf job = new JobConf(conf);

Path path = new Path("hdfs://host:9000/user/test.seq");
job.setInputPath(path);

FileSystem fs = FileSystem.getLocal(conf);

SequenceFile.Writer writer =SequenceFile.createWriter(fs, conf, path,
                            Text.class, BytesWritable.class);

for (int i = 1; i <= numRecords; i++) {
     Text key = new Text(Integer.toString(i));

     BytesWritable value = new BytesWritable(data[i]);
     writer.append(key, value);
  }

}
```

The append() method is used to append to a sequence file. In addition to the org.apache.hadoop.io.SequenceFile.CompressionType class for compression, the SequenceFile class provides the nested classes listed in Table 1-24 and a nested interface.

Table 1-24. SequenceFile Class Nested Classes and Interfaces

Nested Class	Description
SequenceFile.Metadata	Encapsulates the metadata of the sequence file.
SequenceFile.Reader	Used to read key/value pairs from a sequence file.
SequenceFile.Sorter	Used to sort key/value pairs in a sequence file.
SequenceFile.ValueBytes	An interface for the raw values of the sequence file.
SequenceFile.Writer	Used to write key/value pairs to a sequence file.

All three formats of the sequence files have a header, with a common format shown in Figure 1-56.

version	SEQ6 for example
keyClassName	Key class, for example TEXT.class
valueClassName	Value class, for example BytesWritable.class
compression	A boolean indicating if compression is turned on, for example, true
blockCompression	A boolean indicating if block compression is turned on, for example, true
compression codec	CompressionCodec class, for example SnappyCodec
metadata	Sequence file metadata
sync	A sync marker for the end of the header

Figure 1-56. *Sequence file header*

Using the header, the key and value classes can be instantiated by reflection. An uncompressed sequence file format is shown in Figure 1-57. The header has the format described previously.

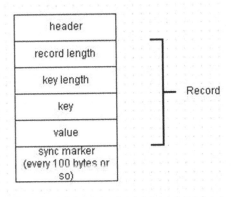

Figure 1-57. *An uncompressed sequence file format*

The format for a record compressed sequence file is shown in Figure 1-58. The record length is the key length plus the value length. Record length and key length are ints.

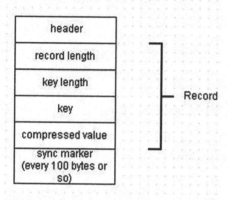

Figure 1-58. *The format for a record compressed sequence file*

The format for a block compressed sequence file is shown in Figure 1-59. The compressed blocks for key lengths and value lengths contain the actual lengths.

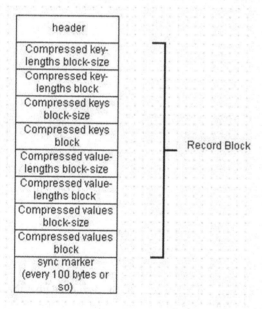

Figure 1-59. *The format for a block-compressed sequence file*

The MapFile is an extension of the sequence file format. A MapFile is a directory with two sequence files—the data file called /data and an index file called /index. MapFiles use SequenceFile.Sorter for sorting. SetFile and ArrayFile are also based on the sequence format.

Compression

Hadoop provides compression of data at three levels.

- Input data
- Intermediate map output data
- Reduce output data

The three levels at which compression is supported are shown in Figure 1-60. The input data is decompressed before being input to the mapper. The intermediate map outputs may be optionally compressed in the Spill buffer before being spilled to disk. Shuffling compressed data to reducers utilizes less network bandwidth. Before being input to the reducer, the compressed intermediate map outputs are again decompressed. The reducer output may be compressed before being stored in the HDFS.

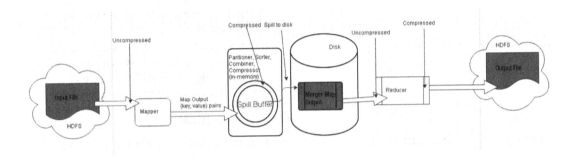

Figure 1-60. *The three levels at which compression is used*

Compression is particularly suitable for I/O bound MR job as it is faster to compress, write to disk, and decompress during read. Storing in compressed form in the HDFS utilizes less disk space. For example, if a 400MB file is compressed by a factor of 10, the actual disk storage used is 40MB. The block replication also has to be taken into account. Compression of intermediate map outputs provides the following benefits:

- Reduces the network I/O overhead as less data has to be shuffled across to the reducers.
- Reduces the disk storage overhead if the map outputs are spilled to disk.
- Increases read and write performance.

The disadvantage of compression is the extra CPU cycles required for compression/decompression. If the CPU resources are limited and the MR job is CPU intensive, compression/decompression may incur an overhead of utilizing the much needed CPU cycles.

The compression at various levels may be configured using configuration properties in mapred-default.xml, as discussed in Table 1-25.

Table 1-25. *Configuration Properties for Configuring*

Property	Description
`mapreduce.output.fileoutputformat.compress`	A Boolean to indicate whether the job outputs should be compressed. Default value is `false`. The output file is in compressed form if set to `true`.
`mapreduce.output.fileoutputformat.compress.type`	If the job outputs are to be compressed as sequence files, which of the sequence file compression type to use: `NONE`, `BLOCK`, or `RECORD`. The default is `RECORD`.
`mapreduce.output.fileoutputformat.compress.codec`	If the job outputs are compressed, which `CompressionCodec` to use: `BZip2Codec`, `DefaultCodec`, `GzipCodec`, `SnappyCodec`. The default is `DefaultCodec`. The `CompressionCodec` is also used during decompression.
`mapreduce.map.output.compress`	Should map outputs be compressed before being sent across the network to the reducer, or before being spilled to disk. Map outputs are compressed as sequence files by default. The default value is `false`. Should be set to `true` for a large job or a large cluster.
`mapreduce.map.output.compress.codec`	If the map outputs are compressed, which `CompressionCodec` to use: `BZip2Codec`, `DefaultCodec`, `GzipCodec`, `SnappyCodec`. The default is `DefaultCodec`.

Compression of job output and map outputs may also be configured using the `JobConf` in the old API. The `CompressionCodec` class for compression may also be set in `JobConf`.

```
JobConf conf = new JobConf(new Configuration(), SampleJob.class);
conf.setCompressMapOutput(true);
conf.setMapOutputCompressorClass(SnappyCodec.class);
conf.setOutputFormatClass(SequenceFileAsBinaryOutputFormat.class);
SequenceFileAsBinaryOutputFormat.setOutputCompressorClass(conf,BZip2Codec.class);
SequenceFileAsBinaryOutputFormat.setCompressOutput(conf, true) ;
conf.setOutputKeyClass(BytesWritable.class);
conf.setOutputValueClass(BytesWritable.class);
```

In the new API map and job output compression is set as follows.

```
Job job = new Job(new Configuration());
job.getConfiguration().setBoolean("mapreduce.map.output.compress", true);
job.getConfiguration().setClass("mapreduce.map.output.compress.codec",
          BZip2Codec.class, CompressionCodec.class);
job.setOutputFormatClass(SequenceFileAsBinaryOutputFormat.class);
SequenceFileAsBinaryOutputFormat.setCompressOutput(job,true);
SequenceFileAsBinaryOutputFormat.setOutputCompressionType(job,SequenceFile.CompressionType.
BLOCK);
SequenceFileAsBinaryOutputFormat.setOutputCompressorClass(job,BZip2Codec.class);
```

Sequence file compression is used by default to compress map outputs. The corresponding getCompressMapOutput() and getMapOutputCompressorClass(Class<? extends CompressionCodec> defaultValue) methods are also provided to get the Boolean for map output compression and the CompressionCodec class used.

Multiple codecs are supported for compression/decompression. Some codecs have a better compression factor but take more time during compression/decompression, while other codecs provide a balance between compression factor and compression/decompression time. Some codecs are more suitable in some particular level of compression, such as compression of input data versus compression of intermediate map outputs. Table 1-26 shows the codecs supported by Hadoop.

Table 1-26. *Codecs Supported by Hadoop*

CompressionCodec	Description
BZip2Codec	A splittable codec suitable for input to a map tasks as input file can be split and processed in parallel using multiple mappers. Capable of compressing/decompressing a stream at an arbitrary start position. Most codecs can decompress a stream only starting from the beginning.
DefaultCodec	The default codec.
GzipCodec	Creates non-splittable gzip compressors/decompressors.
SnappyCodec	Creates snappy compressors/decompressors and the compression factor is also reasonable. Suitable if speed, rather than high compression and compatibility with other compression libraries, is the priority.

Snappy is recommended if fast compression/decompression (especially decompression) is required without compromising too much on the compression ratio. Snappy is generally used for compression/decompression of intermediate map outputs. Snappy provides an effective balance between compression ratio (compressed files are 20% to 100% larger) and speed.

Gzip is recommended when the objective is highest level of compression (10:1) and as a result greatest disk-space savings. Sequence files also support some other codecs such as deflate.

LZO codec is supported by text files only. LZO uses an input buffer for compression to invoke compression less frequently. Compression ratio with LZO is about 4:1 and indexed LZO is splittable, therefore suitable for parallel processing. Snappy is significantly faster than LZO for decompression and comparable for compression as a result the compression/decompression cycle is faster. LZO is an alternative to Snappy for intermediate map output compression. While Snappy is packaged with Hadoop (and easier to enable), LZO has to be installed. Snappy and LZO are not CPU intensive and are comparable in performance with up to 20% improvement in job time. Snappy is generally used for block compression with splittable Hadoop file formats such as sequence files and Avro. LZO is more suitable with plain text, which is not splittable and cannot be processed in parallel in MR. With LZO it is feasible to index compressed files to determine split points for parallel processing.

Outputting large quantities of compressed text data with a non-splittable codec such as zlib/gzip/unindexed, LZO is not suitable for downstream consumers. The entire file is required to be processed as a single file, which results in fewer maps and as a result a load imbalance on maps with a higher probability of map task failure. File formats such as SequenceFile and Tfile are more suitable as they are splittable and compressible.

The io.compression.codecs property in core-default.xml may be used to set a comma-separated list of codec classes that may be used for compression/decompression. In addition to the classes specified with the io.compression.codecsproperty codec, classes on the classpath are discovered using the Java ServiceLoader. The zlib and gzip codecs are available as Hadoop-native libraries. zlib and gzip are available as native libraries because of zlib's performance and because of non-availability of Java libraries.

The minimum block size in the compression of block compressed sequence file is set in the property io.seqfile.compress.blocksize in core-default.xml or core-site.xml. The default value for io.seqfile.compress.blocksize is 1MB. The io.seqfile.lazydecompress property specifies whether values of block compressed sequence files should be decompressed only when necessary; the default value is true.

Summary

This section introduced the Hadoop concepts. Starting in Chapter 1, we will discuss using the Hadoop frameworks. This book uses the Cloudera Hadoop Distribution (CDH5).

CHAPTER 2

■ ■ ■

HDFS and MapReduce

Apache Hadoop is a distributed framework for storing and processing large quantities of data. Going over each of the terms in the previous statement, "distributed" implies that Hadoop is distributed across several (tens, hundreds, or even thousands) of nodes in a cluster. For "storing and processing" means that Hadoop uses two different frameworks: Hadoop Distributed Filesystem (*HDFS*) for storage and *MapReduce* for processing. This is illustrated in Figure 2-1.

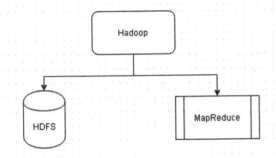

Figure 2-1. *Apache Hadoop components*

What makes Hadoop different from other distributed frameworks is that it can store large quantities of data and process large quantities of data in parallel at a rate much faster than most other frameworks. "Large quantities" implies in the range of 100s and 1000s of terabytes (TB) to several (10s to 100s) petabytes (PB). Yahoo email is hosted on Hadoop and each Yahoo email account is provided with 1TB, which is 1000GB. Most online storage providers provision much less in comparison; for example, Google online storage provides a free starter storage of only 15GB. Yahoo processes 1.42TB in a minute. This chapter has the following sections.

- Hadoop distributed filesystem
- MapReduce framework
- Setting the environment
- Hadoop cluster modes
- Running a MapReduce job with the MR1 framework
- Running MR1 in standalone mode

© Deepak Vohra 2016
D. Vohra, *Practical Hadoop Ecosystem*, DOI 10.1007/978-1-4842-2199-0_2

- Running MR1 in pseudo-distributed mode

- Running MapReduce with the YARN framework

- Running YARN in pseudo-distributed mode

- Running Hadoop Streaming

Hadoop Distributed Filesystem

The Hadoop Distributed Filesystem (HDFS) is a distributed filesystem for storing data in the Hadoop ecosystem. HDFS stores data on commodity hardware and is designed to be fault tolerant, which implies that in a large cluster consisting of several (10s, 100s, or 1000s) nodes, some of the nodes are expected to fail periodically. Data is replicated over the cluster; three times by default in a fully-distributed filesystem. HDFS is different from ordinary distributed filesystems in that it has a much larger storage capacity and is designed to store large datasets. HDFS stores data in blocks, which is an abstraction over the underlying filesystem. The block abstraction is necessary as the size of a block is typically much larger than the size of a block on the underlying filesystem on a disk. An HDFS block is 128MB by default. HDFS consists of two components, called the NameNode and the DataNode. A fully-distributed Hadoop cluster has one NameNode and several DataNodes. The HDFS components are briefly discussed in the following sections.

NameNode

The NameNode is a master component and keeps the naming system of the files and directories managed by a Apache Hadoop cluster. HDFS stores data in blocks and NameNode keeps and manages the block locations of the files/directories. NameNode tracks where data is kept, and when a client requests data, NameNode provides the block locations of the data requested. Similarly, when a client wants to store new data, the NameNode provides the block locations at which the data could be stored. NameNode does not store any data itself, nor does it directly access the DataNodes to read and write data.

DataNodes

The DataNodes store the data in Apache Hadoop. While the NameNode provides the clients with the block locations from which data can be read or at which new data can be stored, the DataNodes read and write requests from the clients. The DataNodes also perform the actual block creation, replication, and deletion duties under instruction from the the NameNode.

MapReduce Framework

As mentioned in the introduction, Apache Hadoop consists of two frameworks: HDFS and MapReduce. A Hadoop application is a MapReduce application consisting of two phases: the *Map phase* and the *Reduce phase*. Data in Hadoop is processed using key/value pairs. During the Map phase, the input dataset is processed using the specified Map function. Data to the Map phase is typically input from HDFS. The Map function could be designed to count the number of unique occurrences of a word in a dataset, as you'll see in a subsequent example. The Map phase generates an intermediate set of key/value pairs, which are sorted and partitioned and then transferred to the Reduce phase to be processed by a Reduce function. The output from the Reduce function is the output from a MapReduce application. The output from a MapReduce application is typically stored in the HDFS.

Two kinds of MapReduce frameworks are provided: *MapReduce 1* (MR1) and *YARN* (MR2). The components in MR1 are *JobTracker* and *TaskTracker*. A fully-distributed Hadoop cluster has one JobTracker and several TaskTrackers and the single JobTracker manages the several TaskTrackers. A MR1 Hadoop cluster is illustrated in Figure 2-2; the HDFS components are also shown.

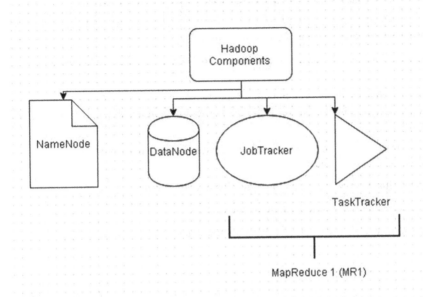

Figure 2-2. *MapReduce 1 (MR1) cluster components*

The MR1 components are briefly discussed in the following sections.

JobTracker

The JobTracker is a master component and it manages the jobs and resources in a Hadoop cluster. Clients submit MapReduce (MR) jobs to be run on Hadoop to the JobTracker and the JobTracker schedules and runs the jobs on TaskTrackers. As a MR job would typically process some data, the JobTracker gets the block locations for the data from the NameNode and schedules the jobs to run on TaskTrackers in proximity of the data. Because large quantities of data are involved, the computation to be performed on a dataset is moved to the data rather than shuffling the dataset to the computation as in a small-scale data processing framework.

TaskTracker

The TaskTrackers run the Map and Reduce tasks for a MapReduce application. A TaskTracker consists of "slots" in which a task runs. The "slots" are Map or Reduce task specific. A *Map slot* runs only a Map task and a *Reduce slot* runs only a Reduce task. The TaskTracker runs tasks under instruction from the JobTracker and, when a task completes, the TaskTracker notifies the JobTracker.

MR1 has the following drawbacks:

- JobTracker manages and monitors both the resources and the MapReduce Job and task scheduling, which makes the JobTracker a single point of failure (SPOF) in a cluster. The cluster cannot be scaled efficiently.

- Underutilization of resources as the slots to run a task are Map and Reduce task specific.

- Non-MapReduce applications cannot be run concurrently.

To overcome these drawbacks, the MR2 (also called YARN) was designed. MR2 has the following advantages over MR1.

- Better scalability as the JobTracker functionality is split between the ResourceManager and ApplicationMaster. Hadoop may be run on much larger clusters with MR2.

- Better cluster utilization as the resource capacity configured for each node may be used by both Map and Reduce tasks.

- Non-MapReduce clusters may be run on the same cluster concurrently.

- Higher throughput uses finer-grained resource scheduling.

A MR2 Hadoop cluster is shown in Figure 2-3. The HDFS components are also shown.

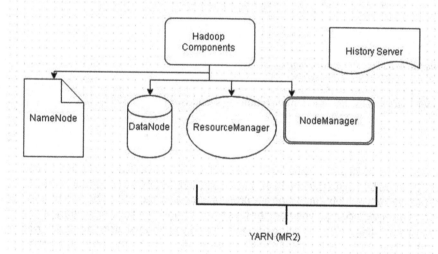

Figure 2-3. *MapReduce 2 (MR2) Hadoop cluster components*

The MR2 components are briefly discussed in the following sections.

ResourceManager

The *ResourceManager* is a master node and it accepts job submissions from clients and starts processes called *ApplicationMaster* to run the jobs. The ResourceManager also assigns resources required for a job. A job could be a MapReduce application or a non-MapReduce application. A ResourceManager consists of two components: *Scheduler* and *ApplicationsManager*. The Scheduler allocates resources and does not participate in running or monitoring an application. Resources are allocated as resource containers, with each resource container assigned a specific memory. The ApplicationsManager component accepts the job submissions from the clients and starts the *ApplicationMaster* to run the submitted applications. The ApplicationsManager also restarts failed ApplicationMaster. The ApplicationMasters are application specific, with one ApplicationMaster for each application. After the ApplicationsManager has obtained the resources for an ApplicationMaster to start an application, the ApplicationMaster obtains additional resources if required from the Scheduler component of the ResourceManager directly.

NodeManager

The *NodeManager* is a per-machine component that runs resource containers on the machine and monitors the resource usage of the applications running in the resource containers on the machine. The NodeManager also reports the resource usage to the ResourceManager. When the ApplicationMasters start/stop or monitor the status of an application on a resource container, they do so via the NodeManager.

Job HistoryServer

Because MR2 does not include a JobTracker to keep information about a MapReduce job and the ApplicationMasters that actually run a MapReduce application terminate on completion, a *Job HistoryServer* is provided in MR2 to keep the information about the MapReduce jobs submitted (whether failed or successful) to a Hadoop cluster.

Setting the Environment

We have used Oracle Linux 6.x installed on Oracle Virtual Box 4.x. A different Linux distribution and setup could be used just as well. The following software is required for this chapter in addition to Oracle Virtual Box.

- Apache Hadoop (version 2.6.0)

- Java (version 7)

These examples use the Cloudera distribution of Apache Hadoop Cdh5.4.7 Hadoop 2.6.0. A later version may also be used. If you do use a different version, some of the configuration files and directory paths could be different, so be sure to modify the filenames and directory paths accordingly. Create a directory (/cdh for example) to install the software and set its permissions to global (777).

```
mkdir /cdh
chmod -R 777 /cdh
cd /cdh
```

Add a group called hadoop and add a user called hadoop to the hadoop group.

```
groupadd hadoop
useradd -g hadoop hadoop
```

Download and install Java 7 from http://www.oracle.com/technetwork/java/javase/downloads/jdk7-downloads-1880260.html. Extract the tar file to the /cdh directory. The Java 7 update version could be different than the one used in this chapter.tar -xvf hadoopv file.

```
tar zxvf jdk-7u55-linux-i586.gz
```

Download and extract the tar file for CDH 5.4.7 Hadoop 2.6.0.

```
wget http://archive-primary.cloudera.com/cdh5/cdh/5/hadoop-2.6.0-cdh5.4.7.tar.gz
tar -xvf hadoop-2.6.0-cdh5.4.7.tar.gz
```

The CDH 5 packaging and built-in references make it necessary to create symlinks between certain directories. Create the following symlinks.

```
ln -s /cdh/hadoop-2.6.0-cdh5.4.7/bin /cdh/hadoop-2.6.0-cdh5.4.7/share/hadoop/mapreduce1/bin
ln -s /cdh/hadoop-2.6.0-cdh5.4.7/etc/hadoop /cdh/hadoop-2.6.0-cdh5.4.7/share/hadoop/mapreduce1/conf
```

A *symlink* is just a pointer from one directory to another, implying that when a certain directory is referenced the pointed to, the directory is invoked. By creating the two symlinks, when the /cdh/hadoop-2.6.0-cdh5.4.7/share/hadoop/mapreduce1/bin is referenced or invoked, the /cdh/hadoop-2.6.0-cdh5.4.7/bin directory is referenced or invoked. Similarly, when the /cdh/hadoop-2.6.0-cdh5.4.7/share/hadoop/mapreduce1/conf directory is referenced, the /cdh/hadoop-2.6.0-cdh5.4.7/etc/hadoop directory is invoked. The symlinks are shown in Figure 2-4.

```
[root@localhost cdh]# ls -l /cdh/hadoop-2.6.0-cdh5.4.7/share/hadoop/mapreduce1/bin
lrwxrwxrwx. 1 root root 30 Sep 25 13:56 /cdh/hadoop-2.6.0-cdh5.4.7/share/hadoop/mapreduce1/bin -> /cdh/hadoop-2.6.0-cdh5.4.7/bin
[root@localhost cdh]# ls -l /cdh/hadoop-2.6.0-cdh5.4.7/share/hadoop/mapreduce1/conf
lrwxrwxrwx. 1 root root 37 Sep 25 08:03 /cdh/hadoop-2.6.0-cdh5.4.7/share/hadoop/mapreduce1/conf -> /cdh/hadoop-2.6.0-cdh5.4.7/etc/hadoop
[root@localhost cdh]# 
```

Figure 2-4. Symlinks

You also need to set the environment variables for Hadoop and Java. In the bash shell, set the following environment variables. HADOOP_NAMENODE_USER runs the NameNode and HADOOP_DATANODE_USER runs the DataNode. For MR1-based MapReduce applications, the Hadoop environment variables are set to MR1 directories. For YARN-based MapReduce applications, you'll see how to set the Hadoop variables to MR2 directories later in the chapter.

```
vi ~/.bashrc
export HADOOP_PREFIX=/cdh/hadoop-2.6.0-cdh5.4.7
export HADOOP_CONF=$HADOOP_PREFIX/etc/hadoop
export JAVA_HOME=/cdh/jdk1.7.0_55
export HADOOP_MAPRED_HOME=/cdh/hadoop-2.6.0-cdh5.4.7/share/hadoop/mapreduce1
export HADOOP_HOME=/cdh/hadoop-2.6.0-cdh5.4.7/share/hadoop/mapreduce1
export HADOOP_CLASSPATH=$HADOOP_HOME/*:$HADOOP_HOME/lib/*:$JAVA_HOME/lib/*
```

```
export PATH=/usr/lib/qt-3.3/bin:/usr/local/sbin:/usr/sbin:/sbin:/usr/local/bin:/usr/bin:/
bin: $HADOOP_HOME/bin:$HADOOP_MAPRED_HOME/bin:$JAVA_HOME/bin
export CLASSPATH=$HADOOP_CLASSPATH
export HADOOP_NAMENODE_USER=hadoop
export HADOOP_DATANODE_USER=hadoop
```

The environment variables in a bash shell are shown in Figure 2-5. Save the bash file with the vi editor command :wq. The environment settings are applied only to new Linux terminals started after you saved the settings.

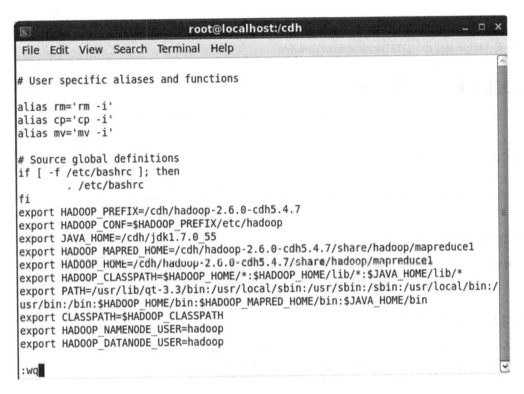

Figure 2-5. *Setting environment variables*

The environment variables should be verified by running the echo command, as some preset values could be appended. For example, the value of the PATH environment variable is output with command echo $PATH, as shown in Figure 2-6.

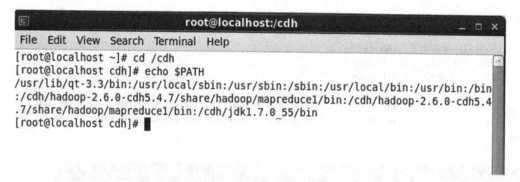

Figure 2-6. Outputting the PATH environment variable

Hadoop Cluster Modes

Hadoop supports three cluster modes: *standalone, pseudo-distributed,* and *fully-distributed.*

Standalone Mode

By default, Hadoop runs in the standalone mode as a single Java process (single JVM). The standalone mode is a non-distributed mode and the HDFS is not used. The local filesystem is used instead.

Pseudo-Distributed Mode

In the pseudo-distributed mode, each component process runs in a separate JVM on the same node. It is called "pseudo-distributed" because only a single node is actually involved.

Fully-Distributed Mode

In fully-distributed mode, Hadoop runs on a cluster of nodes. The Hadoop cluster has more than one node, ranging from two-three to several hundreds or thousands of nodes.

The three modes of a Hadoop cluster are illustrated in Figure 2-7.

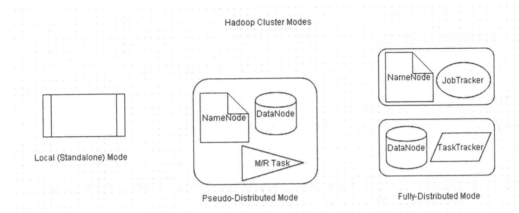

Figure 2-7. *Hadoop cluster modes*

This chapter uses the standalone and pseudo-distributed modes.

Running a MapReduce Job with the MR1 Framework

A MR1 framework based application can run in any of the cluster modes: standalone, pseudo-distributed, or fully-distributed. This section discusses the standalone and pseudo-distributed modes. First, the standalone mode.

Running MR1 in Standalone Mode

In the standalone mode, a MapReduce application is run in a single JVM. This example demonstrates the standalone mode using two different MapReduce applications:

- Grep. A *Grep* job extracts matching regexs (regular expressions) from input files and counts them.

- Word Count. A *Word Count* job counts the occurrences of each word in an input dataset.

First, the Grep MapReduce application.

Running a Grep Application

Running a Grep job involves following these steps:

1. Create a directory on the local filesystem.

2. Copy the files to be used for regular expression matching to the directory.

3. Run a Hadoop command to run the Grep job from the Hadoop examples jar.

4. List the result of the Grep in the output file.

Create a directory (/cdh/input for example).

```
mkdir /cdh/input
```

Copy the .xml files from the Hadoop configuration directory to the /cdh/input directory.

```
cp $HADOOP_CONF/*.xml /cdh/input
```

Run the following command to list the files in the /cdh/input directory.

```
ls -l
```

The XML files copied from the configuration directory are listed, as shown in Figure 2-8. Some other files could also be listed, based on previous use.

```
[root@localhost input]# ls -l
total 44
-rw-r--r--. 1 root root 5041 Sep 25 08:05 capacity-scheduler.xml
-rw-r--r--. 1 root root  178 Sep 25 08:05 core-site.xml
-rw-r--r--. 1 root root 3032 Sep 25 08:05 fair-scheduler.xml
-rw-r--r--. 1 root root 4644 Sep 25 08:05 hadoop-policy.xml
-rw-r--r--. 1 root root  178 Sep 25 08:05 hdfs-site.xml
-rw-r--r--. 1 root root   20 Sep 25 08:14 input1.txt
-rw-r--r--. 1 root root   29 Sep 25 08:15 input2.txt
-rw-r--r--. 1 root root 2033 Sep 25 08:05 mapred-queue-acls.xml
-rw-r--r--. 1 root root  178 Sep 25 08:05 mapred-site.xml
[root@localhost input]# █
```

Figure 2-8. *Listing files in the input directory*

Next you'll run the hadoop command to run the Grep job from the examples packaged in the hadoop-examples-2.6.0-mr1-cdh5.4.7.jar file. The hadoop command syntax is as follows.

```
[root@localhost cdh]# hadoop
Usage: hadoop [--config confdir] COMMAND
       where COMMAND is one of:
  fs                    run a generic filesystem user client
  version               print the version
  jar <jar>             run a jar file
  checknative [-a|-h]   check native hadoop and compression libraries availability
  distcp <srcurl> <desturl> copy file or directories recursively
```

The Grep job may be invoked with the following hadoop jar command. The input directory is the /cdh/input in which the XML files are copied, the output directory is /cdh/output, and the regular expression is dfs[a-z.]+. The parameters to the Grep job are all variables and different values could be used for the input and output directories and the regular expression. The output directory must not already exist when running the Grep.

```
hadoop jar $HADOOP_HOME/hadoop-examples-2.6.0-mr1-cdh5.4.7.jar grep /cdh/input  /cdh/output
'dfs[a-z.]+'
```

The hadoop jar command to run the Grep application on an input dataset is shown in a Linux command shell in Figure 2-9.

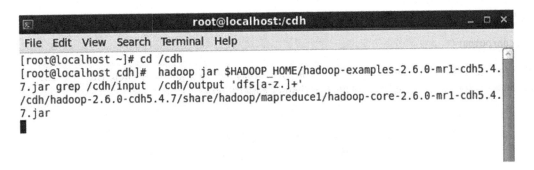

Figure 2-9. Hadoop command for the Grep job

A MR1 job runs to Grep the specified regular expression in the input files. The output from the Hadoop command is shown in Figure 2-10. The output lists the MapReduce job run, the number of file bytes read and written, the number of read, large read, and write operations, as well as the number of map input/output records, map output bytes, input split bytes, reduce input/output records, spilled records, and total bytes read.

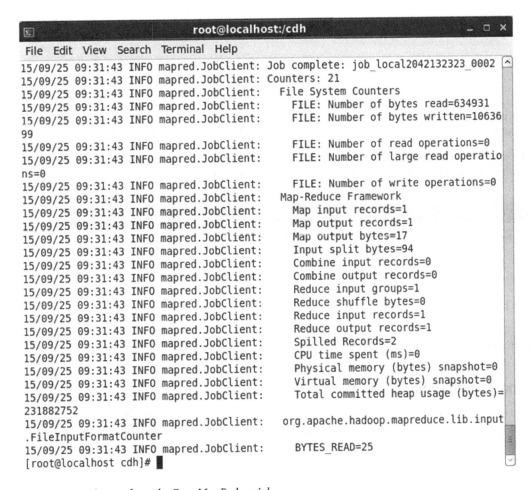

Figure 2-10. Output from the Grep MapReduce job

To list the output, run the following command.

```
ls -l /cdh/output/*
```

Two files are listed, as shown in Figure 2-11. The part-00000 file is a result of the Grep. The _SUCCESS file indicates the successful completion of the MapReduce application.

```
[root@localhost cdh]# ls -l /cdh/output/*
-rw-r--r--. 1 root root 11 Sep 25 09:31 /cdh/output/part-00000
-rw-r--r--. 1 root root  0 Sep 25 09:31 /cdh/output/_SUCCESS
[root@localhost cdh]#
```

Figure 2-11. *Listing the files generated by running MapReduce Job for Grep*

To list the result in the part-00000 file, run the following command.

```
vi /cdh/output/part-00000
```

The result of the Grep is listed, as shown in Figure 2-12.

```
1       dfsadmin
~
~
```

Figure 2-12. *Displaying the output from the Grep application*

The result would be different if a different regular expression is used. For example, if the regular expression is [a-z].xml, the result of the Grep is shown in Figure 2-13.

```
root@localhost:/cdh                    _ □ x
File  Edit  View  Search  Terminal  Help
4       e.xml
2       r.xml
~
```

Figure 2-13. *Grep output with a different regular expression*

Next, you'll see how to run a word count application in standalone mode.

Running a Word Count Application

The word count example counts the occurrences of unique words in a dataset of input files. A word count example is packaged with the examples. Copy the WordCount.java file from the examples directory to the /cdh directory.

```
cd /cdh
/cdh>cp /cdh/hadoop-2.6.0-cdh5.4.7/src/hadoop-mapreduce1-project/src/examples/org/apache/
hadoop/examples/WordCount.java.
```

Compile the WordCount.java Java source file.

```
/cdh>hadoop com.sun.tools.javac.Main WordCount.java
```

Package the .class files generated into a jar file.

```
/cdh>jar cf wordcount.jar WordCount*.class
```

You need to create a dataset to be used as input to the WordCount application. Create two input files with some text in them. Create an input file called input1.txt in the /cdh/input directory, which was also used in the Grep example. Different methods are available for creating a file. The one used in this chapter creates an empty file with the vi command.

```
vi /cdh/input/input1.txt
```

Add some text, for example "Word Count Example", to the input1.txt and save the file with the :wq command in the vi editor, as shown in Figure 2-14.

Figure 2-14. *Creating an input file input1.txt for the WordCount application*

Similarly, create another input file called input2.txt.

```
vi /cdh/input/input2.txt
```

And add some text, With Local (Standalone) Mode, for example, and save the input file with the :wq command, as shown in Figure 2-15.

Figure 2-15. *Creating a WordCount application input file called input2.txt*

Before running the WordCount application, remove the *.xml files that were used for the Grep application from the /cdh/input directory with the following command.

```
rm *.xml
```

The ls -l command should list only the input1.txt and input2.txt files, as shown in Figure 2-16.

```
[root@localhost input]# rm *.xml
rm: remove regular file `capacity-scheduler.xml'? y
rm: remove regular file `core-site.xml'? y
rm: remove regular file `fair-scheduler.xml'? y
rm: remove regular file `hadoop-policy.xml'? y
rm: remove regular file `hdfs-site.xml'? y
rm: remove regular file `mapred-queue-acls.xml'? y
rm: remove regular file `mapred-site.xml'? y
[root@localhost input]# ls -l
total 8
-rw-r--r--. 1 root root 20 Sep 25 08:14 input1.txt
-rw-r--r--. 1 root root 29 Sep 25 08:15 input2.txt
[root@localhost input]#
```

Figure 2-16. *Listing the WordCount application input files in the input directory after removing the XML files*

Run the WordCount application with the following hadoop command. The class name must be specified as the fully qualified class name org/apache/hadoop/examples/WordCount. The input directory is /cdh/input and the output directory is /cdh/output. The output directory must not already exist when you're running the WordCount application.

```
hadoop jar wordcount.jar org/apache/hadoop/examples/WordCount /cdh/input /cdh/output
```

The hadoop command is shown in a Linux command shell in Figure 2-17.

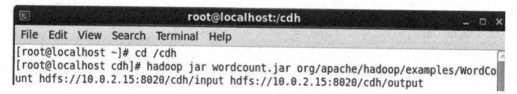

Figure 2-17. *Running the hadoop jar command for the WordCount application*

A MapReduce application runs in standalone mode to count the unique word occurrences in the input files. The MapReduce output from the hadoop jar command is shown in Figure 2-18.

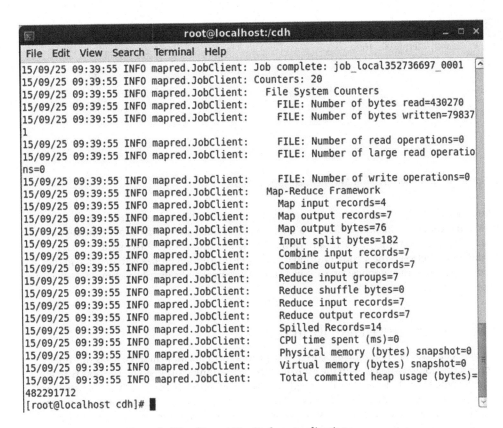

Figure 2-18. Output from the WordCount MapReduce application

You can list the output files in the /cdh/output directory using the following command.

```
/cdh>ls -l /cdh/output
```

Two files are listed, as shown in Figure 2-19. The _SUCCESS file indicates that the Hadoop command completed successfully. The part-r-00000 file is the resulting file with the word count.

```
[root@localhost cdh]# ls -l /cdh/output
total 4
-rw-r--r--. 1 root root 62 Sep 25 09:39 part-r-00000
-rw-r--r--. 1 root root  0 Sep 25 09:39 _SUCCESS
[root@localhost cdh]#
```

Figure 2-19. Listing the files generated by the WordCount MapReduce application

You can list the word count result using the following command.

```
/cdh>vi /cdh/output/part-r-00000
```

The word count for each of the unique words in the input is listed, as shown in Figure 2-20.

```
                                   root@localhost:/cdh                                    _ □ ×

  File   Edit   View   Search   Terminal   Help

(Standalone)    1
Count     1
Example   1
Local     1
Mode      1
With      1
Word      1
~
```

Figure 2-20. *Output from the WordCount MapReduce application*

You saw how to run the Grep and word count examples packaged in the Hadoop examples using the MR1 framework and the standalone mode. Next, you'll run the same Grep and word count examples in pseudo-distributed mode, still using the MR1 framework. (The YARN framework is discussed in a later example.) The difference between the standalone and the pseudo-distributed modes is that, while in the standalone mode, the MapReduce application runs in a single JVM, in pseudo-distributed mode, each of the Hadoop components runs in a separate JVM.

Running MR1 in Pseudo-Distributed Mode

The MR1 framework could run a MapReduce job as a local process with the Map/Reduce tasks running in single JVM or as a distributed process with the Map/Reduce tasks running on TaskTracker slots with a JobTracker managing the Map/Reduce tasks. By default, the Map/Reduce tasks run locally in a single JVM as configured in mapred-site.xml with the mapreduce.framework.name configuration property set to local. If mapreduce.framework.name is set to classic, separate JobTracker and TaskTracker components are used, whether in pseudo-distributed mode or fully-distributed mode. If classic is used, the mapreduce.jobtracker.address configuration property in mapred-site.xml must also be set to a JobTracker URI. the default setting being local. As you'll learn later for the MR2 (YARN) framework, the mapreduce.framework.name must be set to yarn. This chapter uses the local MR1 framework by using the default settings for mapreduce.framework.name and mapreduce.jobtracker.address.

In pseudo-distributed mode, you need to configure some Hadoop core and HDFS properties. You need to specify a NameNode URI in core-site.xml with the fs.defaultFS configuration property and also set the hadoop.tmp.dir property for the temporary directory used by Hadoop during the Map/Reduce processes. In the vi editor, set the fs.defaultFS property to the NameNode URI, which could be different for different setups. However, hdfs://localhost:8020 should be valid in most setups. This example uses the hdfs://10.0.2.15:8020 URI in which 10.0.2.15 is the URI with Oracle Linux installed on Oracle VirtualBox. The URI will differ with different installs and different networking configurations. Set the hadoop.tmp.dir property to /var/lib/hadoop-0.20/cache.

```
vi   $HADOOP_CONF/core-site.xml

<?xml-stylesheet type="text/xsl" href="configuration.xsl"?>

<!-- Put site-specific property overrides in this file. -->mk

<configuration>
<property>
  <name>fs.defaultFS</name>
    <value>hdfs://10.0.2.15:8020</value>
```

```
    </property>
<property>
    <name>hadoop.tmp.dir</name>
    <value>/var/lib/hadoop-0.20/cache</value>
  </property>
</configuration>
```

The core-site.xml file is listed in a vi editor in Figure 2-21. Save core-site.xml with :wq.

Figure 2-21. The core-site.xml configuration file

You now need to create the directory specified in the hadoop.tmp.dir property. Remove the /var/lib/hadoop-0.20/cache directory if it was created in some earlier installation of Hadoop. Create the directory and set its permissions to global (777).

```
rm -rf   /var/lib/hadoop-0.20/cache
mkdir -p /var/lib/hadoop-0.20/cache
chmod -R 777  /var/lib/hadoop-0.20/cache
```

You also need to configure some HDFS properties in the hdfs-site.xml configuration file. At a minimum, you need to set the NameNode storage directory/directories using the dfs.namenode.name.dir property. Since a pseudo-distributed cluster runs on a single machine, you need to modify the default setting for the replication factor from 3 to 1 and set the dfs.replication property. Also set the HDFS superuser group to hadoop with the dfs.permissions.superusergroup property. Setting dfs.permissions to false turns off the permissions checking except that the mode, owner, and group are still verified. The hdfs-site.xml file could be modified using the vi editor.

```
vi $HADOOP_CONF/hdfs-site.xml
<?xml version="1.0" encoding="UTF-8"?>
<?xml-stylesheet type="text/xsl" href="configuration.xsl"?>
<!-- Put site-specific property overrides in this file. -->
<configuration>
<property>
 <name>dfs.permissions.superusergroup</name>
  <value>hadoop</value>
  </property><property>
   <name>dfs.namenode.name.dir</name>
    <value>/data/1/dfs/nn</value>
    </property>
        <property>
                <name>dfs.replication</name>
                    <value>1</value>
        </property>
<property>
<name>dfs.permissions</name>
<value>false</value>
</property>
</configuration>
```

The hdfs-site.xml file is listed in the vi editor in Figure 2-22.

Figure 2-22. *The hdfs-site.xml configuration file*

Remove the directory/directories configured as the NameNode storage directories if they were created in an earlier installation of Hadoop. Create the NameNode storage directory and set its permissions to global (777).

```
rm -rf   /data/1/dfs/nn
mkdir -p /data/1/dfs/nn
chmod -R 777 /data/1/dfs/nn
```

Next, you start the HDFS, which is comprised of the NameNode and the DataNode. The NameNode and DataNode could be started together with the start-dfs.sh script or started separately with an hadoop or hdfs command. The hadoop command is deprecated but can still be used. Alternatively, the hdfs command can be used. The hdfs command has the following syntax; some of the commands have been omitted.

```
[root@localhost cdh]# hdfs
Usage: hdfs [--config confdir] COMMAND
       where COMMAND is one of:
  dfs                  run a filesystem command on the file systems supported in Hadoop.
  namenode -format     format the DFS filesystem
  secondarynamenode    run the DFS secondary namenode
  namenode             run the DFS namenode
  journalnode          run the DFS journalnode
  zkfc                 run the ZK Failover Controller daemon
  datanode             run a DFS datanode
  dfsadmin             run a DFS admin client
  haadmin              run a DFS HA admin client
  fsck                 run a DFS filesystem checking utility
  balancer             run a cluster balancing utility
  version              print the version
```

Most commands print help usage when invoked without parameters.

Before starting the NameNode, it must be formatted. Format the NameNode using one of the following commands.

```
hdfs namenode –format
hadoop namenode –format
```

The NameNode is formatted, as shown in Figure 2-23.

```
                          root@localhost:/cdh                          _ □ ×
minutes = 1,5,25
15/09/25 13:59:32 INFO namenode.FSNamesystem: Retry cache on namenode is enabled
15/09/25 13:59:32 INFO namenode.FSNamesystem: Retry cache will use 0.03 of total
 heap and retry cache entry expiry time is 600000 millis
15/09/25 13:59:32 INFO util.GSet: Computing capacity for map NameNodeRetryCache
15/09/25 13:59:32 INFO util.GSet: VM type        = 32-bit
15/09/25 13:59:32 INFO util.GSet: 0.0299999993329447746% max memory 966.7 MB = 29
7.0 KB
15/09/25 13:59:32 INFO util.GSet: capacity        = 2^16 = 65536 entries
15/09/25 13:59:32 INFO namenode.NNConf: ACLs enabled? false
15/09/25 13:59:32 INFO namenode.NNConf: XAttrs enabled? true
15/09/25 13:59:32 INFO namenode.NNConf: Maximum size of an xattr: 16384
15/09/25 13:59:33 INFO namenode.FSImage: Allocated new BlockPoolId: BP-147144429
8-10.0.2.15-1443203973427
15/09/25 13:59:33 INFO common.Storage: Storage directory /data/1/dfs/nn has been
 successfully formatted.
15/09/25 13:59:35 INFO namenode.NNStorageRetentionManager: Going to retain 1 ima
ges with txid >= 0
15/09/25 13:59:35 INFO util.ExitUtil: Exiting with status 0
15/09/25 13:59:35 INFO namenode.NameNode: SHUTDOWN_MSG:
/************************************************************
SHUTDOWN_MSG: Shutting down NameNode at localhost.oraclelinux/10.0.2.15
************************************************************/
[root@localhost cdh]# █
```

Figure 2-23. *Formatting the NameNode*

Start the NameNode with one of the following commands.

```
hdfs namenode
hadoop namenode
```

The NameNode starts.
Similarly, start the DataNode with one of the following commands.

```
hdfs datanode
hdfs datanode
```

The DataNode also starts.
The HDFS status could be monitored using the NameNode HTTP address, which is http://localhost:50070/ by default. An overview of the HDFS is listed, as shown in Figure 2-24.

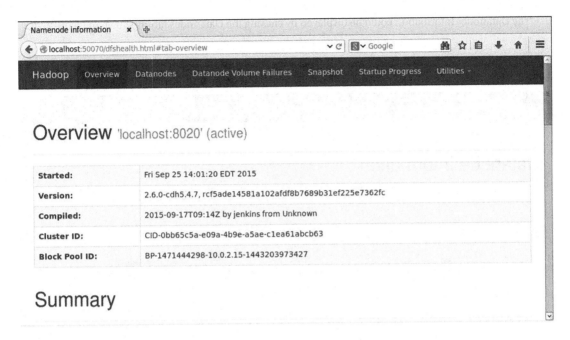

Figure 2-24. *Displaying the HDFS information*

The summary lists the configured capacity for the DFS, the DFS used, the non-DFS used, and the DFS still available, as shown in Figure 2-25. The heap and non-heap memory used are also listed.

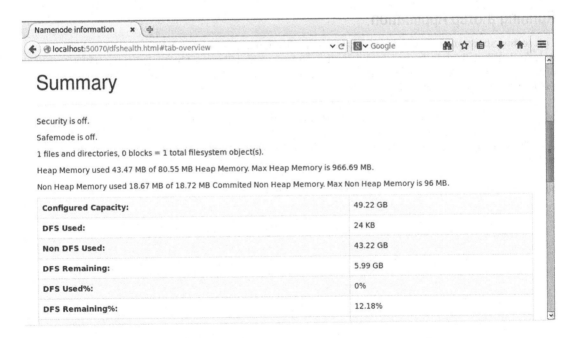

Figure 2-25. *Displaying the HDFS summary*

The Datanodes information could be displayed by clicking the Datanodes tab, as shown in Figure 2-26.

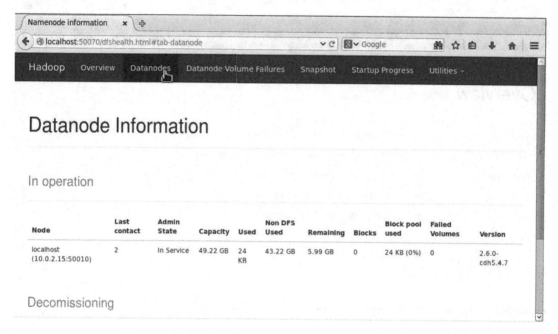

Figure 2-26. *Displaying the datanodes information*

Running a Grep Application

This section shows you how to run the same Grep application that ran in standalone mode, but this time in pseudo-distributed mode. In pseudo-distributed mode, the input files must be copied to the HDFS. Create a directory (/cdh/input) in HDFS for the input files. The filesystem (FS) shell command called -mkdir creates the /cdh/input directory in HDFS.

```
hdfs dfs -mkdir -p hdfs://10.0.2.15:8020/cdh/input
```

The filesystem (FS) shell command called –chmod sets the permissions for the /cdh/input directory to global (777).

```
hdfs dfs -chmod 777 hdfs://10.0.2.15:8020/cdh/input
```

Copy the XML files from the Hadoop configuration directory to the input directory with the filesystem (FS) shell command –put.

```
hdfs dfs -put  $HADOOP_CONF/*.xml hdfs://10.0.2.15:8020/cdh/input
```

Then list the files in the /cdh/input directory with the filesystem (FS) shell command –ls.

```
hdfs dfs -ls hdfs://10.0.2.15:8020/cdh/input
```

The XML files copied to the /cdh/input directory in HDFS are listed, as shown in Figure 2-27.

```
[root@localhost ~]# hdfs dfs -ls hdfs://10.0.2.15:8020/cdh/input
Found 8 items
-rw-r--r--   1 root hadoop       4436 2015-09-25 14:13 hdfs://10.0.2.15:8020/cdh
/input/capacity-scheduler.xml
-rw-r--r--   1 root hadoop        975 2015-09-25 14:13 hdfs://10.0.2.15:8020/cdh
/input/core-site.xml
-rw-r--r--   1 root hadoop       9683 2015-09-25 14:13 hdfs://10.0.2.15:8020/cdh
/input/hadoop-policy.xml
-rw-r--r--   1 root hadoop       1163 2015-09-25 14:13 hdfs://10.0.2.15:8020/cdh
/input/hdfs-site.xml
-rw-r--r--   1 root hadoop        620 2015-09-25 14:13 hdfs://10.0.2.15:8020/cdh
/input/httpfs-site.xml
-rw-r--r--   1 root hadoop       3523 2015-09-25 14:13 hdfs://10.0.2.15:8020/cdh
/input/kms-acls.xml
-rw-r--r--   1 root hadoop       5511 2015-09-25 14:13 hdfs://10.0.2.15:8020/cdh
/input/kms-site.xml
-rw-r--r--   1 root hadoop        690 2015-09-25 14:13 hdfs://10.0.2.15:8020/cdh
/input/yarn-site.xml
[root@localhost ~]#
```

Figure 2-27. *Listing the files in the /cdh/input directory*

Next, run the Hadoop packaged example called Grep using the following Hadoop command. The input and output directories are specified using the HDFS scheme, as the input files are in the HDFS and the output will be generated in the HDFS. The Grep regular expression is dfs[a-z.]+. The /cdh/output directory must not already exist in the HDFS.

```
hadoop jar $HADOOP_HOME/hadoop-examples-2.6.0-mr1-cdh5.4.7.jar grep hdfs://10.0.2.15:8020/
cdh/input  hdfs://10.0.2.15:8020/cdh/output 'dfs[a-z.]+'
```

A MapReduce job runs on the pseudo-distributed cluster to run the Grep example application, as shown in Figure 2-28.

```
root@localhost:/cdh                                          _ □ ×

File   Edit   View   Search   Terminal   Help

15/09/25 14:37:45 INFO mapred.JobClient:        FILE: Number of read operations=0
15/09/25 14:37:45 INFO mapred.JobClient:        FILE: Number of large read operatio
ns=0
15/09/25 14:37:45 INFO mapred.JobClient:        FILE: Number of write operations=0
15/09/25 14:37:45 INFO mapred.JobClient:        HDFS: Number of bytes read=53722
15/09/25 14:37:45 INFO mapred.JobClient:        HDFS: Number of bytes written=624
15/09/25 14:37:45 INFO mapred.JobClient:        HDFS: Number of read operations=86
15/09/25 14:37:45 INFO mapred.JobClient:        HDFS: Number of large read operatio
ns=0
15/09/25 14:37:45 INFO mapred.JobClient:        HDFS: Number of write operations=20
15/09/25 14:37:45 INFO mapred.JobClient:     Map-Reduce Framework
15/09/25 14:37:45 INFO mapred.JobClient:        Map input records=5
15/09/25 14:37:45 INFO mapred.JobClient:        Map output records=5
15/09/25 14:37:45 INFO mapred.JobClient:        Map output bytes=134
15/09/25 14:37:45 INFO mapred.JobClient:        Input split bytes=116
15/09/25 14:37:45 INFO mapred.JobClient:        Combine input records=0
15/09/25 14:37:45 INFO mapred.JobClient:        Combine output records=0
15/09/25 14:37:45 INFO mapred.JobClient:        Reduce input groups=1
15/09/25 14:37:45 INFO mapred.JobClient:        Reduce shuffle bytes=0
15/09/25 14:37:45 INFO mapred.JobClient:        Reduce input records=5
15/09/25 14:37:45 INFO mapred.JobClient:        Reduce output records=5
15/09/25 14:37:46 INFO mapred.JobClient:        Spilled Records=10
15/09/25 14:37:46 INFO mapred.JobClient:        CPU time spent (ms)=0
15/09/25 14:37:46 INFO mapred.JobClient:        Physical memory (bytes) snapshot=0
15/09/25 14:37:46 INFO mapred.JobClient:        Virtual memory (bytes) snapshot=0
15/09/25 14:37:46 INFO mapred.JobClient:        Total committed heap usage (bytes)=
239001600
15/09/25 14:37:46 INFO mapred.JobClient:     org.apache.hadoop.mapreduce.lib.input
.FileInputFormatCounter
15/09/25 14:37:46 INFO mapred.JobClient:        BYTES_READ=174
[root@localhost cdh]# █
```

Figure 2-28. *Running a Grep MapReduce application in pseudo-distributed cluster mode*

You can list the files generated in the /cdh/output directory with the FS shell command -ls.

```
hdfs dfs -ls hdfs://10.0.2.15:8020/cdh/output/*
```

Two files are listed—_SUCCESS and part-00000—as shown in Figure 2-29. The _SUCCESS file indicates that the MapReduce application completed successfully and the part-00000 file is the result of the Grep application.

```
[root@localhost cdh]# hdfs dfs -ls hdfs://10.0.2.15:8020/cdh/output/*
-rw-r--r--   1 root hadoop          0 2015-09-25 14:37 hdfs://10.0.2.15:8020/cdh
/output/_SUCCESS
-rw-r--r--   1 root hadoop        104 2015-09-25 14:37 hdfs://10.0.2.15:8020/cdh
/output/part-00000
[root@localhost cdh]# █
```

Figure 2-29. *Listing files generated by the Grep MapReduce application in pseudo-distributed mode*

List the output generated from the Grep application with the FS shell command -cat, which is applied on the part-00000 file.

```
hdfs dfs -cat hdfs://10.0.2.15:8020/cdh/output/part-00000
```

The output from the Grep application is displayed, as shown in Figure 2-30. All the configuration properties that are Grepped with the regular expression dfs[a-z.]+ are listed.

```
|[root@localhost cdh]# hdfs dfs -cat hdfs://10.0.2.15:8020/cdh/output/part-00000
1        dfs.namenode.name.dir
1        dfs.permissions
1        dfs.permissions.superusergroup
1        dfs.replication
1        dfsadmin
[root@localhost cdh]#
```

Figure 2-30. *Displaying the output from the Grep MapReduce application that's run on a pseudo-distributed mode cluster*

You will be using the same input and output directories for the word count example, so remove the /cdh/input and /cdh/output directories from the HDFS using the FS shell command –rm. Use it recursively with –r.

```
hdfs dfs -rm -r hdfs://10.0.2.15:8020/cdh/input
hdfs dfs -rm -r hdfs://10.0.2.15:8020/cdh/output
```

Running a WordCount Application

Next, you'll run the word count example on a pseudo-cluster with local Map/Reduce tasks. You'll use the same wordcount.jar file generated for the standalone mode. You do need to create input files for the word count example in HDFS. Create an input directory (/cdh/input) in HDFS and set its permissions to global (777).

```
hdfs dfs -mkdir -p hdfs://10.0.2.15:8020/cdh/input
hdfs dfs -chmod 777 hdfs://10.0.2.15:8020/cdh/input
```

Use the same input1.txt file as for the standalone mode or create a new input1.txt file in vi editor. The :wq command saves the file and quits the editor.

```
vi /cdh/input/input1.txt
```

The preceding command creates an empty file to which text could be added and saved, as shown in Figure 2-31.

Figure 2-31. *Creating an input file input1.txt for a WordCount MapReduce application*

Similarly, create a text file called input2.txt.

```
vi /cdh/input/input2.txt
```

Add some text, for example With MR1 Pseudo-distributed (Single Node Cluster) Mode, and save the file with :wq, as shown in Figure 2-32.

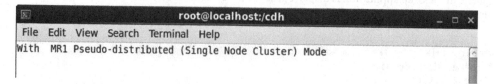

Figure 2-32. *Creating another input file input2.txt for a WordCount MapReduce application*

Unlike with standalone mode, the input files need to be in the HDFS. Put the input1.txt and input2.txt files in the HDFS directory /cdh/input using the FS shell command –put.

```
hdfs dfs -put /cdh/input/* hdfs://10.0.2.15:8020/cdh/input
```

Run the following FS shell command –ls to list the two files copied to HDFS.

```
hdfs dfs -ls hdfs://10.0.2.15:8020/cdh/input
```

The input1.txt and input2.txt files in HDFS are listed, as shown in Figure 2-33.

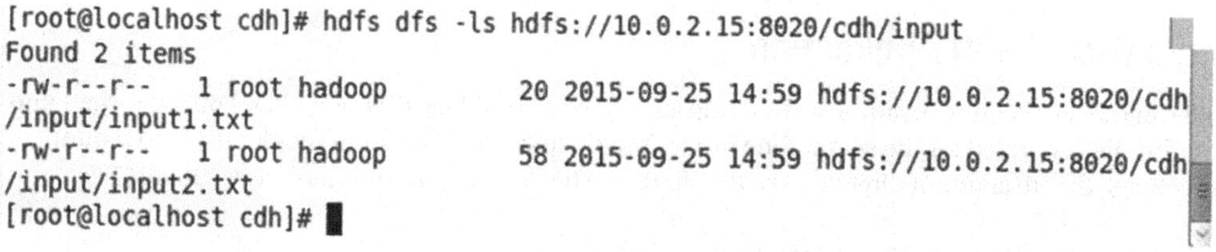

```
[root@localhost cdh]# hdfs dfs -ls hdfs://10.0.2.15:8020/cdh/input
Found 2 items
-rw-r--r--   1 root hadoop         20 2015-09-25 14:59 hdfs://10.0.2.15:8020/cdh
/input/input1.txt
-rw-r--r--   1 root hadoop         58 2015-09-25 14:59 hdfs://10.0.2.15:8020/cdh
/input/input2.txt
[root@localhost cdh]# █
```

Figure 2-33. *Listing the input files for a WordCount MapReduce application*

Next, run the word count example using the following hadoop jar command in which the fully-qualified class name is specified and the hdfs scheme prefixed input and output directories are specified. The /cdh/output output directory must not already exist in the HDFS.

```
hadoop jar wordcount.jar org/apache/hadoop/examples/WordCount hdfs://10.0.2.15:8020/cdh/
input hdfs://10.0.2.15:8020/cdh/output
```

The hadoop command in a Linux command shell is shown in Figure 2-34.

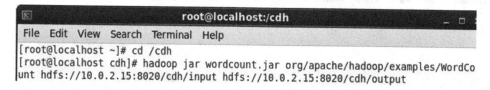

Figure 2-34. *Running the hadoop jar command for a WordCount MapReduce application*

A MapReduce application counts the word occurrences for each unique word in the input dataset and generates the output shown in Figure 2-35.

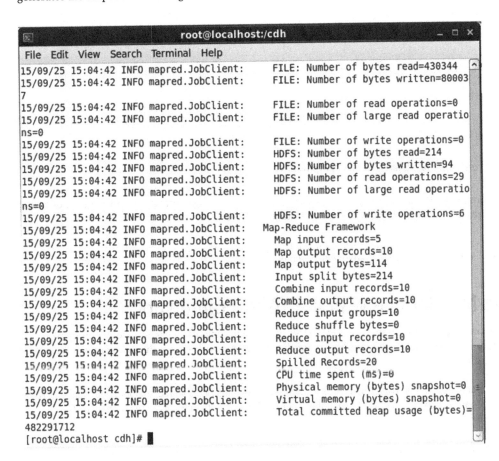

Figure 2-35. Output from the WordCount MapReduce application

The output files generated with the hadoop command could be listed with the FS shell command -ls as before. The _SUCCESS and part-r-00000 files should be listed.

```
hdfs dfs -ls  hdfs://10.0.2.15:8020/cdh/output
```

You can list the result of the WordCount application output to the part-r-00000 file using the FS shell command -cat.

```
hdfs dfs -cat hdfs://10.0.2.15:8020/cdh/output/part-r-00000
```

The result of the word count is listed, as shown in Figure 2-36.

```
[root@localhost cdh]# hdfs dfs -cat hdfs://10.0.2.15:8020/cdh/output/part-r-0000
0
(Single 1
Cluster)        1
Count   1
Example 1
MR1     1
Mode    1
Node    1
Pseudo-distributed      1
With    1
Word    1
[root@localhost cdh]# █
```

Figure 2-36. *Word count for different terms in input files*

Before running MapReduce with the MR2 (YARN) framework, you again need to remove the input and output directories from HDFS using the FS shell commands –rm –r.

```
hdfs dfs -rm -r hdfs://10.0.2.15:8020/cdh/input
hdfs dfs -rm -r hdfs://10.0.2.15:8020/cdh/output
```

Running MapReduce with the YARN Framework

This section shows you how to run the YARN (MR2) MapReduce framework in pseudo-cluster mode. You need to configure Hadoop slightly differently than for the MR1 framework. Create the following symlinks for the MR2 directories.

```
ln -s /cdh/hadoop-2.6.0-cdh5.4.7/bin /cdh/hadoop-2.6.0-cdh5.4.7/share/hadoop/mapreduce2/bin
ln -s /cdh/hadoop-2.6.0-cdh5.4.7/etc/hadoop /cdh/hadoop-2.6.0-cdh5.4.7/share/hadoop/
mapreduce2/conf
```

Also create the following symlink for the YARN bin directory. The symlink /cdh/hadoop-2.6.0-cdh5.4.7/share/hadoop/yarn/bin is created so that when the /cdh/hadoop-2.6.0-cdh5.4.7/share/hadoop/yarn/bin directory is invoked or referenced in preconfigured applications and files, the /cdh/hadoop-2.6.0-cdh5.4.7/bin directory is invoked.

```
ln -s /cdh/hadoop-2.6.0-cdh5.4.7/bin /cdh/hadoop-2.6.0-cdh5.4.7/share/hadoop/yarn/bin
```

Set the environment variables for YARN in the bash shell as follows. In addition to the YARN_HOME environment variable, some other environment variables have been added.

```
vi ~/.bashrc
export HADOOP_PREFIX=/cdh/hadoop-2.6.0-cdh5.4.7
export HADOOP_CONF_DIR=$HADOOP_PREFIX/etc/hadoop
export HADOOP_COMMON_HOME=$HADOOP_PREFIX/share/hadoop/common
export HADOOP_HDFS_HOME=$HADOOP_PREFIX/share/hadoop/hdfs
export YARN_HOME=$HADOOP_PREFIX/share/hadoop/yarn
export JAVA_HOME=/cdh/jdk1.7.0_55
export HADOOP_MAPRED_HOME=/cdh/hadoop-2.6.0-cdh5.4.7/share/hadoop/mapreduce2
```

```
export HADOOP_HOME=/cdh/hadoop-2.6.0-cdh5.4.7/share/hadoop/mapreduce2
export HADOOP_CLASSPATH=$HADOOP_MAPRED_HOME/*:$HADOOP_MAPRED_HOME/lib/*:$JAVA_HOME/
lib/*:$HADOOP_CONF_DIR:$HADOOP_COMMON_HOME/*:$HADOOP_COMMON_HOME/lib/*:$HADOOP_HDFS_
HOME/*:$HADOOP_HDFS_HOME/lib/*:$YARN_HOME/*:$YARN_HOME/lib/*
export PATH=/usr/lib/qt-3.3/bin:/usr/local/sbin:/usr/sbin:/sbin:/usr/local/bin:/usr/bin:/
bin:$HADOOP_HOME/bin:$HADOOP_MAPRED_HOME/bin:$JAVA_HOME/bin:$HADOOP_PREFIX/sbin
export CLASSPATH=$HADOOP_CLASSPATH
export HADOOP_NAMENODE_USER=hadoop
export HADOOP_DATANODE_USER=hadoop
```

The environment variables in the bash shell are shown in a vi editor in Figure 2-37.

Figure 2-37. *Setting environment variables in a bash shell*

Next, you'll see how to run the same Grep and word count examples with the YARN framework in pseudo-distributed mode.

Running YARN in Pseudo-Distributed Mode

The pseudo-distributed mode cluster configuration for YARN is slightly different than for MR1. First, the mapreduce.framework.name configuration property in mapred-site.xml must be set to yarn; the default is local. Create the mapred-site.xml file from the template file.

```
cp /cdh/hadoop-2.6.0-cdh5.4.7/etc/hadoop/mapred-site.xml.template /cdh/hadoop-2.6.0-
cdh5.4.7/etc/hadoop/mapred-site.xml
```

191

Open mapred-site.xml in a vi editor.

```
vi /cdh/hadoop-2.6.0-cdh5.4.7/etc/hadoop/mapred-site.xml
```

Set the mapreduce.framework.name property to yarn.

```
<configuration>
    <property>
        <name>mapreduce.framework.name</name>
        <value>yarn</value>
    </property>
</configuration>
```

The mapred-site.xml is listed in a vi editor in Figure 2-38.

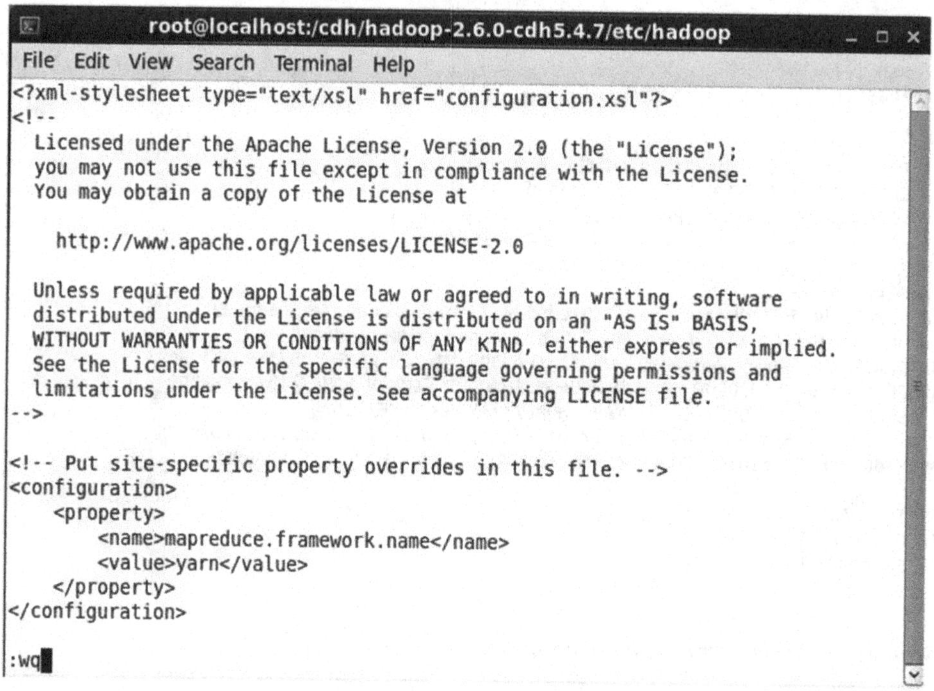

Figure 2-38. *Setting the MapReduce framework to YARN*

The core-site.xml configuration file is the same as in the MR1 framework. The core-site.xml file should not be modified. To the hdfs-site.xml file, add the dfs.client.socket-timeout property with its value set to 3600000, which is much higher than the default setting of 60000. A YARN MapReduce application that tries to connect to the Job HistoryServer after the application is complete could timeout without this higher setting. Open the hdfs-site.xml in a vi editor.

```
vi /cdh/hadoop-2.6.0-cdh5.4.7/etc/hadoop/hdfs-site.xml
```

Set the configuration properties listed:

```
<?xml version="1.0" encoding="UTF-8"?>
<?xml-stylesheet type="text/xsl" href="configuration.xsl"?>

<!-- Put site-specific property overrides in this file. -->

<configuration>
<property>
 <name>dfs.permissions.superusergroup</name>
  <value>hadoop</value>
  </property><property>
   <name>dfs.namenode.name.dir</name>
    <value>/data/1/dfs/nn</value>
    </property>
        <property>
              <name>dfs.replication</name>
                    <value>1</value>
        </property>
<property>
<name>dfs.permissions</name>
<value>false</value>
</property>
<property>
<name>dfs.client.socket-timeout</name>
<value>3600000</value>
</property>
</configuration>
```

The YARN-specific configuration file is yarn-site.xml. You need to set the properties listed in Table 2-1 in the yarn-site.xml file.

Table 2-1. *Configuration Properties for the yarn-site.xml File*

Configuration Property	Description	Value
yarn.nodemanager.aux-services	Auxiliary service name for a pluggable shuffle handler. The shuffle refers to the transfer of the Map task output to the Reducer.	mapreduce_shuffle
yarn.nodemanager.aux-services.mapreduce_shuffle.class	The shuffle handler class.	org.apache.hadoop.mapred.ShuffleHandler
yarn.application.classpath	The YARN application classpath.	$HADOOP_CONF_DIR, $HADOOP_COMMON_HOME/*, $HADOOP_COMMON_HOME/lib/*, $HADOOP_HDFS_HOME/*,$HADOOP_HDFS_HOME/lib/*, $HADOOP_MAPRED_HOME/*,$HADOOP_MAPRED_HOME/lib/*, $YARN_HOME/*,$YARN_HOME/lib/*

Open yarn-site.xml in a vi editor.

```
vi /cdh/hadoop-2.6.0-cdh5.4.7/etc/hadoop/yarn-site.xml
```

The yarn-site.xml file is listed:

```
<configuration>
    <property>
        <name>yarn.nodemanager.aux-services</name>
        <value>mapreduce_shuffle</value>
    </property>
  <property>
        <name>yarn.nodemanager.aux-services.mapreduce_shuffle.class</name>
        <value>org.apache.hadoop.mapred.ShuffleHandler</value>
    </property>
<property>
        <description>Classpath for typical applications.</description>
        <name>yarn.application.classpath</name>
        <value>
        $HADOOP_CONF_DIR,
        $HADOOP_COMMON_HOME/*,$HADOOP_COMMON_HOME/lib/*,
        $HADOOP_HDFS_HOME/*,$HADOOP_HDFS_HOME/lib/*,
        $HADOOP_MAPRED_HOME/*,$HADOOP_MAPRED_HOME/lib/*,
        $YARN_HOME/*,$YARN_HOME/lib/*
        </value>
</property>
</configuration>
```

The yarn-site.xml configuration file is shown in a vi editor in Figure 2-39.

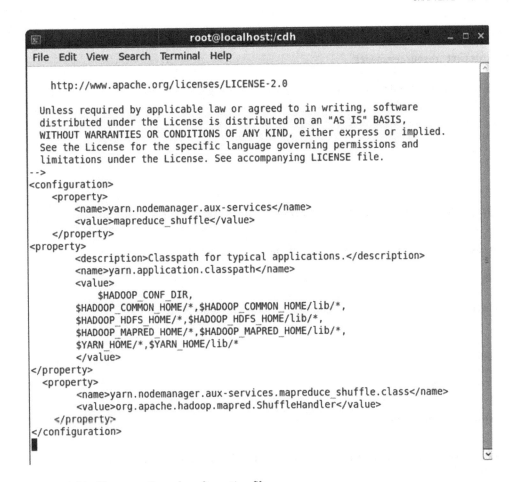

```
http://www.apache.org/licenses/LICENSE-2.0

Unless required by applicable law or agreed to in writing, software
distributed under the License is distributed on an "AS IS" BASIS,
WITHOUT WARRANTIES OR CONDITIONS OF ANY KIND, either express or implied.
See the License for the specific language governing permissions and
limitations under the License. See accompanying LICENSE file.
-->
<configuration>
    <property>
        <name>yarn.nodemanager.aux-services</name>
        <value>mapreduce_shuffle</value>
    </property>
<property>
        <description>Classpath for typical applications.</description>
        <name>yarn.application.classpath</name>
        <value>
            $HADOOP_CONF_DIR,
        $HADOOP_COMMON_HOME/*,$HADOOP_COMMON_HOME/lib/*,
        $HADOOP_HDFS_HOME/*,$HADOOP_HDFS_HOME/lib/*,
        $HADOOP_MAPRED_HOME/*,$HADOOP_MAPRED_HOME/lib/*,
        $YARN_HOME/*,$YARN_HOME/lib/*
        </value>
</property>
  <property>
        <name>yarn.nodemanager.aux-services.mapreduce_shuffle.class</name>
        <value>org.apache.hadoop.mapred.ShuffleHandler</value>
    </property>
</configuration>
```

Figure 2-39. *The yarn-site.xml configuration file*

The YARN ResourceManager and NodeManager daemons must be started before a YARN application can run. You can start the ResourceManager and NodeManager together with the following command.

```
start-yarn.sh
```

First, the ResourceManager starts. Add the password at the prompt. Subsequently, the NodeManager starts, as shown in Figure 2-40.

```
[root@localhost cdh]# start-yarn.sh
starting yarn daemons
starting resourcemanager, logging to /cdh/hadoop-2.6.0-cdh5.4.7/share/hadoop/yar
n/logs/yarn-root-resourcemanager-localhost.oraclelinux.out
root@localhost's password:
localhost: starting nodemanager, logging to /cdh/hadoop-2.6.0-cdh5.4.7/share/had
oop/yarn/logs/yarn-root-nodemanager-localhost.oraclelinux.out
```

Figure 2-40. *Starting YARN*

Alternatively, you can start the ResourceManager separately by using the following command.

```
yarn-daemon.sh start resourcemanager
```

The ResourceManager starts if not already running, as shown in Figure 2-41.

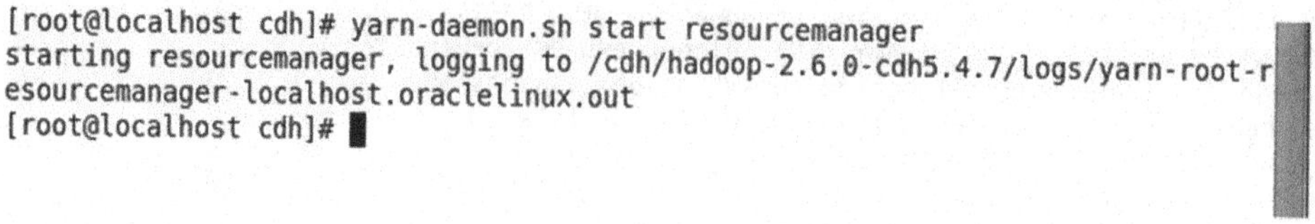

```
[root@localhost cdh]# yarn-daemon.sh start resourcemanager
starting resourcemanager, logging to /cdh/hadoop-2.6.0-cdh5.4.7/logs/yarn-root-r
esourcemanager-localhost.oraclelinux.out
[root@localhost cdh]# 
```

Figure 2-41. *Starting the ResourceManager*

You can also start the NodeManager separately with the following command.

```
yarn-daemon.sh start nodemanager
```

The NodeManager starts if it is not already running, as shown in Figure 2-42.

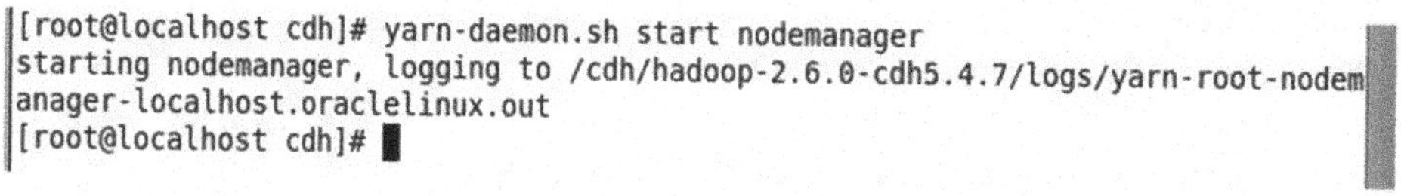

```
[root@localhost cdh]# yarn-daemon.sh start nodemanager
starting nodemanager, logging to /cdh/hadoop-2.6.0-cdh5.4.7/logs/yarn-root-nodem
anager-localhost.oraclelinux.out
[root@localhost cdh]# 
```

Figure 2-42. *Starting the NodeManager*

You also need to start the HistoryServer, which is not a MapReduce daemon and must be started separately with the following command.

```
yarn-daemon.sh start historyserver
```

In later versions of CDH, you use the yarn-daemon.sh start timelineserver command. The HistoryServer starts, as shown in Figure 2-43.

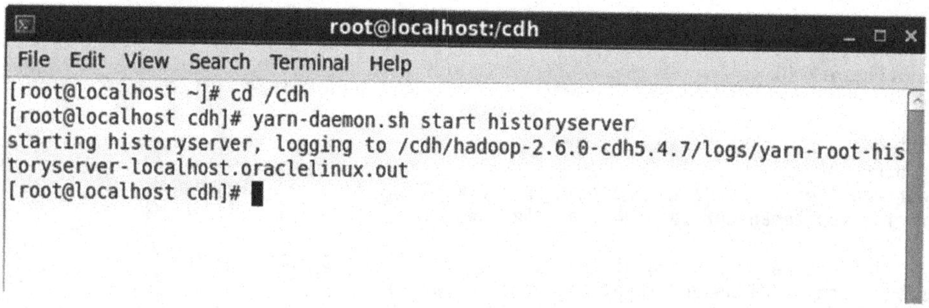

```
root@localhost:/cdh
File  Edit  View  Search  Terminal  Help
[root@localhost ~]# cd /cdh
[root@localhost cdh]# yarn-daemon.sh start historyserver
starting historyserver, logging to /cdh/hadoop-2.6.0-cdh5.4.7/logs/yarn-root-his
toryserver-localhost.oraclelinux.out
[root@localhost cdh]# 
```

Figure 2-43. *Starting the HistoryServer*

The HDFS nodes NameNode and DataNode must also be started as when using MR1. Start NameNode with the following hdfs command.

```
hdfs namenode
```

The NameNode starts.
Start DataNode with the following hdfs command.

```
hdfs datanode
```

The DataNode starts.

Running a Grep Application with YARN

This section runs the same Grep example using the YARN framework instead of the MR1 framework. You still need to create a /cdh/input directory in HDFS and put the XML configuration files in the /cdh/input directory.

```
hdfs dfs -mkdir hdfs://10.0.2.15:8020/cdh/input
hdfs dfs -chmod 777 hdfs://10.0.2.15:8020/cdh/input
hdfs dfs -put  $HADOOP_CONF/*.xml hdfs://10.0.2.15:8020/cdh/input
```

Instead of a hadoop command, you run a yarn command for the Grep application. The syntax for the yarn command is as follows; some of the commands have been omitted.

```
[root@localhost cdh]# yarn
Usage: yarn [--config confdir] COMMAND
where COMMAND is one of:
  resourcemanager -format-state-store   deletes the RMStateStore
  resourcemanager                       run the ResourceManager
  nodemanager                           run a nodemanager on each slave
  timelineserver                        run the timeline server
  rmadmin                               admin tools
  version                               print the version
  jar <jar>                             run a jar file
  CLASSNAME                             run the class named CLASSNAME
```

Run the following yarn command to run the Grep application. The input and output paths are specified using the hdfs scheme. The regular expression is specified as dfs[a-z.]+.

```
yarn jar $HADOOP_HOME/hadoop-mapreduce-examples-2.6.0-cdh5.4.7.jar grep
hdfs://10.0.2.15:8020/cdh/input hdfs://10.0.2.15:8020/cdh/output 'dfs[a-z.]+'
```

A MapReduce application starts, as shown in Figure 2-44.

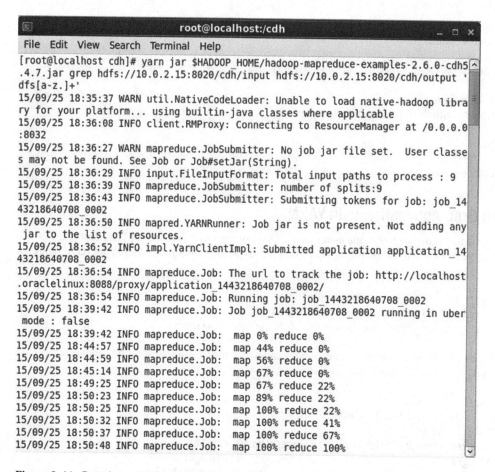

Figure 2-44. Running a YARN Grep application

The YARN output includes the map output records/bytes, input split bytes, reduce input/output records, spilled records, shuffled maps, failed maps, and merged map outputs.

You can list the files generated in the output directory with the FS shell command -ls.

```
hdfs dfs -ls hdfs://10.0.2.15:8020/cdh/output/*
```

The _SUCCESS and part-r-00000 files are listed, as shown in Figure 2-45.

```
[root@localhost cdh]# hdfs dfs -ls  hdfs://10.0.2.15:8020/cdh/output
15/09/25 20:05:08 WARN util.NativeCodeLoader: Unable to load native-hadoop libra
ry for your platform... using builtin-java classes where applicable
Found 2 items
-rw-r--r--   1 root hadoop          0 2015-09-25 19:58 hdfs://10.0.2.15:8020/cdh
/output/_SUCCESS
-rw-r--r--   1 root hadoop        104 2015-09-25 19:58 hdfs://10.0.2.15:8020/cdh
/output/part-r-00000
[root@localhost cdh]# 
```

Figure 2-45. Listing files generated by the YARN Grep application

Output the result of the Grep using the FS shell command –cat, which is used on the result file called part-r-00000.

```
hdfs dfs -cat hdfs://10.0.2.15:8020/cdh/output/part-r-00000
```

The result of the Grep is listed, as shown in Figure 2-46.

```
[root@localhost cdh]# hdfs dfs -cat hdfs://10.0.2.15:8020/cdh/output/part-r-0000
0
15/09/25 20:06:50 WARN util.NativeCodeLoader: Unable to load native-hadoop libra
ry for your platform... using builtin-java classes where applicable
1       dfsadmin
1       dfs.replication
1       dfs.permissions.superusergroup
1       dfs.permissions
1       dfs.namenode.name.dir
[root@localhost cdh]# ▮
```

Figure 2-46. *Grep output*

You again need to remove the input and output directories from HDFS, as you'll be using the same directories for running the word count example in the YARN framework.

```
hdfs dfs -rm r hdfs://10.0.2.15:8020/cdh/input
hdfs dfs -rm r hdfs://10.0.2.15:8020/cdh/output
```

Running a WordCount Application with YARN

Use the same wordcount.jar you generated earlier. Create the /cdh/input directory in HDFS and set its permissions to global (777).

```
hdfs dfs -mkdir hdfs://10.0.2.15:8020/cdh/input
hdfs dfs -chmod 777 hdfs://10.0.2.15:8020/cdh/input
```

Create the input files input1.txt and input2.txt as before. Make the input2.txt file slightly different to distinguish it from the other modes. Create the input2.txt and add some text to the file. Save and quit with the :wq command, as shown in Figure 2-47.

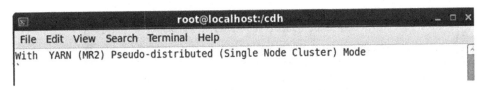

Figure 2-47. *Creating the input2.txt file for the WordCount YARN application*

Put the input files in the /cdh/input directory using the FS shell command –put.

```
hdfs dfs -put /cdh/input/* hdfs://10.0.2.15:8020/cdh/input
```

You can list the input files using the FS shell command –ls.

```
hdfs dfs -ls hdfs://10.0.2.15:8020/cdh/input
```

The input1.txt and input2.txt files are listed, as shown in Figure 2-48.

```
[root@localhost cdh]# hdfs dfs -ls hdfs://10.0.2.15:8020/cdh/input
15/09/25 16:27:04 WARN util.NativeCodeLoader: Unable to load native-hadoop libra
ry for your platform... using builtin-java classes where applicable
Found 2 items
-rw-r--r--   1 root hadoop          20 2015-09-25 16:26 hdfs://10.0.2.15:8020/cdh
/input/input1.txt
-rw-r--r--   1 root hadoop          66 2015-09-25 16:26 hdfs://10.0.2.15:8020/cdh
/input/input2.txt
[root@localhost cdh]# █
```

Figure 2-48. *Listing the input text files for the WordCount YARN application*

The word count example is packaged in the hadoop-mapreduce-examples-2.6.0-cdh5.4.7.jar file and is invoked with a yarn command as follows. The input and output directories are specified as yarn command args. The output directory must not already exist.

```
yarn jar $HADOOP_HOME/hadoop-mapreduce-examples-2.6.0-cdh5.4.7.jar wordcount
hdfs://10.0.2.15:8020/cdh/input hdfs://10.0.2.15:8020/cdh/output
```

The yarn command is shown in the Linux command shell in Figure 2-49.

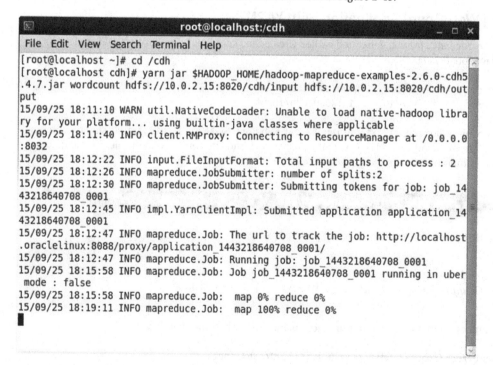

Figure 2-49. *Running the WordCount application with YARN*

The yarn command runs a YARN MapReduce application.

Run the FS shell command –ls to list the generated files, as shown in Figure 2-50.

```
[root@localhost cdh]# hdfs dfs -ls  hdfs://10.0.2.15:8020/cdh/output
15/09/25 18:24:26 WARN util.NativeCodeLoader: Unable to load native-hadoop libra
ry for your platform... using builtin-java classes where applicable
Found 2 items
-rw-r--r--   1 root hadoop          0 2015-09-25 18:21 hdfs://10.0.2.15:8020/cdh
/output/_SUCCESS
-rw-r--r--   1 root hadoop        107 2015-09-25 18:21 hdfs://10.0.2.15:8020/cdh
/output/part-r-00000
[root@localhost cdh]# █
```

Figure 2-50. *Listing the files generated from the YARN application*

```
hdfs dfs -ls  hdfs://10.0.2.15:8020/cdh/output
```

The _SUCCESS and part-r-00000 files are listed; _SUCCESS indicates that the application completed successfully and part-r-00000 is the result of the word count.

Output the result of the word count using the FS shell command –cat, which is applied to the part-r-00000 file.

```
hdfs dfs -cat hdfs://10.0.2.15:8020/cdh/output/part-r-00000
```

The word count result is displayed, as shown in Figure 2-51.

```
[root@localhost cdh]# hdfs dfs -cat hdfs://10.0.2.15:8020/cdh/output/part-r-0000
0
15/09/25 18:26:04 WARN util.NativeCodeLoader: Unable to load native-hadoop libra
ry for your platform... using builtin-java classes where applicable
(MR2)   1
(Single 1
Cluster)        1
Count   1
Example 1
Mode    1
Node    1
Pseudo-distributed      1
With    1
Word    1
YARN    1
`       1
[root@localhost cdh]#
```

Figure 2-51. *Word count result*

Remove the input and output directories, as you'll create the same directories again in the following Hadoop Streaming section.

```
hdfs dfs -rm r hdfs://10.0.2.15:8020/cdh/input
hdfs dfs -rm r hdfs://10.0.2.15:8020/cdh/output
```

Stop the YARN daemons with the following command.

```
stop-yarn.sh
```

Running Hadoop Streaming

This section runs a Hadoop Streaming MapReduce application. Hadoop Streaming is a command-line utility with which a MapReduce job may be run using any executable script. *Mapper* and *Reducer* are specified on the command line as args. Set the environment variables in a bash shell to the MR1 directories and include the Hadoop Streaming jars in the Hadoop classpath.

```
vi ~/.bashrc
export HADOOP_PREFIX=/cdh/hadoop-2.6.0-cdh5.4.7
export HADOOP_CONF=$HADOOP_PREFIX/etc/hadoop-mapreduce1
export JAVA_HOME=/cdh/jdk1.7.0_55
export HADOOP_MAPRED_HOME=/cdh/hadoop-2.6.0-cdh5.4.7/share/hadoop/mapreduce1
export HADOOP_HOME=/cdh/hadoop-2.6.0-cdh5.4.7/share/hadoop/mapreduce1
export HADOOP_CLASSPATH=$HADOOP_HOME/*:$HADOOP_HOME/lib/*:$JAVA_HOME/lib/*:$HADOOP_HOME/
contrib/streaming/*:$HADOOP_HOME/contrib/streaming/lib/*
export PATH=$PATH:$HADOOP_HOME/bin:$HADOOP_MAPRED_HOME/bin:$JAVA_HOME/bin:$HADOOP_PREFIX/
src/hadoop-tools/hadoop-streaming/src/test/bin
export CLASSPATH=$HADOOP_CLASSPATH
export HADOOP_NAMENODE_USER=hadoop
export HADOOP_DATANODE_USER=hadoop
```

Start the HDFS (NameNode and DataNode) as before using the hdfs commands.

```
hdfs namenode
hdfs datanode
```

Create a directory in the HDFS for the input files and set its permissions to global (777), as before.

```
hdfs dfs -mkdir -p hdfs://10.0.2.15:8020/cdh/input
hdfs dfs -chmod 777 hdfs://10.0.2.15:8020/cdh/input
Create the input files input1.txt and input2.txt as before. The vi command opens a vi editor
with an empty file and the :wq command saves and exits the vi editor. The text to add to
input1.txt is the same as before; Word Count Example.
```

```
vi /cdh/input/input1.txt
Word Count Example
:wq
```

The text to add to input2.txt is shown in Figure 2-52.

Figure 2-52. *Hadoop Streaming input file input2.txt*

Put the input text files into the HDFS input directory.

```
hdfs dfs -put /cdh/input/* hdfs://10.0.2.15:8020/cdh/input
```

Next, run the hadoop jar command using the hadoop-streaming-2.6.0-mr1-cdh5.4.7.jar file as an arg. The syntax for Hadoop Streaming is as follows; only input and output are required.

```
[root@localhost cdh]# hadoop jar $HADOOP_HOME/contrib/streaming/hadoop-streaming-2.6.0-mr1-
cdh5.4.7.jar -info
Usage: $HADOOP_HOME/bin/hadoop jar \
        $HADOOP_HOME/hadoop-streaming.jar [options]
Options:
  -input     <path>     DFS input file(s) for the Map step
  -output    <path>     DFS output directory for the Reduce step
  -mapper    <cmd|JavaClassName> The streaming command to run
  -combiner  <cmd|JavaClassName> The streaming command to run
  -reducer   <cmd|JavaClassName> The streaming command to run
  -file      <file>     File/dir to be shipped in the Job jar file
  -inputformat TextInputFormat(default)|SequenceFileAsTextInputFormat|JavaClassName
Optional.
  -outputformat TextOutputFormat(default)|JavaClassName  Optional.
  -partitioner JavaClassName  Optional.
  -numReduceTasks <num>  Optional.
  -inputreader <spec>  Optional.
  -cmdenv    <n>=<v>    Optional. Pass env.var to streaming commands
  -mapdebug <path>  Optional. To run this script when a map task fails
  -reducedebug <path>  Optional. To run this script when a reduce task fails
  -io <identifier>  Optional.
  -verbose


Generic options supported are
-conf <configuration file>     specify an application configuration file
-D <property=value>            use value for given property
-fs <local|namenode:port>      specify a namenode
-jt <local|resourcemanager:port>    specify a ResourceManager
-files <comma separated list of files>    specify comma separated files to be copied to the
                                          map reduce cluster
-libjars <comma separated list of jars>   specify comma separated jar files to include in
                                          the classpath.
-archives <comma separated list of archives>   specify comma separated archives to be
                                                unarchived on the compute machines.


The general command line syntax is
bin/hadoop command [genericOptions] [commandOptions]
```

Run a trivial Hadoop Streaming example with the Mapper as the –cat script in the //hadoop-2.6.0-cdh5.4.7/src/hadoop-tools/hadoop-streaming/src/test/bin directory. The Reducer should be the Linux word count script wc, which outputs the newline count, word count, and byte count in the following format.

```
newlinecount wordcount bytecount
```

Run the following hadoop jar command for the Hadoop Streaming jar.

```
hadoop jar $HADOOP_HOME/contrib/streaming/hadoop-streaming-2.6.0-mr1-cdh5.4.7.jar -input
hdfs://10.0.2.15:8020/cdh/input -output
hdfs://10.0.2.15:8020/cdh/output -mapper cat -reducer /usr/bin/wc
```

The hadoop jar command is shown in a Linux shell in Figure 2-53.

```
[root@localhost cdh]# hadoop jar $HADOOP_HOME/contrib/streaming/hadoop-streaming
-2.6.0-mr1-cdh5.4.7.jar -input hdfs://10.0.2.15:8020/cdh/input -output hdfs://10
.0.2.15:8020/cdh/output -mapper cat -reducer /usr/bin/wc
```

Figure 2-53. *Running a Hadoop Streaming application*

The output from the hadoop jar command is shown in Figure 2-54.

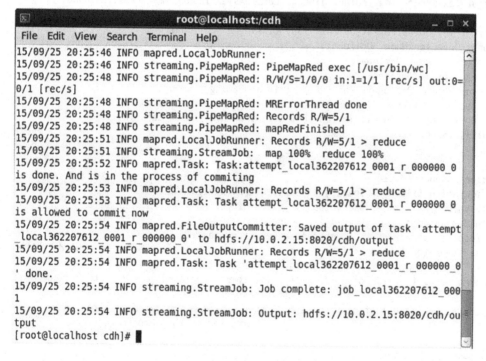

Figure 2-54. *Output from the Hadoop Streaming application*

List the output files generated with the FS shell command -ls.

```
hdfs dfs -ls  hdfs://10.0.2.15:8020/cdh/output
```

Two files—_SUCCESS and part-00000—are listed, as shown in Figure 2-55.

```
|[root@localhost cdh]# hdfs dfs -ls  hdfs://10.0.2.15:8020/cdh/output
Found 2 items
-rw-r--r--   1 root hadoop          0 2015-09-25 20:25 hdfs://10.0.2.15:8020/cdh
/output/_SUCCESS
-rw-r--r--   1 root hadoop         25 2015-09-25 20:25 hdfs://10.0.2.15:8020/cdh
/output/part-00000
```

Figure 2-55. *Listing the files generated via the Hadoop Streaming application*

Run the FS shell command –cat to list the result of the Hadoop Streaming output to the part-r-00000 file.

hdfs dfs -cat hdfs://10.0.2.15:8020/cdh/output/part-00000

The result of Hadoop Streaming is listed in Figure 2-56.

```
|^C[root@localhost cdh]# hdfs dfs -cat hdfs://10.0.2.15:8020/cdh/output/part-0000
|0
|      5       7      51
|[root@localhost cdh]# █
```

Figure 2-56. *Result from the Hadoop Streaming application*

The output indicates that the input has five new lines, seven words, and 51 bytes.

Summary

This chapter introduced the Apache Hadoop components HDFS and MapReduce. It discussed the different MapReduce frameworks called MR1 and MR2, also called YARN. It discussed the standalone and pseudo-distributed modes of the Hadoop cluster. It also demonstrated the different MR frameworks and cluster modes using the Grep and word count examples, which are packaged in the Hadoop distribution. The next chapter discusses the Apache Hive.

PART II

Storing & Querying

CHAPTER 3

Apache Hive

Apache Hive is a data warehouse framework for querying and managing large datasets stored in Hadoop distributed filesystems (HDFS). Hive also provides a SQL-like query language called HiveQL. The HiveQL queries may be run in the Hive CLI shell. By default, Hive stores data in the HDFS, but also supports the Amazon S3 filesystem.

Hive stores data in tables. A Hive table is an abstraction and the metadata for a Hive table is stored in an embedded Derby database called a Derby metastore. Other databases such as MySQL and Oracle Database could also be configured as the Hive metastore. The Apache Hive architecture is illustrated in Figure 3-1.

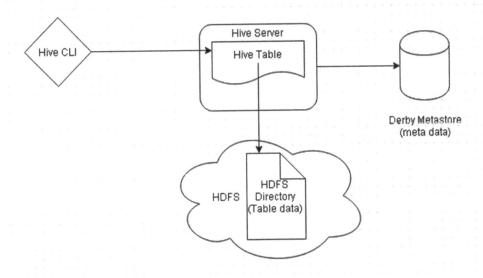

Figure 3-1. *Apache Hive architecture*

© Deepak Vohra 2016
D. Vohra, *Practical Hadoop Ecosystem*, DOI 10.1007/978-1-4842-2199-0_3

Hive supports two types of tables: managed tables and external tables. A managed table is managed by the Hive framework. When a Hive-managed table is deleted, the table's data and the metadata are deleted. In contrast, for a Hive external table, Hive manages only the metadata and the data is stored in some external location not managed by Hive. That location is external to the Hive framework but not external to HDFS, as data for a Hive external table is also stored in HDFS. When a Hive external table is deleted, only the metadata is deleted. The data is retained.

This chapter covers the following topics:

- Setting up the environment
- Configuring Hadoop
- Configuring Hive
- Starting HDFS
- Starting the Hive server
- Starting the Hive CLI
- Creating a database
- Using a database
- Creating a managed table
- Loading data into a table
- Creating a table using LIKE
- Adding data to a table using queries
- Adding data with INSERT INTO TABLE
- Adding data with INSERT OVERWRITE
- Creating a table using AS SELECT
- Altering a table
- Truncating a table
- Dropping a table
- Creating an external table

Setting the Environment

The following software is required for this chapter.

- Apache Hadoop
- Apache Hive
- Java 7

This chapter uses the same setup as Chapter 1 and shows you how to add or install Apache Hive as additional software. In case you did not follow along in Chapter 1 and did not install the software, the procedure is repeated here briefly.

First, create a directory (/cdh, for example) and set its permissions to global (777).

```
mkdir /cdh
chmod -R 777 /cdh
cd /cdh
```

Download and install the Java 7 tar file.

```
tar -xvf jdk-7u55-linux-i586.gz
```

Download the CDH 5.4.7 Hadoop 2.6.0 tar file and extract the file to the /cdh directory.

```
/cdh>wget http://archive-primary.cloudera.com/cdh5/cdh/5/hadoop-2.6.0-cdh5.4.7.tar.gz
/cdh>tar -xvf hadoop-2.6.0-cdh5.4.7.tar.gz
```

Create symlinks for the Hadoop bin and conf directories. Symlinks are required because the CDH distributions can vary slightly with version and some directory and file references are preconfigured. For example, the configuration directory is expected to be $HADOOP_HOME/conf and the directory with the runnable scripts is expected to be $HADOOP_HOME/bin.

```
ln -s /cdh/hadoop-2.6.0-cdh5.4.7/bin /cdh/hadoop-2.6.0-cdh5.4.7/share/hadoop/mapreduce1/bin
ln -s /cdh/hadoop-2.6.0-cdh5.4.7/etc/hadoop  /cdh/hadoop-2.6.0-cdh5.4.7/share/hadoop/
mapreduce1/conf
```

Download and extract the Apache Hive tar file.

```
wget http://archive-primary.cloudera.com/cdh5/cdh/5/hive-0.13.1-cdh5.3.6.tar.gz
tar -xvf hive-0.13.1-cdh5.3.6.tar.gz
```

Set the following environment variables for Hadoop, Hive, and Java in the bash shell.

```
vi ~/.bashrc
export HADOOP_PREFIX=/cdh/ hadoop-2.6.0-cdh5.4.7
export HADOOP_CONF_DIR=$HADOOP_PREFIX/etc/hadoop
export HADOOP_COMMON_HOME=$HADOOP_PREFIX/share/hadoop/common
export HADOOP_HDFS_HOME=$HADOOP_PREFIX/share/hadoop/hdfs
export HIVE_HOME=/cdh/hive-0.13.1-cdh5.3.6
export HIVE_CONF=$HIVE_HOME/conf
export JAVA_HOME=/cdh/jdk1.7.0_55
export HADOOP_MAPRED_HOME=$HADOOP_PREFIX//share/hadoop/mapreduce1
export HADOOP_HOME=$HADOOP_PREFIX/share/hadoop/mapreduce1
export HADOOP_CLASSPATH=$HADOOP_HOME/*:$HADOOP_HOME/lib/*:$JAVA_HOME/lib/*:$HIVE_HOME/
lib/*:$HADOOP_CONF_DIR:$HADOOP_COMMON_HOME/*:$HADOOP_COMMON_HOME/lib/*:$HADOOP_HDFS_
HOME/*:$HADOOP_HDFS_HOME/lib/*:$HADOOP_MAPRED_HOME:$HADOOP_MAPRED_HOME/bin
export PATH=/usr/lib/qt-3.3/bin:/usr/local/sbin:/usr/sbin:/sbin:/usr/local/bin:/usr/bin:/
bin:$HADOOP_HOME/bin:$HADOOP_MAPRED_HOME/bin:$JAVA_HOME/bin:$HIVE_HOME/bin
export CLASSPATH=$HADOOP_CLASSPATH
export HADOOP_NAMENODE_USER=hadoop
export HADOOP_DATANODE_USER=hadoop
```

This section installed Apache Hadoop and Apache Hive and set the environment variables. The next section shows you how to configure Apache Hadoop.

Configuring Hadoop

Configuring Hadoop is done the same way as in Chapter 1. If you already installed and configured Hadoop, you can skip this section.

In the Hadoop core-site.xml configuration file, set the fs.defaultFS property to the NameNode URI hdfs://10.0.2.15:8020, which can vary for different users based on the hostname or IP address. Set the hadoop.tmp.dir property for the Hadoop temporary directory to /var/lib/hadoop-0.20/cache. The configuration properties may be set in vi.

```
vi   $HADOOP_CONF_DIR/core-site.xml
<?xml-stylesheet type="text/xsl" href="configuration.xsl"?>
<!-- Put site-specific property overrides in this file. -->
<configuration>
<property>
  <name>fs.defaultFS</name>
    <value>hdfs://10.0.2.15:8020</value>
    </property>
 <property>
    <name>hadoop.tmp.dir</name>
    <value>/var/lib/hadoop-0.20/cache</value>
  </property>
</configuration>
```

Remove the /var/lib/hadoop-0.20/cache directory if it was previously set for some other application and Apache Hadoop is being reinstalled. Create the /var/lib/hadoop-0.20/cache directory structure and set its permissions to global (777).

```
rm -rf   /var/lib/hadoop-0.20/cache
mkdir -p /var/lib/hadoop-0.20/cache
chmod -R 777   /var/lib/hadoop-0.20/cache
```

Set the dfs.namenode.name.dir configuration property for the NameNode storage directory to /data/1/ dfs/nn. Since a single node is being used, set the dfs.replication to 1. Set the dfs.permissions to false to avoid permissions checking other than the group, mode, and owner permissions, which are still verified.

```
vi $HADOOP_CONF_DIR/hdfs-site.xml
<?xml version="1.0" encoding="UTF-8"?>
<?xml-stylesheet type="text/xsl" href="configuration.xsl"?>
<!-- Put site-specific property overrides in this file. -->
<configuration>
<property>
 <name>dfs.permissions.superusergroup</name>
  <value>hadoop</value>
  </property><property>
   <name>dfs.namenode.name.dir</name>
    <value>/data/1/dfs/nn</value>
    </property>
        <property>
            <name>dfs.replication</name>
                <value>1</value>
        </property>
```

```
<property>
<name>dfs.permissions</name>
<value>false</value>
</property>
</configuration>
```

Remove the NameNode storage directory /data/1/dfs/nn if you previously created it for some other application. Create the /data/1/dfs/nn directory and set its permissions to global (777).

```
rm -rf   /data/1/dfs/nn
mkdir -p /data/1/dfs/nn
chmod -R 777 /data/1/dfs/nn
```

Configuring Hive

Since you did not use Apache Hive in Chapter 1, don't skip this section. Apache Hive is configured in the hive-site.xml configuration file. Create the hive-site.xml file from the template file.

```
cp /cdh/hive-0.13.1-cdh5.3.6/conf/hive-default.xml.template /cdh/hive-0.13.1-cdh5.3.6/conf/
hive-site.xml
```

Open the hive-site.xml file in the vi editor.

```
vi /cdh/hive-0.13.1-cdh5.3.6/conf/hive-site.xml
```

Table 3-1 lists the properties in the hive-site.xml file.

Table 3-1. *Configuration Properties for the hive-site.xml File*

Property	Description	Value
hive.metastore.warehouse.dir	The HDFS directory in which the Hive table data is stored.	hdfs://10.0.2.15:8020/user/hive/warehouse
hive.metastore.uris	The URI for clients to access the Hive metastore.	thrift://localhost:10000

The hostname and IP address for the Hive warehouse directory can be different for different users. The default template (hive-site.xml) contains several settings; the configuration properties that need to be modified in hive-site.xml are as follows:

```
<?xml version="1.0"?>
<?xml-stylesheet type="text/xsl" href="configuration.xsl"?>
<configuration>
<property>
  <name>hive.metastore.warehouse.dir</name>
  <value>hdfs://10.0.2.15:8020/user/hive/warehouse</value>
</property>
<property>
  <name>hive.metastore.uris</name>
  <value>thrift://localhost:10000</value>
</property>
</configuration>
```

Starting HDFS

If you're using the Apache Hadoop installation from Chapter 1 and you skipped the "Configuring Hadoop" section, you don't have to reformat the Hadoop NameNode. The following command may be skipped. The NameNode could still be reformatted, but is not required if you're using the Chapter 1 Hadoop installation.

```
hdfs namenode -format
```

Start the NameNode with the following command.

```
hdfs namenode
```

Start the DataNode with the following command.

```
hdfs datanode
```

Create the HDFS directory configured in the hive.metastore.warehouse.dir property and set the directory permissions to g+w with hadoop dfs. The equivalent hdfs dfs command may be used instead of hadoop dfs in the following and subsequent commands.

```
hadoop dfs -mkdir  -p  hdfs://10.0.2.15:8020/user/hive/warehouse
hadoop dfs -chmod -R g+w hdfs://10.0.2.15:8020/user/hive/warehouse
```

Starting the Hive Server

Next, start the Hive server with the following command.

```
hive --service hiveserver
```

The Hive Thrift Server is started, as shown in Figure 3-2. The Hive server makes it possible for clients to submit requests to Hive.

```
[root@localhost cdh]# hive --service hiveserver
Starting Hive Thrift Server
```

Figure 3-2. *Starting the Hive Thrift Server*

Starting the Hive CLI

Hive CLI is a shell utility for running Hive queries and other HiveQL statements. Start Hive CLI with the following command.

```
>hive
```

Hive CLI is started, as shown in Figure 3-3. The hive> command prompt is displayed.

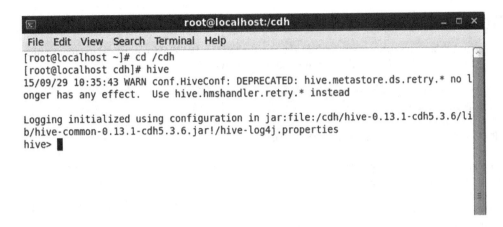

Figure 3-3. *Starting the Hive command line interface (CLI)*

Set the database as default with the following command.

```
use default;
```

Run the show tables command to list the tables in the default database. The tables are listed, as shown in Figure 3-4.

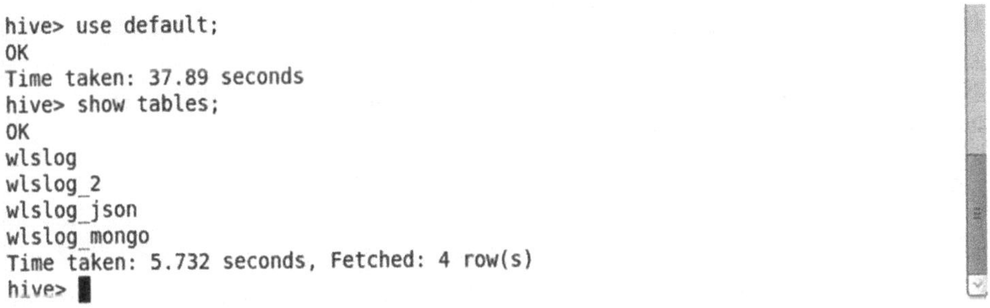

```
hive> use default;
OK
Time taken: 37.89 seconds
hive> show tables;
OK
wlslog
wlslog_2
wlslog_json
wlslog_mongo
Time taken: 5.732 seconds, Fetched: 4 row(s)
hive>
```

Figure 3-4. *Setting the default database and listing the Hive tables*

Initially, no tables may be listed, as shown in Figure 3-5.

```
hive> show tables
    > ;
OK
Time taken: 43.093 seconds
hive>
```

Figure 3-5. *No tables listed*

Creating a Database

If you're going to use a database other than the default, run the CREATE DATABASE command to create a new database. The syntax for the CREATE DATABASE command is as follows.

```
CREATE (DATABASE|SCHEMA) [IF NOT EXISTS] database_name
  [COMMENT database_comment]
  [LOCATION hdfs_path]
  [WITH DBPROPERTIES (property_name=property_value, ...)];
```

For example, to create a database called wlslog at the HDFS location 'hdfs://10.0.2.15:8020/user/hive/warehouse', you use the following command.

```
CREATE DATABASE IF NOT EXISTS WLSLOG
  LOCATION 'hdfs://10.0.2.15:8020/user/hive/warehouse';
```

The wlslog database is created, as shown in Figure 3-6. To avoid open files exceeding the limit, you might need to increase the user file limit (ulimit) setting in /etc/security/limits.conf to 32768.

```
hive> CREATE DATABASE IF NOT EXISTS WLSLOG
    >    LOCATION 'hdfs://10.0.2.15:8020/user/hive/warehouse';
OK
Time taken: 19.987 seconds
hive>
```

Figure 3-6. *Creating the Hive table WLSLOG*

Run the DESCRIBE DATABASE command to list the database name, comments, and location. The EXTENDED clause includes the database properties.

```
DESC DATABASE EXTENDED WLSLOG;
```

The database name, properties, and location are listed, as shown in Figure 3-7.

```
hive> DESC DATABASE EXTENDED WLSLOG;
OK
wlslog              hdfs://10.0.2.15:8020/user/hive/warehouse        root    USER
Time taken: 2.01 seconds, Fetched: 1 row(s)
hive>
```

Figure 3-7. *Describing the WLSLOG database*

Using a Database

Set the database as the current database for subsequent HiveQL statements using the USE database_name command. For example, set the database to WLSLOG as follows.

```
USE WLSLOG;
```

An output of OK indicates that the current table has been set to WLSLOG, as shown in Figure 3-8.

```
hive> USE WLSLOG;
OK
Time taken: 0.302 seconds
hive>
```

Figure 3-8. *Setting the database to use*

To use the default database, run the following command.

```
USE DEFAULT;
```

The current database is set to the default, as shown in Figure 3-9.

```
hive> USE DEFAULT;
OK
Time taken: 0.073 seconds
hive>
```

Figure 3-9. *Setting the current database to the default*

Creating a Managed Table

In this section, you create a managed table to store some data. The data is stored in a text file in HDFS and takes the following format; the complete data file is listed later. The fields in a row are delimited by a , (a comma) and each row is terminated with a newline character (\n).

```
Apr-8-2014-7:06:16-PM-PDT,Notice,WebLogicServer,AdminServer,BEA-000365,Server state changed
to STANDBY
```

Create a managed table called wlslog with the time_stamp, category, type, servername, code, and msg fields, each of type string. The ROW FORMAT is set to DELIMITED, which is used for delimited files. The FIELDS TERMINATED BY clause is set to , and the LINES TERMINATE BY clause is set to \n.

```
CREATE  TABLE  wlslog(time_stamp STRING,category STRING, type STRING,servername STRING,code
STRING,msg STRING) ROW FORMAT DELIMITED FIELDS TERMINATED BY ',' LINES TERMINATED BY '\n';
```

Run the HiveQL statement in Hive CLI to create a managed table, as shown in Figure 3-10.

```
hive> CREATE  TABLE  wlslog(time_stamp STRING,category STRING, type STRING,serve
rname STRING,code STRING,msg STRING) ROW FORMAT DELIMITED FIELDS TERMINATED BY '
,' LINES TERMINATED BY '\n';
OK
Time taken: 14.405 seconds
```

Figure 3-10. *Creating a Hive-managed table*

Subsequently run the show tables command. The wlslog table should be listed, as shown in Figure 3-11.

```
hive> show tables;
OK
wlslog
Time taken: 0.662 seconds, Fetched: 1 row(s)
hive>
```

Figure 3-11. *Listing the wlslog table*

Initially, the wlslog is empty. If you run a SELECT query statement on the wlslog table, no rows would be listed, as shown in Figure 3-12.

```
hive> select * from wlslog;
OK
Time taken: 11.335 seconds
hive>
```

Figure 3-12. *Running a SQL query on the wlslog table*

The wlslog table is created in the Hive warehouse directory 'hdfs://10.0.2.15:8020/user/hive/warehouse'. List the items in the 'hdfs://10.0.2.15:8020/user/hive/warehouse' directory in HDFS using the following command.

```
hadoop dfs -ls hdfs://10.0.2.15:8020/user/hive/warehouse
```

The hdfs://10.0.2.15:8020/user/hive/warehouse/wlslog directory should be listed, as shown in Figure 3-13, because the managed tables in the default database are created in the directory specified in the hive.metastore.warehouse.dir property in the hive-site.xml file.

```
[root@localhost cdh]# hadoop dfs -ls hdfs://10.0.2.15:8020/user/hive/warehouse
Found 1 items
drwxrwxr-x   - root hadoop          0 2015-09-28 15:56 hdfs://10.0.2.15:8020/use
r/hive/warehouse/wlslog
[root@localhost cdh]#
```

Figure 3-13. *Listing the HDFS subdirectories in the Hive warehouse directory*

Loading Data Into a Table

Initially the managed table wlslog is empty. You will load data into the wlslog table. Create a file called wlslog.txt and copy the following data into that file.

```
Apr-8-2014-7:06:16-PM-PDT,Notice,WebLogicServer,AdminServer,BEA-000365,Server state changed
to STANDBY
Apr-8-2014-7:06:17-PM-PDT,Notice,WebLogicServer,AdminServer,BEA-000365,Server state changed
to STARTING
Apr-8-2014-7:06:18-PM-PDT,Notice,WebLogicServer,AdminServer,BEA-000365,Server state changed
to ADMIN
```

```
Apr-8-2014-7:06:19-PM-PDT,Notice,WebLogicServer,AdminServer,BEA-000365,Server state changed
to RESUMING
Apr-8-2014-7:06:20-PM-PDT,Notice,WebLogicServer,AdminServer,BEA-000331,Started WebLogic
AdminServer
Apr-8-2014-7:06:21-PM-PDT,Notice,WebLogicServer,AdminServer,BEA-000365,Server state changed
to RUNNING
Apr-8-2014-7:06:22-PM-PDT,Notice,WebLogicServer,AdminServer,BEA-000360,Server started in
RUNNING mode
```

Run the LOAD DATA command, which has the following syntax, in Hive CLI.

```
LOAD DATA [LOCAL] INPATH 'filepath' [OVERWRITE] INTO TABLE tablename [PARTITION
(partcol1=val1, partcol2=val2 ...)]
```

The LOCAL clause is used if the filesystem is local. The file's path could be a relative path, an absolute path, or a scheme-prefixed URI such as a hdfs: scheme path for an HDFS URI. The OVERWRITE clause should be used if the data in the table will be deleted and replaced with the data being loaded. The OVERWRITE clause does not imply an update. Run the following command to load data from the wlslog.txt file. Include the LOCAL clause because the wlslog.txt file is in the /cdh directory, which is in the local filesystem. Include the OVERWRITE clause to replace the data in the wlslog table.

```
LOAD DATA LOCAL INPATH '/cdh/wlslog.txt' OVERWRITE INTO TABLE wlslog;
```

Data from the wlslog.txt file is loaded into the wlslog table, as shown in Figure 3-14.

```
hive> LOAD DATA LOCAL INPATH '/cdh/wlslog.txt' OVERWRITE INTO TABLE wlslog;
Copying data from file:/cdh/wlslog.txt
Copying file: file:/cdh/wlslog.txt
Loading data to table default.wlslog
Table default.wlslog stats: [numFiles=1, numRows=0, totalSize=724, rawDataSize=0
]
OK
Time taken: 29.294 seconds
hive> █
```

Figure 3-14. Loading data into the wlslog Hive table

Subsequently, run the following SELECT query on the wlslog table.

```
select * from wlslog;
```

The data loaded from the wlslog.txt file is listed, as shown in Figure 3-15. The seven rows of data in wlslog.txt are loaded into seven rows of data in the wlslog table.

```
hive> select * from wlslog;
OK
Apr-8-2014-7:06:16-PM-PDT          Notice  WebLogicServer  AdminServer    BEA-0003
65       Server state changed to STANDBY
Apr-8-2014-7:06:17-PM-PDT          Notice  WebLogicServer  AdminServer    BEA-0003
65       Server state changed to STARTING
Apr-8-2014-7:06:18-PM-PDT          Notice  WebLogicServer  AdminServer    BEA-0003
65       Server state changed to ADMIN
Apr-8-2014-7:06:19-PM-PDT          Notice  WebLogicServer  AdminServer    BEA-0003
65       Server state changed to RESUMING
Apr-8-2014-7:06:20-PM-PDT          Notice  WebLogicServer  AdminServer    BEA-0003
31       Started WebLogic AdminServer
Apr-8-2014-7:06:21-PM-PDT          Notice  WebLogicServer  AdminServer    BEA-0003
65       Server state changed to RUNNING
Apr-8-2014-7:06:22-PM-PDT          Notice  WebLogicServer  AdminServer    BEA-0003
60       Server started in RUNNING mode
Time taken: 27.315 seconds, Fetched: 7 row(s)
```

Figure 3-15. Querying the Hive table data

Creating a Table Using LIKE

If you wanted to copy only the table definition and not the table data from a table, you use the LIKE clause of the CREATE TABLE statement. For example, consider the wlslog table. The following HiveQL statement creates a table called wlslog_2, which has the same table definition as the wlslog table, but the data from the wlslog table is not copied.

CREATE TABLE wlslog_2 LIKE wlslog;

The wlslog_2 table is created, as shown in Figure 3-16.

```
hive> CREATE TABLE wlslog_2 LIKE wlslog;
OK
Time taken: 2.334 seconds
```

Figure 3-16. Creating the Hive table wlslog_2 LIKE wlslog

Initially, the wlslog_2 table is empty. Run a SELECT statement and no rows should be listed, as shown in Figure 3-17.

```
hive> select * from wlslog_2;
OK
Time taken: 1.275 seconds
hive> ▮
```

Figure 3-17. Running a query on the empty wlslog_2 table

Adding Data Into a Table from Queries

In an earlier section, you saw how to load data into an empty table using the LOAD DATA statement. HiveQL also enables you to insert data into a Hive table using queries. Two forms of INSERT statements are provided to insert data into a Hive table, as listed in Table 3-2.

Table 3-2. *Two Forms of INSERT Statements*

INSERT Form	Syntax	Description	TBLPROPERTIES Immutable
INSERT OVERWRITE TABLE	INSERT OVERWRITE TABLE tablename1 [PARTITION (partcol1=val1, partcol2=val2 ...) [IF NOT EXISTS]] select_ statement1 FROM from_ statement;	Overwrites data in a table unless IF NOT EXISTS is specified for a partition. The data added is selected using a SELECT statement.	The immutable property is supported as of Hive 0.13.0 but does not affect INSERT OVERWRITE TABLE. The default is "immutable"="false".
INSERT INTO TABLE	INSERT INTO TABLE tablename1 [PARTITION (partcol1=val1, partcol2=val2 ...)] select_statement1 FROM from_statement;	Appends data into a table or partition. The existing data is retained.	If TBLPROPERTIES ("immutable"="true") is set and a table already has some data, the new data is not added with INSERT INTO statement. If a table is empty, the new data is added with INSERT INTO even if TBLPROPERTIES ("immutable"="true").

The following subsections illustrate how to add data to the empty table called wlslog_2 using each of the INSERT statements.

Adding Data Using INSERT INTO TABLE

The wlslog_2 table was created using the LIKE clause and is initially empty. Using the INSERT INTO statement, you can add data to the wlslog_2 table by selecting from the wlslog table using a SELECT statement.

```
INSERT INTO TABLE wlslog_2  SELECT time_stamp,category,type,servername,code,msg FROM wlslog;
```

The INSERT INTO statement runs using MapReduce jobs. As indicated in the output shown in Figure 3-18, three jobs are started.

```
hive> INSERT INTO TABLE wlslog_2  SELECT time_stamp,category,type,servername,cod
e,msg FROM wlslog;
Total jobs = 3
Launching Job 1 out of 3
Number of reduce tasks is set to 0 since there's no reduce operator
█
```

Figure 3-18. *Running the INSERT INTO statement*

Data is loaded into the wlslog_2 table, as shown in Figure 3-19.

```
Job running in-process (local Hadoop)
Hadoop job information for null: number of mappers: 0; number of reducers: 0
2015-09-28 16:12:57,292 null map = 0%,  reduce = 0%
2015-09-28 16:13:10,319 null map = 100%,  reduce = 0%
Ended Job = job_local1980456990_0001
Execution completed successfully
MapredLocal task succeeded
Stage-4 is selected by condition resolver.
Stage-3 is filtered out by condition resolver.
Stage-5 is filtered out by condition resolver.
Moving data to: hdfs://10.0.2.15:8020/tmp/hive-root/hive_2015-09-28_16-10-03_070
_7287506800930696686-1/-ext-10000
Loading data to table default.wlslog_2
Table default.wlslog_2 stats: [numFiles=1, numRows=7, totalSize=717, rawDataSize
=710]
OK
Time taken: 213.411 seconds
hive> █
```

Figure 3-19. *Loading data into the default.wlslog_2 table*

Subsequently, run a SELECT query on the wlslog_2 table. The seven rows of data copied from the wlslog table are listed, as shown in Figure 3-20.

```
root@localhost:/cdh                              _ □ ×

File  Edit  View  Search  Terminal  Help
2015-09-28 16:13:10,319 null map = 100%,   reduce = 0%
Ended Job = job_local1980456990_0001
Execution completed successfully
MapredLocal task succeeded
Stage-4 is selected by condition resolver.
Stage-3 is filtered out by condition resolver.
Stage-5 is filtered out by condition resolver.
Moving data to: hdfs://10.0.2.15:8020/tmp/hive-root/hive_2015-09-28_16-10-03_070
_7287506800930696686-1/-ext-10000
Loading data to table default.wlslog_2
Table default.wlslog_2 stats: [numFiles=1, numRows=7, totalSize=717, rawDataSize
=710]
OK
Time taken: 213.411 seconds
hive> select * from wlslog_2;
OK
Apr-8-2014-7:06:16-PM-PDT        Notice  WebLogicServer  AdminServer     BEA-0003
65      Server state changed to STANDBY
Apr-8-2014-7:06:17-PM-PDT        Notice  WebLogicServer  AdminServer     BEA-0003
65      Server state changed to STARTING
Apr-8-2014-7:06:18-PM-PDT        Notice  WebLogicServer  AdminServer     BEA-0003
65      Server state changed to ADMIN
Apr-8-2014-7:06:19-PM-PDT        Notice  WebLogicServer  AdminServer     BEA-0003
65      Server state changed to RESUMING
Apr-8-2014-7:06:20-PM-PDT        Notice  WebLogicServer  AdminServer     BEA-0003
31      Started WebLogic AdminServer
Apr-8-2014-7:06:21-PM-PDT        Notice  WebLogicServer  AdminServer     BEA-0003
65      Server state changed to RUNNING
Apr-8-2014-7:06:22-PM-PDT        Notice  WebLogicServer  AdminServer     BEA-0003
60      Server started in RUNNING mode
Time taken: 0.714 seconds, Fetched: 7 row(s)
hive> ▮
```

Figure 3-20. *Running a query on the wlslog_2 table*

Adding Data Using INSERT OVERWRITE

This section shows you how to use the INSERT OVERWRITE statement to add data in the wlslog_2 table. If the wlslog_2 already has data (as it would if the previous statement was run), drop the table and create it again. A table is dropped using the DROP Table statement.

DROP TABLE wlslog_2;

Run the following INSERT OVERWRITE statement to add data to the empty wlslog_2 table.

INSERT OVERWRITE TABLE wlslog_2 SELECT time_stamp,category,type,servername,code,msg FROM wlslog;

The INSERT OVERWRITE statement also runs MapReduce jobs to add data, as shown in Figure 3-21.

223

```
hive> CREATE TABLE wlslog_2 LIKE wlslog;
OK
Time taken: 2.334 seconds
hive> INSERT OVERWRITE TABLE wlslog_2  SELECT time_stamp,category,type,servernam
e,code,msg FROM wlslog;
Total jobs = 3
Launching Job 1 out of 3
Number of reduce tasks is set to 0 since there's no reduce operator
```

Figure 3-21. *Running the INSERT OVERWRITE statement*

Data is loaded into the `wlslog_2` table, as shown in Figure 3-22.

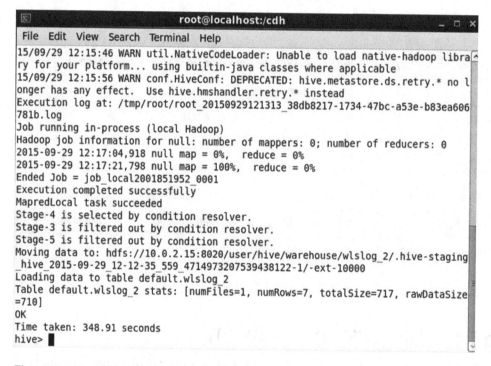

Figure 3-22. *Loading data into the wlslog_2 table*

Run a SQL statement to query the `wlslog_2` table.

```
select * from wlslog_2;
```

The `wlslog_2` table data is listed, as shown in Figure 3-23.

```
hive> select * from wlslog_2;
OK
Apr-8-2014-7:06:16-PM-PDT        Notice  WebLogicServer  AdminServer     BEA-0003
65      Server state changed to STANDBY
Apr-8-2014-7:06:17-PM-PDT        Notice  WebLogicServer  AdminServer     BEA-0003
65      Server state changed to STARTING
Apr-8-2014-7:06:18-PM-PDT        Notice  WebLogicServer  AdminServer     BEA-0003
65      Server state changed to ADMIN
Apr-8-2014-7:06:19-PM-PDT        Notice  WebLogicServer  AdminServer     BEA-0003
65      Server state changed to RESUMING
Apr-8-2014-7:06:20-PM-PDT        Notice  WebLogicServer  AdminServer     BEA-0003
31      Started WebLogic AdminServer
Apr-8-2014-7:06:21-PM-PDT        Notice  WebLogicServer  AdminServer     BEA-0003
65      Server state changed to RUNNING
Apr-8-2014-7:06:22-PM-PDT        Notice  WebLogicServer  AdminServer     BEA-0003
60      Server started in RUNNING mode
Time taken: 5.767 seconds, Fetched: 7 row(s)
hive> █
```

Figure 3-23. *Querying the wlslog_2 table*

Creating a Table Using CREATE TABLE AS SELECT

Sometimes an existing table has the required data and you want to create a new table by selecting some or all of the data from the existing table. HiveQL provides the CREATE TABLE AS SELECT statement to create a table by selecting data from an existing table. The STORED AS clause in a CREATE TABLE statement specifies that the data be stored as a text file. The TEXTFILE is the default storage format. For compressed storage, use the SEQUENCEFILE file format. For ORC file format, use STORED AS ORC. For Parquet columnar format, use STORED AS PARQUET.

The target table should not be a partitioned table, an external table, or a list-bucketing table. The CREATE TABLE statement should not include column names for the target table. The target table gets the same column names and column types as the table in the SELECT statement.

As an example, create a table called wlslog_copy by selecting the data from the wlslog table.

```
CREATE TABLE wlslog_copy
    ROW FORMAT DELIMITED FIELDS TERMINATED BY ',' LINES TERMINATED BY '\n'
    STORED AS TEXTFILE
    AS
SELECT time_stamp,category,type,servername,code,msg
FROM wlslog;
```

MapReduce jobs is started, as shown in Figure 3-24.

```
hive> CREATE TABLE wlslog_copy
    >     ROW FORMAT DELIMITED FIELDS TERMINATED BY ',' LINES TERMINATED BY '\n'
    >     STORED AS TEXTFILE
    >     AS
    > SELECT time_stamp,category,type,servername,code,msg
    > FROM wlslog;
Total jobs = 3
Launching Job 1 out of 3
Number of reduce tasks is set to 0 since there's no reduce operator
```

Figure 3-24. *Creating a Hive table with AS SELECT*

The wlslog_copy table is created, as shown in Figure 3-25.

```
Job running in-process (local Hadoop)
Hadoop job information for null: number of mappers: 0; number of reducers: 0
2015-09-28 16:06:59,005 null map = 0%,  reduce = 0%
2015-09-28 16:07:13,138 null map = 100%,  reduce = 0%
Ended Job = job_local1650395260_0001
Execution completed successfully
MapredLocal task succeeded
Stage-4 is selected by condition resolver.
Stage-3 is filtered out by condition resolver.
Stage-5 is filtered out by condition resolver.
Moving data to: hdfs://10.0.2.15:8020/tmp/hive-root/hive_2015-09-28_16-04-40_205
_8056077517151723327-1/-ext-10001
Moving data to: hdfs://10.0.2.15:8020/user/hive/warehouse/wlslog_copy
Table default.wlslog_copy stats: [numFiles=1, numRows=0, totalSize=717, rawDataS
ize=0]
OK
Time taken: 177.387 seconds
hive>
```

Figure 3-25. *Creating a Hive table called wlslog_copy*

Subsequently, run a SELECT query to list the data in the wlslog_copy table, as shown in Figure 3-26.

```
root@localhost:/cdh                    _ □ ×
File  Edit  View  Search  Terminal  Help
2015-09-28 16:07:13,138 null map = 100%,   reduce = 0%
Ended Job = job_local1650395260_0001
Execution completed successfully
MapredLocal task succeeded
Stage-4 is selected by condition resolver.
Stage-3 is filtered out by condition resolver.
Stage-5 is filtered out by condition resolver.
Moving data to: hdfs://10.0.2.15:8020/tmp/hive-root/hive_2015-09-28_16-04-40_205
_8056077517151723327-1/-ext-10001
Moving data to: hdfs://10.0.2.15:8020/user/hive/warehouse/wlslog_copy
Table default.wlslog_copy stats: [numFiles=1, numRows=0, totalSize=717, rawDataS
ize=0]
OK
Time taken: 177.387 seconds
hive> select * from wlslog_copy;
OK
Apr-8-2014-7:06:16-PM-PDT        Notice  WebLogicServer  AdminServer     BEA-0003
65      Server state changed to STANDBY
Apr-8-2014-7:06:17-PM-PDT        Notice  WebLogicServer  AdminServer     BEA-0003
65      Server state changed to STARTING
Apr-8-2014-7:06:18-PM-PDT        Notice  WebLogicServer  AdminServer     BEA-0003
65      Server state changed to ADMIN
Apr-8-2014-7:06:19-PM-PDT        Notice  WebLogicServer  AdminServer     BEA-0003
65      Server state changed to RESUMING
Apr-8-2014-7:06:20-PM-PDT        Notice  WebLogicServer  AdminServer     BEA-0003
31      Started WebLogic AdminServer
Apr-8-2014-7:06:21-PM-PDT        Notice  WebLogicServer  AdminServer     BEA-0003
65      Server state changed to RUNNING
Apr-8-2014-7:06:22-PM-PDT        Notice  WebLogicServer  AdminServer     BEA-0003
60      Server started in RUNNING mode
Time taken: 0.958 seconds, Fetched: 7 row(s)
hive>
```

Figure 3-26. *Querying a Hive table called wlslog_copy*

Altering a Table

The ALTER TABLE statement could be used to alter a table; for example, you can rename a table, alter table properties, alter table comment, add SerDe properties, or alter table storage properties.

As an example of ALTER TABLE, set the immutable property to true and alter a table comment for the wlslog_copy table.

```
ALTER TABLE wlslog_copy SET TBLPROPERTIES ("immutable"="true",'comment' = 'table altered');
```

As another example, set the field delimiter for the wlslog_copy table to /.
The table and SerDe properties are altered, as shown in Figure 3-27.

```
hive> ALTER TABLE wlslog_copy SET TBLPROPERTIES ("immutable"="true",'comment' =
'table altered');
OK
Time taken: 0.627 seconds
hive> ALTER TABLE wlslog_copy SET SERDEPROPERTIES ('field.delim' = '/');
OK
Time taken: 0.454 seconds
hive>
```

Figure 3-27. *Altering the Hive table called wlslog_copy*

The table and SerDe properties are altered without having to restart the Hive server. To demonstrate, run SELECT query statement on the wlslog_copy table. Because the field delimiter was set to /, the , is not used as a field delimiter and a complete row of data is interpreted as the first column value. The other columns values become NULL, as shown in Figure 3-28.

```
hive> ALTER TABLE wlslog_copy SET TBLPROPERTIES ("immutable"="true",'comment' =
'table altered');
OK
Time taken: 0.627 seconds
hive> ALTER TABLE wlslog_copy SET SERDEPROPERTIES ('field.delim' = '/');
OK
Time taken: 0.454 seconds
hive> select * from wlslog_copy;
OK
Apr-8-2014-7:06:16-PM-PDT,Notice,WebLogicServer,AdminServer,BEA-000365,Server st
ate changed to STANDBY NULL    NULL    NULL    NULL    NULL
Apr-8-2014-7:06:17-PM-PDT,Notice,WebLogicServer,AdminServer,BEA-000365,Server st
ate changed to STARTING NULL    NULL    NULL    NULL    NULL
Apr-8-2014-7:06:18-PM-PDT,Notice,WebLogicServer,AdminServer,BEA-000365,Server st
ate changed to ADMIN    NULL    NULL    NULL    NULL    NULL
Apr-8-2014-7:06:19-PM-PDT,Notice,WebLogicServer,AdminServer,BEA-000365,Server st
ate changed to RESUMING NULL    NULL    NULL    NULL    NULL
Apr-8-2014-7:06:20-PM-PDT,Notice,WebLogicServer,AdminServer,BEA-000331,Started W
ebLogic AdminServer    NULL    NULL    NULL    NULL    NULL
Apr-8-2014-7:06:21-PM-PDT,Notice,WebLogicServer,AdminServer,BEA-000365,Server st
ate changed to RUNNING NULL    NULL    NULL    NULL    NULL
Apr-8-2014-7:06:22-PM-PDT,Notice,WebLogicServer,AdminServer,BEA-000360,Server st
arted in RUNNING mode    NULL    NULL    NULL    NULL    NULL
Time taken: 0.185 seconds, Fetched: 7 row(s)
hive>
```

Figure 3-28. *Querying the altered wlslog_copy table*

Truncating a Table

The TRUNCATE TABLE statement removes all rows from a table but does not drop the table. The syntax for the TRUNCATE TABLE statement is as follows.

```
TRUNCATE TABLE table_name [PARTITION partition_spec];
```

As an example, truncate the wlslog_copy table.

```
TRUNCATE TABLE wlslog_copy;
```

Subsequently run a SELECT query.

```
select * from wlslog_copy;
```

Because the table rows have been removed, no rows are listed, as shown in Figure 3-29.

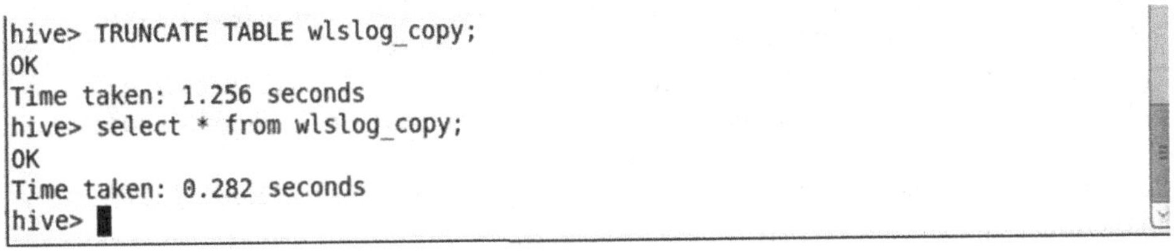

```
hive> TRUNCATE TABLE wlslog_copy;
OK
Time taken: 1.256 seconds
hive> select * from wlslog_copy;
OK
Time taken: 0.282 seconds
hive>
```

Figure 3-29. *Truncating a table*

Dropping a Table

You can drop a Hive table using the DROP TABLE statement, which has the following syntax.

```
DROP TABLE [IF EXISTS] table_name;
```

It is best to include the IF EXISTS clause, as without it, an error is generated if the table does not exist. As an example, drop the wlslog_copy table.

```
DROP TABLE IF EXISTS wlslog_copy;
```

Subsequently run the SHOW TABLES command. The wlslog_copy table is not listed, as shown in Figure 3-30.

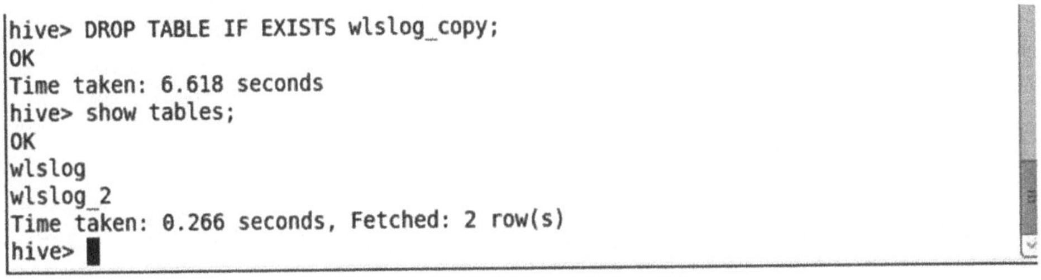

```
hive> DROP TABLE IF EXISTS wlslog_copy;
OK
Time taken: 6.618 seconds
hive> show tables;
OK
wlslog
wlslog_2
Time taken: 0.266 seconds, Fetched: 2 row(s)
hive>
```

Figure 3-30. *Dropping a Hive table*

Creating an External Table

As discussed, an external table differs from a managed table in that an external table is not managed by Hive and its data is isolated from the Hive framework. When an external table is deleted, its data is not deleted; only the table's metadata is deleted. This section shows you how to create an external table using a custom SerDe, the JSON SerDe. Download the jar file for the JSON SerDe.

```
wget https://storage.googleapis.com/google-code-archive-downloads/v2/code.google.com/hive-
json-serde/hive-json-serde-0.2.jar
```

The hive-json-serde-0.2.jar is downloaded.

Let's create an external table using a JSON file stored in HDFS with the LOCATION set to the HDFS URI where the JSON file is stored. Create a JSON file called wlslog.json and copy the following data to that file.

```
{"time_stamp":"Apr-8-2014-7:06:16-PM-PDT","category": "Notice","type":"WebLogicServer",
"servername": "AdminServer","code":"BEA-000365","msg": "Server state changed to STANDBY" }
{"time_stamp":"Apr-8-2014-7:06:17-PM-PDT","category": "Notice","type":"WebLogicServer",
"servername": "AdminServer","code":"BEA-000365","msg": "Server state changed to STARTING" }
{"time_stamp":"Apr-8-2014-7:06:18-PM-PDT","category": "Notice","type":"WebLogicServer",
"servername": "AdminServer","code":"BEA-000360","msg": "Server started in RUNNING mode" }
```

Create a directory in HDFS to store the JSON file. Create the hdfs://localhost:8020/wlslog directory and set its permissions to g+w.

```
hdfs dfs -mkdir -p hdfs://localhost:8020/wlslog
hadoop dfs -chmod -R g+w hdfs://localhost:8020/wlslog
```

Put the wlslog.json file into the HDFS directory using the FS shell command –put.

```
hdfs dfs -put /cdh/wlslog.json hdfs://10.0.2.15:8020/wlslog
```

Subsequently, run the FS shell command –ls to list the wlslog.json file.

```
hdfs dfs -ls /cdh/wlslog.json hdfs://10.0.2.15:8020/wlslog
```

The wlslog.json file is listed, as shown in Figure 3-31.

```
[root@localhost cdh]# hadoop dfs -ls hdfs://10.0.2.15:8020/wlslog

Found 1 items
-rw-r--r--   1 root hadoop        537 2015-09-28 16:23 hdfs://10.0.2.15:8020/wls
log/wlslog.json
[root@localhost cdh]#
[root@localhost cdh]#
```

Figure 3-31. *Listing the wlslog.json file in HDFS*

Start the Hive CLI shell if it is not already running. First, you need to add the hive-json-serde-0.2.jar file to the classpath.

```
ADD JAR hive-json-serde-0.2.jar;
```

The hive-json-serde-0.2.jar file is added, as shown in Figure 3-32.

```
hive> ADD JAR hive-json-serde-0.2.jar;
Added hive-json-serde-0.2.jar to class path
Added resource: hive-json-serde-0.2.jar
hive>
```

Figure 3-32. *Adding the Hive JSON SerDe jar to the classpath*

Create an external table called wlslog_json using the CREATE EXTERNAL TABLE statement with columns TIME_STAMP, CATEGORY, TYPE, SERVERNAME, CODE and MSG all of type string. Set the ROW FORMAT to SerDe class 'org.apache.hadoop.hive.contrib.serde2.JsonSerde'. Set the LOCATION of the external table to 'hdfs://localhost:8020/wlslog', which is the directory at which the wlslog.json file is stored. Run the following CREATE EXTERNAL TABLE statement in the Hive shell.

```
CREATE EXTERNAL TABLE IF NOT EXISTS wlslog_json(TIME_STAMP string,CATEGORY string,TYPE
string,SERVERNAME string,CODE string,MSG string)
     ROW FORMAT SERDE 'org.apache.hadoop.hive.contrib.serde2.JsonSerde'
     LOCATION 'hdfs://localhost:8020/wlslog';
```

The wlslog_json table is created, as shown in Figure 3-33.

```
hive> ADD JAR hive-json-serde-0.2.jar;
Added hive-json-serde-0.2.jar to class path
Added resource: hive-json-serde-0.2.jar
hive> CREATE EXTERNAL TABLE IF NOT EXISTS wlslog_json(TIME_STAMP string,CATEGORY
  string,TYPE string,SERVERNAME string,CODE string,MSG string)
     >       ROW FORMAT SERDE 'org.apache.hadoop.hive.contrib.serde2.JsonSerde'
     >       LOCATION 'hdfs://localhost:8020/wlslog';
OK
Time taken: 2.012 seconds
hive>
```

Figure 3-33. *Creating an external table called wlslog_json*

Subsequently, run a SELECT query statement to list the data in the wlslog_json table, as shown in Figure 3-34.

```
hive> select * from wlslog_json;
OK
Apr-8-2014-7:06:16-PM-PDT        Notice  WebLogicServer  AdminServer     BEA-0003
65      Server state changed to STANDBY
Apr-8-2014-7:06:17-PM-PDT        Notice  WebLogicServer  AdminServer     BEA-0003
65      Server state changed to STARTING
Apr-8-2014-7:06:18-PM-PDT        Notice  WebLogicServer  AdminServer     BEA-0003
60      Server started in RUNNING mode
Time taken: 0.752 seconds, Fetched: 3 row(s)
hive>
```

Figure 3-34. *Querying the wlslog_json table*

Summary

This chapter introduced Apache Hive, which is a data warehousing framework for managing and querying large datasets stored in HDFS. I discussed the difference between a managed table and an external table and you learned how to create a managed table and an external table. I demonstrated using different HiveQL statements such as creating a table LIKE another and using the CREATE TABLE AS SELECT statement. I also discussed the different methods for adding table data, including the LOAD DATA statement and the INSERT INTO and INSERT OVERWRITE statements. You also learned how to alter, truncate, and drop a table. The next chapter discusses Apache HBase.

CHAPTER 4

▪ ▪ ▪

Apache HBase

Apache HBase is a distributed, scalable database designed for Apache Hadoop. HBase is a flexible format NoSQL database. HBase has three main components: *HMaster, ZooKeeper,* and *RegionServers.* The HMaster handles the DDL (create and delete) operations. The ZooKeeper is a distributed coordination service for an HBase cluster. RegionServers manage HBase table data and serve client requests. An HBase table is mapped to one or more *regions* using row key ranges to split the HBase table. More regions are used as a table grows. HMaster manages region assignment. Regions are stored in RegionServers, which serve PUT/GET requests from a client. Each RegionServer is collocated with a DataNode on HDFS. HBase table data is stored in the HDFS. The metadata for the Region ➤ RegionServer mapping is kept in a metatable, which is stored on the ZooKeeper. A client request is first sent to the ZooKeeper, which provides the RegionServer the locations for the requested data. Subsequently, the client GETs/PUTs data directly on a RegionServer. The HBase architecture is illustrated in Figure 4-1.

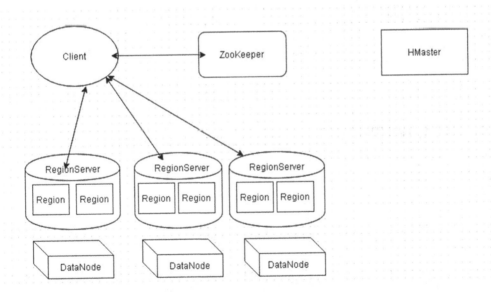

Figure 4-1. *The Apache HBase architecture*

© Deepak Vohra 2016
D. Vohra, *Practical Hadoop Ecosystem*, DOI 10.1007/978-1-4842-2199-0_4

This chapter has the following sections:

- Setting the environment
- Configuring Hadoop
- Configuring HBase
- Configuring Hive
- Starting HBase
- Starting the HBase shell
- Creating an HBase table
- Adding data to a table
- Listing all tables
- Getting a row of data
- Scanning a table
- Counting the number of rows in a table
- Altering a table
- Deleting a table row
- Deleting a table column
- Disabling and enabling a table
- Truncating a table
- Dropping a table
- Determining if a table exists
- Creating a Hive external table stored by HBase

Setting the Environment

The following software is required for this chapter.

- Apache Hadoop
- Apache HBase
- Apache Hive
- Java 7

Oracle Linux is used, but you can use another Linux distribution if you want. Add a group called hadoop and then add the hadoop, hbase, and hdfs users if they have not already been added.

```
groupadd hadoop
useradd -g hadoop hadoop
useradd -g hadoop hbase
useradd -g hadoop hdfs
```

Some of the software is the same as in earlier chapters. If you installed that software in other chapters, you only need to install Apache HBase for this chapter. The complete installation is discussed, including software that might have been installed previously. You can skip the sections that cover any software you have already installed.

Create a directory (/cdh) to install Apache Hadoop, Hbase, and Hive and set the permissions to global (777).

```
mkdir /cdh
chmod -R 777 /cdh
cd /cdh
```

Download and extract the tar file for Java 7.

```
tar zxvf jdk-7u55-linux-i586.gz
```

Download and extract the tar file for Apache Hadoop CDH 5.4.7 Hadoop 2.6.0.

```
wget http://archive-primary.cloudera.com/cdh5/cdh/5/hadoop-2.6.0-cdh5.4.7.tar.gz
tar -xvf hadoop-2.6.0-cdh5.4.7.tar.gz
```

Create symlinks for the Hadoop bin and conf directories. Symlink /cdh/hadoop-2.6.0-cdh5.4.7/share/hadoop/mapreduce1/bin references the /cdh/hadoop-2.6.0-cdh5.4.7/bin directory. Symlink /cdh/hadoop-2.6.0-cdh5.4.7/share/hadoop/mapreduce1/conf references the /cdh/hadoop-2.6.0-cdh5.4.7/etc/hadoop directory.

```
ln -s /cdh/hadoop-2.6.0-cdh5.4.7/bin /cdh/hadoop-2.6.0-cdh5.4.7/share/hadoop/mapreduce1/bin
ln -s /cdh/hadoop-2.6.0-cdh5.4.7/etc/hadoop  /cdh/hadoop-2.6.0-cdh5.4.7/share/hadoop/mapreduce1/conf
```

Download and extract the Apache Hive 0.13.1 CDH 5.3.6 tar file.

```
wget http://archive-primary.cloudera.com/cdh5/cdh/5/hive-0.13.1-cdh5.3.6.tar.gz
tar -xvf hive-0.13.1-cdh5.3.6.tar.gz
```

Download and extract the HBase 1.0.0 CDH 5.4.7 tar file.

```
wget http://archive-primary.cloudera.com/cdh5/cdh/5/hbase-1.0.0-cdh5.4.7.tar.gz
tar -xvf hbase-1.0.0-cdh5.4.7.tar.gz
```

Set the environment variables for Apache Hadoop, Apache Hbase, and Apache Hive.

```
vi ~/.bashrc
export HADOOP_PREFIX=/cdh/hadoop-2.6.0-cdh5.4.7
export HADOOP_CONF_DIR=$HADOOP_PREFIX/etc/hadoop
export HADOOP_COMMON_HOME=$HADOOP_PREFIX/share/hadoop/common
export HADOOP_HDFS_HOME=$HADOOP_PREFIX/share/hadoop/hdfs
export HIVE_HOME=/cdh/hive-0.13.1-cdh5.3.6
export HIVE_CONF=$HIVE_HOME/conf
export HBASE_HOME=/cdh/hbase-1.0.0-cdh5.4.7
export HBASE_CONF=$HBASE_HOME/conf
export JAVA_HOME=/cdh/jdk1.7.0_55
export HADOOP_MAPRED_HOME=$HADOOP_PREFIX/share/hadoop/mapreduce1
export HADOOP_HOME=$HADOOP_PREFIX/share/hadoop/mapreduce1
```

```
export HADOOP_CLASSPATH=$HADOOP_HOME/*:$HADOOP_HOME/lib/*:$JAVA_HOME/lib/*:$HIVE_CONF:$HIVE_
HOME/lib/*:$HADOOP_CONF_DIR:$HADOOP_COMMON_HOME/*:$HBASE_HOME/lib/*:$HBASE_CONF:$HADOOP_
COMMON_HOME/lib/*:$HADOOP_HDFS_HOME/*:$HADOOP_HDFS_HOME/lib/*:
export PATH=$PATH:$HADOOP_HOME/bin:$HADOOP_MAPRED_HOME/bin:$JAVA_HOME/bin:$HIVE_HOME/
bin:$HBASE_HOME/bin
export CLASSPATH=$HADOOP_CLASSPATH
export HADOOP_NAMENODE_USER=hadoop
export HADOOP_DATANODE_USER=hadoop
```

Configuring Hadoop

Set the Hadoop configuration properties fs.defaultFS (NameNode URI) and hadoop.tmp.dir (temporary directory) in the core-site.xml. The IP address of the host can be different for different users.

```
vi   $HADOOP_CONF_DIR/core-site.xml

<?xml-stylesheet type="text/xsl" href="configuration.xsl"?>

<!-- Put site-specific property overrides in this file. -->

<configuration>
<property>
  <name>fs.defaultFS</name>
    <value>hdfs://10.0.2.15:8020</value>
    </property>
 <property>
    <name>hadoop.tmp.dir</name>
    <value>/var/lib/hadoop-0.20/cache</value>
  </property>
</configuration>
```

Create the directory specified in the hadoop.tmp.dir property and set its permissions to global (777). If NameNode is to be reformatted, remove the previously created directory.

```
rm -rf   /var/lib/hadoop-0.20/cache
mkdir -p /var/lib/hadoop-0.20/cache
chmod -R 777  /var/lib/hadoop-0.20/cache
```

In the hdfs-site.xml file, set the dfs.permissions.superusergroup (superuser group), dfs.namenode.name.dir (NameNode storage directory), dfs.replication (replication factor), dfs.permissions (HDFS permissions), and dfs.datanode.max.xcievers properties. The dfs.datanode.max.xcievers property indicates the number of files served concurrently by the DataNode. The higher value is recommended so that sufficient resources are available to HBase. A lower value could cause IOExceptions and the RegionServer to shutdown.

```
vi $HADOOP_CONF_DIR/hdfs-site.xml

<?xml version="1.0" encoding="UTF-8"?>
<?xml-stylesheet type="text/xsl" href="configuration.xsl"?>
```

```xml
<!-- Put site-specific property overrides in this file. -->

<configuration>
<property>
 <name>dfs.permissions.superusergroup</name>
  <value>hadoop</value>
  </property><property>
   <name>dfs.namenode.name.dir</name>
    <value>/data/1/dfs/nn</value>
    </property>
        <property>
             <name>dfs.replication</name>
                   <value>1</value>
        </property>
<property>
<name>dfs.permissions</name>
<value>false</value>
</property>
<property>
  <name>dfs.datanode.max.xcievers</name>
  <value>4096</value>
</property>
</configuration>
```

Create the NameNode storage directory and set its permissions to global (777). First, remove the NameNode storage directory if it was created previously and NameNode is to be reformatted.

```
rm -rf   /data/1/dfs/nn
mkdir -p /data/1/dfs/nn
chmod -R 777 /data/1/dfs/nn
```

Format the NameNode. If you're prompted with a message about reformatting, select Y.

```
hdfs namenode -format
```

Start the NameNode.

```
hdfs namenode
```

Start the DataNode.

```
hdfs datanode
```

Configuring HBase

HBase is configured in the $HBASE_CONF/hbase-site.xml configuration file. Set the properties listed in Table 4-1 in the hbase-site.xml file.

Table 4-1. *Configuration Properties for the hbase-site.xml File*

Property	Description	Value
hbase.rootdir	The directory in which HBase stores data. Should be prefixed with the fully qualified HDFS NameNode URI.	hdfs://10.0.2.15:8020/hbase
hbase.zookeeper.property. dataDir	The data directory for the ZooKeeper. The directory path must start with a /.	/zookeeper
hbase.zookeeper.property. clientPort	The port at which clients connect.	2181
hbase.zookeeper.quorum	Servers in the ZooKeeper ensemble.	localhost
hbase.regionserver.port	The port that the HBase RegionServer binds to.	60020
hbase.master.port	The port that the HBase master binds to.	60000

The hbase-site.xml file may be modified in the vi editor.

```
vi /cdh/hbase-1.0.0-cdh5.4.7/conf/hbase-site.xml
```

Here is the hbase-site.xml file:

```
<?xml version="1.0"?>
<?xml-stylesheet type="text/xsl" href="configuration.xsl"?>
<configuration>
  <property>
    <name>hbase.rootdir</name>
    <value>hdfs://10.0.2.15:8020/hbase</value>
  </property>
  <property>
    <name>hbase.zookeeper.property.dataDir</name>
    <value>/zookeeper</value>
  </property>

  <property>
    <name>hbase.zookeeper.property.clientPort</name>
    <value>2181</value>
  </property>
  <property>
    <name>hbase.zookeeper.quorum</name>
    <value>localhost</value>
  </property>
<property>
<name>hbase.regionserver.port</name>
<value>60020</value>
 </property>
```

```
<property>
<name>hbase.master.port</name>
<value>60000</value>
 </property>
</configuration>
```

Create the HBase data directory configured in the `hbase.zookeeper.property.dataDir` property and set its permissions to global (777). First, remove the `/zookeeper` directory if it was previously created for some other application.

```
rm -rf  /zookeeper
mkdir -p /zookeeper
chmod -R 777 /zookeeper
```

Since HBase uses a lot of files concurrently, increase the user file limit (`ulimit`) to avoid errors similar to the following:

```
java.io.IOException...(Too many open files)
```

To the `/etc/security/limits.conf` file, add the following lines for the `hbase` and `hdfs` users.

```
hdfs   -       nofile  32768
hbase -       nofile  32768
```

You also need to create the HDFS directory configured in the `hbase.rootdir` property. Create the directory and set its permissions to global (777).

```
hadoop dfs -mkdir -p hdfs://10.0.2.15:8020/hbase
hadoop dfs -chmod -R 777 hdfs://10.0.2.15:8020/hbase
```

The `hdfs dfs` command may be used instead of the `hadoop dfs` command in the preceding and subsequent commands.

Configuring Hive

Configuring Hive is not required for HBase but because one example creates a Hive external table stored as Hbase, you need to configure Hive. Create the `hive-site.xml` configuration file by copying the `hive-default.xml.template` template file.

```
cp /cdh/hive-0.13.1-cdh5.3.6/conf/hive-default.xml.template /cdh/hive-0.13.1-cdh5.3.6/conf/
hive-site.xml
```

Set the `hive.metastore.warehouse.dir` property (the HDFS directory in which Hive data is stored) and the `hive.metastore.uris` property (the Thrift Server URI for clients).

```
vi /cdh/hive-0.13.1-cdh5.3.6/conf/hive-site.xml
<?xml version="1.0"?>
<?xml-stylesheet type="text/xsl" href="configuration.xsl"?>
<configuration>
<property>
  <name>hive.metastore.warehouse.dir</name>
```

```
  <value>hdfs://10.0.2.15:8020/user/hive/warehouse</value>
</property>
<property>
  <name>hive.metastore.uris</name>
  <value>thrift://localhost:10001</value>
</property>

</configuration>
```

Create the directory configured in the `hive.metastore.warehouse.dir` property and set its permissions to global (777).

```
hadoop dfs -mkdir  -p hdfs://10.0.2.15:8020/user/hive/warehouse
hadoop dfs -chmod -R g+w hdfs://10.0.2.15:8020/user/hive/warehouse
```

Starting HBase

Start HBase with the following command, which starts the HBase Master, ZooKeeper, and RegionServer.

```
start-hbase.sh
```

HBase starts, as shown in Figure 4-2.

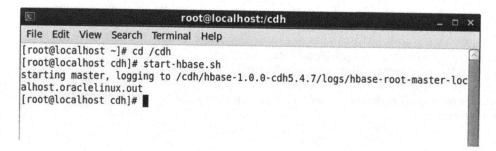

Figure 4-2. *Starting Apache HBase*

Starting the HBase Shell

HBase provides JRuby's IRB-based shell for running commands on HBase. Connect to the HBase instance using the following command.

```
hbase shell
```

The `hbase>` prompt is displayed, as shown in Figure 4-3.

```
[root@localhost cdh]# hbase shell
HBase Shell; enter 'help<RETURN>' for list of supported commands.
Type "exit<RETURN>" to leave the HBase Shell
Version 1.0.0-cdh5.4.7, rUnknown, Thu Sep 17 02:19:27 PDT 2015

hbase(main):001:0> █
```

Figure 4-3. *Starting the HBase shell*

Creating an HBase Table

An HBase table is created using the create command. You must specify the table name and at least one column family name. For example, here's how to create a table called wlslog with column families log and log2.

```
create 'wlslog' , 'log', 'log2'
```

The HBase table wlslog is created, as shown in Figure 4-4.

```
hbase(main):001:0> create 'wlslog' , 'log', 'log2'
0 row(s) in 17.0570 seconds

=> Hbase::Table - wlslog
hbase(main):002:0> █
```

Figure 4-4. *Creating an HBase table called wlslog*

The column family names can also be specified using a dictionary of column family specifications. In the following command, the wlslog table has the column families log and cf.

```
create 'wlslog2', {NAME=>'log'}, {NAME=>'cf'}
```

The HBase table wlslog2 is created, as shown in Figure 4-5.

```
hbase(main):001:0> create 'wlslog' , 'log', 'log2'
0 row(s) in 17.0570 seconds

=> Hbase::Table - wlslog
hbase(main):002:0> create 'wlslog2', {NAME=>'log'}, {NAME=>'cf'}
0 row(s) in 5.4070 seconds

=> Hbase::Table - wlslog2
hbase(main):003:0> █
```

Figure 4-5. *Creating an HBase table wlslog2 demonstrating another syntax to specify column families*

The HBase table definition does not specify the columns in a column family and any columns may be added. Different rows can have different columns.

Adding Data to a Table

The put command is used to add data to a table. A row of data with row key log1 and the columns time_
stamp, category, type, servername, code, and msg is added to the wlslog table, which has a column family
called log, as follows.

```
put 'wlslog', 'log1', 'log:time_stamp', 'Apr-8-2014-7:06:16-PM-PDT'
put 'wlslog', 'log1', 'log:category', 'Notice'
put 'wlslog', 'log1', 'log:type', 'WeblogicServer'
put 'wlslog', 'log1', 'log:servername', 'AdminServer'
put 'wlslog', 'log1', 'log:code', 'BEA-000365'
put 'wlslog', 'log1', 'log:msg', 'Server state changed to STANDBY'
```

The output from the preceding commands is shown in Figure 4-6.

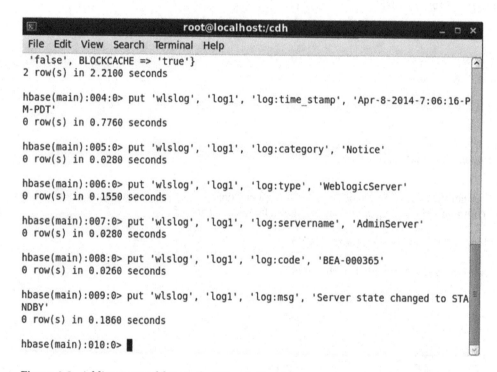

Figure 4-6. *Adding a row of data to the HBase table wlslog*

Similarly, add more rows to the wlslog table.

```
put 'wlslog', 'log2', 'log:time_stamp', 'Apr-8-2014-7:06:17-PM-PDT'
put 'wlslog', 'log2', 'log:category', 'Notice'
put 'wlslog', 'log2', 'log:type', 'WeblogicServer'
put 'wlslog', 'log2', 'log:servername', 'AdminServer'
put 'wlslog', 'log2', 'log:code', 'BEA-000365'
put 'wlslog', 'log2', 'log:msg', 'Server state changed to STARTING'

put 'wlslog', 'log3', 'log:time_stamp', 'Apr-8-2014-7:06:18-PM-PDT'
put 'wlslog', 'log3', 'log:category', 'Notice'
put 'wlslog', 'log3', 'log:type', 'WeblogicServer'
put 'wlslog', 'log3', 'log:servername', 'AdminServer'
put 'wlslog', 'log3', 'log:code', 'BEA-000365'
put 'wlslog', 'log3', 'log:msg', 'Server state changed to ADMIN'

put 'wlslog', 'log4', 'log:time_stamp', 'Apr-8-2014-7:06:19-PM-PDT'
put 'wlslog', 'log4', 'log:category', 'Notice'
put 'wlslog', 'log4', 'log:type', 'WeblogicServer'
put 'wlslog', 'log4', 'log:servername', 'AdminServer'
put 'wlslog', 'log4', 'log:code', 'BEA-000365'
put 'wlslog', 'log4', 'log:msg', 'Server state changed to RESUMING'

put 'wlslog', 'log5', 'log:time_stamp', 'Apr-8-2014-7:06:20-PM-PDT'
put 'wlslog', 'log5', 'log:category', 'Notice'
put 'wlslog', 'log5', 'log:type', 'WeblogicServer'
put 'wlslog', 'log5', 'log:servername', 'AdminServer'
put 'wlslog', 'log5', 'log:code', 'BEA-000331'
put 'wlslog', 'log5', 'log:msg', 'Started Weblogic AdminServer'

put 'wlslog', 'log6', 'log:time_stamp', 'Apr-8-2014-7:06:21-PM-PDT'
put 'wlslog', 'log6', 'log:category', 'Notice'
put 'wlslog', 'log6', 'log:type', 'WeblogicServer'
put 'wlslog', 'log6', 'log:servername', 'AdminServer'
put 'wlslog', 'log6', 'log:code', 'BEA-000365'
put 'wlslog', 'log6', 'log:msg', 'Server state changed to RUNNING'

put 'wlslog', 'log7', 'log:time_stamp', 'Apr-8-2014-7:06:22-PM-PDT'
put 'wlslog', 'log7', 'log:category', 'Notice'
put 'wlslog', 'log7', 'log:type', 'WeblogicServer'
put 'wlslog', 'log7', 'log:servername', 'AdminServer'
put 'wlslog', 'log7', 'log:code', 'BEA-000360'
put 'wlslog', 'log7', 'log:msg', 'Server started in RUNNING mode'
```

The output from adding the row with row key log7 is shown in Figure 4-7.

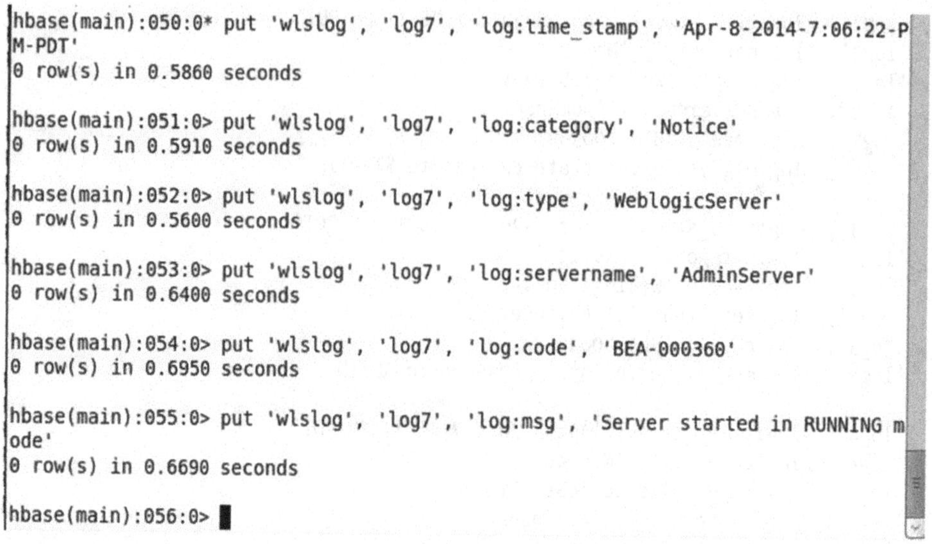

```
hbase(main):050:0* put 'wlslog', 'log7', 'log:time_stamp', 'Apr-8-2014-7:06:22-P
M-PDT'
0 row(s) in 0.5860 seconds

hbase(main):051:0> put 'wlslog', 'log7', 'log:category', 'Notice'
0 row(s) in 0.5910 seconds

hbase(main):052:0> put 'wlslog', 'log7', 'log:type', 'WeblogicServer'
0 row(s) in 0.5600 seconds

hbase(main):053:0> put 'wlslog', 'log7', 'log:servername', 'AdminServer'
0 row(s) in 0.6400 seconds

hbase(main):054:0> put 'wlslog', 'log7', 'log:code', 'BEA-000360'
0 row(s) in 0.6950 seconds

hbase(main):055:0> put 'wlslog', 'log7', 'log:msg', 'Server started in RUNNING m
ode'
0 row(s) in 0.6690 seconds

hbase(main):056:0> ▮
```

Figure 4-7. *Adding more data to the HBase Table wlslog*

Listing All Tables

The list command is used to list all the tables. Run the list command in the HBase shell.

hbase>list

The wlslog and wlslog2 tables are listed, as shown in Figure 4-8.

```
hbase(main):056:0> list
TABLE
wlslog
wlslog2
2 row(s) in 0.1570 seconds

=> ["wlslog", "wlslog2"]
hbase(main):057:0> ▮
```

Figure 4-8. *Listing the HBase tables*

Getting a Row of Data

The get command is used to get a row of data. For example, the following command gets the row with row key log3 from the wlslog table.

get 'wlslog', 'log3'

The row data for the row key log3 is listed, as shown in Figure 4-9.

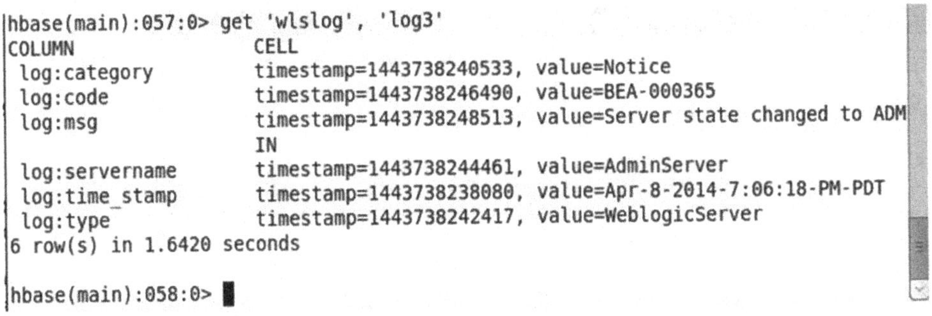

```
hbase(main):057:0> get 'wlslog', 'log3'
COLUMN                    CELL
 log:category             timestamp=1443738240533, value=Notice
 log:code                 timestamp=1443738246490, value=BEA-000365
 log:msg                  timestamp=1443738248513, value=Server state changed to ADM
                          IN
 log:servername           timestamp=1443738244461, value=AdminServer
 log:time_stamp           timestamp=1443738238080, value=Apr-8-2014-7:06:18-PM-PDT
 log:type                 timestamp=1443738242417, value=WeblogicServer
6 row(s) in 1.6420 seconds

hbase(main):058:0> █
```

Figure 4-9. *Getting a row of data*

Particular column values are fetched by specifying a dictionary of columns. For example, you would fetch the column value for the msg column for the row key log1 in the column family called log in the wlslog table as follows.

```
get 'wlslog', 'log1', {COLUMNS=>['log:msg']}
```

The msg column value is output, as shown in Figure 4-10.

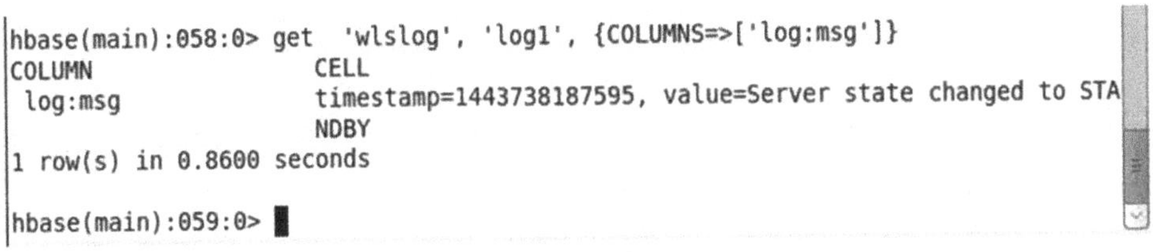

```
hbase(main):058:0> get 'wlslog', 'log1', {COLUMNS=>['log:msg']}
COLUMN                    CELL
 log:msg                  timestamp=1443738187595, value=Server state changed to STA
                          NDBY
1 row(s) in 0.8600 seconds

hbase(main):059:0> █
```

Figure 4-10. *Getting column data*

Scanning a Table

The scan command is used to scan all the data in a table by default. The following command scans all the data in the wlslog table.

```
scan 'wlslog'
```

The scan command output in the HBase shell is shown in Figure 4-11.

```
root@localhost:/cdh                              _  □  ×
File  Edit  View  Search  Terminal  Help

hbase(main):060:0> scan 'wlslog'
ROW                       COLUMN+CELL
 log1                     column=log:category, timestamp=1443738185479, value=Notice
 log1                     column=log:code, timestamp=1443738187081, value=BEA-000365
 log1                     column=log:msg, timestamp=1443738187595, value=Server stat
                          e changed to STANDBY
 log1                     column=log:servername, timestamp=1443738186620, value=Admi
                          nServer
 log1                     column=log:time_stamp, timestamp=1443738184648, value=Apr-
                          8-2014-7:06:16-PM-PDT
 log1                     column=log:type, timestamp=1443738185980, value=WeblogicSe
                          rver
 log2                     column=log:category, timestamp=1443738227370, value=Notice
 log2                     column=log:code, timestamp=1443738231075, value=BEA-000365
 log2                     column=log:msg, timestamp=1443738233173, value=Server stat
                          e changed to STARTING
 log2                     column=log:servername, timestamp=1443738228326, value=Admi
                          nServer
 log2                     column=log:time_stamp, timestamp=1443738226903, value=Apr-
                          8-2014-7:06:17-PM-PDT
 log2                     column=log:type, timestamp=1443738227678, value=WeblogicSe
                          rver
 log3                     column=log:category, timestamp=1443738240533, value=Notice
 log3                     column=log:code, timestamp=1443738246490, value=BEA-000365
 log3                     column=log:msg, timestamp=1443738248513, value=Server stat
                          e changed to ADMIN
```

Figure 4-11. *Scanning an HBase table using the scan command*

The seven rows of data in the wlslog table are listed, as shown in Figure 4-12.

```
                              root@localhost:/cdh                      _  □  ×
 File   Edit   View   Search   Terminal   Help
 log5                       column=log:time_stamp, timestamp=1443738319368, value=Apr-
                           8-2014-7:06:20-PM-PDT
 log5                       column=log:type, timestamp=1443738323403, value=WeblogicSe
                           rver
 log6                       column=log:category, timestamp=1443738335672, value=Notice
 log6                       column=log:code, timestamp=1443738341292, value=BEA-000365
 log6                       column=log:msg, timestamp=1443738343539, value=Server stat
                           e changed to RUNNING
 log6                       column=log:servername, timestamp=1443738339555, value=Admi
                           nServer
 log6                       column=log:time_stamp, timestamp=1443738333722, value=Apr-
                           8-2014-7:06:21-PM-PDT
 log6                       column=log:type, timestamp=1443738337557, value=WeblogicSe
                           rver
 log7                       column=log:category, timestamp=1443738351875, value=Notice
 log7                       column=log:code, timestamp=1443738357749, value=BEA-000360
 log7                       column=log:msg, timestamp=1443738359718, value=Server star
                           ted in RUNNING mode
 log7                       column=log:servername, timestamp=1443738355842, value=Admi
                           nServer
 log7                       column=log:time_stamp, timestamp=1443738349755, value=Apr-
                           8-2014-7:06:22-PM-PDT
 log7                       column=log:type, timestamp=1443738353841, value=WeblogicSe
                           rver
 7 row(s) in 5.9580 seconds

 hbase(main):061:0> ▌
```

Figure 4-12. *Output from the scan command*

Scanner specification, which may include COLUMNS, STARTROW, ENDROW, LIMIT, and TIMESTAMP, could also be specified in the scan command. For example, you could scan the wlslog table, starting from row log5 in column family log.

```
scan 'wlslog', {STARTROW => 'log5', COLUMNS=>['log'] }
```

The output from the scan command lists the rows starting from row log5, as shown in Figure 4-13.

```
root@localhost:/cdh                              _ □ ×
File  Edit  View  Search  Terminal  Help
hbase(main):061:0>  scan  'wlslog',  {STARTROW => 'log5', COLUMNS=>['log'] }
ROW                    COLUMN+CELL
 log5                  column=log:category, timestamp=1443738321304, value=Notice
 log5                  column=log:code, timestamp=1443738327380, value=BEA-000331
 log5                  column=log:msg, timestamp=1443738329422, value=Started Web
                       logic AdminServer
 log5                  column=log:servername, timestamp=1443738325328, value=Admi
                       nServer
 log5                  column=log:time_stamp, timestamp=1443738319368, value=Apr-
                       8-2014-7:06:20-PM-PDT
 log5                  column=log:type, timestamp=1443738323403, value=WeblogicSe
                       rver
 log6                  column=log:category, timestamp=1443738335672, value=Notice
 log6                  column=log:code, timestamp=1443738341292, value=BEA-000365
 log6                  column=log:msg, timestamp=1443738343539, value=Server stat
                       e changed to RUNNING
 log6                  column=log:servername, timestamp=1443738339555, value=Admi
                       nServer
 log6                  column=log:time_stamp, timestamp=1443738333722, value=Apr-
                       8-2014-7:06:21-PM-PDT
 log6                  column=log:type, timestamp=1443738337557, value=WeblogicSe
                       rver
 log7                  column=log:category, timestamp=1443738351875, value=Notice
 log7                  column=log:code, timestamp=1443738357749, value=BEA-000360
 log7                  column=log:msg, timestamp=1443738359718, value=Server star
                       ted in RUNNING mode
 log7                  column=log:servername, timestamp=1443738355842, value=Admi
                       nServer
 log7                  column=log:time_stamp, timestamp=1443738349755, value=Apr-
                       8-2014-7:06:22-PM-PDT
 log7                  column=log:type, timestamp=1443738353841, value=WeblogicSe
```

Figure 4-13. *Running scan with STARTROW from the log5 row*

All rows in the range starting from log5 to the end of the table are listed, as shown in Figure 4-14.

```
┌─────────────────────────────────────────────────────────────────────┐
│ ⊠                         root@localhost:/cdh                _  □  ✕ │
├─────────────────────────────────────────────────────────────────────┤
│ File  Edit  View  Search  Terminal  Help                            │
│ log5                    column=log:msg, timestamp=1443738329422, value=Started Web⌃ │
│                         logic AdminServer                           │
│ log5                    column=log:servername, timestamp=1443738325328, value=Admi │
│                         nServer                                      │
│ log5                    column=log:time_stamp, timestamp=1443738319368, value=Apr- │
│                         8-2014-7:06:20-PM-PDT                        │
│ log5                    column=log:type, timestamp=1443738323403, value=WeblogicSe │
│                         rver                                         │
│ log6                    column=log:category, timestamp=1443738335672, value=Notice │
│ log6                    column=log:code, timestamp=1443738341292, value=BEA-000365 │
│ log6                    column=log:msg, timestamp=1443738343539, value=Server stat │
│                         e changed to RUNNING                         │
│ log6                    column=log:servername, timestamp=1443738339555, value=Admi │
│                         nServer                                      │
│ log6                    column=log:time_stamp, timestamp=1443738333722, value=Apr- │
│                         8-2014-7:06:21-PM-PDT                        │
│ log6                    column=log:type, timestamp=1443738337557, value=WeblogicSe │
│                         rver                                         │
│ log7                    column=log:category, timestamp=1443738351875, value=Notice │
│ log7                    column=log:code, timestamp=1443738357749, value=BEA-000360 │
│ log7                    column=log:msg, timestamp=1443738359718, value=Server star │
│                         ted in RUNNING mode                          │
│ log7                    column=log:servername, timestamp=1443738355842, value=Admi │
│                         nServer                                      │
│ log7                    column=log:time_stamp, timestamp=1443738349755, value=Apr- │
│                         8-2014-7:06:22-PM-PDT                        │
│ log7                    column=log:type, timestamp=1443738353841, value=WeblogicSe │
│                         rver                                         │
│ 3 row(s) in 0.4850 seconds                                          │
│                                                                     │
│ hbase(main):062:0> ▌                                                ⌄│
└─────────────────────────────────────────────────────────────────────┘
```

Figure 4-14. *The output from scanning an HBase table from the log5 row*

While the STARTROW row key is inclusive, the STOPROW row key is excluded. For example, scan the wlslog table starting from log3 and ending with log5.

```
scan 'wlslog', { STARTROW => 'log3', STOPROW => 'log5'}
```

The log3 and log4 rows are listed, but the log5 row is not, as shown in Figure 4-15.

```
hbase(main):062:0> scan  'wlslog',  { STARTROW => 'log3', STOPROW => 'log5'}
ROW                    COLUMN+CELL
 log3                  column=log:category, timestamp=1443738240533, value=Notice
 log3                  column=log:code, timestamp=1443738246490, value=BEA-000365
 log3                  column=log:msg, timestamp=1443738248513, value=Server stat
                       e changed to ADMIN
 log3                  column=log:servername, timestamp=1443738244461, value=Admi
                       nServer
 log3                  column=log:time_stamp, timestamp=1443738238080, value=Apr-
                       8-2014-7:06:18-PM-PDT
 log3                  column=log:type, timestamp=1443738242417, value=WeblogicSe
                       rver
 log4                  column=log:category, timestamp=1443738254406, value=Notice
 log4                  column=log:code, timestamp=1443738260328, value=BEA-000365
 log4                  column=log:msg, timestamp=1443738276347, value=Server stat
                       e changed to RESUMING
 log4                  column=log:servername, timestamp=1443738258582, value=Admi
                       nServer
 log4                  column=log:time_stamp, timestamp=1443738252419, value=Apr-
                       8-2014-7:06:19-PM-PDT
 log4                  column=log:type, timestamp=1443738256571, value=WeblogicSe
                       rver
2 row(s) in 2.0090 seconds

hbase(main):063:0> ▉
```

Figure 4-15. *Using STOPROW in scan command*

Counting the Number of Rows in a Table

The count command is used to count the number of rows in a table. For example, you can count the number of rows in the wlslog table.

count 'wlslog'

Since the wlslog table has seven rows, the number 7 is listed, as shown in Figure 4-16.

```
hbase(main):063:0> count 'wlslog'
7 row(s) in 0.2110 seconds

=> 7
hbase(main):064:0> ▉
```

Figure 4-16. *Running the count command to count rows in an HBase table*

Altering a Table

The alter command is used to alter a table with a dictionary specifying the column family schema. As an example, alter the wlslog table and set number of versions in the log column family to 5.

```
alter 'wlslog', {NAME => 'log', VERSIONS => 5}
```

As another example, delete the log2 column family from the wlslog table.

```
alter 'wlslog', {NAME => 'log2', METHOD => 'delete'}
```

The output from the preceding command in the HBase shell is shown in Figure 4-17.

```
hbase(main):064:0> alter 'wlslog', {NAME => 'log', VERSIONS => 5}
Updating all regions with the new schema...
0/1 regions updated.
0/1 regions updated.
1/1 regions updated.
Done.
0 row(s) in 4.4190 seconds

hbase(main):065:0> alter 'wlslog', {NAME => 'log2', METHOD => 'delete'}
Updating all regions with the new schema...
0/1 regions updated.
1/1 regions updated.
Done.
0 row(s) in 3.3750 seconds

hbase(main):066:0> █
```

Figure 4-17. *Altering an HBase table*

Deleting a Table Row

The deleteall command is used to delete all the column data in a row when it's provided a table name and a row key. The following command deletes row log1 in the wlslog table.

```
deleteall   'wlslog',  'log1'
```

The output from the command in the HBase shell is shown in Figure 4-18.

```
hbase(main):125:0> deleteall    'wlslog',  'log1'
0 row(s) in 0.2020 seconds
```

Figure 4-18. *Using the deleteall command*

If you run the scan command after deleting the log1 row, you'd see that the log1 row data would not be listed. Row data starting from row log2 is listed, as shown in Figure 4-19.

```
root@localhost:/cdh                              _  □  ×

File   Edit   View   Search   Terminal   Help

hbase(main):129:0> scan 'wlslog'
ROW                      COLUMN+CELL
 log2                    column=log:category, timestamp=1443739060093, value=Notice
 log2                    column=log:code, timestamp=1443739065685, value=BEA-000365
 log2                    column=log:msg, timestamp=1443739067603, value=Server stat
                         e changed to STARTING
 log2                    column=log:servername, timestamp=1443739063796, value=Admi
                         nServer
 log2                    column=log:time_stamp, timestamp=1443739057780, value=Apr-
                         8-2014-7:06:17-PM-PDT
 log2                    column=log:type, timestamp=1443739061858, value=WeblogicSe
                         rver
 log3                    column=log:category, timestamp=1443739073612, value=Notice
 log3                    column=log:code, timestamp=1443739079101, value=BEA-000365
 log3                    column=log:msg, timestamp=1443739081088, value=Server stat
                         e changed to ADMIN
 log3                    column=log:servername, timestamp=1443739077332, value=Admi
                         nServer
 log3                    column=log:time_stamp, timestamp=1443739071577, value=Apr-
                         8-2014-7:06:18-PM-PDT
 log3                    column=log:type, timestamp=1443739075416, value=WeblogicSe
                         rver
 log4                    column=log:category, timestamp=1443739087284, value=Notice
 log4                    column=log:code, timestamp=1443739130917, value=BEA-000365
 log4                    column=log:msg, timestamp=1443739133049, value=Server stat
                         e changed to RESUMING
 log4                    column=log:servername, timestamp=1443739129097, value=Admi
                         nServer
 log4                    column=log:time_stamp, timestamp=1443739085181, value=Apr-
                         8-2014-7:06:19-PM-PDT
```

Figure 4-19. *Scanning the HBase table wlslog subsequent to deleting row log1*

Optionally, the column coordinates may also be specified in the deleteall command.

Deleting a Table Column

The delete command is used to delete a column data when it's provided the table/row/column coordinates. For example, the following command deletes the category column in the column family log in row log5 in the wlslog table:

```
delete   'wlslog',  'log5',  'log:category'
```

The output from this delete command is shown in Figure 4-20.

```
hbase(main):126:0> delete     'wlslog',  'log5',  'log:category'
0 row(s) in 0.6730 seconds

hbase(main):127:0> █
```

Figure 4-20. *Deleting a column in row log5*

Subsequently to running the `deleteall` and `delete` commands, you could run `get` commands to fetch data for the `log1` and `log5` rows. No rows would be listed for the the `log1` row because the `log1` rows were deleted with `deleteall`. Row data for `log5` is listed, but the `category` column data is not listed, as shown in Figure 4-21.

```
hbase(main):125:0> deleteall   'wlslog', 'log1'
0 row(s) in 0.2020 seconds

hbase(main):126:0> delete   'wlslog', 'log5', 'log:category'
0 row(s) in 0.6730 seconds

hbase(main):127:0> get 'wlslog', 'log1'
COLUMN                CELL
0 row(s) in 0.1140 seconds

hbase(main):128:0> get 'wlslog', 'log5'
COLUMN                CELL
 log:code             timestamp=1443739144412, value=BEA-000331
 log:msg              timestamp=1443739146240, value=Started Weblogic AdminServe
                      r
 log:servername       timestamp=1443739142647, value=AdminServer
 log:time_stamp       timestamp=1443739137002, value=Apr-8-2014-7:06:20-PM-PDT
 log:type             timestamp=1443739140784, value=WeblogicServer
5 row(s) in 0.1560 seconds

hbase(main):129:0> ▋
```

Figure 4-21. *Column data for the category column is now shown, as it has been deleted*

Disabling and Enabling a Table

A table may be disabled with the `disable` command and enabled with the `enable` command. Certain commands, such as to truncate a table or drop a table, require the table to be first disabled. For example, the following command disables the `wlslog` table.

```
disable 'wlslog'
```

The following command enables the `wlslog` table.

```
enable 'wlslog'
```

The output from the preceding commands is shown in Figure 4-22.

```
hbase(main):131:0> disable 'wlslog'
0 row(s) in 3.1750 seconds

hbase(main):132:0> enable 'wlslog'
0 row(s) in 2.6950 seconds

hbase(main):133:0> ▋
```

Figure 4-22. *Disabling and enabling an HBase table*

Truncating a Table

The truncate command truncates a table. When a table is truncated, all the table data is deleted but the table is not dropped. For example, the following command truncates the wlslog table.

```
truncate 'wlslog'
```

You could subsequently run a scan on the wlslog table. No table rows would be listed, as shown in Figure 4-23. The wlslog table is automatically disabled before getting truncated.

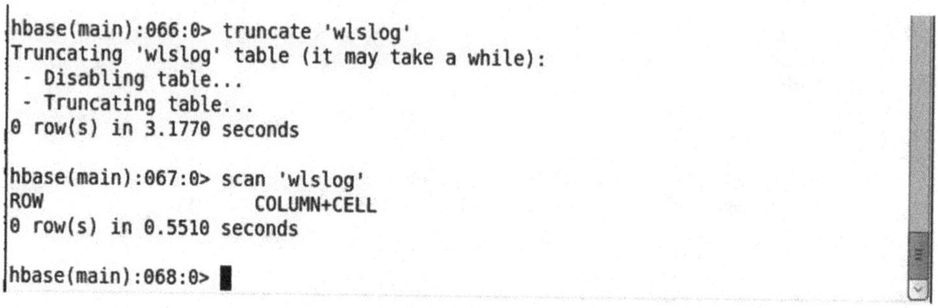

```
hbase(main):066:0> truncate 'wlslog'
Truncating 'wlslog' table (it may take a while):
 - Disabling table...
 - Truncating table...
0 row(s) in 3.1770 seconds

hbase(main):067:0> scan 'wlslog'
ROW                      COLUMN+CELL
0 row(s) in 0.5510 seconds

hbase(main):068:0>
```

Figure 4-23. Truncating the wlslog table

Dropping a Table

The drop command drops a table. The table must first be disabled. The following commands run in sequence to disable and drop the wlslog table.

```
disable 'wlslog'
drop 'wlslog'
```

The wlslog table is dropped, as shown in Figure 4-24.

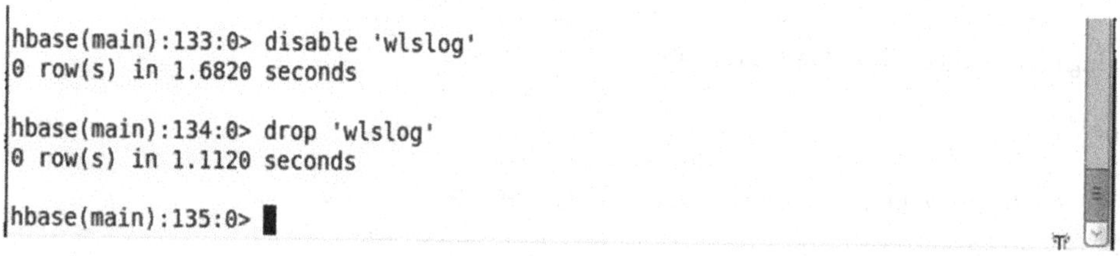

```
hbase(main):133:0> disable 'wlslog'
0 row(s) in 1.6820 seconds

hbase(main):134:0> drop 'wlslog'
0 row(s) in 1.1120 seconds

hbase(main):135:0>
```

Figure 4-24. Dropping the HBase wlslog table

Determining if a Table Exists

The exists command is used to determine whether a table exists. For example, after dropping the wlslog table, you could run the exists command on it.

```
exists 'wlslog'
```

Because the wlslog table has been dropped, the message Table wlslog does not exist is displayed, as shown in Figure 4-25.

```
hbase(main):134:0> drop 'wlslog'
0 row(s) in 1.1120 seconds

hbase(main):135:0> exists 'wlslog'
Table wlslog does not exist
0 row(s) in 0.7990 seconds

hbase(main):136:0> █
```

Figure 4-25. *Determining if wlslog table exists*

Creating a Hive External Table Stored By HBase

Chapter 2 discussed the Apache Hive framework. It also discussed creating an external table stored as JSON in HDFS. This section discusses creating a Hive table stored by HBase. First, you start the Hive server.

```
hive --service hiveserver
```

The Hive server is started.
Then start the Hive CLI (command line interface) shell.

```
hive
```

Set the database to default.

```
hive>use default;
```

Drop the wlslog table if it exists. Drop the Hive wlslog table, not the HBase wlslog table.

```
hive>drop table wlslog;
```

The output from the preceding commands is shown in Figure 4-26.

```
hive> use default;
OK
Time taken: 0.408 seconds
hive> drop table wlslog;
OK
Time taken: 25.249 seconds
hive> █
```

Figure 5-26. *Dropping HBase table default.wlslog*

Next, create an external table called wlslog on the HBase table wlslog. The STORED BY clause is set to 'org.apache.hadoop.hive.hbase.HBaseStorageHandler', which is the Hive storage handler for HBase. In SERDEPROPERTIES, specify the HBase columns mapping for the Hive table columns with the hbase.columns. mapping string. The hbase.columns.mapping should not include extra spaces, as those would be interpreted as included in a column name.

The first column in the `hbase.columns.mapping` must be `:key`, as it maps the row key of the HBase table row to the first column (of type `string` or `struct`) of the Hive table. If the HBase table name is the same as the Hive table name, the HBase table name is not required in the `TBLPROPERTIES`, but it can be specified. Run the following `CREATE EXTERNAL TABLE` command to create a Hive external table called `wlslog` over the HBase table `wlslog`.

```
CREATE EXTERNAL TABLE wlslog(key string,time_stamp string,category string,type
string,servername string,code string,msg string) STORED BY 'org.apache.hadoop.hive.hbase.
HBaseStorageHandler'
WITH SERDEPROPERTIES ("hbase.columns.mapping" =":key,log:time_stamp,log:category,log:type,lo
g:servername,log:code,log:msg")
TBLPROPERTIES ("hbase.table.name" = "wlslog");
```

The Hive `wlslog` table is created, as shown in Figure 4-27.

```
hive> use default;
OK
Time taken: 0.408 seconds
hive> drop table wlslog;
OK
Time taken: 25.249 seconds
hive> CREATE EXTERNAL TABLE wlslog(key string,time_stamp string,category string,
type string,servername string,code string,msg string)
    > STORED BY 'org.apache.hadoop.hive.hbase.HBaseStorageHandler'
    > WITH SERDEPROPERTIES ("hbase.columns.mapping" =":key,log:time_stamp,log:ca
tegory,log:type,log:servername,log:code,log:msg")
    > TBLPROPERTIES ("hbase.table.name" = "wlslog");
OK
Time taken: 15.941 seconds
hive> █
```

Figure 4-27. *Creating the Hive external table wlslog*

Run a `SELECT` query in the Hive shell on the `wlslog` table.

```
hive>select * from wlslog;
```

The seven rows stored in the Hive table stored by the HBase `wlslog` table are listed, as shown in Figure 4-28.

```
                        root@localhost:/cdh                      _ □ ×

 File  Edit  View  Search  Terminal  Help
hive> drop table wlslog;
OK
Time taken: 25.249 seconds
hive> CREATE EXTERNAL TABLE wlslog(key string,time_stamp string,category string,
type string,servername string,code string,msg string)
    > STORED BY 'org.apache.hadoop.hive.hbase.HBaseStorageHandler'
    > WITH SERDEPROPERTIES ("hbase.columns.mapping" =":key,log:time_stamp,log:ca
tegory,log:type,log:servername,log:code,log:msg")
    > TBLPROPERTIES ("hbase.table.name" = "wlslog");
OK
Time taken: 15.941 seconds
hive> select * from wlslog;
OK
log1    Apr-8-2014-7:06:16-PM-PDT        Notice  WeblogicServer  AdminServer   B
EA-000365       Server state changed to STANDBY
log2    Apr-8-2014-7:06:17-PM-PDT        Notice  WeblogicServer  AdminServer   B
EA-000365       Server state changed to STARTING
log3    Apr-8-2014-7:06:18-PM-PDT        Notice  WeblogicServer  AdminServer   B
EA-000365       Server state changed to ADMIN
log4    Apr-8-2014-7:06:19-PM-PDT        Notice  WeblogicServer  AdminServer   B
EA-000365       Server state changed to RESUMING
log5    Apr-8-2014-7:06:20-PM-PDT        Notice  WeblogicServer  AdminServer   B
EA-000331       Started Weblogic AdminServer
log6    Apr-8-2014-7:06:21-PM-PDT        Notice  WeblogicServer  AdminServer   B
EA-000365       Server state changed to RUNNING
log7    Apr-8-2014-7:06:22-PM-PDT        Notice  WeblogicServer  AdminServer   B
EA-000360       Server started in RUNNING mode
Time taken: 34.262 seconds, Fetched: 7 row(s)
hive>
```

Figure 4-28. *Querying the Hive external table wlslog*

Summary

This chapter introduced the Apache HBase framework to store and query data. It discussed the various HBase shell commands to create an HBase table, put data in the table, get data from the table, and perform other CRUD operations such as delete a column or a row, truncate a table, and drop a table. It also covered creating a Hive external table stored by HBase. The next chapter discusses Apache Sqoop.

Bulk Transferring & Streaming

PART III

Bulk Transferring & Streaming

CHAPTER 5

■ ■ ■

Apache Sqoop

Apache Sqoop is a tool for transferring large quantities of data between a relational database, such as MySQL and Oracle database, and the Hadoop ecosystem, which includes the Hadoop Distributed File System (HDFS), Apache Hive, and Apache HBase. While Sqoop supports transfer between a relational database and HDFS bi-directionally, Sqoop only supports transfer from a relational database to Apache Hive and Apache HBase uni-directionally. The data transfer paths supported by Apache Sqoop are illustrated in Figure 5-1.

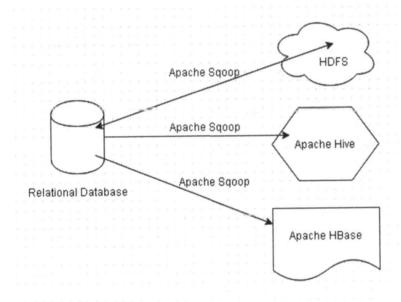

Figure 5-1. *Apache Sqoop data transfer paths*

The main commands supported by Apache Sqoop are listed in Table 5-1.

© Deepak Vohra 2016
D. Vohra, *Practical Hadoop Ecosystem*, DOI 10.1007/978-1-4842-2199-0_5

Table 5-1. *Apache Sqoop Commands*

Command	Description	Syntax
`sqoop import`	Imports from a RDMS table to HDFS with each row in a relational database table being transferred as a HDFS record in plain text by default. Import to a Avro data file and the sequence file is also supported. Supported databases are HSQLDB 1.8.0+, MySQL 5.0+, Oracle 10.2.0+, and PostgreSQL 8.3+. Other databases could also be used. Transfer from RDBMS to Apache Hive and Apache HBase are also supported.	`sqoop import [GENERIC-ARGS] [TOOL-ARGS]`
`sqoop export`	Exports a set of files from HDFS to RDBMS. The target table must be created prior to running the Sqoop export tool. Direct transfer from Apache Hive and Apache HBase to RDBMS is not supported.	`sqoop export (generic-args) (export-args)`
`sqoop import-all-tables`	Imports all tables in RDBS to HDFS.	`sqoop import-all-tables (generic-args) (import-args)`
`sqoop job`	Creates, runs, and deletes a MapReduce job.	`sqoop job (generic-args) (job-args)`
`sqoop metastore`	Creates a metastore instance to run MapReduce jobs.	`sqoop metastore (generic-args) (metastore-args)`
`sqoop merge`	Merges a newer dataset with an older dataset.	`sqoop merge (generic-args) (merge-args)`
`sqoop codegen`	Creates code to run HQL statements to create table and load data.	`sqoop codegen (generic-args) (codegen-args)`
`sqoop create-hive-table`	Creates a Hive table to which data may be imported from RDBMS.	`sqoop create-hive-table (generic-args) (create-hive-table-args)`
`sqoop eval`	Evaluate SQL.	`sqoop eval (generic-args) (eval-args)`
`sqoop list-databases`	Lists databases.	`sqoop list-databases (generic-args) (list-databases-args)`
`sqoop list-tables`	Lists tables.	`sqoop list-tables (generic-args) (list-tables-args)`
`sqoop version`	Lists the Sqoop version.	`sqoop version`
`sqoop help`	Lists the Sqoop tools.	`sqoop help [tool-name]`

This chapter discusses the `sqoop import` and `sqoop export` commands to transfer data from the MySQL database to HDFS, transfer data from HDFS to the MySQL database, transfer data from the MySQL database to Apache Hive, and transfer data from the MySQL database to the Apache HBase. This chapter has the following sections.

- Installing MySQL database
- Creating MySQL database tables
- Setting the environment
- Configuring Hadoop
- Starting HDFS
- Configuring Hive
- Configuring HBase
- Importing into HDFS
- Exporting from HDFS
- Importing into Hive
- Importing into HBase

Installing MySQL Database

First, you need to install MySQL database. Create a directory (`/mysql` for example) to install MySQL database and set its permissions to global (777).

```
mkdir /mysql
chmod  -R 777 /mysql
```

Download the MySQL Server 5.6.19 `tar.gz` file (or alter the version, such as to 5.6.31) `mysql-5.6.19-linux-glibc2.5-i686.tar.gz` for the Linux Generic platform from `http://dev.mysql.com/downloads/mysql/`. Extract the `tar.gz` file to the `/mysql` directory.

```
tar zxvf mysql-5.6.19-linux-glibc2.5-i686.tar.gz
```

Add a group called `mysql` and a user `mysql` to the group.

```
groupadd mysql
useradd -r -g mysql mysql
```

Create a symlink for the MySQL installation directory.

```
ln -s /mysql/mysql-5.6.19-linux-glibc2.5-i686 mysql
cd mysql
```

Run the following commands to install the MySQL database and set the owner/group for the database to `mysql`.

```
chown -R mysql.
```

```
chgrp -R mysql.
scripts/mysql_install_db --user=mysql
chown -R root.
chown -R mysql data
```

Start MySQL Server with the following command.

```
bin/mysqld_safe --user=mysql &
```

MySQL Server starts, as shown in Figure 5-2.

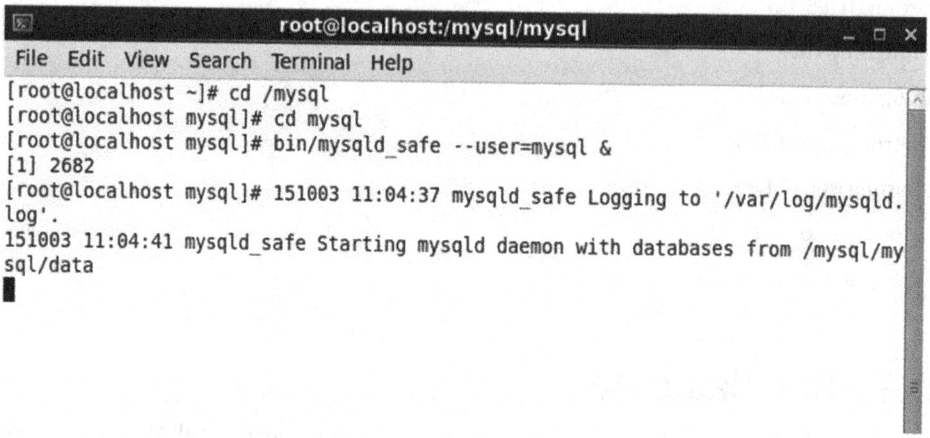

root@localhost:/mysql/mysql

File   Edit   View   Search   Terminal   Help
```
[root@localhost ~]# cd /mysql
[root@localhost mysql]# cd mysql
[root@localhost mysql]# bin/mysqld_safe --user=mysql &
[1] 2682
[root@localhost mysql]# 151003 11:04:37 mysqld_safe Logging to '/var/log/mysqld.
log'.
151003 11:04:41 mysqld_safe Starting mysqld daemon with databases from /mysql/my
sql/data
```

Figure 5-2. *Starting MySQL Server*

Creating MySQL Database Tables

Log in to the MySQL CLI shell using the following command and then specify the root password when prompted. The root user does not require a password by default.

```
cd /mysql
cd mysql
bin/mysql -u root
```

The MySQL command line shell starts, as shown in Figure 5-3. Set the database to use test.

```
mysql> use test
```

The database is set to test, which is shown in Figure 5-3.

```
[root@localhost mysql]# bin/mysql
Welcome to the MySQL monitor.  Commands end with ; or \g.
Your MySQL connection id is 1
Server version: 5.6.19 MySQL Community Server (GPL)

Copyright (c) 2000, 2014, Oracle and/or its affiliates. All rights reserved.

Oracle is a registered trademark of Oracle Corporation and/or its
affiliates. Other names may be trademarks of their respective
owners.

Type 'help;' or '\h' for help. Type '\c' to clear the current input statement.

mysql> use test
Reading table information for completion of table and column names
You can turn off this feature to get a quicker startup with -A

Database changed
mysql>
```

Figure 5-3. *Starting the MySQL CLI shell*

Create a MySQL database table called wlslog with the following SQL script. A primary key is required to be set for the sqoop import tool.

```
CREATE TABLE wlslog(time_stamp VARCHAR(255) PRIMARY KEY,category VARCHAR(255),type
VARCHAR(255),servername VARCHAR(255), code VARCHAR(255),msg VARCHAR(255));
```

The wlslog table is created, as shown in Figure 5-4.

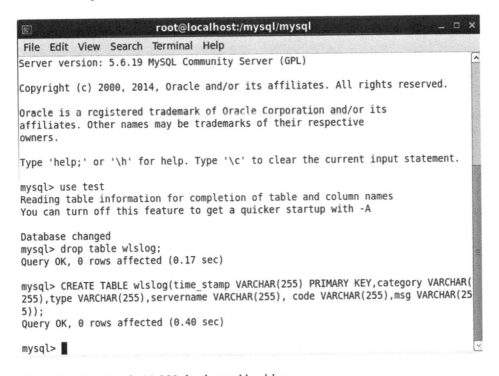

Figure 5-4. *Creating the MySQL database table wlslog*

265

Add seven rows of data to the wlslog table using the following SQL script.

```
INSERT INTO wlslog(time_stamp,category,type,servername,code,msg) VALUES('Apr-8-2014-7:06:16-
PM-PDT','Notice','WebLogicServer','AdminServer','BEA-000365','Server state changed to
STANDBY');
INSERT INTO wlslog(time_stamp,category,type,servername,code,msg) VALUES('Apr-8-2014-7:06:17-
PM-PDT','Notice','WebLogicServer','AdminServer','BEA-000365','Server state changed to
STARTING');
INSERT INTO wlslog(time_stamp,category,type,servername,code,msg) VALUES('Apr-8-2014-7:06:18-
PM-PDT','Notice','WebLogicServer','AdminServer','BEA-000365','Server state changed to
ADMIN');
INSERT INTO wlslog(time_stamp,category,type,servername,code,msg) VALUES('Apr-8-2014-7:06:19-
PM-PDT','Notice','WebLogicServer','AdminServer','BEA-000365','Server state changed to
RESUMING');
INSERT INTO wlslog(time_stamp,category,type,servername,code,msg) VALUES('Apr-8-2014-
7:06:20-PM-PDT','Notice','WebLogicServer','AdminServer','BEA-000361','Started WebLogic
AdminServer');
INSERT INTO wlslog(time_stamp,category,type,servername,code,msg) VALUES('Apr-8-2014-7:06:21-
PM-PDT','Notice','WebLogicServer','AdminServer','BEA-000365','Server state changed to
RUNNING');
INSERT INTO wlslog(time_stamp,category,type,servername,code,msg) VALUES('Apr-8-2014-7:06:22-
PM-PDT','Notice','WebLogicServer','AdminServer','BEA-000360','Server started in RUNNING
mode');
```

The output from the SQL script is shown in Figure 5-5.

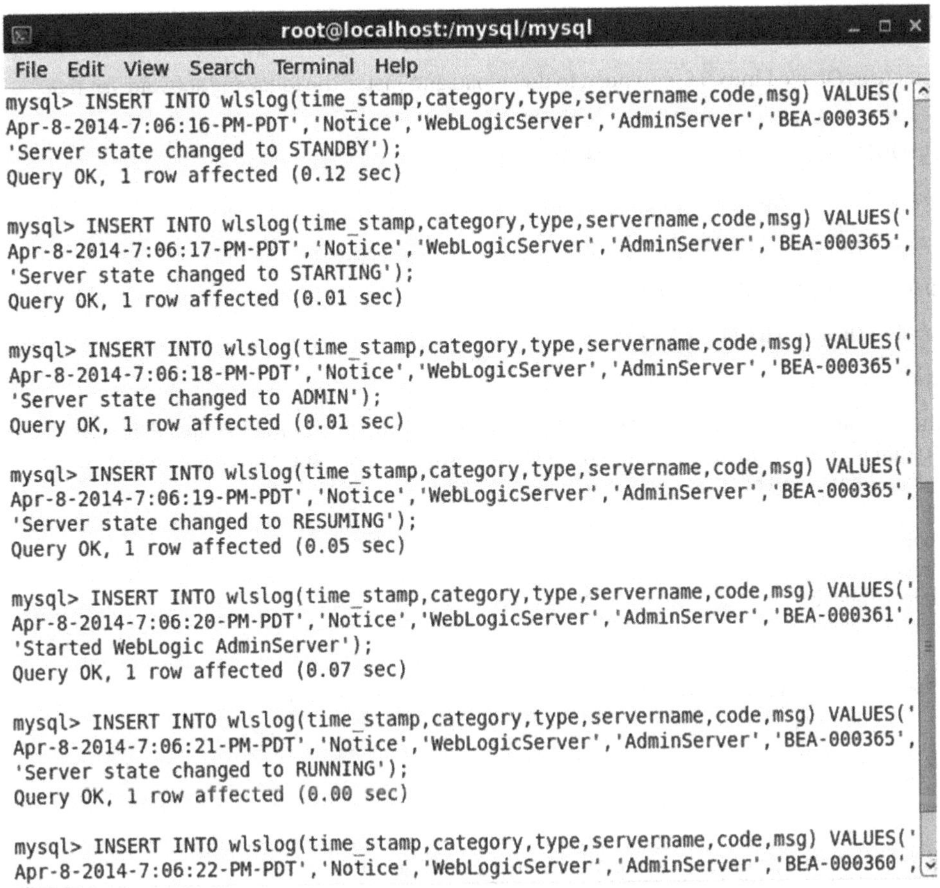

Figure 5-5. Adding data to MySQL wlslog table

The wlslog table is used to import into HDFS. Create another table called WLSLOG_COPY for exporting from HDFS to the MySQL database. The table definition for the WLSLOG_COPY table should be the same as the WLSLOG table.

```
CREATE TABLE WLSLOG_COPY(time_stamp VARCHAR(255) PRIMARY KEY,category VARCHAR(255),type
VARCHAR(255),servername VARCHAR(255), code VARCHAR(255),msg VARCHAR(255));
```

The WLSLOG_COPY table is created, as shown in Figure 5-6.

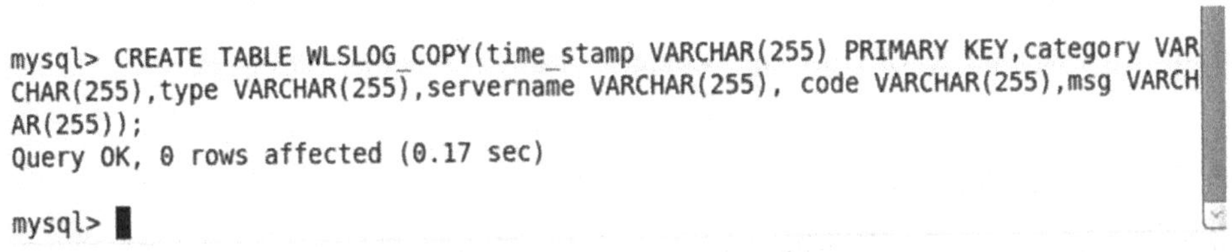

Figure 5-6. Creating the MySQL database table called WLSLOG_COPY

Setting the Environment

Since this chapter uses Oracle Linux 6.6, you need to download and install the following software for this tutorial.

- MySQL Database 5.0 or later (5.6.x used)

- Apache Hadoop 2.6.0 CDH 5.4.7

- Apache Sqoop 1.4.5 CDH 5.4.7

- Apache Hive 0.13.1 CDH 5.3.6

- Apache HBase 1.0.0 CDH 5.4.7

- Java 7

Some of the software is the same as used in earlier chapters and you don't have to reinstall it. The section does explain how to install all the required software, however. Create the hadoop group and add the users called hadoop, hbase, and hdfs.

```
groupadd hadoop
useradd -g hadoop hadoop
useradd -g hadoop hbase
useradd -g hadoop hdfs
```

Create a directory to install the software and set its permissions to global (777).

```
mkdir /cdh
chmod -R 777 /cdh
cd /cdh
```

Download the Java 7 tar.gz file and extract the file to the /cdh directory.

```
tar zxvf jdk-7u55-linux-i586.tar.gz
```

Download the Hadoop 2.6.0 tar file and extract the tar.gz file to the /cdh directory.

```
wget http://archive-primary.cloudera.com/cdh5/cdh/5/hadoop-2.6.0-cdh5.4.7.tar.gz
tar -xvf hadoop-2.6.0-cdh5.4.7.tar.gz
```

Create symlinks for the Hadoop installation bin and conf directories.

```
ln -s /cdh/hadoop-2.6.0-cdh5.4.7/bin /cdh/hadoop-2.6.0-cdh5.4.7/share/hadoop/mapreduce1/bin
ln -s /cdh/hadoop-2.6.0-cdh5.4.7/etc/hadoop  /cdh/hadoop-2.6.0-cdh5.4.7/share/hadoop/
mapreduce1/conf
```

Download and install Sqoop 1.4.5 CDH 5.4.7 and extract the tar.gz file to the /cdh directory.

```
wget http://archive-primary.cloudera.com/cdh5/cdh/5/sqoop-1.4.5-cdh5.4.7.tar.gz
tar -xvf sqoop-1.4.5-cdh5.4.7.tar.gz
```

Copy the JDBC jar for MySQL database to the Sqoop lib directory. The JDBC jar may be downloaded separately or obtained from the database installations.

```
cp mysql-connector-java-5.1.31-bin.jar   /cdh/sqoop-1.4.5-cdh5.4.7/lib
```

Download and extract Hive 0.13.1 tar file to the /cdh directory.

```
wget http://archive-primary.cloudera.com/cdh5/cdh/5/hive-0.13.1-cdh5.3.6.tar.gz
tar -xvf hive-0.13.1-cdh5.3.6.tar.gz
```

Download and extract the HBase tar file to the /cdh directory.

```
wget http://archive-primary.cloudera.com/cdh5/cdh/5/hbase-1.0.0-cdh5.4.7.tar.gz
tar -xvf hbase-1.0.0-cdh5.4.7.tar.gz
```

Set the environment variables for MySQL, Sqoop, Hadoop, Hbase, and Hive in the bash shell file.

```
vi ~/.bashrc
export MYSQL_HOME=/mysql/mysql-5.6.19-linux-glibc2.5-i686
export HADOOP_PREFIX=/cdh/hadoop-2.6.0-cdh5.4.7
export HADOOP_CONF_DIR=$HADOOP_PREFIX/etc/hadoop
export HADOOP_COMMON_HOME=$HADOOP_HOME
export HADOOP_HDFS_HOME=$HADOOP_PREFIX/share/hadoop/hdfs
export HIVE_HOME=/cdh/hive-0.13.1-cdh5.3.6
export HIVE_CONF=$HIVE_HOME/conf
export HBASE_HOME=/cdh/hbase-1.0.0-cdh5.4.7
export SQOOP_HOME=/cdh/sqoop-1.4.5-cdh5.4.7
export HBASE_CONF=$HBASE_HOME/conf
export JAVA_HOME=/cdh/jdk1.7.0_55
export HADOOP_MAPRED_HOME=$HADOOP_PREFIX/share/hadoop/mapreduce1
export HADOOP_HOME=$HADOOP_PREFIX/share/hadoop/mapreduce1
export HADOOP_CLASSPATH=$HADOOP_HOME/*:$HADOOP_HOME/lib/*:$JAVA_HOME/lib/*:$HIVE_CONF:$HIVE_
HOME/lib/*:$HADOOP_CONF_DIR:$HADOOP_COMMON_HOME/*:$HBASE_HOME/lib/*:$HBASE_CONF:$HADOOP_
COMMON_HOME/lib/*:$HADOOP_HDFS_HOME/*:$HADOOP_HDFS_HOME/lib/*:$SQOOP_HOME/lib/*
export PATH=$PATH:$HADOOP_HOME/bin:$HADOOP_MAPRED_HOME/bin:$JAVA_HOME/bin:$HIVE_HOME/
bin:$HBASE_HOME/bin:$MYSQL_HOME/bin:$SQOOP_HOME/bin
export CLASSPATH=$HADOOP_CLASSPATH
export HADOOP_NAMENODE_USER=hadoop
export HADOOP_DATANODE_USER=hadoop
```

Configuring Hadoop

Set the Hadoop core properties fs.defaultFS and hadoop.tmp.dir in the core-site.xml file.

```
vi   $HADOOP_CONF_DIR/core-site.xml
<?xml-stylesheet type="text/xsl" href="configuration.xsl"?>

<!-- Put site-specific property overrides in this file. -->

<configuration>
<property>
  <name>fs.defaultFS</name>
    <value>hdfs://10.0.2.15:8020</value>
    </property>
```

```
<property>
    <name>hadoop.tmp.dir</name>
    <value>/var/lib/hadoop-0.20/cache</value>
  </property>
</configuration>
```

Create the directory specified in the hadoop.tmp.dir property and set its permissions to global (777). Remove the /var/lib/hadoop-0.20/cache directory first if the Hadoop is to be reconfigured.

```
rm -rf   /var/lib/hadoop-0.20/cache
mkdir -p /var/lib/hadoop-0.20/cache
chmod -R 777  /var/lib/hadoop-0.20/cache
```

Set the HDFS configuration properties called dfs.permissions.superusergroup, dfs.namenode.name.dir, dfs.replication, dfs.permissions, and dfs.datanode.max.xcievers in the hdfs-site.xml file.

```
vi $HADOOP_CONF_DIR/hdfs-site.xml
<?xml version="1.0" encoding="UTF-8"?>
<?xml-stylesheet type="text/xsl" href="configuration.xsl"?>

<!-- Put site-specific property overrides in this file. -->

<configuration>
<property>
 <name>dfs.permissions.superusergroup</name>
  <value>hadoop</value>
  </property><property>
   <name>dfs.namenode.name.dir</name>
    <value>/data/1/dfs/nn</value>
    </property>
        <property>
               <name>dfs.replication</name>
                    <value>1</value>
        </property>
<property>
<name>dfs.permissions</name>
<value>false</value>
</property>
<property>
  <name>dfs.datanode.max.xcievers</name>
  <value>4096</value>
</property>
</configuration>
```

If NameNode is to be reformatted, remove any previously created NameNode storage directory, create a new directory, and set its permissions to global (777).

```
rm -rf   /data/1/dfs/nn
mkdir -p /data/1/dfs/nn
chmod -R 777 /data/1/dfs/nn
```

Starting HDFS

Formatting the NameNode is optional if it was already formatted in an earlier chapter. But if the NameNode storage directory or the Hadoop temp directory has been removed and created again, the NameNode needs to be reformatted.

```
hdfs namenode –format
```

Start the NameNode.

```
hdfs namenode
```

Start the DataNode.

```
hdfs datanode
```

Configuring Hive

Create the `hive-site.xml` configuration file from the `hive-default.xml.template` template file.

```
cp /cdh/hive-0.13.1-cdh5.3.6/conf/hive-default.xml.template /cdh/hive-0.13.1-cdh5.3.6/conf/
hive-site.xml
```

Set the `hive.metastore.warehouse.dir` and `hive.metastore.uris` Hive configuration properties in the `hive-site.xml` file.

```
vi /cdh/hive-0.13.1-cdh5.3.6/conf/hive-site.xml
```

```xml
<?xml version="1.0"?>
<?xml-stylesheet type="text/xsl" href="configuration.xsl"?>
<configuration>
<property>
  <name>hive.metastore.warehouse.dir</name>
  <value>hdfs://10.0.2.15:8020/user/hive/warehouse</value>
</property>
<property>
  <name>hive.metastore.uris</name>
  <value>thrift://localhost:10001</value>
</property>

</configuration>
```

Create the directory specified in the `hive.metastore.warehouse.dir` property in `hive-site.xml` and set its permissions.

```
hadoop dfs -mkdir  hdfs://10.0.2.15:8020/user/hive/warehouse
hadoop dfs -chmod -R g+w hdfs://10.0.2.15:8020/user/hive/warehouse
```

Start the Hive Server.

```
hive --service hiveserver
```

The Hive server service starts, as shown in Figure 5-7.

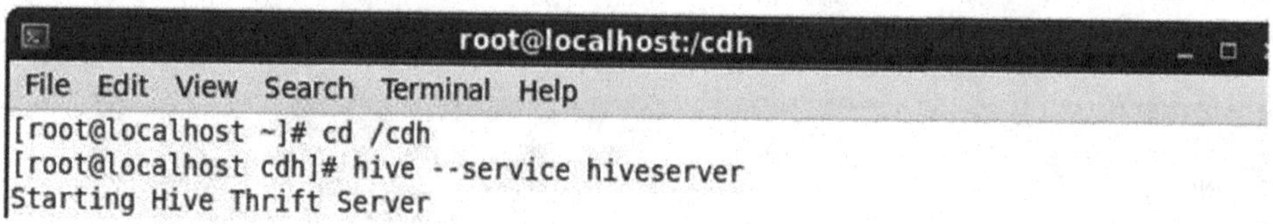

Figure 5-7. *Starting the Hive Thrift server*

Configuring HBase

Set the hbase.rootdir, hbase.zookeeper.property.dataDir, hbase.zookeeper.property.clientPort, hbase.zookeeper.quorum, hbase.regionserver.port, and hbase.master.port HBase configuration properties in the hbase-site.xml file.

```
vi /cdh/hbase-1.0.0-cdh5.4.7/conf/hbase-site.xml
<?xml version="1.0"?>
<?xml-stylesheet type="text/xsl" href="configuration.xsl"?>
<configuration>
  <property>
    <name>hbase.rootdir</name>
    <value>hdfs://10.0.2.15:8020/hbase</value>
  </property>
  <property>
    <name>hbase.zookeeper.property.dataDir</name>
    <value>/zookeeper</value>
  </property>

  <property>
      <name>hbase.zookeeper.property.clientPort</name>
      <value>2181</value>
  </property>
  <property>
    <name>hbase.zookeeper.quorum</name>
    <value>localhost</value>
  </property>
<property>
<name>hbase.regionserver.port</name>
<value>60020</value>
 </property>
<property>
<name>hbase.master.port</name>
<value>60000</value>
 </property>
</configuration>
```

Create the directory specified in the `hbase.zookeeper.property.dataDir` property and set its permissions.

```
mkdir -p /zookeeper
chmod -R 777 /zookeeper
```

Create the directory specified in the `hbase.rootdir` property and set its permissions to global (777).

```
hadoop dfs -mkdir hdfs://10.0.2.15:8020/hbase
hadoop dfs -chmod -R 777 hdfs://10.0.2.15:8020/hbase
```

The `hadoop dfs` command may be replaced with `hdfs dfs`. As root user, set the maximum number of file handles for hbase and hdfs users in the `/etc/security/limits.conf` file.

```
vi /etc/security/limits.conf
hdfs  -        nofile  32768
hbase -        nofile  32768
```

Start HBase with the following command.

```
start-hbase.sh
```

HBase starts, as shown in Figure 5-8.

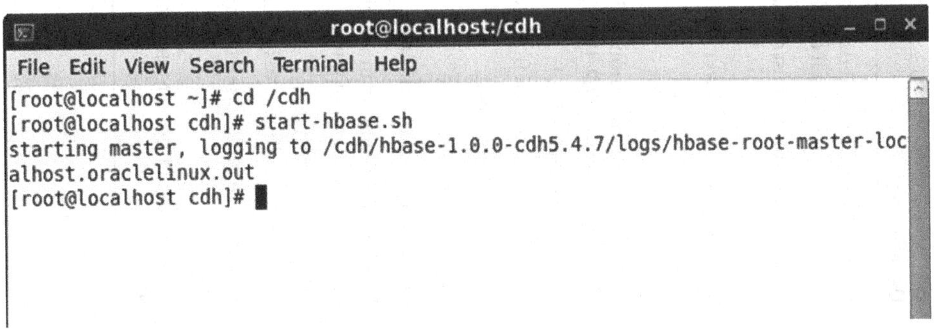

Figure 5-8. *The HBase server starts*

Importing Into HDFS

The Sqoop `import` tool is used to import a single table from a relational database, MySQL database in this chapter, into HDFS. Each row in the relational database table is imported as a single record and stored as a text file (one record per line). The `import` tool is run with the `sqoop import` command; some of the command arguments are listed in Table 5-2.

Table 5-2. Sqoop Import Command Arguments

Command Argument	Description	MySQL Value Used
`--connect <jdbc-uri>`	Specifies the JDBC URI used to connect to the relational database.	`jdbc:mysql://localhost/test`
`--connection-manager <class-name>`	Specifies the connection manager class.	Not used
`--driver <class-name>`	Specifies the JDBC driver class.	`com.mysql.jdbc.Driver` inferred automatically and not required to be specified for MySQL database
`--hadoop-home <dir>`	Specifies the Hadoop home directory to override the $HADOOP_HOME environment variable.	`"/cdh/hadoop-2.6.0-cdh5.4.7/share/hadoop/mapreduce1"`
`-P`	Specifies the password from console.	Not used
`--password <password>`	Specifies the password.	`""`
`--username <username>`	Specifies the username.	`"root"`
`--verbose`	Outputs verbose information.	Not used
`--connection-param-file <filename>`	Specifies the filename in which additional connection parameters may be specified.	Not used
`--columns <col,col,col...>`	Specifies the columns to import.	`time_stamp,category,type,servername, code,msg`
`--table <table-name>`	Specifies the table name to import from.	`wlslog`
`--target-dir <dir>`	Specifies the target directory in HDFS.	`/mysql/import`

With the MySQL Server and HDFS running, use the following command to import using Sqoop.

```
sqoop import --connect "jdbc:mysql://localhost/test" --hadoop-home "/cdh/hadoop-2.6.0-
cdh5.4.7/share/hadoop/mapreduce1"  --password "" --username "root" --table "wlslog"
--columns "time_stamp,category,type,servername, code,msg" --target-dir "/mysql/import"
--verbose
```

An error associated with commons-io could get generated because Sqoop is using commons-io-1.4.jar; this needs to be replaced with commons-io-2.4.jar, which is used by the rest of the Hadoop install.

The Sqoop import tool starts, as shown in Figure 5-9.

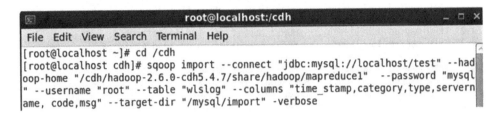

Figure 5-9. *Running the Sqoop import tool*

A MapReduce job runs to import the MySQL database table data into HDFS, as shown in Figure 5-10. As the output indicates the MapReduce job "Retrieved 7 records".

```
root@localhost:/cdh
File Edit View Search Terminal Help
15/10/03 11:29:27 INFO mapred.JobClient: Job complete: job_local2119115423_0001
15/10/03 11:29:27 INFO mapred.JobClient: Counters: 18
15/10/03 11:29:27 INFO mapred.JobClient:   File System Counters
15/10/03 11:29:27 INFO mapred.JobClient:     FILE: Number of bytes read=17777898
15/10/03 11:29:27 INFO mapred.JobClient:     FILE: Number of bytes written=18074
188
15/10/03 11:29:27 INFO mapred.JobClient:     FILE: Number of read operations=0
15/10/03 11:29:27 INFO mapred.JobClient:     FILE: Number of large read operatio
ns=0
15/10/03 11:29:27 INFO mapred.JobClient:     FILE: Number of write operations=0
15/10/03 11:29:27 INFO mapred.JobClient:     HDFS: Number of bytes read=0
15/10/03 11:29:27 INFO mapred.JobClient:     HDFS: Number of bytes written=717
15/10/03 11:29:27 INFO mapred.JobClient:     HDFS: Number of read operations=1
15/10/03 11:29:27 INFO mapred.JobClient:     HDFS: Number of large read operatio
ns=0
15/10/03 11:29:27 INFO mapred.JobClient:     HDFS: Number of write operations=2
15/10/03 11:29:27 INFO mapred.JobClient:   Map-Reduce Framework
15/10/03 11:29:27 INFO mapred.JobClient:     Map input records=7
15/10/03 11:29:27 INFO mapred.JobClient:     Map output records=7
15/10/03 11:29:27 INFO mapred.JobClient:     Input split bytes=87
15/10/03 11:29:27 INFO mapred.JobClient:     Spilled Records=0
15/10/03 11:29:27 INFO mapred.JobClient:     CPU time spent (ms)=0
15/10/03 11:29:27 INFO mapred.JobClient:     Physical memory (bytes) snapshot=0
15/10/03 11:29:27 INFO mapred.JobClient:     Virtual memory (bytes) snapshot=0
15/10/03 11:29:27 INFO mapred.JobClient:     Total committed heap usage (bytes)=
88903680
15/10/03 11:29:28 INFO mapreduce.ImportJobBase: Transferred 717 bytes in 120.342
 seconds (5.958 bytes/sec)
15/10/03 11:29:28 INFO mapreduce.ImportJobBase: Retrieved 7 records.
15/10/03 11:29:28 DEBUG util.ClassLoaderStack: Restoring classloader: sun.misc.L
auncher$AppClassLoader@10f243b
[root@localhost cdh]#
```

Figure 5-10. *MapReduce job to import the MySQL database table data to HDFS*

You can list the output generated with the following command.

```
hdfs dfs -ls /mysql/import
```

The _SUCCESS and `part-m-00000` files are listed, as shown in Figure 5-11.

```
[root@localhost cdh]# hdfs dfs -ls /mysql/import
Found 2 items
-rw-r--r--   1 root hadoop          0 2015-10-03 11:29 /mysql/import/_SUCCESS
-rw-r--r--   1 root hadoop        717 2015-10-03 11:29 /mysql/import/part-m-0000
0
[root@localhost cdh]#
```

Figure 5-11. *Files generated by the Sqoop import command*

The _SUCCESS file indicates that the Sqoop command completed successfully and the `part-m-00000` file is the text data file generated from the MySQL table, as shown in Figure 5-12.

```
[root@localhost cdh]# hdfs dfs -cat /mysql/import/part-m-00000
Apr-8-2014-7:06:16-PM-PDT,Notice,WebLogicServer,AdminServer,BEA-000365,Server st
ate changed to STANDBY
Apr-8-2014-7:06:17-PM-PDT,Notice,WebLogicServer,AdminServer,BEA-000365,Server st
ate changed to STARTING
Apr-8-2014-7:06:18-PM-PDT,Notice,WebLogicServer,AdminServer,BEA-000365,Server st
ate changed to ADMIN
Apr-8-2014-7:06:19-PM-PDT,Notice,WebLogicServer,AdminServer,BEA-000365,Server st
ate changed to RESUMING
Apr-8-2014-7:06:20-PM-PDT,Notice,WebLogicServer,AdminServer,BEA-000361,Started W
ebLogic AdminServer
Apr-8-2014-7:06:21-PM-PDT,Notice,WebLogicServer,AdminServer,BEA-000365,Server st
ate changed to RUNNING
Apr-8-2014-7:06:22-PM-PDT,Notice,WebLogicServer,AdminServer,BEA-000360,Server st
arted in RUNNING mode
[root@localhost cdh]# █
```

Figure 5-12. *HDFS data imported by Sqoop from the MySQL table*

Exporting from HDFS

This section shows you how to export HDFS data to a MySQL table WLSLOG_COPY, which should be empty to start with. Specify the arguments listed in Table 5-3 to the sqoop export command; be sure to set the argument values in double quotes.

Table 5-3. *Sqoop Export Command Arguments to Export to MySQL Table*

Argument	Description	Value
-connect	The connection URL for MySQL database.	"jdbc:mysql://localhost/test"
--username	Username for MySQL database.	"root"
--password	Password for MySQL database.	""
--table	MySQL table name, which is case-sensitive.	"WLSLOG_COPY"
--hadoop-home	Hadoop home directory.	/cdh/hadoop-2.6.0-cdh5.4.7/share/hadoop/mapreduce1"
--export-dir	HDFS directory from which MySQL data is exported.	"/mysql/import"
-verbose	Set command output to verbose.	

Run the following sqoop export command.

```
sqoop export --connect "jdbc:mysql://localhost/test"  --hadoop-home "/cdh/hadoop-2.6.0-
cdh5.4.7/share/hadoop/mapreduce1" --password "" --username "root"  --export-dir "/mysql/
import" --table "WLSLOG_COPY"    --verbose
```

The Sqoop export tool starts, as shown in Figure 5-13.

```
[root@localhost ~]# cd /cdh
[root@localhost cdh]# sqoop export --connect "jdbc:mysql://localhost/test"  --ha
doop-home "/cdh/hadoop-2.6.0-cdh5.4.7/share/hadoop/mapreduce1" --password "" --u
sername "root"  --export-dir "/mysql/import" --table "WLSLOG_COPY"   --verbose
```

Figure 5-13. *Running the Sqoop export command*

The HDFS data is exported to the test.WLSLOG_COPY table. The output from the MapReduce job indicates "Exported 7 records", as shown in Figure 5-14.

```
                        root@localhost:/cdh                          _ □ ×
 File  Edit  View  Search  Terminal  Help
15/10/03 11:40:28 INFO mapred.JobClient: Job complete: job_local2001218582_0001
15/10/03 11:40:29 INFO mapred.JobClient: Counters: 18
15/10/03 11:40:29 INFO mapred.JobClient:   File System Counters
15/10/03 11:40:29 INFO mapred.JobClient:     FILE: Number of bytes read=71117466
15/10/03 11:40:29 INFO mapred.JobClient:     FILE: Number of bytes written=72294
052
15/10/03 11:40:29 INFO mapred.JobClient:     FILE: Number of read operations=0
15/10/03 11:40:29 INFO mapred.JobClient:     FILE: Number of large read operatio
ns=0
15/10/03 11:40:29 INFO mapred.JobClient:     FILE: Number of write operations=0
15/10/03 11:40:29 INFO mapred.JobClient:     HDFS: Number of bytes read=4720
15/10/03 11:40:29 INFO mapred.JobClient:     HDFS: Number of bytes written=0
15/10/03 11:40:29 INFO mapred.JobClient:     HDFS: Number of read operations=78
15/10/03 11:40:29 INFO mapred.JobClient:     HDFS: Number of large read operatio
ns=0
15/10/03 11:40:29 INFO mapred.JobClient:     HDFS: Number of write operations=0
15/10/03 11:40:29 INFO mapred.JobClient:   Map-Reduce Framework
15/10/03 11:40:29 INFO mapred.JobClient:     Map input records=7
15/10/03 11:40:29 INFO mapred.JobClient:     Map output records=7
15/10/03 11:40:29 INFO mapred.JobClient:     Input split bytes=576
15/10/03 11:40:29 INFO mapred.JobClient:     Spilled Records=0
15/10/03 11:40:29 INFO mapred.JobClient:     CPU time spent (ms)=0
15/10/03 11:40:29 INFO mapred.JobClient:     Physical memory (bytes) snapshot=0
15/10/03 11:40:29 INFO mapred.JobClient:     Virtual memory (bytes) snapshot=0
15/10/03 11:40:29 INFO mapred.JobClient:     Total committed heap usage (bytes)=
358383616
15/10/03 11:40:30 INFO mapreduce.ExportJobBase: Transferred 4.6094 KB in 77.9222
 seconds (60.5732 bytes/sec)
15/10/03 11:40:30 INFO mapreduce.ExportJobBase: Exported 7 records.
15/10/03 11:40:30 DEBUG util.ClassLoaderStack: Restoring classloader: sun.misc.L
auncher$AppClassLoader@10f243b
[root@localhost cdh]# █
```

Figure 5-14. *The MapReduce job to export seven records to the MySQL WLSLOG_COPY table*

Run a SELECT statement in the MySQL command-line shell to query the exported data in the WLSLOG_COPY table, as shown in Figure 5-15.

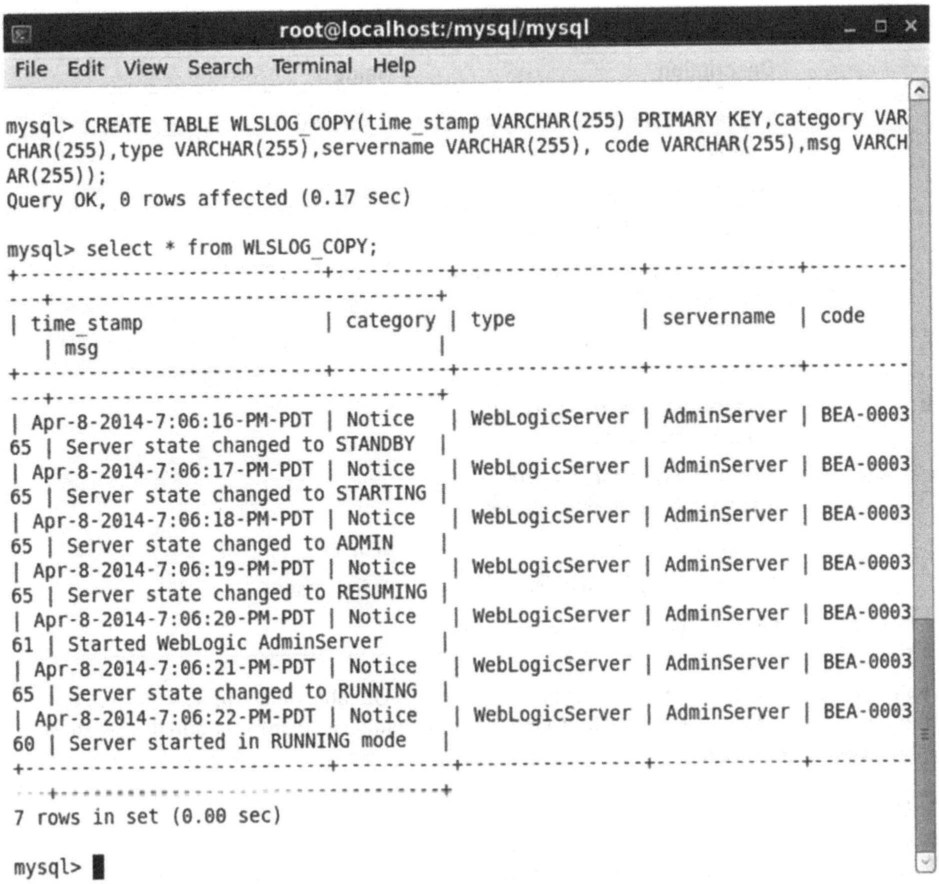

Figure 5-15. *Querying the MySQL table data exported from HDFS*

Importing Into Hive

This section shows you how to import MySQL table data into Hive using the sqoop import tool. Specify the arguments in Table 5-4 to the sqoop import command; be sure to set the argument values in double quotes.

Table 5-4. *Sqoop Import Command Arguments to Import Into Hive*

Argument	Description	Value
-connect	The connection URL for MySQL database.	"jdbc:mysql://localhost/test"
--username	Username for MySQL database.	"root"
--password	Password for MySQL database.	""
--table	MySQL table name, which is case-sensitive.	"WLSLOG_COPY"
--hadoop-home	Hadoop home directory.	"/cdh/hadoop-2.6.0-cdh5.4.7/share/hadoop/mapreduce1"
--hive-import	Import into Hive instead of the default, which is HDFS.	
--create-hive-table	Create the Hive table to which MySQL table is to be imported.	
--hive-table	Hive table to create.	WLSLOG
--split-by	MySQL table primary key.	"time_stamp"
-verbose	Set command output to verbose.	

Since you will be creating the Hive table wlslog to which the MySQL table data is to be exported, you need to delete the wlslog table if it exists in the HBase table. Set the database to default and list the Hive tables with the show tables command.

```
hive>use default;
hive>show tables;
```

If the wlslog table is listed, drop the table with the following command.

```
hive>drop table wlslog;
```

The output from the preceding commands is shown in Figure 5-16.

```
hive> use default;
OK
Time taken: 84.87 seconds
hive> show tables;
OK
wlslog
wlslog_2
wlslog_json
wlslog_mongo
wlslogmongo
wlsmongo
Time taken: 2.429 seconds, Fetched: 6 row(s)
hive> drop table wlslog;
OK
Time taken: 40.521 seconds
hive> █
```

Figure 5-16. *Dropping the Hive wlslog table*

Run the following sqoop import command to import from MySQL to Hive.

```
sqoop import --connect "jdbc:mysql://localhost/test"    --hadoop-home "/cdh/hadoop-2.6.0-
cdh5.4.7/share/hadoop/mapreduce1" --password "" --username "root" --hive-import --create-
hive-table  --hive-table "WLSLOG" --table "WLSLOG_COPY" --split-by "time_stamp" --verbose
```

The default database may be added to the --hive-table setting explicitly as default.wlslog. The MySQL table data is imported into Hive as indicated by the message "Loading data to table default. wlslog" in Figure 5-17.

```
G, `code` STRING, `msg` STRING) COMMENT 'Imported by sqoop on 2015/10/03 12:00:4
1' ROW FORMAT DELIMITED FIELDS TERMINATED BY '\001' LINES TERMINATED BY '\012' S
TORED AS TEXTFILE
15/10/03 12:00:42 DEBUG hive.TableDefWriter: Load statement: LOAD DATA INPATH 'h
dfs://10.0.2.15:8020/user/root/WLSLOG_COPY' INTO TABLE `WLSLOG`
15/10/03 12:00:42 INFO hive.HiveImport: Loading uploaded data into Hive
15/10/03 12:00:48 DEBUG hive.HiveImport: Using in-process Hive instance.
Logging initialized using configuration in jar:file:/cdh/hive-0.13.1-cdh5.3.6/li
b/hive-common-0.13.1-cdh5.3.6.jar!/hive-log4j.properties
OK
Time taken: 59.939 seconds
Loading data to table default.wlslog
Table default.wlslog stats: [numFiles=1, numRows=0, totalSize=717, rawDataSize=0
]
OK
Time taken: 27.94 seconds
[root@localhost cdh]# █
```

Figure 5-17. *Importing data into Hive from the MySQL table*

Run the following SELECT statement to query the Hive table.

```
hive>SELECT * FROM WLSLOG
```

The MySQL data imported into Hive is listed, as shown in Figure 5-18.

```
hive> drop table wlslog;
OK
Time taken: 40.521 seconds
hive> SELECT * FROM WLSLOG
    > ;
OK
Apr-8-2014-7:06:16-PM-PDT       Notice  WebLogicServer  AdminServer     BEA-0003
65      Server state changed to STANDBY
Apr-8-2014-7:06:17-PM-PDT       Notice  WebLogicServer  AdminServer     BEA-0003
65      Server state changed to STARTING
Apr-8-2014-7:06:18-PM-PDT       Notice  WebLogicServer  AdminServer     BEA-0003
65      Server state changed to ADMIN
Apr-8-2014-7:06:19-PM-PDT       Notice  WebLogicServer  AdminServer     BEA-0003
65      Server state changed to RESUMING
Apr-8-2014-7:06:20-PM-PDT       Notice  WebLogicServer  AdminServer     BEA-0003
61      Started WebLogic AdminServer
Apr-8-2014-7:06:21-PM-PDT       Notice  WebLogicServer  AdminServer     BEA-0003
65      Server state changed to RUNNING
Apr-8-2014-7:06:22-PM-PDT       Notice  WebLogicServer  AdminServer     BEA-0003
60      Server started in RUNNING mode
Time taken: 26.019 seconds, Fetched: 7 row(s)
hive> █
```

Figure 5-18. *Querying data imported into Hive*

Importing Into HBase

This section shows you how to import MySQL table data into HBase using the sqoop import tool. Specify the arguments in Table 5-5 to the sqoop import command; be sure to set the argument values in double quotes.

Table 5-5. *Sqoop Import Command Arguments to Import Into HBase*

Argument	Description	Value
-connect	The connection URL for MySQL database.	"jdbc:mysql://localhost/test"
--username	Username for MySQL database.	"root"
--password	Password for MySQL database.	""
--table	MySQL table name, which is case-sensitive.	"wlslog"
--hadoop-home	Hadoop home directory.	"/cdh/hadoop-2.6.0-cdh5.4.7/share/hadoop/mapreduce1"
--hbase-create-table	Create the HBase table to which MySQL table is to be imported.	
--hbase-table	HBase table name.	WLSLOG
--column-family	HBase column family.	"wls"
-verbose	Set command output to verbose.	

Because the HBase table wlslog is to be created by the sqoop command, the wlslog table must not already exist in HBase. Start the HBase shell if it's not already started.

```
hbase shell
```

HBase shell starts, as shown in Figure 5-19.

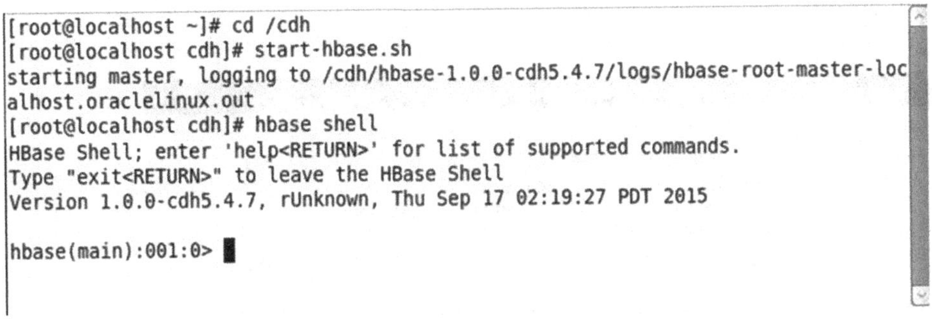

```
[root@localhost ~]# cd /cdh
[root@localhost cdh]# start-hbase.sh
starting master, logging to /cdh/hbase-1.0.0-cdh5.4.7/logs/hbase-root-master-loc
alhost.oraclelinux.out
[root@localhost cdh]# hbase shell
HBase Shell; enter 'help<RETURN>' for list of supported commands.
Type "exit<RETURN>" to leave the HBase Shell
Version 1.0.0-cdh5.4.7, rUnknown, Thu Sep 17 02:19:27 PDT 2015

hbase(main):001:0>
```

Figure 5-19. *Starting the HBase shell*

List the tables in HBase using the list command.

```
list
```

The wlslog table is listed, as shown in Figure 5-20.

```
hbase(main):003:0> list
TABLE
wlslog
wlslog2
2 row(s) in 9.9960 seconds

=> ["wlslog", "wlslog2"]
```

Figure 5-20. *Listing HBase tables*

Disable and drop the wlslog table.

```
disable table 'wlslog'
drop table 'wlslog'
```

The wlslog table is dropped, as shown in Figure 5-21.

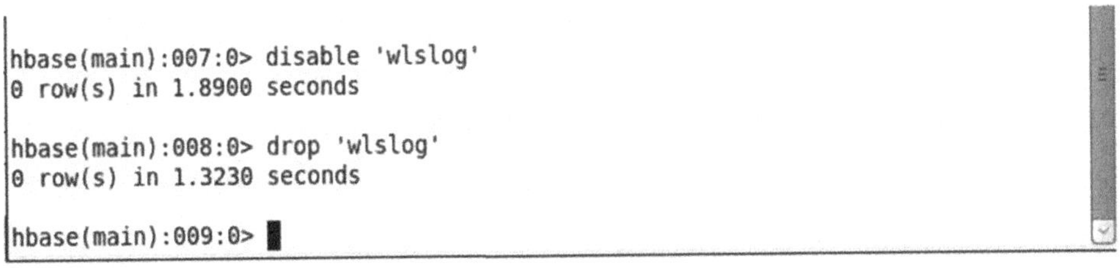

```
hbase(main):007:0> disable 'wlslog'
0 row(s) in 1.8900 seconds

hbase(main):008:0> drop 'wlslog'
0 row(s) in 1.3230 seconds

hbase(main):009:0>
```

Figure 5-21. *Dropping the HBase table wlslog*

283

Run the following sqoop import command.

```
sqoop import --connect "jdbc:mysql://localhost/test"  --hadoop-home "/cdh/hadoop-2.6.0-
cdh5.4.7/share/hadoop/mapreduce1" --password "" --username "root" --hbase-create-table
--hbase-table "WLSLOG" --column-family "wls" --table "wlslog" --verbose
```

The MySQL table data is imported to Hbase, as shown in Figure 5-22. As indicated in the output, the MR job "Retrieved 7 records".

Figure 5-22. *MapReduce job to import the MySQL table data to HBase*

Start the HBase shell if it's not already started.

```
hbase shell
```

Run the scan "WLSLOG" command to list the data in the wlslog table.

```
hbase>scan "WLSLOG"
```

The HBase table data is scanned, as shown in Figure 5-23.

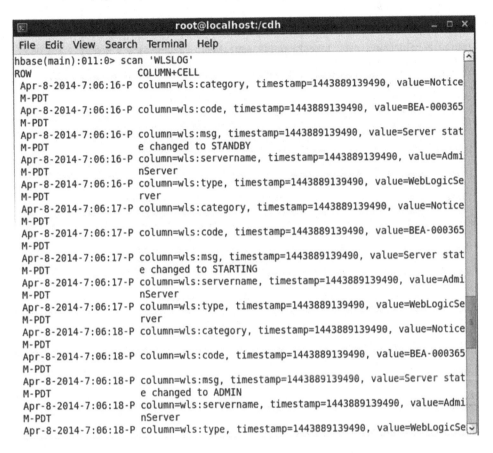

Figure 5-23. *Scanning the HBase table data imported from the MySQL table*

The seven records imported into HBase are listed, as shown in Figure 5-24.

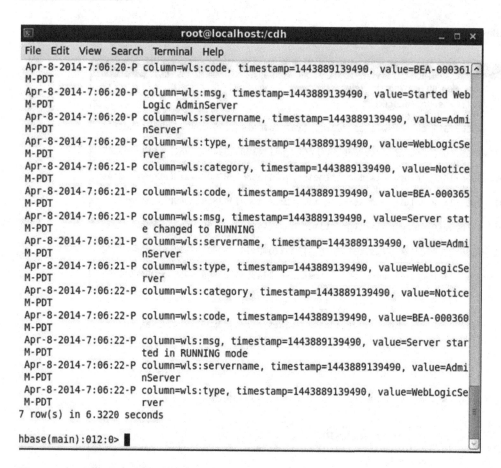

Figure 5-24. *The seven records imported into HBase*

Summary

This chapter introduced the Apache Sqoop framework, which is used to bulk transfer data from a relational database to a HDFS, Apache Hive, and Apache HBase. You used the MySQL database as the relational database. First, you imported MySQL table data into HDFS. Subsequently, you exported the data back to another MySQL table. You imported the MySQL table data into Apache Hive and Apache HBase. The next chapter shows you how to start Apache Flume.

CHAPTER 6

■ ■ ■

Apache Flume

Apache Flume is a framework based on streaming data flows for collecting, aggregating, and transferring large quantities of data. Flume is an efficient and reliable distributed service. A unit of data flow in Flume is called an *event*. The main components in Flume architecture are *Flume source, Flume channel,* and *Flume sink,* all of which are hosted by a *Flume agent*. A Flume source consumes events from an external source such as a log file or a web server. A Flume source stores the events it receives in a passive data store called a Flume channel. Examples of Flume channel types are a JDBC channel, a file channel, and a memory channel. The Flume sink component removes the events from the Flume channel and puts them in an external storage such as HDFS. A Flume sink can also forward events to another Flume source to be processed by another Flume agent. The Flume architecture for a single-hop data flow is shown in Figure 6-1.

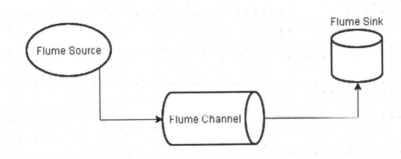

Figure 6-1. *Apache Flume architecture*

Different types of sources, channels, and sinks are supported by the Apache Flume framework. Some of the supported source types are Avro Source, Thrift Source, Exec Source, and HTTP Source. Some of the supported channel types are Memory Channel, JDBC Channel, and File Channel. Some of the supported Sink types are HDFS Sink, MorphlineSolr Sink, and HBase Sink. This chapter discusses two Flume examples. In the first example, the Flume source is of type Exec, the channel is of type Memory, and the sink is of type HDFS. In the second example, the Flume source is of type Exec, the Flume channel is of type Memory, and the sink is of type HBase. This chapter covers the following topics:

Setting the Environment

- Configuring Hadoop

© Deepak Vohra 2016
D. Vohra, *Practical Hadoop Ecosystem*, DOI 10.1007/978-1-4842-2199-0_6

- Starting HDFS
- Configuring HBase
- Configuring Flume
- Running a Flume agent
- Configuring Flume for an HBase sink
- Streaming a MySQL log to an HBase sink

Setting the Environment

The following software is required for this chapter:

- Apache Hadoop
- Apache Flume
- Apache HBase
- Java 7
- MySQL database

Apache Hadoop, Apache HBase, Java 7, and MySQL don't have to be reinstalled if they are already installed, but they could be reinstalled and reconfigured by deleting an older installation. MySQL database is required only for the log file to be used in the Flume examples and is not used for its database. An alternative log file or sample file may also be used instead of the MySQL log file. Create a directory to install the software and set its permissions to global (777).

```
mkdir /cdh
chmod -R 777 /cdh
cd /cdh
```

Download and extract the Java 7 tar file.

```
tar zxvf jdk-7u55-linux-i586.gz
```

Download and extract the Hadoop 2.6.0 tar file.

```
wget http://archive-primary.cloudera.com/cdh5/cdh/5/hadoop-2.6.0-cdh5.4.7.tar.gz
tar -xvf hadoop-2.6.0-cdh5.4.7.tar.gz
```

Create symlinks for the Hadoop bin and conf directories.

```
ln -s /cdh/hadoop-2.6.0-cdh5.4.7/bin /cdh/hadoop-2.6.0-cdh5.4.7/share/hadoop/mapreduce1/bin
ln -s /cdh/hadoop-2.6.0-cdh5.4.7/etc/hadoop  /cdh/hadoop-2.6.0-cdh5.4.7/share/hadoop/
mapreduce1/conf
```

Download and extract the Flume 1.5.0 CDH 5.4.7 tar file.

```
wget http://archive-primary.cloudera.com/cdh5/cdh/5/flume-ng-1.5.0-cdh5.4.7.tar.gz
tar -xvf flume-ng-1.5.0-cdh5.4.7.tar.gz
```

Download and extract the HBase 10.0.0 CDH 5.4.7 tar file.

```
wget http://archive-primary.cloudera.com/cdh5/cdh/5/hbase-1.0.0-cdh5.4.7.tar.gz
tar -xvf hbase-1.0.0-cdh5.4.7.tar.gz
```

Set the environment variables for MySQL, Hadoop, HBase, Flume, and Java.

```
export MYSQL_HOME=/mysql/mysql-5.6.19-linux-glibc2.5-i686
export HADOOP_PREFIX=/cdh/hadoop-2.6.0-cdh5.4.7
export HADOOP_CONF_DIR=$HADOOP_PREFIX/etc/hadoop
export HADOOP_COMMON_HOME=$HADOOP_PREFIX/share/hadoop/common
export HADOOP_HDFS_HOME=$HADOOP_PREFIX/share/hadoop/hdfs
export FLUME_HOME=/cdh/apache-flume-1.5.0-cdh5.4.7-bin
export HBASE_HOME=/cdh/hbase-1.0.0-cdh5.4.7
export HBASE_CONF=$HBASE_HOME/conf
export JAVA_HOME=/cdh/jdk1.7.0_55
export HADOOP_MAPRED_HOME=$HADOOP_PREFIX/share/hadoop/mapreduce1
export HADOOP_HOME=$HADOOP_PREFIX/share/hadoop/mapreduce1
export HADOOP_CLASSPATH=$HADOOP_HOME/*:$HADOOP_HOME/lib/*:$JAVA_HOME/lib/*:$HADOOP_CONF_
DIR:$HADOOP_COMMON_HOME/*:$HBASE_HOME/lib/*:$HBASE_CONF:$HADOOP_COMMON_HOME/lib/*:$HADOOP_
HDFS_HOME/*:$HADOOP_HDFS_HOME/lib/*:$FLUME_HOME/lib/*
export PATH=$PATH:$HADOOP_HOME/bin:$HADOOP_MAPRED_HOME/bin:$JAVA_HOME/bin:$HBASE_HOME/
bin:$MYSQL_HOME/bin:$FLUME_HOME/bin
export CLASSPATH=$HADOOP_CLASSPATH
export HADOOP_NAMENODE_USER=hadoop
export HADOOP_DATANODE_USER=hadoop
```

Configuring Hadoop

You don't have to reinstalled and reconfigured Hadoop if it was installed/configured in an earlier chapter. The Hadoop configuration is the same as in earlier chapters. Set the fs.defaultFS and hadoop.tmp.dir properties in the core-site.xml file.

```
vi    $HADOOP_CONF_DIR/core-site.xml

<?xml-stylesheet type="text/xsl" href="configuration.xsl"?>

<!-- Put site-specific property overrides in this file. -->

<configuration>
<property>
  <name>fs.defaultFS</name>
    <value>hdfs://10.0.2.15:8020</value>
    </property>
 <property>
     <name>hadoop.tmp.dir</name>
     <value>/var/lib/hadoop-0.20/cache</value>
   </property>
 </configuration>
```

Remove the /var/lib/hadoop-0.20/cache directory using the rm -rf command if it was created in an earlier chapter. Create the Hadoop temporary directory and set its permissions to global (777).

```
mkdir -p /var/lib/hadoop-0.20/cache
chmod -R 777  /var/lib/hadoop-0.20/cache
```

Configure the dfs.namenode.name.dir, dfs.replication,dfs.permissions, dfs.permissions.superusergroup, and dfs.datanode.max.xcievers properties in the hdfs-site.xml configuration file.

```
vi $HADOOP_CONF_DIR/hdfs-site.xml

<?xml version="1.0" encoding="UTF-8"?>
<?xml-stylesheet type="text/xsl" href="configuration.xsl"?>

<!-- Put site-specific property overrides in this file. -->

<configuration>
<property>
 <name>dfs.permissions.superusergroup</name>
  <value>hadoop</value>
  </property><property>
   <name>dfs.namenode.name.dir</name>
    <value>/data/1/dfs/nn</value>
    </property>
        <property>
                <name>dfs.replication</name>
                     <value>1</value>
        </property>
<property>
<name>dfs.permissions</name>
<value>false</value>
</property>
<property>
  <name>dfs.datanode.max.xcievers</name>
  <value>4096</value>
</property>
</configuration>
```

Remove the /data/1/dfs/nn directory using the rm -rf command if it was created in an earlier chapter. Create the NameNode storage directory and set its permission to global (777).

```
mkdir -p /data/1/dfs/nn
chmod -R 777 /data/1/dfs/nn
```

Starting HDFS

Start HDFS, which is comprised of the NameNode and DataNode. NameNode is not required to be reformatted if it was formatted in an earlier chapter.

```
hdfs namenode
hdfs datanode
```

Create the HDFS directory configured in the hbase.rootdir property and set its permissions to global (777).

```
hadoop dfs -mkdir hdfs://10.0.2.15:8020/hbase
hadoop dfs -chmod -R 777 hdfs://10.0.2.15:8020/hbase
```

Create the HDFS directory hdfs://10.0.2.15:8020/flume to stream MySQL log data in one of the Flume examples.

```
hadoop dfs -mkdir -p hdfs://10.0.2.15:8020/flume
hadoop dfs -chmod -R 777 hdfs://10.0.2.15:8020/flume
```

Creating an HBase Table

The HBase configuration is the same as shown in earlier chapters. Configure the hbase.rootdir, hbase.zookeeper.property.dataDir, hbase.zookeeper.property.clientPort, hbase.zookeeper.quorum, hbase.regionserver.port, and hbase.master.por properties in the hbase-site.xml file.

```
vi /cdh/hbase-1.0.0-cdh5.4.7/conf/hbase-site.xml
```

```
<?xml version="1.0"?>
<?xml-stylesheet type="text/xsl" href="configuration.xsl"?>
<configuration>
  <property>
    <name>hbase.rootdir</name>
    <value>hdfs://10.0.2.15:8020/hbase</value>
  </property>
  <property>
    <name>hbase.zookeeper.property.dataDir</name>
    <value>/zookeeper</value>
  </property>

  <property>
    <name>hbase.zookeeper.property.clientPort</name>
    <value>2181</value>
  </property>
  <property>
    <name>hbase.zookeeper.quorum</name>
    <value>localhost</value>
  </property>
<property>
<name>hbase.regionserver.port</name>
<value>60020</value>
 </property>
<property>
<name>hbase.master.port</name>
<value>60000</value>
 </property>
</configuration>
```

Remove the /zookeeper directory using the rm -rf command if it was created in an earlier chapter. Create the /zookeeper directory configured in the hbase.zookeeper.property.dataDir property and set its permissions to global (777).

291

```
mkdir -p /zookeeper
chmod -R 777 /zookeeper
```

Configure the ulimit limits for hdfs and hbase users in the /etc/security/limits.conf file.

```
vi /etc/security/limits.conf
```

```
hdfs  -        nofile  32768
hbase -        nofile  32768
```

Start HBase.

```
start-hbase.sh
```

Start the HBase shell.

```
hbase shell
```

Create an HBase table called 'flume' with the column family 'mysqllog' to which MySQL log will be streamed in one of the Flume examples.

```
create 'flume','mysqllog'
```

The HBase table 'flume' is created, as shown in Figure 6-2.

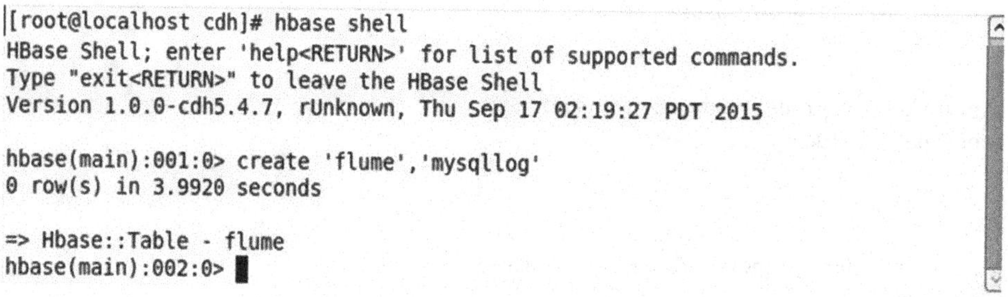

```
[root@localhost cdh]# hbase shell
HBase Shell; enter 'help<RETURN>' for list of supported commands.
Type "exit<RETURN>" to leave the HBase Shell
Version 1.0.0-cdh5.4.7, rUnknown, Thu Sep 17 02:19:27 PDT 2015

hbase(main):001:0> create 'flume','mysqllog'
0 row(s) in 3.9920 seconds

=> Hbase::Table - flume
hbase(main):002:0> █
```

Figure 6-2. *Starting HBase and the HBase Shell*

Configuring Flume

The Flume Agent uses a configuration file in which the Flume source, channel, and sink are configured. The format for configuring a Flume source, channel, and sink is the following.

```
<agent_name>.sources=<source_name>
<agent_name>.sinks=<sink_name>
<agent_name>.channels=<channel_name>
```

The Flume source, channel, and sink have properties, some of which are required and are configured using the following format.

```
<agent_name>.sources.<source_name>.<property_name>=<property_value>
<agent_name>.sinks.<sink_name>.<property_name>=<property_value>
<agent_name>.channels.<channel_name>.<property_name>=<property_value>
```

Some of the properties are common to all types of sources and sinks, such as the type and channels properties. Some of the other properties are specific to the Flume source or sink type. Create a Flume configuration file called flume.conf (although the name is arbitrary). Add the properties listed in Table 6-1 to this flume.conf file.

Table 6-1. *Configuration Properties for the flume.conf File*

Property	Description	Value
agent.sources	Sets the Flume source name	MySQLLog
agent.sources.MySQLLog.type	Sets the Flume source type	exec
agent.sinks	Sets the Flume sink name	HDFSSink
agent.sinks.HDFSSink.type	Sets the Flume sink type	hdfs
agent.channels	Sets the Flume channel name	ch1
agent.channels.ch1.capacity	Sets the channel capacity	1000000
agent.channels.ch1.transactionCapacity	Sets the channel transaction capacity	1000
agent.channels.ch1.type	Sets the channel type	memory
agent.sources.MySQLLog.channels	Sets the channel on the source	ch1
agent.sources.MySQLLog.command	Sets the source exec command	cat /var/log/mysqld.log
agent.sinks.HDFSSink.channel	Sets the channel on the sink	ch1
agent.sinks.HDFSSink.hdfs.path	Sets the HDFS path for the sink	hdfs://10.0.2.15:8020/flume/
agent.sinks.HDFSSink.hdfs.file.Type	Sets the HDFS file type	DataStream

Here is the flume.conf file:

```
agent.sources=MySQLLog
agent.sources.MySQLLog.type=exec

agent.sinks=HDFSSink
agent.sinks.HDFSSink.type = hdfs
```

```
agent.channels=ch1
agent.channels.ch1.capacity = 1000000
agent.channels.ch1.transactionCapacity = 1000
agent.channels.ch1.type=memory

agent.sources.MySQLLog.channels=ch1
agent.sources.MySQLLog.command=cat /var/log/mysqld.log

agent.sinks.HDFSSink.channel = ch1
agent.sinks.HDFSSink.hdfs.path = hdfs://10.0.2.15:8020/flume/
agent.sinks.HDFSSink.hdfs.file.Type = DataStream
```

Copy the flume.conf file to the Flume configuration directory (the conf directory).

```
cp flume.conf $FLUME_HOME/conf/flume.conf
```

Running a Flume Agent

This section runs the Flume agent and streams MySQL log data to HDFS. Run the following Flume agent command in which the -conf option specifies the Flume configuration directory and the -f option specifies the Flume configuration filename. The Flume agent name is specified using the -n option. The Flume agent name is configured in the flume.conf file as the prefix to all settings.

```
flume-ng agent  --conf $FLUME_HOME/conf -f $FLUME_HOME/conf/flume.conf -n agent  -Dflume.
root.logger=INFO,console
```

The Flume agent is started and the Hadoop libraries are added to the classpath for HDFS access, as shown in Figure 6-3.

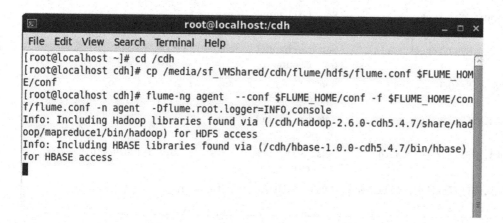

Figure 6-3. *Starting the Flume agent*

MySQL log data is streamed to HDFS and the data files called FlumeData.<file#>.tmp are generated in the hdfs://10.0.2.15:8020/flume directory, which is configured in the flume.conf file. The detailed output from the Flume agent lists the channels, source, and sink being created and started:

```
[root@localhost cdh]# flume-ng agent  --conf $FLUME_HOME/conf -f $FLUME_HOME/conf/flume.conf
-n agent  -Dflume.root.logger=INFO,console
Info: Including Hadoop libraries found via (/cdh/hadoop-2.6.0-cdh5.4.7/share/hadoop/
mapreduce1/bin/hadoop) for HDFS access
Info: Including HBASE libraries found via (/cdh/hbase-1.0.0-cdh5.4.7/bin/hbase) for HBASE
access
org.apache.flume.node.Application -f /cdh/apache-flume-1.5.0-cdh5.4.7-bin/conf/flume.conf -n
agent
2015-10-04 12:32:28,712 (conf-file-poller-0) [INFO - org.apache.flume.conf.FlumeConfiguratio
n$AgentConfiguration.addProperty(FlumeConfiguration.java:931)] Added sinks: HDFSSink Agent:
agent
2015-10-04 12:32:29,888 (conf-file-poller-0) [INFO - org.apache.flume.node.
AbstractConfigurationProvider.loadChannels(AbstractConfigurationProvider.java:145)] Creating
channels
2015-10-04 12:32:30,508 (conf-file-poller-0) [INFO - org.apache.flume.node.
AbstractConfigurationProvider.loadChannels(AbstractConfigurationProvider.java:200)] Created
channel ch1
2015-10-04 12:32:30,559 (conf-file-poller-0) [INFO - org.apache.flume.source.
DefaultSourceFactory.create(DefaultSourceFactory.java:41)] Creating instance of source
MySQLLog, type exec
2015-10-04 12:32:31,022 (conf-file-poller-0) [INFO - org.apache.flume.sink.
DefaultSinkFactory.create(DefaultSinkFactory.java:42)] Creating instance of sink: HDFSSink,
type: hdfs
2015-10-04 12:32:31,692 (conf-file-poller-0) [INFO - org.apache.flume.node.
AbstractConfigurationProvider.getConfiguration(AbstractConfigurationProvider.java:114)]
Channel ch1 connected to [MySQLLog, HDFSSink]
2015-10-04 12:32:34,640 (lifecycleSupervisor-1-1) [INFO - org.apache.flume.instrumentation.
MonitoredCounterGroup.start(MonitoredCounterGroup.java:96)] Component type: CHANNEL, name:
ch1 started
2015-10-04 12:32:34,818 (lifecycleSupervisor-1-3) [INFO - org.apache.flume.instrumentation.
MonitoredCounterGroup.start(MonitoredCounterGroup.java:96)] Component type: SINK, name:
HDFSSink started
2015-10-04 12:32:34,887 (lifecycleSupervisor-1-0) [INFO - org.apache.flume.instrumentation.
MonitoredCounterGroup.start(MonitoredCounterGroup.java:96)] Component type: SOURCE, name:
MySQLLog started
```

You can list the FlumeData files in HDFS using the following command.

```
hdfs dfs -ls hdfs://10.0.2.15:8020/flume
```

The FlumeData files are listed. One FlumeData file is generated for each Flume event, as shown in Figure 6-4.

```
                           root@localhost:/cdh                         _  □  ×
File   Edit   View   Search   Terminal   Help
me/FlumeData.1443976356331
-rw-r--r--   1 root hadoop       1169 2015-10-04 12:39 hdfs://10.0.2.15:8020/flu
me/FlumeData.1443976356332
-rw-r--r--   1 root hadoop       1161 2015-10-04 12:39 hdfs://10.0.2.15:8020/flu
me/FlumeData.1443976356333
-rw-r--r--   1 root hadoop       1014 2015-10-04 12:39 hdfs://10.0.2.15:8020/flu
me/FlumeData.1443976356334
-rw-r--r--   1 root hadoop       1153 2015-10-04 12:40 hdfs://10.0.2.15:8020/flu
me/FlumeData.1443976356335
-rw-r--r--   1 root hadoop       1152 2015-10-04 12:40 hdfs://10.0.2.15:8020/flu
me/FlumeData.1443976356336
-rw-r--r--   1 root hadoop       1109 2015-10-04 12:40 hdfs://10.0.2.15:8020/flu
me/FlumeData.1443976356337
-rw-r--r--   1 root hadoop       1157 2015-10-04 12:40 hdfs://10.0.2.15:8020/flu
me/FlumeData.1443976356338
-rw-r--r--   1 root hadoop       1033 2015-10-04 12:40 hdfs://10.0.2.15:8020/flu
me/FlumeData.1443976356339
-rw-r--r--   1 root hadoop       1138 2015-10-04 12:40 hdfs://10.0.2.15:8020/flu
me/FlumeData.1443976356340
-rw-r--r--   1 root hadoop       1138 2015-10-04 12:40 hdfs://10.0.2.15:8020/flu
me/FlumeData.1443976356341
-rw-r--r--   1 root hadoop       1018 2015-10-04 12:40 hdfs://10.0.2.15:8020/flu
me/FlumeData.1443976356342
-rw-r--r--   1 root hadoop       1178 2015-10-04 12:40 hdfs://10.0.2.15:8020/flu
me/FlumeData.1443976356343
-rw-r--r--   1 root hadoop       1150 2015-10-04 12:40 hdfs://10.0.2.15:8020/flu
me/FlumeData.1443976356344
-rw-r--r--   1 root hadoop        985 2015-10-04 12:40 hdfs://10.0.2.15:8020/flu
me/FlumeData.1443976356345
-rw-r--r--   1 root hadoop        201 2015-10-04 12:40 hdfs://10.0.2.15:8020/flu
me/FlumeData.1443976356346.tmp
[root@localhost cdh]# █
```

Figure 6-4. *Listing the FlumeData files in HDFS*

MySQL log data streamed in the FlumeData files may be listed with the following command. The following command lists the data streamed in the FlumeData.1443976356172 file.

```
hdfs dfs -cat hdfs://10.0.2.15:8020/flume/FlumeData.1443976356172
```

The MySQL log data is listed, as shown in Figure 6-5.

```
/mysql/mysql/bin/mysqld: ready for connections.[root@localhost cdh]# hdfs dfs -c
6356172://10.0.2.15:8020/flume/FlumeData.144397
SEQ░░org.apache.hadoop.io.LongWritable"org.apache.hadoop.io.BytesWritable░░]X░x
.B5;P░/░░30░B2015-01-18 17:12:16 2816 [Note] Server socket created on IP: '::'.░
P3░░░2015-01-18 17:12:16 2816 [ERROR] /mysql/mysql/bin/mysqld: Can't create/wri
te to file '/var/run/mysqld/mysqld.pid' (Errcode: 2 - No such file or directory)
░░3░░e2015-01-18 17:12:16 2816 [ERROR] Can't start server: can't create PID fil
e: No such file or directory░░3░░Q150118 17:12:17 mysqld_safe mysqld from pid f
ile /var/run/mysqld/mysqld.pid ended░░3░░@150118 17:47:42 mysqld_safe The file
/usr/local/mysql/bin/mysqld░░3░░Hdoes not exist or is not executable. Please cd
 to the mysql installation░░30░░8directory and restart this script from there as
 follows:░░3░░░░/bin/mysqld_safe&░░3░░KSee http://dev.mysql.com/doc/mysql/en/m
ysqld-safe.html for more information░░3░░U150118 18:01:31 mysqld_safe Starting
mysqld daemon with databases from /var/lib/mysql[root@localhost cdh]# ▮
```

Figure 6-5. Displaying MySQL log data streamed to HDFS with Flume

Configuring Flume for HBase Sink

The preceding example used an HDFS sink. Several types of sinks are supported and this section shows you how to configure a sink of type HBase. Create another flume.conf file or modify the same configuration file to add the properties in Table 6-2 to flume.conf for a source of type exec, a channel of type memory, and a sink of type HDFS.

Table 6-2. Configuration Properties in the flume.conf File

Property	Description	Value
hbase-agent.sources	Sets the Flume source name	MySQLLog
hbase-agent.sources.MySQLLog.type	Sets the Flume source type	exec
hbase-agent.sinks	Sets the Flume sink name	HBaseSink
hbase-agent.sinks.HDFSSink.type	Sets the Flume sink type for HBase	org.apache.flume.sink. hbase.HBaseSink
hbase-agent.channels	Sets the Flume channel name	ch1
hbase-agent.channels.ch1.capacity	Sets the channel capacity	1000000
hbase-agent.channels.ch1. transactionCapacity	Sets the channel transaction capacity	1000
hbase-agent.channels.ch1.type	Sets the channel type	memory
hbase-agent.sources.MySQLLog.channels	Sets the channel on the source	ch1
hbase-agent.sources.MySQLLog.command	Sets the source exec command	cat /var/log/mysqld. log
hbase-agent.sinks.HDFSSink.channel	Sets the channel on the sink	ch1
hbase-agent.sinks.HBaseSink.table	Sets the HBase table for the sink	flume
hbase-agent.sinks.HBaseSink.columnFamily	Sets the column family for the HBase table	mysqllog

The `flume.conf` file is listed:

```
hbase-agent.sources=MySQLLog

hbase-agent.sinks=HBaseSink
hbase-agent.channels=ch1
hbase-agent.channels.ch1.capacity = 1000000
hbase-agent.channels.ch1.transactionCapacity = 1000
hbase-agent.channels.ch1.type=memory
hbase-agent.sources.MySQLLog.type=exec
hbase-agent.sources.MySQLLog.command=cat /var/log/mysqld.log
hbase-agent.sources.MySQLLog.channels=ch1
hbase-agent.sinks.HBaseSink.type=org.apache.flume.sink.hbase.HBaseSink
hbase-agent.sinks.HBaseSink.channel=ch1
hbase-agent.sinks.HBaseSink.table=flume
hbase-agent.sinks.HBaseSink.columnFamily=mysqllog
```

Copy the `flume.conf` to the Flume configuration directory `conf`.

```
cp flume.conf $FLUME_HOME/conf/flume.conf
```

Streaming MySQL Logs to an HBase Sink

This section shows you how to run the Flume agent to stream MySQL logs to HBase. Run the following command in which the agent name is specified as `hbase-agent`, which is configured in the `flume.conf` file.

```
flume-ng agent  --conf $FLUME_HOME/conf -f $FLUME_HOME/conf/flume.conf -n hbase-
agent  -Dflume.root.logger=INFO,console
```

The Flume agent is started and the HBase libraries are added to the classpath, as shown in Figure 6-6.

Figure 6-6. *Starting the Flume agent to stream MySQL log data to HBase*

The HBase sink is started as well, as shown in Figure 6-7.

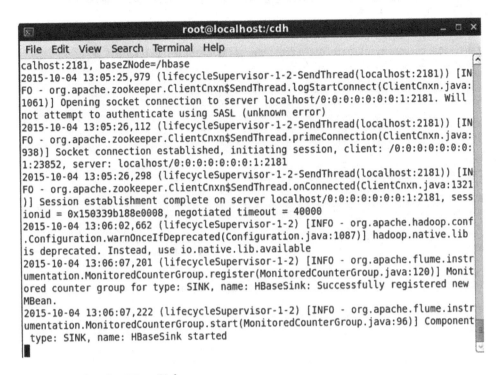

```
root@localhost:/cdh                          _  □  ×

File  Edit  View  Search  Terminal  Help
calhost:2181, baseZNode=/hbase
2015-10-04 13:05:25,979 (lifecycleSupervisor-1-2-SendThread(localhost:2181)) [IN
FO - org.apache.zookeeper.ClientCnxn$SendThread.logStartConnect(ClientCnxn.java:
1061)] Opening socket connection to server localhost/0:0:0:0:0:0:0:1:2181. Will
not attempt to authenticate using SASL (unknown error)
2015-10-04 13:05:26,112 (lifecycleSupervisor-1-2-SendThread(localhost:2181)) [IN
FO - org.apache.zookeeper.ClientCnxn$SendThread.primeConnection(ClientCnxn.java:
938)] Socket connection established, initiating session, client: /0:0:0:0:0:0:0:
1:23852, server: localhost/0:0:0:0:0:0:0:1:2181
2015-10-04 13:05:26,298 (lifecycleSupervisor-1-2-SendThread(localhost:2181)) [IN
FO - org.apache.zookeeper.ClientCnxn$SendThread.onConnected(ClientCnxn.java:1321
)] Session establishment complete on server localhost/0:0:0:0:0:0:0:1:2181, sess
ionid = 0x150339b188e0008, negotiated timeout = 40000
2015-10-04 13:06:02,662 (lifecycleSupervisor-1-2) [INFO - org.apache.hadoop.conf
.Configuration.warnOnceIfDeprecated(Configuration.java:1087)] hadoop.native.lib
is deprecated. Instead, use io.native.lib.available
2015-10-04 13:06:07,201 (lifecycleSupervisor-1-2) [INFO - org.apache.flume.instr
umentation.MonitoredCounterGroup.register(MonitoredCounterGroup.java:120)] Monit
ored counter group for type: SINK, name: HBaseSink: Successfully registered new
MBean.
2015-10-04 13:06:07,222 (lifecycleSupervisor-1-2) [INFO - org.apache.flume.instr
umentation.MonitoredCounterGroup.start(MonitoredCounterGroup.java:96)] Component
 type: SINK, name: HBaseSink started
```

Figure 6-7. Starting HBase Sink

Subsequently, run the following command in the HBase shell. It will list the data streamed to the HBase table called 'flume'.

```
scan 'flume'
```

The MySQL logs streamed to the HBase table 'flume' are then listed, as shown in Figure 6-8.

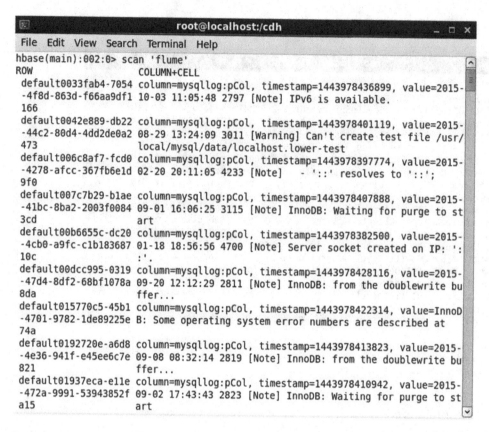

Figure 6-8. MySQL logs streamed to HBase

Summary

This chapter introduced the Apache Flume framework. Flume is designed for streaming large quantities of log data from different types and sources to sinks of different types. Although Flume is designed mainly for log data, it can also be used for other types of data. The main components of Flume are source, channel, and sink, all of which are processed by a Flume agent as configured in a configuration file. The next chapter discusses Apache Avro.

PART IV

■ ■ ■

Serializing

Serializing

CHAPTER 7

■ ■ ■

Apache Avro

Apache Avro is a compact binary data serialization format providing varied data structures. Avro uses JSON notation schemas to serialize/deserialize data. Avro data is stored in a container file (an .avro file) and its schema (the .avsc file) is stored with the data file. Unlike some other similar systems such as Protocol buffers, Avro does not require code generation and uses dynamic typing. Data is untagged because the schema is accompanied with the data, resulting in a compact data file. Avro supports versioning; different versions (having different columns) of Avro data files may coexist along with their schemas. Another benefit of Avro is interoperability with other languages because of its efficient binary format. The Apache Hadoop ecosystem supports Apache Avro in several of its projects. Apache Hive provides support to store a table as Avro. The Apache sqoop import command supports importing relational data to an Avro data file. Apache Flume supports Avro as a source and sink type.

This chapter discusses creating a Hive external table stored as Avro. In another example, you'll see how to import a MySQL table data to HDFS as an Avro data file. This chapter covers the following topics:

- Setting the environment
- Creating an Avro schema
- Creating a Hive-managed table
- Creating a Hive (prior to version 0.14) external table stored as Avro
- Creating a Hive (version 0.14 and later) external table stored as Avro
- Transferring MySQL table data as an Avro data file with Sqoop

Setting the Environment

This chapter requires the following software.

- Apache Hadoop
- Apache Hive
- Apache Sqoop
- MySQL database
- Java 7

Create a directory to install the software and set its permissions to global (777).

```
mkdir /cdh
chmod -R 777 /cdh
cd /cdh
```

© Deepak Vohra 2016
D. Vohra, *Practical Hadoop Ecosystem*, DOI 10.1007/978-1-4842-2199-0_7

303

Download and extract the Hadoop tar file.

```
wget http://archive-primary.cloudera.com/cdh5/cdh/5/hadoop-2.6.0-cdh5.4.7.tar.gz
tar -xvf hadoop-2.6.0-cdh5.4.7.tar.gz
```

Create symlinks for the Hadoop bin and conf directories.

```
ln -s /cdh/hadoop-2.6.0-cdh5.4.7/bin /cdh/hadoop-2.6.0-cdh5.4.7/share/hadoop/mapreduce1/bin
ln -s /cdh/hadoop-2.6.0-cdh5.4.7/etc/hadoop /cdh/hadoop-2.6.0-cdh5.4.7/share/hadoop/
mapreduce1/conf
```

Download and extract the Hive tar file.

```
wget http://archive-primary.cloudera.com/cdh5/cdh/5/hive-0.13.1-cdh5.3.6.tar.gz
tar -xvf hive-0.13.1-cdh5.3.6.tar.gz
```

Download and extract the Sqoop tar file.

```
wget http://archive-primary.cloudera.com/cdh5/cdh/5/sqoop-1.4.5-cdh5.4.7.tar.gz
tar -xvf sqoop-1.4.5-cdh5.4.7.tar.gz
```

Copy the MySQL JDBC jar file to the Sqoop lib directory.

```
cp mysql-connector-java-5.1.31-bin.jar  /cdh/sqoop-1.4.5-cdh5.4.7/lib
```

Set environment variables for Hadoop, Hive, Sqoop, MySQL, and Java. Some of the PATH variable built-in settings might be different than those listed here.

```
vi ~/.bashrc
export MYSQL_HOME=/mysql/mysql-5.6.19-linux-glibc2.5-i686
export HADOOP_PREFIX=/cdh/hadoop-2.6.0-cdh5.4.7
export HADOOP_CONF_DIR=$HADOOP_PREFIX/etc/hadoop
export HADOOP_COMMON_HOME=$HADOOP_HOME
export HADOOP_HDFS_HOME=$HADOOP_PREFIX/share/hadoop/hdfs
export HIVE_HOME=/cdh/hive-0.13.1-cdh5.3.6
export HIVE_CONF=$HIVE_HOME/conf
export SQOOP_HOME=/cdh/sqoop-1.4.5-cdh5.4.7
export JAVA_HOME=/cdh/jdk1.7.0_55
export HADOOP_MAPRED_HOME=$HADOOP_PREFIX/share/hadoop/mapreduce1
export HADOOP_HOME=$HADOOP_PREFIX/share/hadoop/mapreduce1
export HADOOP_CLASSPATH=$HADOOP_HOME/*:$HADOOP_HOME/lib/*:$JAVA_HOME/lib/*:$HIVE_HOME/
lib/*:$HADOOP_CONF_DIR:$HADOOP_COMMON_HOME/*:$HADOOP_COMMON_HOME/lib/*:$HADOOP_HDFS_
HOME/*:$HADOOP_HDFS_HOME/lib/*:$SQOOP_HOME/lib/*
export PATH=$JAVA_HOME/bin:/usr/lib/qt-3.3/bin:/usr/local/sbin:/usr/sbin:/sbin:/usr/local/
bin:/usr/bin:/bin:$HADOOP_HOME/bin:$HADOOP_MAPRED_HOME/bin:$HIVE_HOME/bin:$SQOOP_HOME/
bin:$MYSQL_HOME/bin:$HADOOP_PREFIX/bin
export CLASSPATH=$HADOOP_CLASSPATH
export HADOOP_NAMENODE_USER=hadoop
export HADOOP_DATANODE_USER=hadoop
export HADOOP_VERSION=2.6.0
export HADOOP_USER_CLASSPATH_FIRST=true
```

Configure Hadoop and Hive as discussed in earlier chapters. (Chapter 1 covers Hadoop and Chapter 2 covers Hive.) The ulimit might also need to be increased; for example, **ulimit -n 70000**. Start the NameNode.

```
hdfs namenode
```

Start the DataNode.

```
hdfs datanode
```

Creating an Avro Schema

An Avro schema is in JavaScript Object Notation (JSON) format and describes the fields allowed in a value, including their data types. An Avro schema describes a record and has the following format.

```
{
 "type": "record",
 "namespace": "schema.namespace",
 "name": "schema.name",
 "fields": [
 { "name": "field1", "type": "string" },
 { "name": "field2", "type": "int" }
 ]
}
```

The record has four fields: type, namespace, name, and fields. The type describes the JSON field type and is "record" for Avro schemas. The namespace differentiates one schema group from another. The name is the schema name. The name and namespace are arbitrary values. The fields are the actual schema definitions and describe the fields in a record value including their types. A field type is a primitive type (null, int, long, string, boolean, float, double, and bytes). A schema definition may consist of a single field or multiple fields.

This example uses a multi-field schema to store log data. The schema has six fields—timestamp, category, type, servername, code, and msg—each of type string. The default attribute is recommended. It's not the default value used if a value is not provided, but it is used in schema evolution. When referring to a schema, the qualified name of the schema is used, which is the name prefixed with the namespace. Create a wlslog.avsc schema to represent WebLogic server log and copy the following listing to the wlslog.avsc file.

```
{
 "type" : "record",
 "name" : "wlslog",
 "namespace" : "wlslog.example.schema",
 "fields" : [{"name" : "timestamp",
 "type" : "string",
 "default" : "NONE"},
 {"name" : "category",
 "type" : "string",
 "default" : "NONE"},
 {"name" : "type",
 "type" : "string",
 "default" : "NONE"},
 {"name" : "servername",
```

```
"type" : "string",
"default" : "NONE"},
{"name" : "code",
"type" : "string",
"default" : "NONE"},
{"name" : "msg",
"type" : "string",
"default" : "NONE"}]
}
```

When the HDFS (NameNode and DataNode) starts, create a directory in HDFS to copy the Avro schema and set its permissions to global. You might need to delete the directory first if it was created for another application.

```
hdfs dfs -rm -r hdfs://localhost:8020/wlslog
hdfs dfs -mkdir -p hdfs://localhost:8020/wlslog
hdfs dfs -chmod -R 777 hdfs://localhost:8020/wlslog
```

Put the wlslog.avsc file in the HDFS directory.

```
hdfs dfs -put wlslog.avsc  hdfs://localhost:8020/wlslog
```

Creating a Hive-Managed Table

The following sample log data taken from WebLogic Server log is used to create a Hive external table stored as Avro. Store the following listing in the wlslog.txt file.

```
Apr-8-2014-7:06:16-PM-PDT,Notice,WebLogicServer,AdminServer,BEA-000365,Server state changed
to STANDBY
Apr-8-2014-7:06:17-PM-PDT,Notice,WebLogicServer,AdminServer,BEA-000365,Server state changed
to STARTING
Apr-8-2014-7:06:18-PM-PDT,Notice,WebLogicServer,AdminServer,BEA-000365,Server state changed
to ADMIN
Apr-8-2014-7:06:19-PM-PDT,Notice,WebLogicServer,AdminServer,BEA-000365,Server state changed
to RESUMING
Apr-8-2014-7:06:20-PM-PDT,Notice,WebLogicServer,AdminServer,BEA-000331,Started WebLogic
AdminServer
Apr-8-2014-7:06:21-PM-PDT,Notice,WebLogicServer,AdminServer,BEA-000365,Server state changed
to RUNNING
Apr-8-2014-7:06:22-PM-PDT,Notice,WebLogicServer,AdminServer,BEA-000360,Server started in
RUNNING mode
```

First, you need to create a Hive-managed table from which you'll transfer the data to a Hive external table stored as Avro. Start the Hive server.

```
hive --service hiveserver
```

Start the Hive shell.

```
hive
```

Set the database to use as the default.

```
use default;
```

Create a Hive-managed table called wlslog with columns timestamp, category, type, servername, code, and msg.

```
CREATE  TABLE  wlslog(time_stamp STRING,category STRING,type STRING,servername STRING,code
STRING,msg STRING) ROW FORMAT DELIMITED FIELDS TERMINATED BY ',' LINES TERMINATED BY '\n';
```

Load data into the Hive-managed table from the wlslog.txt file using the LOAD DATA command. Refer to the section entitled "Loading Data Into a Table" in Chapter 2 for information about the wlslog.txt file.

```
LOAD DATA LOCAL INPATH '/cdh/wlslog.txt' OVERWRITE INTO TABLE wlslog;
```

Run a query (a SELECT HiveQL statement) in Hive to list the wlslog table data, as shown in Figure 7-1.

```
hive> select * from wlslog;
OK
Apr-8-2014-7:06:16-PM-PDT        Notice  WebLogicServer  AdminServer     BEA-0003
65      Server state changed to STANDBY
Apr-8-2014-7:06:17-PM-PDT        Notice  WebLogicServer  AdminServer     BEA-0003
65      Server state changed to STARTING
Apr-8-2014-7:06:18-PM-PDT        Notice  WebLogicServer  AdminServer     BEA-0003
65      Server state changed to ADMIN
Apr-8-2014-7:06:19-PM-PDT        Notice  WebLogicServer  AdminServer     BEA-0003
65      Server state changed to RESUMING
Apr-8-2014-7:06:20-PM-PDT        Notice  WebLogicServer  AdminServer     BEA-0003
31      Started WebLogic AdminServer
Apr-8-2014-7:06:21-PM-PDT        Notice  WebLogicServer  AdminServer     BEA-0003
65      Server state changed to RUNNING
Apr-8-2014-7:06:22-PM-PDT        Notice  WebLogicServer  AdminServer     BEA-0003
60      Server started in RUNNING mode
Time taken: 43.677 seconds, Fetched: 7 row(s)
hive>
```

Figure 7-1. *Running a SELECT HiveQL statement*

The HiveQL syntax for creating a Hive external table stored as Avro is different for Hive versions prior to 0.14.0. The chapter first discusses using Hive 0.13.1 and then using Hive 1.1.0 (renamed from 0.15.0). Hive 0.14.1 was renamed Hive 1.0.0 and Hive 0.15.0 was renamed Hive 1.1.0.

Creating a Hive (Prior to Version 0.14.0) External Table Stored as Avro

The Hive versions prior to 0.14.0 use the classes listed in Table 6-1 to store data as Avro.

Table 7-1. *Hive Avro Classes for Versions Prior to 0.14.0*

Class	Description	Clause Used In
`org.apache.hadoop.hive.serde2.avro.` `AvroSerDe`	The Hive SerDe class to store data as Avro.	`ROW FORMAT SERDE`
`org.apache.hadoop.hive.ql.io.avro.` `AvroContainerInputFormat`	Input format for Avro container.	`STORED AS`
`org.apache.hadoop.hive.ql.io.avro.` `AvroContainerOutputFormat`	Output format for Avro container.	`STORED AS`

Run the following `CREATE EXTERNAL TABLE` command to create an external table stored as an Avro data file. The Avro schema is specified in TBLPROPERTIES with the `avro.schema.url` property. The `hdfs://localhost:8020/wlslog/wlslog.avsc` URL points to the `wlslog.avsc` schema file placed into HDFS earlier.

```
CREATE EXTERNAL TABLE IF NOT EXISTS wlslog_avro(TIME_STAMP string,CATEGORY string,TYPE
string,SERVERNAME string,CODE string,MSG string)ROW FORMAT SERDE 'org.apache.hadoop.hive.
serde2.avro.AvroSerDe'
  STORED AS INPUTFORMAT
  'org.apache.hadoop.hive.ql.io.avro.AvroContainerInputFormat'
  OUTPUTFORMAT
  'org.apache.hadoop.hive.ql.io.avro.AvroContainerOutputFormat'
  TBLPROPERTIES (
    'avro.schema.url'='hdfs://localhost:8020/wlslog/wlslog.avsc');
```

If the preceding command generates an error that cautions you about running out of heap space. Increase the heap space; for example, use **export HADOOP_HEAPSIZE=2000**. The `wlslog_avro` table is created, as shown in Figure 7-2.

```
hive> CREATE EXTERNAL TABLE IF NOT EXISTS wlslog_avro(TIME_STAMP string,CATEGORY
 string,TYPE string,SERVERNAME string,CODE string,MSG string)ROW FORMAT SERDE
    >    'org.apache.hadoop.hive.serde2.avro.AvroSerDe'
    >    STORED AS INPUTFORMAT
    >    'org.apache.hadoop.hive.ql.io.avro.AvroContainerInputFormat'
    >    OUTPUTFORMAT
    >    'org.apache.hadoop.hive.ql.io.avro.AvroContainerOutputFormat'
    >    TBLPROPERTIES (
    >      'avro.schema.url'='hdfs://localhost:8020/wlslog/wlslog.avsc');
OK
Time taken: 23.248 seconds
hive> select * from  wlslog_avro;
OK
Time taken: 5.416 seconds
hive>
```

Figure 7-2. *Creating an external table in Hive for Avro data*

Use an INSERT OVERWRITE TABLE command to add data to the wlslog_avro table from the wlslog table.

```
INSERT OVERWRITE TABLE wlslog_avro SELECT time_stamp,category,type,servername,code,msg   FROM
wlslog;
```

MapReduce jobs are launched to add data to the wlslog_avro table, as shown in Figure 7-3.

```
hive> INSERT OVERWRITE TABLE wlslog_avro SELECT time_stamp,category,type,servern
ame,code,msg  FROM wlslog;
Total jobs = 3
Launching Job 1 out of 3
Number of reduce tasks is set to 0 since there's no reduce operator
```

Figure 7-3. *Running the INSERT OVERWRITE HiveQL statement*

As indicated by the output in Figure 7-4, the data is loaded into the wlslog_avro table.

```
Job running in-process (local Hadoop)
Hadoop job information for null: number of mappers: 0; number of reducers: 0
2015-10-05 22:16:12,448 null map = 0%,  reduce = 0%
2015-10-05 22:16:39,650 null map = 100%,  reduce = 0%
Ended Job = job_local522902006_0001
Execution completed successfully
MapredLocal task succeeded
Stage-4 is selected by condition resolver.
Stage-3 is filtered out by condition resolver.
Stage-5 is filtered out by condition resolver.
Moving data to: hdfs://10.0.2.15:8020/user/hive/warehouse/wlslog_avro/.hive-stag
ing_hive_2015-10-05_22-12-12_247_2767187710634411410-1/-ext-10000
Loading data to table default.wlslog_avro
Table default.wlslog_avro stats: [numFiles=1, numRows=7, totalSize=1160, rawData
Size=0]
OK
Time taken: 314.218 seconds
hive>
```

Figure 7-4. *Loading data into the wlslog_avro Hive table stored as Avro*

Run a SELECT query in the Hive shell to list the new data.

```
select * from wlslog_avro;
```

The data loaded into the wlslog_avro table is listed, as shown in Figure 7-5.

```
hive> select * from wlslog_avro;
OK
Apr-8-2014-7:06:16-PM-PDT          Notice  WebLogicServer  AdminServer      BEA-0003
65       Server state changed to STANDBY
Apr-8-2014-7:06:17-PM-PDT          Notice  WebLogicServer  AdminServer      BEA-0003
65       Server state changed to STARTING
Apr-8-2014-7:06:18-PM-PDT          Notice  WebLogicServer  AdminServer      BEA-0003
65       Server state changed to ADMIN
Apr-8-2014-7:06:19-PM-PDT          Notice  WebLogicServer  AdminServer      BEA-0003
65       Server state changed to RESUMING
Apr-8-2014-7:06:20-PM-PDT          Notice  WebLogicServer  AdminServer      BEA-0003
31       Started WebLogic AdminServer
Apr-8-2014-7:06:21-PM-PDT          Notice  WebLogicServer  AdminServer      BEA-0003
65       Server state changed to RUNNING
Apr-8-2014-7:06:22-PM-PDT          Notice  WebLogicServer  AdminServer      BEA-0003
60       Server started in RUNNING mode
Time taken: 5.773 seconds, Fetched: 7 row(s)
hive> █
```

Figure 7-5. *Querying the Hive table wlslog_avro*

The Avro data file is stored in a sub-directory (called `wlslog_avro`) in the Hive warehouse directory. To list the data file, run the following command.

```
hdfs dfs -ls hdfs://10.0.2.15:8020/user/hive/warehouse/wlslog_avro
```

The Avro data file 000000_0 is listed, as shown in Figure 7-6.

```
[root@localhost cdh]# hdfs dfs -ls hdfs://10.0.2.15:8020/user/hive/warehouse/wls
log_avro
15/10/05 22:21:58 WARN util.NativeCodeLoader: Unable to load native-hadoop libra
ry for your platform... using builtin-java classes where applicable
Found 1 items
-rwxr-xr-x   1 root hadoop       1160 2015-10-05 22:16 hdfs://10.0.2.15:8020/use
r/hive/warehouse/wlslog_avro/000000_0
[root@localhost cdh]# █
```

Figure 7-6. *Listing the Avro data file*

To list the data in the 000000_0 data file, run the following command.

```
hdfs dfs -cat hdfs://10.0.2.15:8020/user/hive/warehouse/wlslog_avro/000000_0
```

The Avro data on which the Hive external table `wlslog_avro` is based is listed, as shown in Figure 7-7. The listing starts with the schema for the Avro data followed by the Avro data. The data appears to be incorrectly formatted, with squares overwritten on top of the text, but this happens because the data is in Avro format.

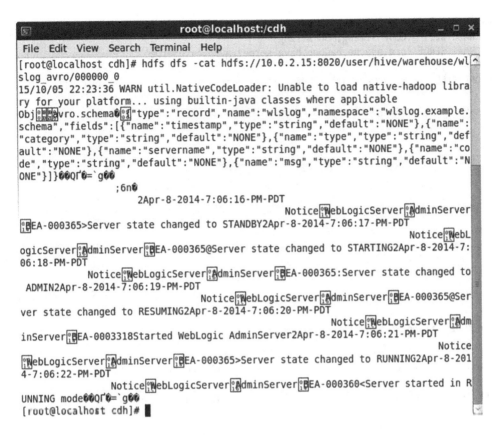

Figure 7-7. Listing Avro data

Creating a Hive (Version 0.14.0 and Later) External Table Stored as Avro

This section discusses creating a Hive external table using the syntax in Hive 0.14.0 and later. Download Hive 1.1.0 (same as 0.15.0) and extract the tar file.

```
wget http://archive-primary.cloudera.com/cdh5/cdh/5/hive-1.1.0-cdh5.4.7.tar.gz
tar -xvf hive-1.1.0-cdh5.4.7.tar.gz
```

Modify the environment variable for Hive to reference the installation directory for Hive 1.1.0.

```
export HIVE_HOME=/cdh/hive-1.1.0-cdh5.4.7
```

Run the following CREATE EXTERNAL TABLE HiveQL statement to create the external table wlslogavro. Instead of using the input format and output format classes, the new syntax uses the STORED AS AVRO clause.

```
CREATE EXTERNAL TABLE IF NOT EXISTS wlslogavro(TIME_STAMP string,CATEGORY string,TYPE
string,SERVERNAME string,CODE string,MSG string)
        ROW FORMAT SERDE 'org.apache.hadoop.hive.serde2.avro.AvroSerDe'
        STORED AS AVRO
        TBLPROPERTIES ('avro.schema.url'='hdfs://localhost:8020/wlslog/wlslog.avsc');
```

The Hive external table wlslogavro is created, as shown in Figure 7-8.

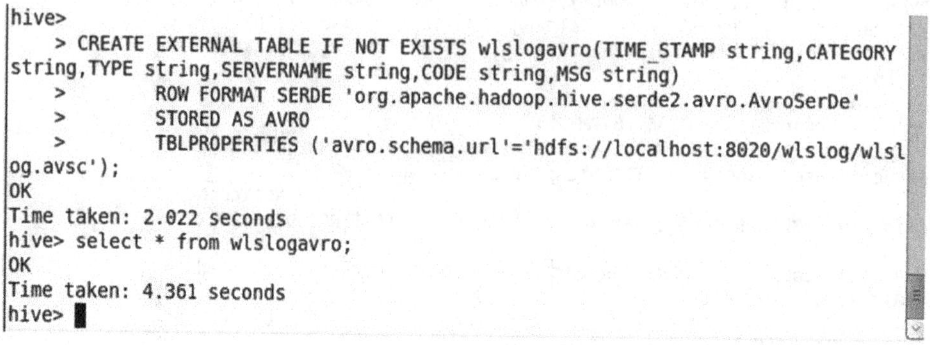

```
hive>
    > CREATE EXTERNAL TABLE IF NOT EXISTS wlslogavro(TIME_STAMP string,CATEGORY
string,TYPE string,SERVERNAME string,CODE string,MSG string)
    >        ROW FORMAT SERDE 'org.apache.hadoop.hive.serde2.avro.AvroSerDe'
    >        STORED AS AVRO
    >        TBLPROPERTIES ('avro.schema.url'='hdfs://localhost:8020/wlslog/wlsl
og.avsc');
OK
Time taken: 2.022 seconds
hive> select * from wlslogavro;
OK
Time taken: 4.361 seconds
hive>
```

Figure 7-8. *Creating the Hive external table wlslogavro*

Add data to the wlslogavro table using an INSERT OVERWRITE TABLE command as before.

```
INSERT OVERWRITE TABLE wlslogavro SELECT time_stamp,category,type,servername,code,msg FROM
wlslog;
```

MapReduce jobs are launched to load data into the Hive external table wlslog, as shown in Figure 7-9.

Figure 7-9. Running the INSERT OVERWRITE HiveQL statement to load data into a Hive table

Run a SELECT statement in the Hive shell to list the data added.

```
select * from wlslogavro;
```

The seven data rows are listed, as shown in Figure 7-10.

```
hive> select * from wlslogavro;
OK
Apr-8-2014-7:06:16-PM-PDT        Notice  WebLogicServer  AdminServer     BEA-0003
65      Server state changed to STANDBY
Apr-8-2014-7:06:17-PM-PDT        Notice  WebLogicServer  AdminServer     BEA-0003
65      Server state changed to STARTING
Apr-8-2014-7:06:18-PM-PDT        Notice  WebLogicServer  AdminServer     BEA-0003
65      Server state changed to ADMIN
Apr-8-2014-7:06:19-PM-PDT        Notice  WebLogicServer  AdminServer     BEA-0003
65      Server state changed to RESUMING
Apr-8-2014-7:06:20-PM-PDT        Notice  WebLogicServer  AdminServer     BEA-0003
31      Started WebLogic AdminServer
Apr-8-2014-7:06:21-PM-PDT        Notice  WebLogicServer  AdminServer     BEA-0003
65      Server state changed to RUNNING
Apr-8-2014-7:06:22-PM-PDT        Notice  WebLogicServer  AdminServer     BEA-0003
60      Server started in RUNNING mode
Time taken: 1.595 seconds, Fetched: 7 row(s)
hive>
```

Figure 7-10. Querying the Hive table wlslogavro

List the data file generated for the Hive external table.

```
hdfs dfs -ls hdfs://10.0.2.15:8020/user/hive/warehouse/wlslogavro
```

The Avro data file 000000_0 is listed, as shown in Figure 7-11.

```
[root@localhost cdh]# hdfs dfs -ls hdfs://10.0.2.15:8020/user/hive/warehouse/wls
logavro
15/10/05 22:59:23 WARN util.NativeCodeLoader: Unable to load native-hadoop libra
ry for your platform... using builtin-java classes where applicable
Found 1 items
-rwxr-xr-x   1 root hadoop       1160 2015-10-05 22:54 hdfs://10.0.2.15:8020/use
r/hive/warehouse/wlslogavro/000000_0
[root@localhost cdh]# █
```

Figure 7-11. *Listing the Avro data file in HDFS*

List the Avro data in the 000000_0 file using the following command.

```
hdfs dfs -cat hdfs://10.0.2.15:8020/user/hive/warehouse/wlslogavro/000000_0
```

The Avro data, including the Avro schema, is listed, as shown in Figure 7-12.

```
[root@localhost cdh]# hdfs dfs -cat hdfs://10.0.2.15:8020/user/hive/warehouse/wl
slogavro/000000_0
15/10/05 23:00:36 WARN util.NativeCodeLoader: Unable to load native-hadoop libra
ry for your platform... using builtin-java classes where applicable
Obj░░░░vro.schema░░░"type":"record","name":"wlslog","namespace":"wlslog.example.
schema","fields":[{"name":"timestamp","type":"string","default":"NONE"},{"name":
"category","type":"string","default":"NONE"},{"name":"type","type":"string","def
ault":"NONE"},{"name":"servername","type":"string","default":"NONE"},{"name":"co
de","type":"string","default":"NONE"},{"name":"msg","type":"string","default":"N
ONE"}]}░░░░:G░░ ░░K-h░
                      2Apr-8-2014-7:06:16-PM-PDT
                                        Notice░WebLogicServer░AdminServe
r░BEA-000365>Server state changed to STANDBY2Apr-8-2014-7:06:17-PM-PDT
                                                        Notice░Web
LogicServer░AdminServer░BEA-000365@Server state changed to STARTING2Apr-8-2014-7
:06:18-PM-PDT
            Notice░WebLogicServer░AdminServer░BEA-000365:Server state changed t
o ADMIN2Apr-8-2014-7:06:19-PM-PDT
                            Notice░WebLogicServer░AdminServer░BEA-000365@Se
rver state changed to RESUMING2Apr-8-2014-7:06:20-PM-PDT
                                        Notice░WebLogicServer░Ad
minServer░BEA-0003318Started WebLogic AdminServer2Apr-8-2014-7:06:21-PM-PDT
                                                        Notic
e░WebLogicServer░AdminServer░BEA-000365>Server state changed to RUNNING2Apr-8-20
14-7:06:22-PM-PDT
                Notice░WebLogicServer░AdminServer░BEA-000360<Server started in
RUNNING mode░░░░:G░░   ░░K-h[root@localhost cdh]# █
```

Figure 7-12. *Listing the Avro data*

Transferring the MySQL Table Data as an Avro Data File with Sqoop

This section transfers the MySQL table data to HDFS as an Avro data file using the Apache `sqoop import` command. First, you need to create a MySQL table. Start MySQL server.

```
bin/mysqld_safe --user=mysql &
```

MySQL database is started, as shown in Figure 7-13.

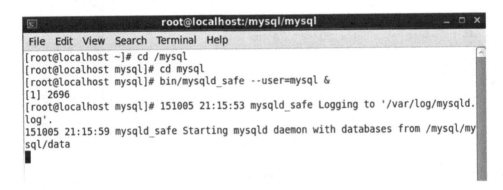

Figure 7-13. *Starting MySQL Server*

Start the MySQL CLI shell.

```
bin/mysql
```

Set the database to `test`.

```
mysql> use test
```

Drop the `wlslog` table if it already exists.

```
drop table wlslog;
```

The output from the preceding commands is shown in Figure 7-14.

```
[root@localhost mysql]# bin/mysql
Welcome to the MySQL monitor.  Commands end with ; or \g.
Your MySQL connection id is 1
Server version: 5.6.19 MySQL Community Server (GPL)

Copyright (c) 2000, 2014, Oracle and/or its affiliates. All rights reserved.

Oracle is a registered trademark of Oracle Corporation and/or its
affiliates. Other names may be trademarks of their respective
owners.

Type 'help;' or '\h' for help. Type '\c' to clear the current input statement.

mysql> use test
Reading table information for completion of table and column names
You can turn off this feature to get a quicker startup with -A

Database changed
mysql> drop table wlslog;
Query OK, 0 rows affected (0.22 sec)

mysql>
```

Figure 7-14. Starting MySQL CLI, setting the MySQL database, and dropping the MySQL table wlslog

Run the following SQL script to create the MySQL table wlslog.

```
CREATE TABLE wlslog(time_stamp VARCHAR(255) PRIMARY KEY,category VARCHAR(255),type
VARCHAR(255),servername VARCHAR(255), code VARCHAR(255),msg VARCHAR(255));
```

The MySQL table wlslog is created, as shown in Figure 7-15.

```
root@localhost:/mysql/mysql                      _ □ x
File  Edit  View  Search  Terminal  Help
mysql> CREATE TABLE wlslog(time_stamp VARCHAR(255) PRIMARY KEY,category VARCHAR(
255),type VARCHAR(255),servername VARCHAR(255), code VARCHAR(255),msg VARCHAR(25
5));
Query OK, 0 rows affected (0.33 sec)
```

Figure 7-15. Creating the MySQL table wlslog

Add data to the wlslog table using the following SQL script.

```
INSERT INTO wlslog(time_stamp,category,type,servername,code,msg) VALUES('Apr-8-2014-7:06:16-
PM-PDT','Notice','WebLogicServer','AdminServer','BEA-000365','Server state changed to
STANDBY');
INSERT INTO wlslog(time_stamp,category,type,servername,code,msg) VALUES('Apr-8-2014-7:06:17-
PM-PDT','Notice','WebLogicServer','AdminServer','BEA-000365','Server state changed to
STARTING');
INSERT INTO wlslog(time_stamp,category,type,servername,code,msg) VALUES('Apr-8-2014-7:06:18-
PM-PDT','Notice','WebLogicServer','AdminServer','BEA-000365','Server state changed to
ADMIN');
```

```
INSERT INTO wlslog(time_stamp,category,type,servername,code,msg) VALUES('Apr-8-2014-7:06:19-
PM-PDT','Notice','WebLogicServer','AdminServer','BEA-000365','Server state changed to
RESUMING');
INSERT INTO wlslog(time_stamp,category,type,servername,code,msg) VALUES('Apr-8-2014-
7:06:20-PM-PDT','Notice','WebLogicServer','AdminServer','BEA-000361','Started WebLogic
AdminServer');
INSERT INTO wlslog(time_stamp,category,type,servername,code,msg) VALUES('Apr-8-2014-7:06:21-
PM-PDT','Notice','WebLogicServer','AdminServer','BEA-000365','Server state changed to
RUNNING');
INSERT INTO wlslog(time_stamp,category,type,servername,code,msg) VALUES('Apr-8-2014-7:06:22-
PM-PDT','Notice','WebLogicServer','AdminServer','BEA-000360','Server started in RUNNING
mode');
```

Data is added to the wlslog table, as shown in Figure 7-16.

```
mysql> INSERT INTO wlslog(time_stamp,category,type,servername,code,msg) VALUES('
Apr-8-2014-7:06:16-PM-PDT','Notice','WebLogicServer','AdminServer','BEA-000365',
'Server state changed to STANDBY');
Query OK, 1 row affected (0.10 sec)

mysql> INSERT INTO wlslog(time_stamp,category,type,servername,code,msg) VALUES('
Apr-8-2014-7:06:17-PM-PDT','Notice','WebLogicServer','AdminServer','BEA-000365',
'Server state changed to STARTING');
Query OK, 1 row affected (0.07 sec)

mysql> INSERT INTO wlslog(time_stamp,category,type,servername,code,msg) VALUES('
Apr-8-2014-7:06:18-PM-PDT','Notice','WebLogicServer','AdminServer','BEA-000365',
'Server state changed to ADMIN');
Query OK, 1 row affected (0.05 sec)

mysql> INSERT INTO wlslog(time_stamp,category,type,servername,code,msg) VALUES('
Apr-8-2014-7:06:19-PM-PDT','Notice','WebLogicServer','AdminServer','BEA-000365',
'Server state changed to RESUMING');
Query OK, 1 row affected (0.14 sec)

mysql> INSERT INTO wlslog(time_stamp,category,type,servername,code,msg) VALUES('
Apr-8-2014-7:06.20-PM-PDT','Notice','WebLogicServer','AdminServer','BEA-000361',
'Started WebLogic AdminServer');
Query OK, 1 row affected (0.07 sec)

mysql> INSERT INTO wlslog(time_stamp,category,type,servername,code,msg) VALUES('
Apr-8-2014-7:06:21-PM-PDT','Notice','WebLogicServer','AdminServer','BEA-000365',
```

Figure 7-16. *Adding data to the wlslog table*

Run a SELECT query to list the data that was added.

```
select * from wlslog;
```

The wlslog table data is listed, as shown in Figure 7-17.

```
mysql> select * from wlslog;
+----------------------------+----------+-----------------+--------------+---------
---+----------------------------------+
| time_stamp                 | category | type            | servername   | code
   | msg                              |
+----------------------------+----------+-----------------+--------------+---------
---+----------------------------------+
| Apr-8-2014-7:06:16-PM-PDT | Notice   | WebLogicServer | AdminServer | BEA-0003
65 | Server state changed to STANDBY  |
| Apr-8-2014-7:06:17-PM-PDT | Notice   | WebLogicServer | AdminServer | BEA-0003
65 | Server state changed to STARTING |
| Apr-8-2014-7:06:18-PM-PDT | Notice   | WebLogicServer | AdminServer | BEA-0003
65 | Server state changed to ADMIN    |
| Apr-8-2014-7:06:19-PM-PDT | Notice   | WebLogicServer | AdminServer | BEA-0003
65 | Server state changed to RESUMING |
| Apr-8-2014-7:06:20-PM-PDT | Notice   | WebLogicServer | AdminServer | BEA-0003
61 | Started WebLogic AdminServer     |
| Apr-8-2014-7:06:21-PM-PDT | Notice   | WebLogicServer | AdminServer | BEA-0003
65 | Server state changed to RUNNING  |
| Apr-8-2014-7:06:22-PM-PDT | Notice   | WebLogicServer | AdminServer | BEA-0003
60 | Server started in RUNNING mode   |
+----------------------------+----------+-----------------+--------------+---------
---+----------------------------------+
7 rows in set (0.00 sec)

mysql>
```

Figure 7-17. *Querying the MySQL table wlslog*

Run the sqoop import command to transfer the MySQL table data to HDFS. Specify the args listed in Table 6-2 to the sqoop import command.

Table 7-2. Sqoop Import Command Arguments

Arg	Description	Value
--as-avrodatafile	Specifies that data be imported as Avro. The --direct option must not be specified with --as-avrodatafile.	
--connect	Specifies the connection URL for the MySQL database.	"jdbc:mysql://localhost/test"
--hadoop-home	Specifies the Hadoop home directory.	"/cdh/hadoop-2.6.0-cdh5.4.7/share/hadoop/mapreduce1"
--username	Specifies the username to connect to MySQL database.	"root"
--password	Specifies the password for the MySQL database.	""
--table	Specifies the MySQL table.	"wlslog"
--columns	Specifies the columns for the MySQL table.	"time_stamp,category,type,servername, code,msg"
--target-dir	Specifies the target directory in HDFS. The target directory must not exist already. Run the hdfs dfs -rm -r hdfs://10.0.2.15:8020/mysql/import command to remove the /mysql/import directory if it exists.	"/mysql/import"
-verbose	Sets the verbose output mode.	

Run the following `sqoop import` command.

```
sqoop import --as-avrodatafile --connect "jdbc:mysql://localhost/test" --hadoop-home "/cdh/
hadoop-2.6.0-cdh5.4.7/share/hadoop/mapreduce1"  --password "" --username "root" --table
"wlslog" --columns "time_stamp,category,type,servername,code,msg" --target-dir "/mysql/
import"  -verbose
```

The `commons-io-1.4.jar` file may have to be removed from the Sqoop `lib` directory in order for the command to run. The Sqoop import tool is started, as shown in Figure 7-18.

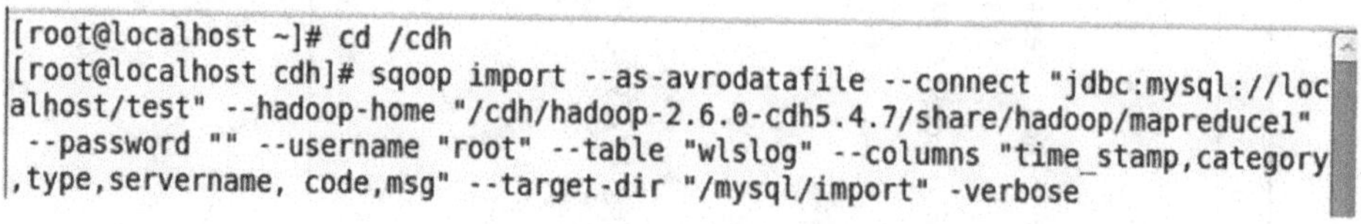

```
[root@localhost ~]# cd /cdh
[root@localhost cdh]# sqoop import --as-avrodatafile --connect "jdbc:mysql://loc
alhost/test" --hadoop-home "/cdh/hadoop-2.6.0-cdh5.4.7/share/hadoop/mapreduce1"
 --password "" --username "root" --table "wlslog" --columns "time_stamp,category
,type,servername, code,msg" --target-dir "/mysql/import" -verbose
```

Figure 7-18. *Running the sqoop import command as avrodatafile*

A MapReduce job runs to transfer MySQL table data to HDFS, as indicated by the "`Retrieved 7 records`" message shown in Figure 7-19.

```
                          root@localhost:/cdh                    _ □ ✕

 File  Edit  View  Search  Terminal  Help
15/10/05 21:54:47 INFO mapred.JobClient: Job complete: job_local1516384002_0001
15/10/05 21:54:48 INFO mapred.JobClient: Counters: 18
15/10/05 21:54:48 INFO mapred.JobClient:    File System Counters
15/10/05 21:54:48 INFO mapred.JobClient:      FILE: Number of bytes read=17777898
15/10/05 21:54:48 INFO mapred.JobClient:      FILE: Number of bytes written=18075
198
15/10/05 21:54:48 INFO mapred.JobClient:      FILE: Number of read operations=0
15/10/05 21:54:48 INFO mapred.JobClient:      FILE: Number of large read operatio
ns=0
15/10/05 21:54:48 INFO mapred.JobClient:      FILE: Number of write operations=0
15/10/05 21:54:48 INFO mapred.JobClient:      HDFS: Number of bytes read=0
15/10/05 21:54:48 INFO mapred.JobClient:      HDFS: Number of bytes written=1486
15/10/05 21:54:48 INFO mapred.JobClient:      HDFS: Number of read operations=1
15/10/05 21:54:48 INFO mapred.JobClient:      HDFS: Number of large read operatio
ns=0
15/10/05 21:54:48 INFO mapred.JobClient:      HDFS: Number of write operations=2
15/10/05 21:54:48 INFO mapred.JobClient:    Map-Reduce Framework
15/10/05 21:54:48 INFO mapred.JobClient:      Map input records=7
15/10/05 21:54:48 INFO mapred.JobClient:      Map output records=7
15/10/05 21:54:48 INFO mapred.JobClient:      Input split bytes=87
15/10/05 21:54:48 INFO mapred.JobClient:      Spilled Records=0
15/10/05 21:54:48 INFO mapred.JobClient:      CPU time spent (ms)=0
15/10/05 21:54:48 INFO mapred.JobClient:      Physical memory (bytes) snapshot=0
15/10/05 21:54:48 INFO mapred.JobClient:      Virtual memory (bytes) snapshot=0
15/10/05 21:54:48 INFO mapred.JobClient:      Total committed heap usage (bytes)=
71798784
15/10/05 21:54:49 INFO mapreduce.ImportJobBase: Transferred 1.4512 KB in 109.659
 seconds (13.5511 bytes/sec)
15/10/05 21:54:49 INFO mapreduce.ImportJobBase: Retrieved 7 records.
15/10/05 21:54:49 DEBUG util.ClassLoaderStack: Restoring classloader: sun.misc.L
auncher$AppClassLoader@10f243b
[root@localhost cdh]# ▮
```

Figure 7-19. *Running a MapReduce job to import data into HDFS*

Run one of the following equivalent commands to list the data files in HDFS to which the MySQL table data is transferred.

```
hdfs dfs -ls hdfs://localhost:8020/mysql/import
hdfs dfs -ls /mysql/import
```

The _SUCCESS and part-m-00000.avro files are listed, as shown in Figure 7-20. The _SUCCESS file indicates that the sqoop import command completed successfully. The part-m-00000.avro file contains the data transferred from the MySQL database.

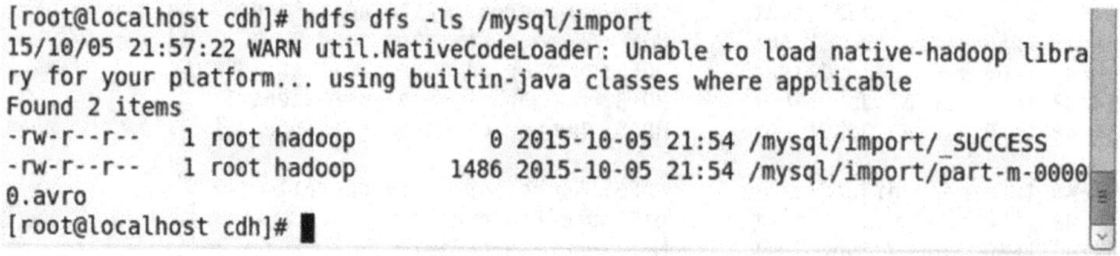

```
[root@localhost cdh]# hdfs dfs -ls /mysql/import
15/10/05 21:57:22 WARN util.NativeCodeLoader: Unable to load native-hadoop libra
ry for your platform... using builtin-java classes where applicable
Found 2 items
-rw-r--r--   1 root hadoop          0 2015-10-05 21:54 /mysql/import/_SUCCESS
-rw-r--r--   1 root hadoop       1486 2015-10-05 21:54 /mysql/import/part-m-0000
0.avro
[root@localhost cdh]# ▮
```

Figure 7-20. *Listing the files generated by the sqoop import command*

List the Avro data file using one of the following commands.

```
hdfs dfs -cat hdfs://localhost:8020/mysql/import/part-m-00000.avro
hdfs dfs -cat /mysql/import/part-m-00000.avro
```

The data in the Avro file part-m-00000.avro is listed, as shown in Figure 7-21.

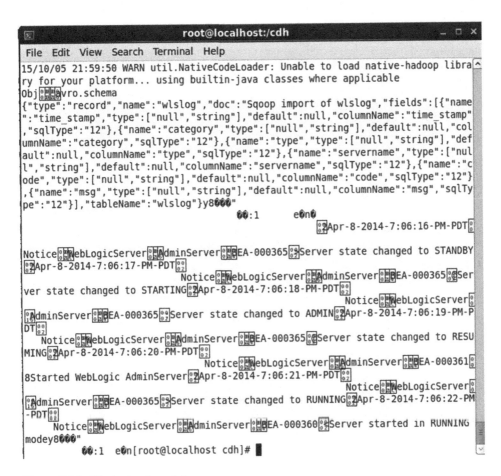

Figure 7-21. *Displaying Avro data*

Summary

This chapter introduced the Apache Avro binary data format and explained the support for it in the Hadoop ecosystem. It discussed two examples of Avro support in Hadoop. First, you created a Hive external table stored as Avro. Second, you used the sqoop import command to transfer MySQL table data to HDFS as an Avro data file. The next chapter introduces another data format called Apache Parquet.

CHAPTER 8

■ ■ ■

Apache Parquet

Apache Parquet is an efficient, structured, column-oriented (also called columnar storage), compressed, binary file format. Parquet supports several compression codecs, including Snappy, GZIP, deflate, and BZIP2. Snappy is the default. Structured file formats such as RCFile, Avro, SequenceFile, and Parquet offer better performance with compression support, which reduces the size of the data on the disk and consequently the I/O and CPU resources required to deserialize data.

In columnar storage, all the column data for a particular column is stored adjacently instead of by row. Columnar storage offers the following advantages:

- Data is stored by column instead of by row and the compression is applied more efficiently because the column data is the same type.

- Query processing is more efficient as the columns are stored together. The query engine can skip the columns it does not need for a particular query.

Apache Parquet can be used with any project in the Hadoop ecosystem. This chapter discusses creating a Hive external table stored as an Apache Parquet file. The following topics are discussed:

- Setting the environment

- Configuring Hadoop

- Configuring Hive

- Starting HDFS

- Creating a Hive-managed table

- Creating a Hive external table

- Loading data into a Hive external table

- Listing the Parquet data file

Setting the Environment

The following software is required for this chapter.

- Apache Hadoop

- Apache Hive

- Parquet Hive Storage Handler

- Java 7

© Deepak Vohra 2016
D. Vohra, *Practical Hadoop Ecosystem*, DOI 10.1007/978-1-4842-2199-0_8

Create a directory (/cdh) for installing the software and set its permissions to global (777).

```
mkdir /cdh
chmod -R 777 /cdh
cd /cdh
```

Download and extract the Java 7 tar file.

```
tar zxvf jdk-7u55-linux-i586.gz
```

Download and extract the Hadoop 2.6.0 CDH 5.4.7 tar file.

```
wget http://archive-primary.cloudera.com/cdh5/cdh/5/hadoop-2.6.0-cdh5.4.7.tar.gz
tar -xvf hadoop-2.6.0-cdh5.4.7.tar.gz
```

Create symlinks for the Hadoop bin and conf directories.

```
ln -s /cdh/hadoop-2.6.0-cdh5.4.7/bin /cdh/hadoop-2.6.0-cdh5.4.7/share/hadoop/mapreduce1/bin
ln -s /cdh/hadoop-2.6.0-cdh5.4.7/etc/hadoop  /cdh/hadoop-2.6.0-cdh5.4.7/share/hadoop/
mapreduce1/conf
```

Download and extract the Hive 0.13.1 CDH 5.3.6 tar file.

```
wget http://archive-primary.cloudera.com/cdh5/cdh/5/hive-0.13.1-cdh5.3.6.tar.gz
tar -xvf hive-0.13.1-cdh5.3.6.tar.gz
```

Download the Parquet Hive storage handler jar file called parquet-hive-storage-handler-1.6.0.jar from http://mvnrepository.com/artifact/com.twitter/parquet-hive-storage-handler/1.6.0. The parquet-hive-storage-handler-1.6.0.jar file must not be copied to the Hive lib directory and should be loaded into classpath with the ADD JAR command in the Hive shell. See the "Creating a Hive External Table" section.

Set the environment variables for Hadoop, Hive, and Java 7.

```
vi ~/.bashrc
export HADOOP_PREFIX=/cdh/hadoop-2.6.0-cdh5.4.7
export HADOOP_CONF_DIR=$HADOOP_PREFIX/etc/hadoop
export HADOOP_COMMON_HOME=$HADOOP_PREFIX/share/hadoop/common
export HADOOP_HDFS_HOME=$HADOOP_PREFIX/share/hadoop/hdfs
export HIVE_HOME=/cdh/hive-0.13.1-cdh5.3.6
export HIVE_CONF=$HIVE_HOME/conf
export JAVA_HOME=/cdh/jdk1.7.0_55
export HADOOP_MAPRED_HOME=$HADOOP_PREFIX/share/hadoop/mapreduce1
export HADOOP_HOME=$HADOOP_PREFIX/share/hadoop/mapreduce1
export HADOOP_CLASSPATH=$HADOOP_HOME/*:$HADOOP_HOME/lib/*:$JAVA_HOME/lib/*:$HIVE_HOME/
lib/*:$HADOOP_CONF_DIR:$HADOOP_COMMON_HOME/*:$HADOOP_COMMON_HOME/lib/*:$HADOOP_HDFS_
HOME/*:$HADOOP_HDFS_HOME/lib/*:
export PATH=/usr/local/sbin:/usr/sbin:/sbin:/usr/local/bin:/usr/bin:/bin:$HADOOP_PREFIX/
bin:$HADOOP_HOME/bin:$HADOOP_MAPRED_HOME/bin:$JAVA_HOME/bin:$HIVE_HOME/bin
export CLASSPATH=$HADOOP_CLASSPATH
export HADOOP_NAMENODE_USER=hadoop
export HADOOP_DATANODE_USER=hadoop
```

Configuring Hadoop

The Hadoop configuration is the same as in earlier chapters. Add the `fs.defaultFS` and `hadoop.tmp.dir` configuration properties to the `core-site.xml` file. The NameNode URI host IP address could be different for different users.

```
vi    $HADOOP_CONF_DIR/core-site.xml
<?xml-stylesheet type="text/xsl" href="configuration.xsl"?>

<!-- Put site-specific property overrides in this file. -->

<configuration>
<property>
  <name>fs.defaultFS</name>
    <value>hdfs://10.0.2.15:8020</value>
    </property>
  <property>
     <name>hadoop.tmp.dir</name>
     <value>/var/lib/hadoop-0.20/cache</value>
   </property>
</configuration>
```

Create the Hadoop temp directory and set its permissions to global (777).

```
mkdir -p /var/lib/hadoop-0.20/cache
chmod -R 777   /var/lib/hadoop-0.20/cache
```

Set the `dfs.permissions.superusergroup`, `dfs.namenode.name.dir`, `dfs.replication`, and `dfs.permissions` configuration properties in the `hdfs-site.xml` file.

```
vi $HADOOP_CONF_DIR/hdfs-site.xml

<?xml version="1.0" encoding="UTF-8"?>
<?xml-stylesheet type="text/xsl" href="configuration.xsl"?>

<!-- Put site-specific property overrides in this file. -->

<configuration>
<property>
 <name>dfs.permissions.superusergroup</name>
  <value>hadoop</value>
  </property><property>
   <name>dfs.namenode.name.dir</name>
    <value>/data/1/dfs/nn</value>
    </property>
        <property>
            <name>dfs.replication</name>
                <value>1</value>
        </property>
<property>
<name>dfs.permissions</name>
```

```
<value>false</value>
</property>
</configuration>
```

Create the NameNode storage directory and set its permissions to global (777).

```
mkdir -p /data/1/dfs/nn
chmod -R 777 /data/1/dfs/nn
```

Configuring Hive

Next, configure Hive in the `hive-site.xml` file. Create the `hive-site.xml` file from the `hive-default.xml.template` template file.

```
cp /cdh/hive-0.13.1-cdh5.3.6/conf/hive-default.xml.template /cdh/hive-0.13.1-cdh5.3.6/conf/
hive-site.xml
```

Set the `hive.metastore.warehouse.dir` (directory in which Hive stores data) and `hive.metastore.uris` (Hive Thrift Server Client URI) configuration properties in the `hive-site.xml` file.

```
vi /cdh/hive-0.13.1-cdh5.3.6/conf/hive-site.xml
<?xml version="1.0"?>
<?xml-stylesheet type="text/xsl" href="configuration.xsl"?>
<configuration>
<property>
  <name>hive.metastore.warehouse.dir</name>
  <value>hdfs://10.0.2.15:8020/user/hive/warehouse</value>
</property>
<property>
  <name>hive.metastore.uris</name>
  <value>thrift://localhost:10000</value>
</property>

</configuration>
```

Start the Hive Thrift Server.

```
hive --service hiveserver
```

The heap size may need to be increased for the previous command; run the export `HADOOP_HEAPSIZE=2000` command. Hive Thrift Server is started, as shown in Figure 8-1.

Figure 8-1. *Starting Hive Thrift Server*

Starting HDFS

Start the HDFS, which comprises NameNode and DataNode. First, start the NameNode.

```
hdfs namenode
```

Subsequently, start the DataNode.

```
hdfs datanode
```

Create the Hive warehouse directory in HDFS and set its permissions to global (777).

```
hadoop dfs -mkdir  hdfs://10.0.2.15:8020/user/hive/warehouse
hadoop dfs -chmod -R g+w hdfs://10.0.2.15:8020/user/hive/warehouse
```

Create the /wlslog directory in HDFS. This is where the Hive external table stored as a Parquet file will store the data file in the Parquet format. First, remove the /wlslog file if it exists. Set the directory permissions to global (777).

```
hdfs dfs -rm -r hdfs://localhost:8020/wlslog
hdfs dfs -mkdir -p hdfs://localhost:8020/wlslog
hdfs dfs -chmod -R 777 hdfs://localhost:8020/wlslog
```

This example loads data into the Hive external table from another Hive-managed table. First, you'll create a Hive-managed table from which data will be loaded into the Hive external table based on Parquet storage.

Creating a Hive-Managed Table

In this section, you'll create a Hive-managed table stored as a text file. Load the following data into the Hive-managed table and store this data in a wlslog.txt file.

```
Apr 8 2014-7:06:16-PM-PDT,Notice,WebLogicServer,AdminServer,BEA-000365,Server state changed
to STANDBY
Apr-8-2014-7:06:17-PM-PDT,Notice,WebLogicServer,AdminServer,BEA-000365,Server state changed
to STARTING
Apr-8-2014-7:06:18-PM-PDT,Notice,WebLogicServer,AdminServer,BEA-000365,Server state changed
to ADMIN
Apr-8-2014-7:06:19-PM-PDT,Notice,WebLogicServer,AdminServer,BEA-000365,Server state changed
to RESUMING
Apr-8-2014-7:06:20-PM-PDT,Notice,WebLogicServer,AdminServer,BEA-000331,Started WebLogic
AdminServer
Apr-8-2014-7:06:21-PM-PDT,Notice,WebLogicServer,AdminServer,BEA-000365,Server state changed
to RUNNING
Apr-8-2014-7:06:22-PM-PDT,Notice,WebLogicServer,AdminServer,BEA-000360,Server started in
RUNNING mode
```

Start the Hive shell and set the database to the default.

```
hive
```

329

```
use default;
```

Next, create a table called wlslog. Drop the wlslog table if it already exists.

```
drop table wlslog;
```

The output from the preceding Hive shell commands is shown in Figure 8-2.

```
hive> use default;
OK
Time taken: 81.586 seconds
hive> drop table wlslog;
OK
Time taken: 44.373 seconds
hive>
```

Figure 8-2. *Setting the database as the default*

Create a managed table called wlslog with the following CREATE TABLE statement.

```
CREATE  TABLE  wlslog(time_stamp STRING,category STRING,type STRING,servername STRING,code
STRING,msg STRING) ROW FORMAT DELIMITED FIELDS TERMINATED BY ',' LINES TERMINATED BY '\n';
```

Load data into the wlslog table from the wlslog.txt file using the following LOAD DATA command.

```
LOAD DATA LOCAL INPATH '/cdh/wlslog.txt' OVERWRITE INTO TABLE wlslog;
```

The Hive-managed table called wlslog is created, as shown in Figure 8-3.

```
hive> CREATE  TABLE  wlslog(time_stamp STRING,category STRING,type STRING,server
name STRING,code STRING,msg STRING) ROW FORMAT DELIMITED FIELDS TERMINATED BY ',
' LINES TERMINATED BY '\n';
OK
Time taken: 32.468 seconds
hive> LOAD DATA LOCAL INPATH '/cdh/wlslog.txt' OVERWRITE INTO TABLE wlslog;
Loading data to table default.wlslog
Table default.wlslog stats: [numFiles=1, numRows=0, totalSize=724, rawDataSize=0
]
OK
Time taken: 29.27 seconds
hive>
```

Figure 8-3. *Creating a Hive-managed table*

Creating a Hive External Table

Next, you'll create a Hive external table stored on a Parquet data file. Add the parquet-hive-storage-handler-1.6.0.jar file to the classpath in the Hive shell using the ADD JAR command. The syntax for creating a Hive external table stored as a Parquet file was modified in Hive 0.13.0. First, I will discuss using the syntax prior to Hive 0.13.0.

Hive Version Prior to 0.13.0

The classes listed in Table 8-1 are used to create a Hive external table stored as a Parquet data file in Hive versions 0.10, 0.11, and 0.12.

Table 8-1. *Hive Classes to Create a Hive External Table Stored as Parquet Format Data*

Class	Description	CREATE EXTERNAL TABLE Clause in Which It's Used
parquet.hive.serde.ParquetHiveSerDe	Defines the format in which data is stored.	ROW FORMAT SERDE
parquet.hive.DeprecatedParquetInputFormat	Defines the Parquet input format.	STORED AS
parquet.hive.DeprecatedParquetOutputFormat	Defines the Parquet output format.	STORED AS

Run the following CREATE EXTERNAL TABLE statement in the Hive shell to create a Hive external table stored as a parquet data file in the 'hdfs://localhost:8020/wlslog' directory.

```
CREATE EXTERNAL TABLE IF NOT EXISTS wlslog_parquet(TIME_STAMP string,CATEGORY string,TYPE
string,SERVERNAME string,CODE string,MSG string)ROW FORMAT SERDE 'parquet.hive.serde.
ParquetHiveSerDe'
        stored as inputformat 'parquet.hive.DeprecatedParquetInputFormat'
        outputformat 'parquet.hive.DeprecatedParquetOutputFormat'
        LOCATION 'hdfs://localhost:8020/wlslog';
```

The Hive external table wlslog_parquet is created, as shown in Figure 8-4.

```
hive> CREATE EXTERNAL TABLE IF NOT EXISTS wlslog_parquet(TIME_STAMP string,CATEG
ORY string,TYPE string,SERVERNAME string,CODE string,MSG string)ROW FORMAT SERDE
 'parquet.hive.serde.ParquetHiveSerDe'
    >          stored as inputformat 'parquet.hive.DeprecatedParquetInputFormat'
    >          outputformat 'parquet.hive.DeprecatedParquetOutputFormat'
    >          LOCATION 'hdfs://localhost:8020/wlslog';
OK
Time taken: 1.074 seconds
hive>
```

Figure 8-4. *Creating a Hive external table*

Hive Version 0.13.0 and Later

The CREATE EXTERNAL TABLE command for creating a Hive external table stored as Parquet is as follows.

```
CREATE EXTERNAL TABLE IF NOT EXISTS wlslog_parquet(TIME_STAMP string,CATEGORY string,TYPE
string,SERVERNAME string,CODE string,MSG string)
        ROW FORMAT SERDE 'parquet.hive.serde.ParquetHiveSerDe'
        STORED AS PARQUET
        LOCATION 'hdfs://localhost:8020/wlslog';
```

First, drop the `wlslog_parquet` table if it was created using the earlier syntax. Subsequently run the `CREATE EXTERNAL TABLE` statement in the Hive shell, as shown in Figure 8-5.

```
hive> drop table wlslog_parquet;
OK
Time taken: 53.986 seconds
hive> CREATE EXTERNAL TABLE IF NOT EXISTS wlslog_parquet(TIME_STAMP string,CATEG
ORY string,TYPE string,SERVERNAME string,CODE string,MSG string)
    >         ROW FORMAT SERDE 'parquet.hive.serde.ParquetHiveSerDe'
    >         STORED AS PARQUET
    >         LOCATION 'hdfs://localhost:8020/wlslog';
OK
Time taken: 13.985 seconds
hive> █
```

Figure 8-5. *Creating a Hive external table for Hive 0.13.0*

Loading Data Into a Hive External Table

Next, load data into the `wlslog_parquet` table using the `INSERT OVERWRITE TABLE` command in the Hive shell.

```
hive>INSERT OVERWRITE TABLE wlslog_parquet SELECT time_stamp,category,type,servername,code,
msg  FROM wlslog;
```

`MapReduce` jobs are started and they load data into the `wlslog_parquet` table, as shown in Figure 8-6.

```
hive> INSERT OVERWRITE TABLE wlslog_parquet SELECT time_stamp,category,type,serv
ername,code,msg  FROM wlslog;
Total jobs = 3
Launching Job 1 out of 3
Number of reduce tasks is set to 0 since there's no reduce operator
Job running in-process (local Hadoop)
Hadoop job information for null: number of mappers: 0; number of reducers: 0
2015-10-05 15:44:58,600 null map = 0%,  reduce = 0%
SLF4J: Failed to load class "org.slf4j.impl.StaticLoggerBinder".
SLF4J: Defaulting to no-operation (NOP) logger implementation
SLF4J: See http://www.slf4j.org/codes.html#StaticLoggerBinder for further detail
s.
2015-10-05 15:45:37,294 null map = 100%,  reduce = 0%
Ended Job = job_local1431208511_0001
Oct 5, 2015 3:45:13 PM INFO: parquet.hadoop.codec.CodecConfig: Compression set t
o false
Oct 5, 2015 3:45:13 PM INFO: parquet.hadoop.codec.CodecConfig: Compression: UNCO
MPRESSED
Oct 5, 2015 3:45:13 PM INFO: parquet.hadoop.ParquetOutputFormat: Parquet block s
```

Figure 8-6. *Running the INSERT OVERWRITE HiveQL Statement*

Data from the `wlslog` table is loaded into the `wlslog_parquet` table, as shown in Figure 8-7.

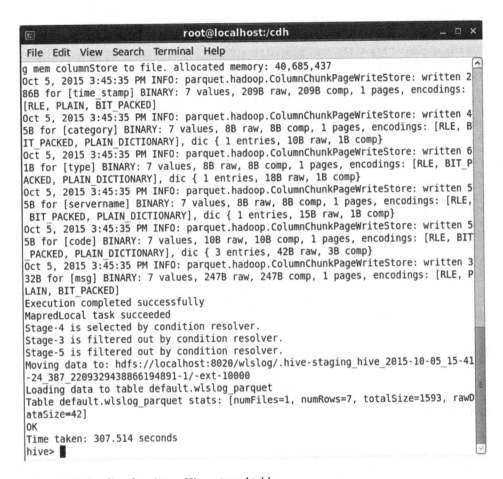

Figure 8-7. Loading data into a Hive external table

Run a SELECT statement in the Hive shell to query the data in the wlslog_parquet table.

```
select * from wlslog_parquet;
```

The wlslog_parquet table data is listed, as shown in Figure 8-8.

```
hive> select * from wlslog_parquet;
OK
SLF4J: Failed to load class "org.slf4j.impl.StaticLoggerBinder".
SLF4J: Defaulting to no-operation (NOP) logger implementation
SLF4J: See http://www.slf4j.org/codes.html#StaticLoggerBinder for further detail
s.
Apr-8-2014-7:06:16-PM-PDT        Notice  WebLogicServer  AdminServer    BEA-0003
65      Server state changed to STANDBY
Apr-8-2014-7:06:17-PM-PDT        Notice  WebLogicServer  AdminServer    BEA-0003
65      Server state changed to STARTING
Apr-8-2014-7:06:18-PM-PDT        Notice  WebLogicServer  AdminServer    BEA-0003
65      Server state changed to ADMIN
Apr-8-2014-7:06:19-PM-PDT        Notice  WebLogicServer  AdminServer    BEA-0003
65      Server state changed to RESUMING
Apr-8-2014-7:06:20-PM-PDT        Notice  WebLogicServer  AdminServer    BEA-0003
31      Started WebLogic AdminServer
Apr-8-2014-7:06:21-PM-PDT        Notice  WebLogicServer  AdminServer    BEA-0003
65      Server state changed to RUNNING
Apr-8-2014-7:06:22-PM-PDT        Notice  WebLogicServer  AdminServer    BEA-0003
60      Server started in RUNNING mode
Time taken: 3.4 seconds, Fetched: 7 row(s)
hive> 
```

Figure 8-8. *Querying a Hive external table*

Listing the Parquet Data File

The data for the Hive external table is actually stored as a Parquet data file in the HDFS. List the data files in the 'hdfs://localhost:8020/wlslog' directory, which is specified in the LOCATION clause of the CREATE EXTERNAL TABLE command.

```
hdfs dfs -ls 'hdfs://localhost:8020/wlslog'
```

The Parquet data file is listed, as shown in Figure 8-9.

```
[root@localhost cdh]# hdfs dfs -ls hdfs://localhost:8020/wlslog
Found 1 items
-rwxrwxrwx   1 root hadoop       1593 2015-10-05 12:13 hdfs://localhost:8020/wls
log/000000_0
[root@localhost cdh]# 
```

Figure 8-9. *Listing the Parquet data file*

List the data in the data file with the following Hive shell command.

```
hdfs dfs -cat  'hdfs://localhost:8020/wlslog/000000_0'
```

The Parquet data file data is listed, as shown in Figure 8-10. The Parquet format file displayed as text may appear to be incorrectly formatted, overwritten with squares that are filled with numbers. The data is stored as column-oriented, with data for all columns being stored adjacently.

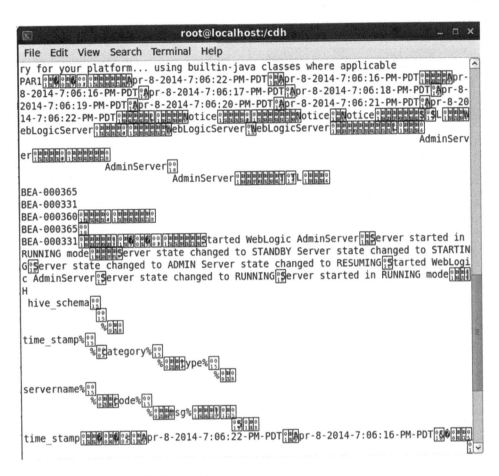

Figure 8-10. *Displaying the Parquet data*

Summary

This chapter introduced the Apache Parquet storage format, which is an efficient, structured, columnar storage format. You saw how to create a Hive external table stored as a Parquet data file. In the next chapter, you learn about Apache Kafka.

Messaging & Indexing

CHAPTER 9

▪ ▪ ▪

Apache Kafka

Apache Kafka is publish-subscribe, high-throughput, distributed messaging system. Kafka is fast with a single broker handling hundreds of MB (terabytes)/sec of reads and writes from several clients. Messages are replicated across the cluster and persisted to disk. Kafka can be used for stream processing, web site activity tracking, metrics collection and monitoring, and log aggregation.

The main components of Kafka architecture are *Producer*, *Broker*, *Topic,* and *Consumer*. Kafka keeps feeds of messages in topics. Producers send (or write) messages to topics and consumers, who subscribe to those topics, consume (or read) messages from topics. Topics are partitioned and a key can be attached to each message guaranteeing that messages with the same key arrive at the same partition. A topic partition is like a log. Messages are byte arrays of data and can be in any format, with String, JSON, and Avro being the most common. Messages are retained for a specified amount of time. A ZooKeeper coordinates the Kafka cluster. A Kafka cluster consists of one or more servers called *brokers*.

Kafka is similar to Flume in that it streams messages, but Kafka is designed for a different purpose. While Flume is designed to stream messages to a sink such as HDFS or HBase, Kafka is designed for messages to be consumed by several applications. The Apache Kafka architecture is shown in Figure 9-1.

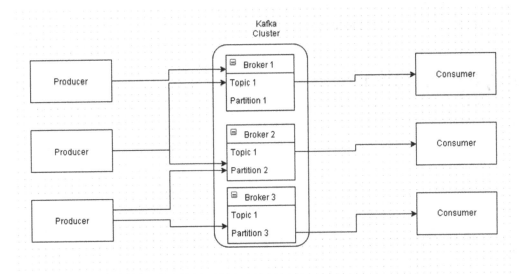

Figure 9-1. *Apache Kafka architecture*

© Deepak Vohra 2016
D. Vohra, *Practical Hadoop Ecosystem*, DOI 10.1007/978-1-4842-2199-0_9

In this chapter, you learn how to create a Kafka cluster consisting of a single broker. A single producer sends messages to a topic and a single consumer consumes messages from the topic. The simplified, single producer, single topic, single consumer Kafka cluster is represented in Figure 9-2.

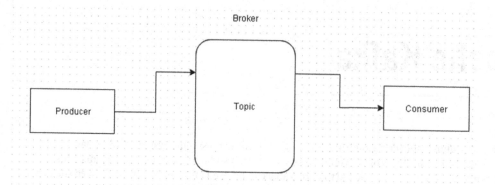

Figure 9-2. *Single producer-broker-consumer Kafka architecture*

This chapter covers the following topics:

- Setting the environment
- Starting the Kafka server
- Creating a Kafka topic
- Starting a Kafka producer
- Starting a Kafka consumer
- Producing and consuming messages

Setting the Environment

This section shows you how to download and install Apache Kafka on Oracle Linux 6.6. Create a directory (/kafka for example) and set its permissions to global (777).

```
mkdir /kafka
chmod -R 777 /kafka
cd /kafka
```

Download the Kafka 2.10-0.8.2.1 tgz file and extract the file to a directory.

```
wget http://apache.mirror.iweb.ca/kafka/0.8.2.1/kafka_2.10-0.8.2.1.tgz
tar -xvf kafka_2.10-0.8.2.1.tgz
```

Set the environment variable KAFKA_HOME in the bash shell and add the bin directory to the PATH.

```
vi ~/.bashrc
export KAFKA_HOME=/kafka/kafka_2.10-0.8.2.1
export PATH=$PATH:$KAFKA_HOME/bin
```

Start the ZooKeeper server.

```
/kafka>zookeeper-server-start.sh config/zookeeper.properties
```

The ZooKeeper starts on localhost:2181, as shown in Figure 9-3.

Figure 9-3. *Starting ZooKeeper*

Starting the Kafka Server

This section shows how to start the Kafka server. The configuration properties for the Kafka server are set in the config/server.properties file. The configuration properties are divided into sections. Table 9-1 shows the main configuration properties, including the value used.

Table 9-1. *Configuration Properties for the Kafka Server*

Property	Description	Value	Section
broker.id	A unique broker ID for each broker. By default, only one broker is configured.	0	Server Basics
controlled.shutdown.retry.backoff.ms	Backoff time in ms between shutdown retries. Default value is 5000.	10000	Server Basics
auto.create.topics.enable	Whether to create topics automatically if not created before sending producer messages.	true	Server Basics
delete.topic.enable	Whether to enable topic deletion.	true	Server Basics
port	The port the socket server listens on.	9092	Socket Server Settings
host.name	Hostname the broker binds on. If not set, the server binds on all interfaces.	Not set	Socket Server Settings
advertised.host.name	Hostname the broker advertises to producers and consumers. If not set, the value of host.name is used.	Not set	Socket Server Settings
advertised.port	The port advertised to ZooKeeper. If not set, the port where the broker binds.	Not set	Socket Server Settings
num.network.threads	Number of threads handling network threads.	3	Socket Server Settings
num.io.threads	Number of input/output threads.	8	Socket Server Settings
socket.send.buffer.bytes	Send buffer used by the socket server.	102400	Socket Server Settings
socket.receive.buffer.bytes=102400	Receive buffer used by socket server.	102400	Socket Server Settings
socket.request.max.bytes	Maximum size of a socket server request.	104857600	Socket Server Settings
log.dirs	Directories (separated by "," to store log files)	/tmp/kafka-logs	Log Basics

(continued)

Table 9-1. (*continued*)

Property	Description	Value	Section
`num.partitions`	Default number of log partitions per topic.	1	Log Basics
`num.recovery.threads.per.data.dir`	Number of threads per data directory to be used for log recovery.	1	Log Basics
`log.flush.interval.messages`	Number of messages to accept before forcing a flush of data to disk.	10000	Log Flush Policy
`log.flush.interval.ms`	Maximum amount of time a log message can be retained before flushing.	1000	Log Flush Policy
`log.retention.hours`	Minimum age of a log file to be eligible for deletion.	168	Log Retention Policy
`log.retention.bytes`	The minimum size of logs to be retained. Logs are not pruned below the setting.	1073741824	Log Retention Policy
`log.segment.bytes`	Maximum size of a log segment file.	1073741824	Log Retention Policy
`log.retention.check.interval.ms`	The interval at which log segments are checked to determine if they need to be deleted.	300000	Log Retention Policy
`log.cleaner.enable`	Whether to enable log cleaner, which marks individual logs for log compaction.	`false`	Log Retention Policy
`zookeeper.connection.timeout.ms`	Timeout for connecting to ZooKeeper.	6000	ZooKeeper

The configuration properties must be set before starting the Kafka server. Start the Kafka server.

```
kafka-server-start.sh config/server.properties
```

The Kafka server starts, as shown in Figure 9-4.

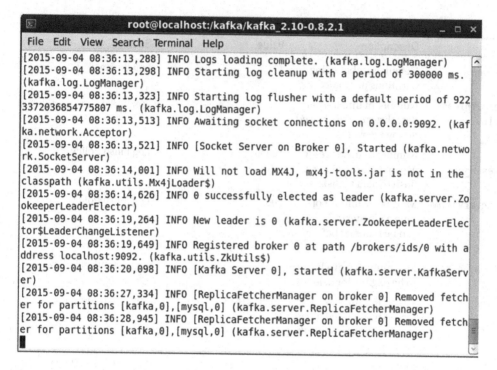

Figure 9-4. *Starting the Kafka server*

Creating a Kafka Topic

Next, create a topic called kafka using the following command. Set the number of partitions to 1 and replication factor to 1.

```
kafka-topics.sh --create --zookeeper localhost:2181 --replication-factor 1 --partitions 1
--topic kafka
```

A message Created topic "kafka" should be displayed, as shown in Figure 9-5.

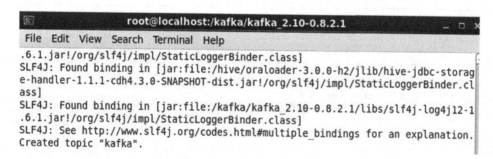

Figure 9-5. *Creating the Kafka topic "kafka"*

The topics can be listed using the following command.

```
bin/kafka-topics.sh --list --zookeeper localhost:2181
```

The kafka topic is listed, as shown in Figure 9-6.

```
[root@localhost kafka]# cd kafka_2.10-0.8.2.1
[root@localhost kafka_2.10-0.8.2.1]# bin/kafka-topics.sh --list --zookeeper loca
lhost:2181

kafka
mysql
[root@localhost kafka 2.10-0.8.2.1]#
```

Figure 9-6. *Listing Kafka topics*

Because you have enabled topic deletion, a topic may even be deleted with the following command.

```
kafka-topics.sh --delete --zookeeper localhost:2181 --replication-factor 1 --partitions 1
--topic kafka
```

As auto.create.topics.enable is set to true by default if a topic is not created prior to a producer sending messages to, the topic is created automatically.

Starting a Kafka Producer

Having started the ZooKeeper and the Kafka server, start the Kafka producer. Specify the topic with the -topic option as kafka.

```
kafka-console-producer.sh --broker-list localhost:9092 --topic kafka
```

A Kafka producer starts, as shown in Figure 9-7.

```
root@localhost:/kafka/kafka_2.10-0.8.2.1                    _ □ x
File  Edit  View  Search  Terminal  Help
[root@localhost ~]# cd /kafka/kafka_2.10-0.8.2.1
[root@localhost kafka_2.10-0.8.2.1]# kafka-console-producer.sh --broker-list loc
alhost:9092 --topic kafka
```

Figure 9-7. *Starting a Kafka producer*

Starting a Kafka Consumer

Start the Kafka consumer using the following command.

```
kafka-console-consumer.sh --zookeeper localhost:2181 --topic kafka --from-beginning
```

A Kafka consumer starts, as shown in Figure 9-8.

```
[root@localhost kafka_2.10-0.8.2.1]# kafka-console-consumer.sh --zookeeper local
host:2181 --topic kafka --from-beginning
```

Figure 9-8. *Starting a Kafka consumer*

Producing and Consuming Messages

Having started the producer and the consumer, you can now produce message(s) at the producer and consume message(s) at the consumer. At the producer add a message, for example "Message from kafka producer", and then click the Enter button, as shown in Figure 9-9. The message is sent.

```
[root@localhost kafka_2.10-0.8.2.1]# kafka-console-producer.sh --broker-list loc
alhost:9092 --topic kafka
MEssage from Kafka producer
[]
```

Figure 9-9. *Producing a message*

At the consumer, the message is consumed, as shown in Figure 9-10.

```
[root@localhost kafka_2.10-0.8.2.1]# kafka-console-consumer.sh --zookeeper local
host:2181 --topic kafka --from-beginning
MEssage from Kafka producer
```

Figure 9-10. *Consuming a message*

Send another message at the producer. The message is consumed at the consumer, as shown in Figure 9-11.

```
Created topic "kafka".
[root@localhost kafka_2.10-0.8.2.1]# kafka-console-producer.sh --broker-list loc
alhost:9092 --topic kafka
[2015-09-03 18:22:57,327] WARN Property topic is not valid (kafka.utils.Verifiab
leProperties)
SLF4J: Class path contains multiple SLF4J bindings.
SLF4J: Found binding in [jar:file:/hive/hive-0.10.0-cdh4.6.0/lib/slf4j-log4j12-1
.6.1.jar!/org/slf4j/impl/StaticLoggerBinder.class]
SLF4J: Found binding in [jar:file:/hive/oraloader-3.0.0-h2/jlib/hive-jdbc-storag
e-handler-1.1.1-cdh4.3.0-SNAPSHOT-dist.jar!/org/slf4j/impl/StaticLoggerBinder.cl
ass]
SLF4J: Found binding in [jar:file:/kafka/kafka_2.10-0.8.2.1/libs/slf4j-log4j12-1
.6.1.jar!/org/slf4j/impl/StaticLoggerBinder.class]
SLF4J: See http://www.slf4j.org/codes.html#multiple_bindings for an explanation.
MEssage from Kafka producer
Message from Kafka Producer
```

```
[root@localhost kafka_2.10-0.8.2.1]# kafka-console-consumer.sh --zookeeper local
host:2181 --topic kafka --from-beginning
SLF4J: Class path contains multiple SLF4J bindings.
SLF4J: Found binding in [jar:file:/hive/hive-0.10.0-cdh4.6.0/lib/slf4j-log4j12-1
.6.1.jar!/org/slf4j/impl/StaticLoggerBinder.class]
SLF4J: Found binding in [jar:file:/hive/oraloader-3.0.0-h2/jlib/hive-jdbc-storag
e-handler-1.1.1-cdh4.3.0-SNAPSHOT-dist.jar!/org/slf4j/impl/StaticLoggerBinder.cl
ass]
SLF4J: Found binding in [jar:file:/kafka/kafka_2.10-0.8.2.1/libs/slf4j-log4j12-1
.6.1.jar!/org/slf4j/impl/StaticLoggerBinder.class]
SLF4J: See http://www.slf4j.org/codes.html#multiple_bindings for an explanation.
MEssage from Kafka producer
Message from Kafka Producer
[]
```

Figure 9-11. *Producing and consuming messages*

Summary

This chapter introduced Apache Kafka, a distributed messaging system. Apache Kafka comprises four main components: a Kafka producer, Kafka broker, Kafka topic, and Kafka consumer. A Kafka broker is a Kafka server. A Kafka producer produces messages that are saved in a Kafka topic. A Kafka consumer that subscribes to that topic consumes the messages. The next chapter discusses Apache Solr.

CHAPTER 10

■ ■ ■

Apache Solr

Apache Solr is a Apache Lucene-based enterprise search platform providing features such as full-text search, near real-time indexing, and database integration. The Apache Hadoop ecosystem provides support for Solr in several of its projects. Apache Hive Storage Handler for Solr can be used to index Hive table data in Solr. Apache HBase-Solr supports indexing of HBase table data. Apache Flume provides a `MorphlineSolrSink` for streaming data to Apache Solr for indexing. This chapter introduces Apache Solr and creates a Hive table stored by Solr. This chapter has the following sections:

- Setting the environment
- Configuring the Solr schema
- Starting the Solr server
- Indexing a document in Solr
- Deleting a document from Solr
- Indexing a document in Solr with a Java client
- Searching a document in Solr
- Creating a Hive-managed table
- Creating a Hive external table
- Loading Hive external table data
- Searching Hive table data indexed in Solr

Setting the Environment

The following software is required for this chapter.

- Apache Hadoop
- Apache Hive
- Apache Solr
- Apache ZooKeeper
- Hive Storage Handler for Solr
- Java 7

© Deepak Vohra 2016
D. Vohra, *Practical Hadoop Ecosystem*, DOI 10.1007/978-1-4842-2199-0_10

Apache Solr runs as a full-text search server within a servlet container. You can use any of the commonly used servlet containers, such as WebLogic Server, WebSphere Application Server, JBoss Application Server, GlassFish Server, and Apache Tomcat. The default is Jetty, which is included with the Solr installation. This chapter's examples use the embedded Jetty server.

Create a directory (/cdh) to install the software (if not already created in earlier chapters) and set its permissions to global (777).

```
mkdir /cdh
chmod -R 777 /cdh
cd /cdh
```

Download and extract the Java 7 tar file.

```
tar zxvf jdk-7u55-linux-i586.gz
```

Download and extract the Hadoop 2.6.0 tar file.

```
wget http://archive-primary.cloudera.com/cdh5/cdh/5/hadoop-2.6.0-cdh5.4.7.tar.gz
tar -xvf hadoop-2.6.0-cdh5.4.7.tar.gz
```

Create symlinks for the Hadoop bin and conf directories.

```
ln -s /cdh/hadoop-2.6.0-cdh5.4.7/bin /cdh/hadoop-2.6.0-cdh5.4.7/share/hadoop/mapreduce1/bin
ln -s /cdh/hadoop-2.6.0-cdh5.4.7/etc/hadoop  /cdh/hadoop-2.6.0-cdh5.4.7/share/hadoop/
mapreduce1/conf
```

Download and extract the Hive 1.1.0 tar file.

```
wget  http://archive-primary.cloudera.com/cdh5/cdh/5/hive-1.1.0-cdh5.4.7.tar.gz
tar -xvf hive-1.1.0-cdh5.4.7.tar.gz
```

Download and extract the Apache Solr tar file.

```
wget http://archive-primary.cloudera.com/cdh5/cdh/5/solr-4.10.3-cdh5.4.7.tar.gz
tar -xvf solr-4.10.3-cdh5.4.7.tar.gz
```

Download and extract the Apache ZooKeeper tar file.

```
wget http://archive-primary.cloudera.com/cdh5/cdh/5/zookeeper-3.4.5-cdh5.4.7.tar.gz
tar -xvf zookeeper-3.4.5-cdh5.4.7.tar.gz
```

Create the zoo.cfg configuration file by copying the sample configuration file /cdh/zookeeper-3.4.5-cdh5.4.7/conf/zoo_sample.cfg.

```
cp /cdh/zookeeper-3.4.5-cdh5.4.7/conf/zoo_sample.cfg /cdh/zookeeper-3.4.5-cdh5.4.7/conf/zoo.cfg
```

Download, compile, and package the Hive storage handler for Hive.

```
git clone http://github.org/chimpler/hive-solr
cd hive-solr
mvn compile
mvn package
```

Copy the jar file to the Hive lib directory, adding the jar to the classpath of Hive.

```
cp hive-solr-0.0.1-SNAPSHOT-jar-with-dependencies.jar /cdh/hive-1.1.0-cdh5.4.7/lib
```

Set the environment variables for Apache Hadoop, Apache Hive, Apache ZooKeeper, Apache Solr, and Java 7.

```
vi ~/.bashrc
export SOLR_HOME=/cdh/solr-4.10.3-cdh5.4.7
export ZOOKEEPER_HOME=/cdh/zookeeper-3.4.5-cdh5.4.7
export HADOOP_PREFIX=/cdh/hadoop-2.6.0-cdh5.4.7
export HADOOP_CONF_DIR=$HADOOP_PREFIX/etc/hadoop
export HADOOP_COMMON_HOME=$HADOOP_PREFIX/share/hadoop/common
export HADOOP_HDFS_HOME=$HADOOP_PREFIX/share/hadoop/hdfs
export HIVE_HOME=/cdh/hive-1.1.0-cdh5.4.7
export HIVE_CONF=$HIVE_HOME/conf
export JAVA_HOME=/cdh/jdk1.7.0_55
export HADOOP_MAPRED_HOME=$HADOOP_PREFIX/share/hadoop/mapreduce1
export HADOOP_HOME=$HADOOP_PREFIX/share/hadoop/mapreduce1
export HADOOP_CLASSPATH=$HADOOP_HOME/*:$HADOOP_HOME/lib/*:$JAVA_HOME/lib/*:$HIVE_HOME/
lib/*:$HIVE_CONF:$HADOOP_CONF_DIR:$HADOOP_COMMON_HOME/*:$HADOOP_COMMON_HOME/lib/*:$HADOOP_
HDFS_HOME/*:$HADOOP_HDFS_HOME/lib/*:$SOLR_HOME/dist/*:$SOLR_HOME/lib/hive-solr-0.0.1-
SNAPSHOT-jar-with-dependencies.jar
export PATH=$JAVA_HOME/bin:/usr/local/sbin:/usr/sbin:/sbin:/usr/local/bin:/usr/bin:/
bin:$HADOOP_PREFIX/bin:$HADOOP_HOME/bin:$HADOOP_MAPRED_HOME/bin:$HIVE_HOME/bin:$SQOOP_HOME/
bin/*:$MYSQL_HOME/bin:$SOLR_HOME/bin:$ZOOKEEPER_HOME/bin
export CLASSPATH=$HADOOP_CLASSPATH
export HADOOP_NAMENODE_USER=hadoop
export HADOOP_DATANODE_USER=hadoop
export HADOOP_VERSION=2.6.0
```

Configuring the Solr Schema

The Solr configuration is specified in the schema.xml file in the /cdh/solr-4.10.3-cdh5.4.7/example/ solr/conf directory. The schema configuration includes the field names in the documents indexed in Solr and the different types of fields. Every document that is to be indexed for searching in Apache Solr must specify its fields in the schema.xml file. Each document indexed for search must include the id field by default. Table 10-1 lists the elements found in the schema.xml file.

Table 10-1. *Elements in the schema.xml File*

Element	Description	Example
`<field/>`	Specifies a field that may be used in a document indexed in Solr. The field name must not be duplicate.	`<field name="id" type="string" indexed="true" stored="true" required="true" multiValued="false" />`
`<uniqueKey/>`	The unique key field used to determine the uniqueness of a document. Required by default.	`<uniqueKey>id</uniqueKey>`
`<fieldType/>`	Specifies a field type used in a field name.	`<fieldType name="string" class="solr.StrField" sortMissingLast="true" />`

The `<field/>` element provides several attributes, with some of the attributes listed in Table 10-2.

Table 10-2. *Attributes in the <field/> Element*

Attribute	Description
`name`	Field name.
`default`	Field default value.
`indexed`	A Boolean (true/false) indicating if the field is to be indexed. Only an indexed field is searchable and sortable.
`stored`	A Boolean (true/false) indicating if the field value is retrievable during search.
`multiValued`	A Boolean (true/false) indicating if the field may have multiple values in a document.

The examples in this chapter store documents with the fields time_stamp, category, type, servername, code, and msg. You therefore need to specify these elements in the schema.xml file. Open the schema.xml file in the vi editor.

```
vi /cdh/solr-4.10.3-cdh5.4.7/example/solr/collection1/conf/schema.xml
```

Add the `<field/>` elements called time_stamp, category, type, servername, code, and msg. A section of the schema.xml file is listed.

```
<?xml version="1.0" encoding="UTF-8" ?>
<schema name="example" version="1.5">
<field name="time_stamp" type="string" indexed="true"  stored="true"  multiValued="false" />
<field name="category" type="string" indexed="true"  stored="true"  multiValued="false" />
<field name="type" type="string" indexed="true"  stored="true"  multiValued="false" />
<field name="servername" type="string" indexed="true"  stored="true"  multiValued="false" />
<field name="code" type="string" indexed="true"  stored="true"  multiValued="false" />
<field name="msg" type="string" indexed="true"  stored="true"  multiValued="false" />
```

The section of the added schema.xml file is shown in Figure 10-1.

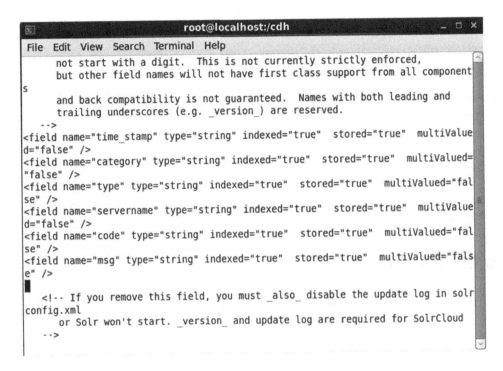

Figure 10-1. *Updated schema.xml*

Some of the fields are required and should not be removed. These fields are id and _version_. The uniqueKey element is set to id.

```
<field name="_version_" type="long" indexed="true" stored="true"/>
    <field name="id" type="string" indexed="true" stored="true" required="true"
multiValued="false" />
 <uniqueKey>id</uniqueKey>
```

The fieldType elements specify the field types, such as the string and boolean types.

```
    <fieldType name="string" class="solr.StrField" sortMissingLast="true" />
    <fieldType name="boolean" class="solr.BoolField" sortMissingLast="true"/>
</schema>
```

The schema.xml file cannot contain any duplicated fields. For example, you can't add an element called category, because schema.xml includes an element called category. Remove the duplicate category element, as shown in Figure 10-2.

```
    <field name="title" type="text_general" indexed="true" stored="true" multiVal
ued="true"/>
    <field name="subject" type="text_general" indexed="true" stored="true"/>
    <field name="description" type="text_general" indexed="true" stored="true"/>
    <field name="comments" type="text_general" indexed="true" stored="true"/>
    <field name="author" type="text_general" indexed="true" stored="true"/>
    <field name="keywords" type="text_general" indexed="true" stored="true"/>
    <!-- <field name="category" type="text_general" indexed="true" stored="true"/>
-->
```

Figure 10-2. *Commenting out the duplicate <category/> element*

The Solr server must be restarted after you modify the schema.xml file. You'll learn how to start the Solr server in the next section.

Starting the Solr Server

This section shows you how to start the Solr server and log in to the Solr Admin console. Before starting Solr, you need to start the ZooKeeper server. Run the following command to start the ZooKeeper server.

```
zkServer.sh start
```

ZooKeeper starts, as shown in Figure 10-3.

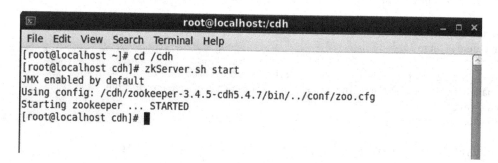

```
root@localhost:/cdh                          _ □ ✕
File  Edit  View  Search  Terminal  Help
[root@localhost ~]# cd /cdh
[root@localhost cdh]# zkServer.sh start
JMX enabled by default
Using config: /cdh/zookeeper-3.4.5-cdh5.4.7/bin/../conf/zoo.cfg
Starting zookeeper ... STARTED
[root@localhost cdh]# ▮
```

Figure 10-3. *Starting ZooKeeper*

Change (cd) to the /cdh/solr-4.10.3-cdh5.4.7/example/ directory and start the Apache Solr search server with the following command.

```
cd /cdh/solr-4.10.3-cdh5.4.7/example
example>java -jar start.jar
```

The Jetty server starts and the container configuration is loaded from the solr.xml configuration file. A new Searcher is registered, as shown in Figure 10-4.

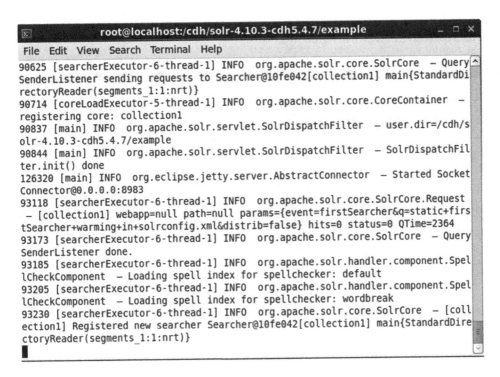

Figure 10-4. *Starting the Apache Solr server*

Log in to the Solr Admin console with the http://localhost:8983/solr/ URL. The Admin Dashboard displays information such as the version and JVM, and the system properties such as physical memory and swap space, as shown in Figure 10-5.

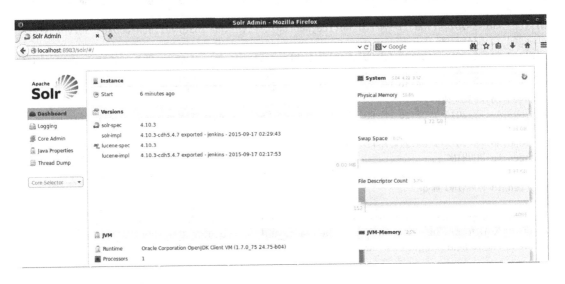

Figure 10-5. *Solr Admin Dashboard*

In the Core selector, select the `collection1` collection. The Overview tab lists the statistics about the Solr server and data collection, as shown in Figure 10-6.

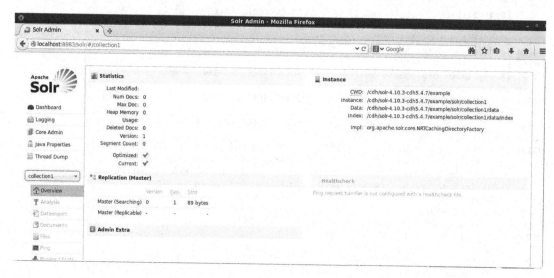

Figure 10-6. *Overview of collection1*

Indexing a Document in Solr

Solr supports indexing structured documents in the CSV, XML, JSON formats and in binary. This section shows you how to index the following sample log data and then store the file as `wlslog.txt`.

```
wlslog1,Apr-8-2014-7:06:16-PM-PDT,Notice,WebLogicServer,AdminServer,BEA-000365,Server state
changed to STANDBY
wlslog2,Apr-8-2014-7:06:17-PM-PDT,Notice,WebLogicServer,AdminServer,BEA-000365,Server state
changed to STARTING
wlslog3,Apr-8-2014-7:06:18-PM-PDT,Notice,WebLogicServer,AdminServer,BEA-000365,Server state
changed to ADMIN
wlslog4,Apr-8-2014-7:06:19-PM-PDT,Notice,WebLogicServer,AdminServer,BEA-000365,Server state
changed to RESUMING
wlslog5,Apr-8-2014-7:06:20-PM-PDT,Notice,WebLogicServer,AdminServer,BEA-000331,Started
WebLogic AdminServer
wlslog6,Apr-8-2014-7:06:21-PM-PDT,Notice,WebLogicServer,AdminServer,BEA-000365,Server state
changed to RUNNING
wlslog7,Apr-8-2014-7:06:22-PM-PDT,Notice,WebLogicServer,AdminServer,BEA-000360,Server
started in RUNNING mode
```

This example indexes the document as an XML document. Convert the preceding listing to the following XML form. The root element must be `<add/>` and each document must be enclosed in the `<doc/>` element. The `id` field is required in each `<doc/>` element.

```
<add>
<doc>
  <field name="id">wlslog1</field>
```

```
  <field name="time_stamp">Apr-8-2014-7:06:16-PM-PDT</field>
  <field name="category">Notice</field>
  <field name="type">WebLogicServer</field>

  <field name="servername">AdminServer</field>
  <field name="code">BEA-000365</field>
  <field name="msg">Server state changed to STANDBY</field>
</doc>
<doc>
  <field name="id">wlslog2</field>

  <field name="time_stamp">Apr-8-2014-7:06:17-PM-PDT</field>
  <field name="category">Notice</field>
  <field name="type">WebLogicServer</field>
  <field name="servername">AdminServer</field>
  <field name="code">BEA-000365</field>
  <field name="msg">Server state changed to STARTING</field>
</doc>
<doc>
  <field name="id">wlslog3</field>

  <field name="time_stamp">Apr-8-2014-7:06:18-PM-PDT</field>
  <field name="category">Notice</field>
  <field name="type">WebLogicServer</field>

  <field name="servername">AdminServer</field>
  <field name="code">BEA-000365</field>
  <field name="msg">Server state changed to ADMIN</field>
</doc>
<doc>
<field name="id">wlslog4</field>

  <field name="time_stamp">Apr-8-2014-7:06:19-PM-PDT</field>
  <field name="category">Notice</field>
  <field name="type">WebLogicServer</field>

  <field name="servername">AdminServer</field>
  <field name="code">BEA-000365</field>
  <field name="msg">Server state changed to RESUMING</field>
</doc>

<doc>
<field name="id">wlslo5</field>

  <field name="time_stamp">Apr-8-2014-7:06:20-PM-PDT</field>
  <field name="category">Notice</field>
  <field name="type">WebLogicServer</field>

  <field name="servername">AdminServer</field>
  <field name="code">BEA-000331</field>
  <field name="msg">Started WebLogic AdminServer</field>
```

```
</doc>
<doc>
<field name="id">wlslog6</field>

  <field name="time_stamp">Apr-8-2014-7:06:21-PM-PDT</field>
  <field name="category">Notice</field>
  <field name="type">WebLogicServer</field>
  <field name="servername">AdminServer</field>
  <field name="code">BEA-000365</field>
  <field name="msg">Server state changed to RUNNING</field>
</doc>
<doc>
<field name="id">wlslog7</field>

  <field name="time_stamp">Apr-8-2014-7:06:22-PM-PDT</field>
  <field name="category">Notice</field>
  <field name="type">WebLogicServer</field>
  <field name="servername">AdminServer</field>
  <field name="code">BEA-000360</field>
  <field name="msg">Server started in RUNNING mode</field>

</doc>
</add>
```

In the Solr Admin console, select the Documents tab for collection1. In the Request-Handler field, select /update. The different options available in Document Type are CSV, Document Builder, File Upload, JSON, Solr Command (raw XML or JSON), and XML. Select the Solr Command (raw XML or JSON) option. In the document field, add the XML document listed previously. Click on Submit Document, as shown in Figure 10-7.

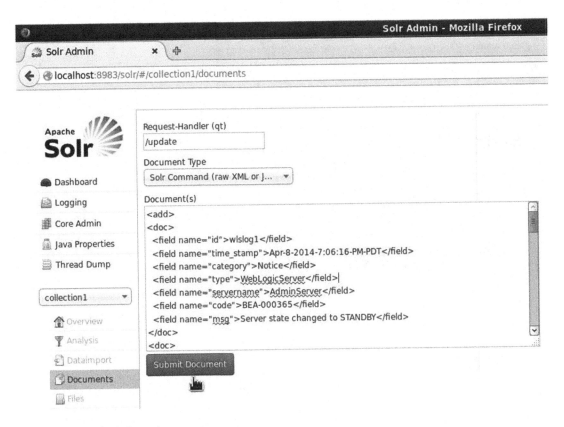

Figure 10-7. Submitting a document

If the document is added to Solr, a Status: success message is returned, as shown in Figure 10-8.

Figure 10-8. Status "success" for submitting a document

The added documents are not available for searching until the Solr server is restarted. Shut down the Solr server and restart it.

```
java -jar start.jar
```

Searching a Document in Solr

This section shows you how to query the documents indexed in the previous section. Specify the http://localhost:8983/solr/#/collection1/query URL in a browser. Specify the Request-Handler as /select, as shown in Figure 10-9. In the q field, specify the query. The default query of *:* returns all the documents and all the fields. The Start, Rows field specifies the index of the start document and the number of documents to select.

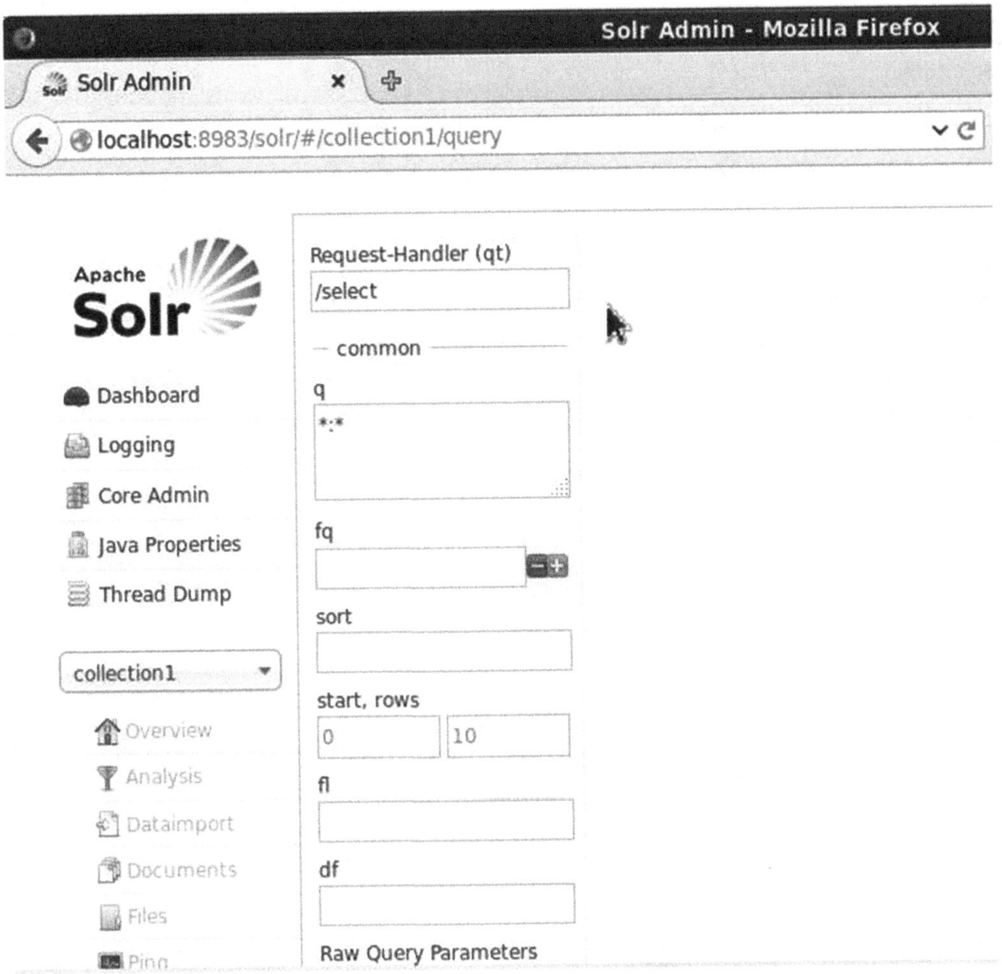

Figure 10-9. *Settings for a Solr query*

The wt (writer type) format field specifies the format of the response document and is set to json by default. The wt selection specifies the format of the returned document. Some of the supported response document formats are JSON, XML, and CSV, the default being JSON. Click on Execute Query to run the query, as shown in Figure 10-10.

Figure 10-10. *Submitting a Solr query*

The result of the query is returned and displayed as JSON. The numFound field in the response JSON object indicates the number of documents found. The documents are returned as a JSON array doc. As all documents were selected to be searched, the seven documents added previously are listed in JSON format, as shown in Figure 10-11.

Figure 10-11. *Result of the Solr query*

All the fields in each document are returned by default. The _version_ field is added to each of the documents index in Solr automatically and are listed in the search, as shown in Figure 10-12.

Figure 10-12. *Query result with the _version_ field added to each document*

The complete JSON document returned by the search is listed here:

```json
{
  "responseHeader": {
    "status": 0,
    "QTime": 104,
    "params": {
      "indent": "true",
      "q": "*:*",
      "_": "1444223313860",
      "wt": "json"
    }
  },
  "response": {
    "numFound": 7,
    "start": 0,
    "docs": [
      {
        "id": "wlslog1",
        "time_stamp": "Apr-8-2014-7:06:16-PM-PDT",
        "category": "Notice",
        "type": "WebLogicServer",
        "servername": "AdminServer",
        "code": "BEA-000365",
        "msg": "Server state changed to STANDBY",
        "_version_": 1514377153434615800
      },
      {
        "id": "wlslog2",
        "time_stamp": "Apr-8-2014-7:06:17-PM-PDT",
        "category": "Notice",
        "type": "WebLogicServer",
        "servername": "AdminServer",
        "code": "BEA-000365",
        "msg": "Server state changed to STARTING",
        "_version_": 1514377153530036200
      },
      {
        "id": "wlslog3",
        "time_stamp": "Apr-8-2014-7:06:18-PM-PDT",
        "category": "Notice",
        "type": "WebLogicServer",
        "servername": "AdminServer",
        "code": "BEA-000365",
        "msg": "Server state changed to ADMIN",
        "_version_": 1514377153532133400
      },
      {
        "id": "wlslog4",
        "time_stamp": "Apr-8-2014-7:06:19-PM-PDT",
        "category": "Notice",
```

```
      "type": "WebLogicServer",
      "servername": "AdminServer",
      "code": "BEA-000365",
      "msg": "Server state changed to RESUMING",
      "_version_": 1514377153533182000
    },
    {
      "id": "wlslog5",
      "time_stamp": "Apr-8-2014-7:06:20-PM-PDT",
      "category": "Notice",
      "type": "WebLogicServer",
      "servername": "AdminServer",
      "code": "BEA-000331",
      "msg": "Started WebLogic AdminServer",
      "_version_": 1514377153537376300
    },
    {
      "id": "wlslog6",
      "time_stamp": "Apr-8-2014-7:06:21-PM-PDT",
      "category": "Notice",
      "type": "WebLogicServer",
      "servername": "AdminServer",
      "code": "BEA-000365",
      "msg": "Server state changed to RUNNING",
      "_version_": 1514377153538424800
    },
    {
      "id": "wlslog7",
      "time_stamp": "Apr-8-2014-7:06:22-PM-PDT",
      "category": "Notice",
      "type": "WebLogicServer",
      "servername": "AdminServer",
      "code": "BEA-000360",
      "msg": "Server started in RUNNING mode",
      "_version_": 1514377153539473400
    }
  ]
 }
}
```

Deleting a Document from Solr

You can delete one or more documents from the Solr index. Select the Request-Handler as /update. In the Documents field, you specify all documents to be deleted with the following XML document.

```
<delete><query>*:*</query></delete>
```

Click on Submit Document, as shown in Figure 10-13.

Figure 10-13. *Submitting an update request to delete all documents*

The response status of "success" indicates that the documents were deleted successfully, as shown in Figure 10-14.

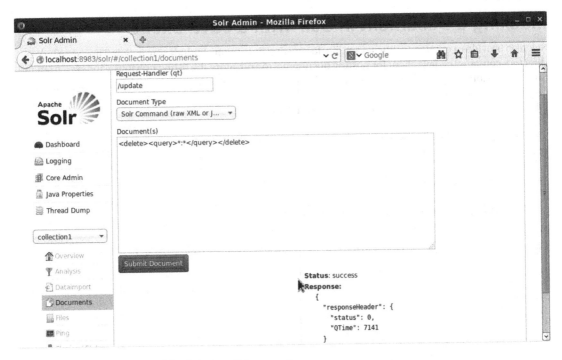

Figure 10-14. *Status "success" for deleting all documents*

The Solr server must be restarted before the documents are deleted. If a search is performed on the documents that are still indexed in Solr, no document is returned, as shown in Figure 10-15.

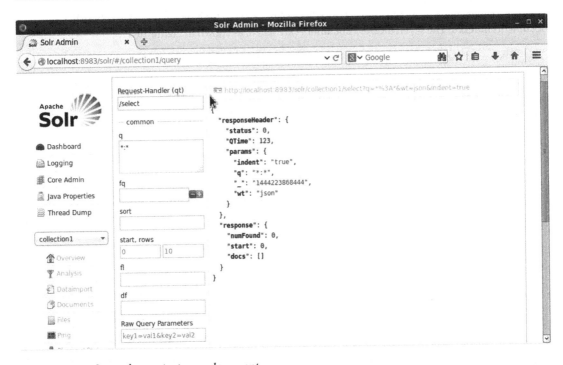

Figure 10-15. *Query does not return a document*

Indexing a Document in Solr with a Java Client

Solr also provides a command-line Java utility for posting documents for indexing in Solr. The exampledocs directory contains the Java client for posting documents to Solr. Store the listing previously indexed from the Solr Admin Console as wlslog.xml. Change (cd) to the exampledocs directory.

```
cd /cdh/solr-4.10.3-cdh5.4.7/example/exampledocs
```

The documents to be indexed must be specified as XML files on the command-line arg. Run the following command on the command line.

```
java -jar post.jar wlslog.xml
```

The wlslog.xml file is indexed, as shown in Figure 10-16.

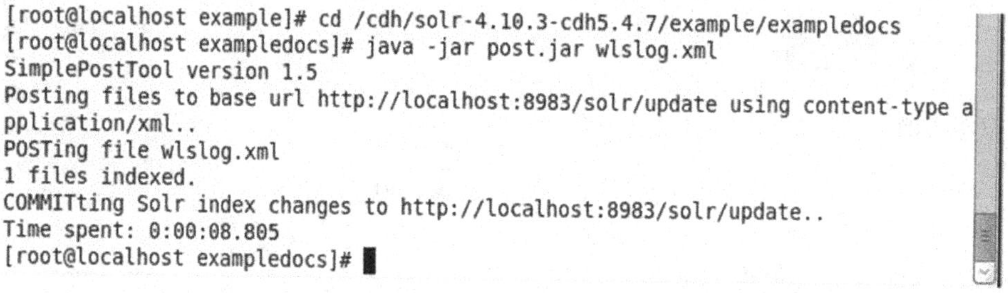

```
[root@localhost example]# cd /cdh/solr-4.10.3-cdh5.4.7/example/exampledocs
[root@localhost exampledocs]# java -jar post.jar wlslog.xml
SimplePostTool version 1.5
Posting files to base url http://localhost:8983/solr/update using content-type a
pplication/xml..
POSTing file wlslog.xml
1 files indexed.
COMMITting Solr index changes to http://localhost:8983/solr/update..
Time spent: 0:00:08.805
[root@localhost exampledocs]# █
```

Figure 10-16. *Posting the wlslog.xml file to a Solr index*

Run a search query from the http://localhost:8983/solr/#/collection1/query URL to list the documents indexed. The seven indexed documents are listed, as shown in Figure 10-17.

Figure 10-17. *Listing indexed documents*

In subsequent sections, you'll be indexing Hive table data. Delete the documents again, as discussed before.

Creating a Hive-Managed Table

This section shows you how to create a managed table from which you can then load data into a Hive external table defined from documents stored in Solr. First, start the HDFS NameNode and DataNode, as discussed in earlier chapters (Chapters 2 and 7). Then, log in to the Hive shell.

```
hive
```

Set the database to use as default.

```
hive>use default;
```

Since you'll be creating a Hive table called wlslog, drop that table if it already exists.

```
hive>drop table wlslog;
```

The output from the preceding commands is shown in Figure 10-18.

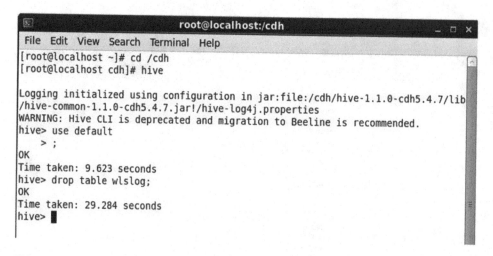

Figure 10-18. Starting Hive CLI, setting the database to use as the default, and dropping the wlslog table

Run the following CREATE TABLE command to create a Hive-managed table. The Hive table must have the same number and types of fields as in the data (wlslog.txt) to be loaded into the table.

```
CREATE  TABLE  wlslog(id STRING,time_stamp STRING,category STRING,type STRING,servername
STRING,code STRING,msg STRING) ROW FORMAT DELIMITED FIELDS TERMINATED BY ',' LINES
TERMINATED BY '\n';
```

A Hive-managed table called wlslog is created, as shown in Figure 10-19.

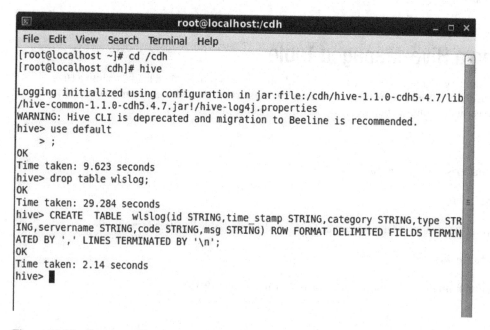

Figure 10-19. Creating a Hive-managed table called wlslog

Load data into the wlslog table from the /wlslog.txt file using the LOAD DATA command in the Hive shell.

```
LOAD DATA LOCAL INPATH '/cdh/wlslog.txt' OVERWRITE INTO TABLE wlslog;
```

The data is loaded into the wlslog table, as shown in Figure 10-20.

Figure 10-20. *Loading data into the Hive-managed table called wlslog*

Run a SELECT query to list the new data, as shown in Figure 10-21.

```
hive> select * from wlslog;
OK
wlslog1 Apr-8-2014-7:06:16-PM-PDT          Notice  WebLogicServer  AdminServer    B
EA-000365       Server state changed to STANDBY
wlslog2 Apr-8-2014-7:06:17-PM-PDT          Notice  WebLogicServer  AdminServer    B
EA-000365       Server state changed to STARTING
wlslog3 Apr-8-2014-7:06:18-PM-PDT          Notice  WebLogicServer  AdminServer    B
EA-000365       Server state changed to ADMIN
wlslog4 Apr-8-2014-7:06:19-PM-PDT          Notice  WebLogicServer  AdminServer    B
EA-000365       Server state changed to RESUMING
wlslog5 Apr-8-2014-7:06:20-PM-PDT          Notice  WebLogicServer  AdminServer    B
EA-000331       Started WebLogic AdminServer
wlslog6 Apr-8-2014-7:06:21-PM-PDT          Notice  WebLogicServer  AdminServer    B
EA-000365       Server state changed to RUNNING
wlslog7 Apr-8-2014-7:06:22-PM-PDT          Notice  WebLogicServer  AdminServer    B
EA-000360       Server started in RUNNING mode
Time taken: 2.417 seconds, Fetched: 7 row(s)
hive> █
```

Figure 10-21. *Querying a Hive table called wlslog*

Creating a Hive External Table

This section shows you how to create a Hive external table over the Solr collection. One of the differences between loading data from a data source such as JSON and XML and Solr is that while OLH can load data from a Hive external table created over a JSON/XML file, OLH cannot load data from a Hive external table created over a Solr collection. You'll be creating a Hive external table over Solr and then creating another Hive table (managed or external) from the data in the first Hive external table. To create a Hive external table over Solr, you use the com.chimpler.hive.solr.SolrStorageHandler storage handler class. Use the SerDe property listed in Table 10-3 for mapping the Solr data into Hive.

Table 10-3. *SerDe Property for Mapping Solr Data into Hive*

SerDe Property	Description	Value
solr.column.mapping	Specifies the mapping of Solr fields to Hive columns.	time_stamp,category,type, servername,code,msg

Specify the tblproperties listed in Table 10-4.

Table 10-4. *Tblproperties*

Table Property	Description	Value
solr.url	Specifies the Solr collection URL.	http://localhost:8983/solr/ collection1
solr.buffer.input.rows	Specifies the number of rows to load in bulk when loading rows into Solr. Property is optional.	10000
solr.buffer.output.rows	Specifies the number of rows to store in bulk when storing rows in Solr. Default is 10000. Property is optional.	10000

Add the hive-solr-0.0.1-SNAPSHOT-jar-with-dependencies.jar file to the Hive classpath with the ADD JAR command; the following command is for the jar file in the root directory. Specify a relative path if the jar is in a different directory.

```
hive>ADD JAR hive-solr-0.0.1-SNAPSHOT-jar-with-dependencies.jar;
```

Run the following CREATE EXTERNAL TABLE command in a Hive shell to create an external table called wlslog_solr. The STORED BY clause specifies the Hive storage handler class for Solr as com.chimpler.hive. solr.SolrStorageHandler.

```
hive>CREATE EXTERNAL TABLE wlslog_solr (id STRING,
    time_stamp STRING,
    category STRING,
    type STRING,
    servername STRING,
    code STRING,
    msg STRING) STORED BY "com.chimpler.hive.solr.SolrStorageHandler"
with serdeproperties ("solr.column.mapping"="id,time_stamp,category,type,servername,code,
msg")
tblproperties ("solr.url" = "http://localhost:8983/solr/collection1","solr.buffer.input.
rows"="10000","solr.buffer.output.rows"="10000");
```

The Hive external table wlslog_solr is created, as shown in Figure 10-22.

```
hive> ADD JAR hive-solr-0.0.1-SNAPSHOT-jar-with-dependencies.jar;
Added [hive-solr-0.0.1-SNAPSHOT-jar-with-dependencies.jar] to class path
Added resources: [hive-solr-0.0.1-SNAPSHOT-jar-with-dependencies.jar]
hive> create external table wlslog_solr (id STRING,
    >       time_stamp STRING,
    >       category STRING,
    >       type STRING,
    >       servername STRING,
    >       code STRING,
    >       msg STRING) stored by "com.chimpler.hive.solr.SolrStorageHandler"
    > with serdeproperties ("solr.column.mapping"="id,time_stamp,category,type,s
ervername,code,msg")
    > tblproperties ("solr.url" = "http://localhost:8983/solr/collection1","solr
.buffer.input.rows"="10000","solr.buffer.output.rows"="10000");
OK
Time taken: 0.603 seconds
hive> select * from wlslog_solr;
OK
Time taken: 3.673 seconds
hive> █
```

Figure 10-22. *Creating a Hive external table*

Loading Hive External Table Data

This section shows you how to load data into the Hive external table in a Hive shell. Run the following INSERT OVERWRITE TABLE command to load data from the wlslog table to the wlslog_solr table.

INSERT OVERWRITE TABLE wlslog_solr SELECT id,time_stamp,category,type,servername,code, msg FROM wlslog;

The MapReduce job loads the data from the wlslog table to the wlslog_solr table, as shown in Figure 10-23.

```
hive> INSERT OVERWRITE TABLE wlslog_solr SELECT id,time_stamp,category,type,serv
ername,code,msg FROM wlslog;
Query ID = root_20151007094242_2f86b492-b949-447b-b4ea-07537b2d7955
Total jobs = 1
Launching Job 1 out of 1
Number of reduce tasks is set to 0 since there's no reduce operator
Job running in-process (local Hadoop)
2015-10-07 09:43:09,689 Stage-0 map = 0%,   reduce = 0%
2015-10-07 09:43:20,836 Stage-0 map = 100%,   reduce = 0%
Ended Job = job_local74841939_0001
MapReduce Jobs Launched:
Stage-Stage-0:  HDFS Read: 1556 HDFS Write: 778 SUCCESS
Total MapReduce CPU Time Spent: 0 msec
OK
Time taken: 59.134 seconds
hive> █
```

Figure 10-23. *Loading data into a Hive external table*

Next, run the following query in a Hive shell.

```
select * from wlslog_solr;
```

The wlslog_solr table data is listed, as shown in Figure 10-24.

```
hive> select * from wlslog_solr;
OK
wlslog1 Apr-8-2014-7:06:16-PM-PDT        Notice  WebLogicServer  AdminServer   B
EA-000365        Server state changed to STANDBY
wlslog2 Apr-8-2014-7:06:17-PM-PDT        Notice  WebLogicServer  AdminServer   B
EA-000365        Server state changed to STARTING
wlslog3 Apr-8-2014-7:06:18-PM-PDT        Notice  WebLogicServer  AdminServer   B
EA-000365        Server state changed to ADMIN
wlslog4 Apr-8-2014-7:06:19-PM-PDT        Notice  WebLogicServer  AdminServer   B
EA-000365        Server state changed to RESUMING
wlslog5 Apr-8-2014-7:06:20-PM-PDT        Notice  WebLogicServer  AdminServer   B
EA-000331        Started WebLogic AdminServer
wlslog6 Apr-8-2014-7:06:21-PM-PDT        Notice  WebLogicServer  AdminServer   B
EA-000365        Server state changed to RUNNING
wlslog7 Apr-8-2014-7:06:22-PM-PDT        Notice  WebLogicServer  AdminServer   B
EA-000360        Server started in RUNNING mode
Time taken: 3.912 seconds, Fetched: 7 row(s)
hive> █
```

Figure 10-24. *Querying a Hive external table*

Searching a Hive Table Data Indexed in Solr

The Hive external table wlslog_solr data is indexed in Apache Solr. To select the indexed data, run a query from URL:

```
http://localhost:8983/solr/#/collection1/query as before.
```

Specify /select in the Request-Handler field, *.* in the q field, and json in the wt field. Click on Execute Query, as shown in Figure 10-25.

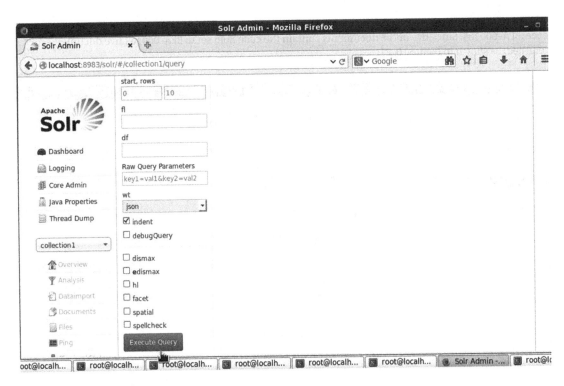

Figure 10-25. *Querying a Solr collection called collection1*

The seven documents indexed in Solr are listed, as shown in Figure 10-26.

Figure 10-26. *Query result lists seven documents*

As another example, search for documents with the code field set to BEA-000365. Specify the query as code:BEA-000365. Since five of the documents contain the code field set to BEA-000365, five documents are returned, as shown in Figure 10-27.

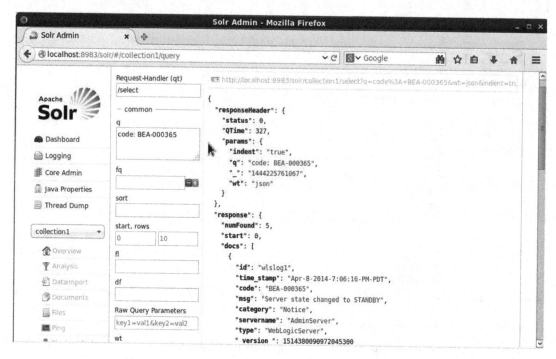

Figure 10-27. Search result for the query with the code field set to BEA-000365

Summary

This chapter introduced the Apache Solr framework in the CDH 5 distribution. It also used the Apache ZooKeeper in CDH 5. You learned how to index a few documents in Solr from the Solr Admin console and search for the indexed documents. You created a Hive external table stored by Solr and loaded data into it. The Hive external table data was indexed in Solr. The next chapter discusses Apache Mahout.

CHAPTER 11

■ ■ ■

Apache Mahout

Apache Mahout is a scalable machine learning library with support for several classification, clustering, and collaborative filtering algorithms. Mahout runs on top of Hadoop using the MapReduce model. Mahout also provides a Java API. This chapter explains how to get started with Mahout; you'll install Mahout and run some sample Mahout applications. You will also see how to develop a user recommender system using the Mahout Java API. This chapter covers the following topics:

- Setting the environment
- Configuring and starting HDFS
- Setting the Mahout environment
- Running a Mahout classification sample
- Running a Mahout clustering sample
- Developing a user-based recommender system with the Mahout Java API

Setting the Environment

This chapter requires the following software.

- Apache Mahout
- Eclipse Java IDE
- Apache Hadoop
- Java 7

The chapter's examples use the Oracle Linux 6 OS, although you can use a different Linux OS. First, create a directory called /mahout to install the required software. Set the directory permissions to global (777).

```
mkdir /mahout
chmod -R 777 /mahout
cd /mahout
```

Create a group called hadoop and add a user called mahout to the hadoop group.

```
groupadd hadoop
useradd -g hadoop mahout
```

© Deepak Vohra 2016
D. Vohra, *Practical Hadoop Ecosystem*, DOI 10.1007/978-1-4842-2199-0_11

Download and install Java 7 from http://www.oracle.com/technetwork/java/javase/downloads/ java-archive-downloads-javase7-521261.html. The Java 7 update could vary.

```
/mahout>tar -xvf jdk-7u55-linux-i586.gz
```

Download CDH 5.2 Hadoop 2.5.0 (or a later version) and extract the tar.gz file to the /mahout directory.

```
/mahout>wget http://archive-primary.cloudera.com/cdh5/cdh/5/hadoop-2.5.0-cdh5.2.0.tar.gz
/mahout>tar -xvf hadoop-2.5.0-cdh5.2.0.tar.gz
```

Create symlinks for the Hadoop bin and conf directories.

```
/mahout>ln -s /mahout/hadoop-2.5.0-cdh5.2.0/bin-mapreduce1 /mahout/hadoop-2.5.0-cdh5.2.0/
share/hadoop/mapreduce1/bin
/mahout>ln -s /mahout/hadoop-2.5.0-cdh5.2.0/etc/hadoop /mahout/hadoop-2.5.0-cdh5.2.0/share/
hadoop/mapreduce1/conf
```

Download and install Mahout 0.9. The CDH version could vary, such as 5.2.0, 5.4.7, or later.

```
/mahout>wget http://archive.cloudera.com/cdh5/cdh/5/mahout-0.9-cdh5.2.0.tar.gz
/mahout>tar -xvf mahout-0.9-cdh5.2.0.tar.gz
```

Add environment variables for Hadoop, Mahout, and Java to the shell bash file.

```
vi ~/.bashrc
export HADOOP_PREFIX=/mahout/hadoop-2.5.0-cdh5.2.0
export JAVA_HOME=/mahout/jdk1.7.0_55
export MAHOUT_HOME=/mahout/mahout-0.9-cdh5.2.0
export MAHOUT_CONF=$MAHOUT_HOME/conf
export MAHOUT_LOCAL=true
export HADOOP_MAPRED_HOME=/mahout/hadoop-2.5.0-cdh5.2.0/share/hadoop/mapreduce1
export HADOOP_HOME=/mahout/hadoop-2.5.0-cdh5.2.0/share/hadoop/mapreduce1
export HADOOP_CONF=$HADOOP_PREFIX/etc/hadoop
export HADOOP_CLASSPATH=$HADOOP_HOME/*:$HADOOP_HOME/lib/*:$MAHOUT_HOME/lib/*:$HADOOP_PREFIX/
share/hadoop/hdfs/*:$HADOOP_PREFIX/share/hadoop/hdfs/lib/*
export PATH=$JAVA_HOME/bin:$PATH:$HADOOP_HOME/bin:$MAHOUT_HOME/bin
export CLASSPATH=$HADOOP_CLASSPATH
export HADOOP_NAMENODE_USER=mahout
export HADOOP_DATANODE_USER=mahout
```

Since Eclipse IDE will be used only for developing a user recommender system, create a directory called /recosystem to install Eclipse and set its permissions to global (777).

```
mkdir /recosystem
chmod -R 777 /recosystem
cd /recosystem
```

To install the Eclipse IDE, download and extract the Eclipse tar.gz file.

```
tar xvf eclipse-java-luna-SR1a-linux-gtk.tar.gz
```

Configuring and Starting HDFS

Next, configure and start HDFS, which is comprised of NameNode and DataNode. The core Hadoop properties are set in the core-site.xml file. Set the fs.defaultFS property for the URI of the HDFS filesystem. Set the hadoop.tmp.dir property as the base for Hadoop's temporary files.

```
vi $HADOOP_CONF/core-site.xml
<?xml-stylesheet type="text/xsl" href="configuration.xsl"?>

<!-- Put site-specific property overrides in this file. -->

<configuration>
<property>
  <name>fs.defaultFS</name>
    <value>hdfs://10.0.2.15:8020</value>
    </property>
 <property>
    <name>hadoop.tmp.dir</name>
    <value>file:///var/lib/hadoop-0.20/cache</value>
  </property>
</configuration>
```

Create the directory specified in the hadoop.tmp.dir property and set its permissions to global (777).

```
rm -rf /var/lib/hadoop-0.20/cache
mkdir -p /var/lib/hadoop-0.20/cache
chmod R 777 /var/lib/hadoop-0.20/cache
```

Set the HDFS configuration properties in the hdfs-site.xml file.

```
vi $HADOOP_CONF/hdfs-site.xml
```

Set the superuser group to hadoop using the dfs.permissions.superusergroup property. Set the NameNode storage directory file:///data/1/dfs/nn to use the dfs.namenode.name.dir property. Set the replication factor to 1 with the dfs.replication property. The permissions checking in HDFS is modulated with the dfs.permissions property. Even when the dfs.permissions is set to false, the file/directory mode, owner, and group are still verified.

```
<?xml version="1.0" encoding="UTF-8"?>
<?xml-stylesheet type="text/xsl" href="configuration.xsl"?>

<!-- Put site-specific property overrides in this file. -->

<configuration>
 <property>
   <name>dfs.permissions.superusergroup</name>
   <value>hadoop</value>
  </property>
  <property>
    <name>dfs.namenode.name.dir</name>
    <value>file:///data/1/dfs/nn</value>
```

```
</property>
<property>
  <name>dfs.replication</name>
  <value>1</value>
</property>
<property>
  <name>dfs.permissions</name>
  <value>false</value>
</property>
</configuration>
```

Create the NameNode storage directory and set its permissions to global (777).

```
rm -rf /data/1/dfs/nn
mkdir -p /data/1/dfs/nn
chmod -R 777 /data/1/dfs/nn
```

Format the NameNode and start the NameNode and DataNode, which comprise the HDFS.

```
hadoop namenode -format
hadoop namenode
hadoop datanode
```

Setting the Mahout Environment

You need to put the Mahout lib jars into HDFS so they are available at runtime. Create a directory called /mahout/mahout-0.9-cdh5.2.0/lib in HDFS and set its permissions to g+w. Put the Mahout lib jars to the /mahout/mahout-0.9-cdh5.2.0/lib directory.

```
hadoop dfs -mkdir -p hdfs://10.0.2.15:8020/mahout/mahout-0.9-cdh5.2.0/lib
hadoop dfs -chmod -R g+w hdfs://10.0.2.15:8020/mahout/mahout-0.9-cdh5.2.0/lib
hadoop dfs -put /mahout/mahout-0.9-cdh5.2.0/lib/*  hdfs://10.0.2.15:8020/mahout/mahout-0.9-cdh5.2.0/lib
```

When Mahout runs, the following error could get generated if there is not enough space available to create an object heap for the Java Virtual Machine. To prevent/fix the error, you need to lower the Java heap memory requirement in the Mahout application. Change (cd) to the Mahout installation directory mahout-0.9-cdh5.2.0.

```
cd mahout-0.9-cdh5.2.0
```

Open the bin/mahout application file.

```
vi bin/mahout
```

The default value of JAVA_HEAP_MAX is 3g, as shown in Figure 11-1.

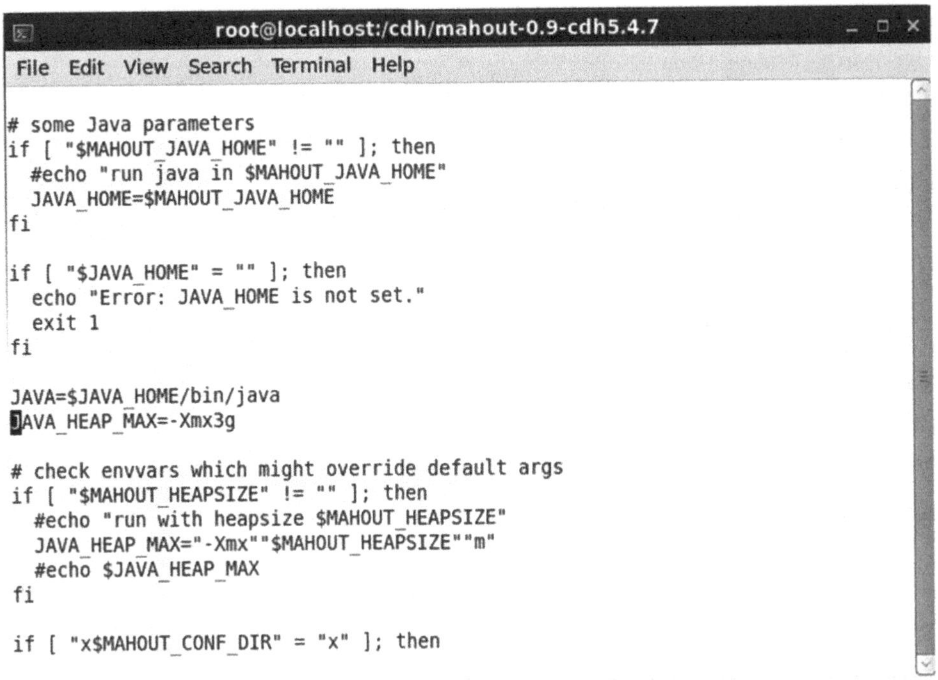

```
root@localhost:/cdh/mahout-0.9-cdh5.4.7                    _ □ ×

File  Edit  View  Search  Terminal  Help

# some Java parameters
if [ "$MAHOUT_JAVA_HOME" != "" ]; then
  #echo "run java in $MAHOUT_JAVA_HOME"
  JAVA_HOME=$MAHOUT_JAVA_HOME
fi

if [ "$JAVA_HOME" = "" ]; then
  echo "Error: JAVA_HOME is not set."
  exit 1
fi

JAVA=$JAVA_HOME/bin/java
JAVA_HEAP_MAX=-Xmx3g

# check envvars which might override default args
if [ "$MAHOUT_HEAPSIZE" != "" ]; then
  #echo "run with heapsize $MAHOUT_HEAPSIZE"
  JAVA_HEAP_MAX="-Xmx""$MAHOUT_HEAPSIZE""m"
  #echo $JAVA_HEAP_MAX
fi

if [ "x$MAHOUT_CONF_DIR" = "x" ]; then
```

Figure 11-1. *The default Java heap max is 3g*

Lower the JAVA_HEAP_MAX setting to 1g.

```
JAVA_HEAP_MAX = -Xmx1g
```

The modified setting is shown in Figure 11-2.

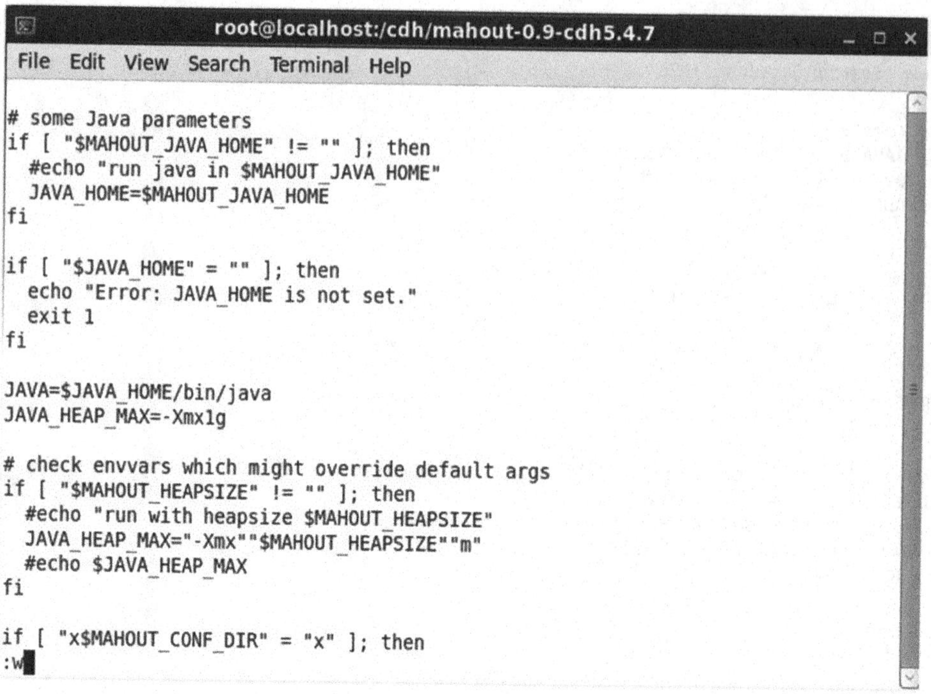

```
root@localhost:/cdh/mahout-0.9-cdh5.4.7
File  Edit  View  Search  Terminal  Help

# some Java parameters
if [ "$MAHOUT_JAVA_HOME" != "" ]; then
  #echo "run java in $MAHOUT_JAVA_HOME"
  JAVA_HOME=$MAHOUT_JAVA_HOME
fi

if [ "$JAVA_HOME" = "" ]; then
  echo "Error: JAVA_HOME is not set."
  exit 1
fi

JAVA=$JAVA_HOME/bin/java
JAVA_HEAP_MAX=-Xmx1g

# check envvars which might override default args
if [ "$MAHOUT_HEAPSIZE" != "" ]; then
  #echo "run with heapsize $MAHOUT_HEAPSIZE"
  JAVA_HEAP_MAX="-Xmx""$MAHOUT_HEAPSIZE""m"
  #echo $JAVA_HEAP_MAX
fi

if [ "x$MAHOUT_CONF_DIR" = "x" ]; then
:w
```

Figure 11-2. *The modified Java heap max is 1g*

Running a Mahout Classification Sample

Mahout provides several examples for the different types of machine learning algorithms. This section shows you how to run the Classification example. Run the following command to invoke the classify sample classify-20newsgroups.sh.

./examples/bin/classify-20newsgroups.sh

Three Classification algorithms are listed: cnaivebayes, naivebayes, and sgd. Select one of the Classification algorithms, for example, Naïve Bayes (selection 2), as shown in Figure 11-3.

The working directory /tmp/mahout-work-root is created and the sample data on which the classification algorithm is trained is downloaded. This is also shown in Figure 11-3.

```
[root@localhost mahout-0.9-cdh5.4.7]# ./examples/bin/classify-20newsgroups.sh
Please select a number to choose the corresponding task to run
1. cnaivebayes
2. naivebayes
3. sgd
4. clean -- cleans up the work area in /tmp/mahout-work-root
Enter your choice : 2
ok. You chose 2 and we'll use naivebayes
creating work directory at /tmp/mahout-work-root
Downloading 20news-bydate
  % Total    % Received % Xferd  Average Speed   Time    Time     Time  Current
                                 Dload  Upload   Total   Spent    Left  Speed
  61 13.7M   61 8688k    0     0   191k      0  0:01:13 0:00:45 0:00:28  230k
```

Figure 11-3. *Running a classification application based on Naïve Bayes*

The Naïve Bayes algorithm runs on the data. The data is split between training and holdout test data, as indicated by the following message.

```
'Creating training and holdout set with a random 80-20 split of the generated vector
dataset'
```

The Naïve Bayes model runs on the training data, as indicated by the following message.

```
Training Naive Bayes model
```

After the Naïve Bayes model has been trained, the program runs a self test on the training set and a test on the holdout set, as indicated by the following messages.

```
Self testing on training set
Testing on holdout set
```

A summary of the Naïve Bayes results is displayed, as shown in Figure 11-4.

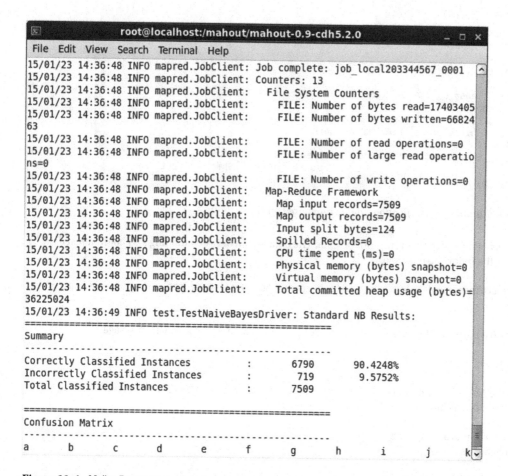

```
root@localhost:/mahout/mahout-0.9-cdh5.2.0                    _ □ ×

File  Edit  View  Search  Terminal  Help

15/01/23 14:36:48 INFO mapred.JobClient: Job complete: job_local203344567_0001
15/01/23 14:36:48 INFO mapred.JobClient: Counters: 13
15/01/23 14:36:48 INFO mapred.JobClient:    File System Counters
15/01/23 14:36:48 INFO mapred.JobClient:      FILE: Number of bytes read=17403405
15/01/23 14:36:48 INFO mapred.JobClient:      FILE: Number of bytes written=66824
63
15/01/23 14:36:48 INFO mapred.JobClient:      FILE: Number of read operations=0
15/01/23 14:36:48 INFO mapred.JobClient:      FILE: Number of large read operatio
ns=0
15/01/23 14:36:48 INFO mapred.JobClient:      FILE: Number of write operations=0
15/01/23 14:36:48 INFO mapred.JobClient:    Map-Reduce Framework
15/01/23 14:36:48 INFO mapred.JobClient:      Map input records=7509
15/01/23 14:36:48 INFO mapred.JobClient:      Map output records=7509
15/01/23 14:36:48 INFO mapred.JobClient:      Input split bytes=124
15/01/23 14:36:48 INFO mapred.JobClient:      Spilled Records=0
15/01/23 14:36:48 INFO mapred.JobClient:      CPU time spent (ms)=0
15/01/23 14:36:48 INFO mapred.JobClient:      Physical memory (bytes) snapshot=0
15/01/23 14:36:48 INFO mapred.JobClient:      Virtual memory (bytes) snapshot=0
15/01/23 14:36:48 INFO mapred.JobClient:      Total committed heap usage (bytes)=
36225024
15/01/23 14:36:49 INFO test.TestNaiveBayesDriver: Standard NB Results:
=========================================================
Summary
-------------------------------------------------
Correctly Classified Instances       :     6790       90.4248%
Incorrectly Classified Instances     :      719        9.5752%
Total Classified Instances           :     7509

=========================================================
Confusion Matrix
-------------------------------------------------
a      b      c      d      e      f      g      h      i      j      k
```

Figure 11-4. Naïve Bayes summary

Running a Mahout Clustering Sample

This section runs a clustering algorithm. Run the following command to invoke the `cluster-reuters.sh` shell script, which runs a Clustering demo.

```
./examples/bin/cluster-reuters.sh
```

Select one of the clustering algorithms from the list. For example, select the k-means clustering algorithm, which is choice 1, as shown in Figure 11-5.

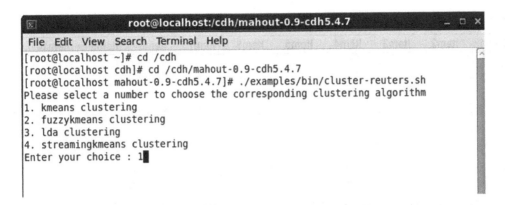

Figure 11-5. Running a k-means clustering application

A Mahout working directory /tmp/mahout-work-root is created and the sample data is downloaded. Mahout driver.MahoutDriver runs MapReduce on the sample data to cluster the data.

The clustering output is generated, including the top terms and the inter-cluster density.

```
Inter-Cluster Density: 0.5890881732810521
Intra-Cluster Density: 0.7102817655357396
CDbw Inter-Cluster Density: 0.0
CDbw Intra-Cluster Density: 19.413235604460176
CDbw Separation: 227.28512875123707
```

Developing a User-Based Recommender System with the Mahout Java API

A user-based recommender system can make recommendations about items to users based on user similarity. Item preference and buying data is available for some users based on what they bought or considered buying in the past. For example, five users bought or considered buying some of the 10 items available from an online store listed in Table 11-1.

Table 11-1. Matrix of User Buys or Considered Buys

	Item1	Item2	Item3	Item4	Item5	Item6	Item7	Item8	Item9	Item10
User1	x			x		x			x	
User2	x		x	x			x			x
User3		x			x	x		x	x	
User4			x	x		x		x		x
User5		x	x		x		x		x	

The user ID/item ID matrix would most likely be sparse as not all users would have bought or considered buying all the items. The problem a user-based recommender system can solve is which items would a new user who buys/considers buying an item be interested in? Also, which other items would past purchasers be interested in, based on their past interest? Consider the new user (User6), who buys Item1, as shown in Table 11-2.

Table 11-2. *Matrix of User Preferences with an Additional User6*

	Item1	Item2	Item3	Item4	Item5	Item6	Item7	Item8	Item9	Item10
User1	x			x		x		x		
User2	x		x	x			x	x		x
User3		x			x	x		x	x	
User4			x	x		x		x		x
User5		x	x		x		x		x	
User6	x									

A user-based recommender system recommends other items to User6 based on User6's similarity with other users. For example, User1 and User2 also bought Item1 and both of the users also bought Item4 and Item9. A user-based recommender system would recommend Item4 and Item9 to User1. A user-based recommender system may also recommend some items that one but not both of the users bought, but with a lower recommendation preference. This section explains a user-based recommender system using data on users who have provided ratings for some items. The user-based recommender system recommends items to users based on user similarity. You'll use Mahout's Java API for recommender systems to develop a user-based recommender system. You'll see how to create an Eclipse Maven project and provide the Mahout libraries as a Maven dependency.

The Sample Data

The sample data used by the user-based recommender system is provided in a .csv file. The first value in each row is the user ID, the second value is the item ID, and the third value is the rating. The ratings.csv sample data file is listed here:

```
1,10,1.0
1,11,2.0
1,12,5.0
1,13,5.0
1,14,5.0
1,15,4.0
1,16,5.0
1,17,1.0
1,18,5.0
2,10,1.0
2,11,2.0
2,15,5.0
2,16,4.5
2,17,1.0
2,18,5.0
3,11,2.5
3,12,4.5
3,13,4.0
3,14,3.0
3,15,3.5
3,16,4.5
3,17,4.0
```

```
3,18,5.0
4,10,5.0
4,11,5.0
4,12,5.0
4,13,0.0
4,14,2.0
4,15,3.0
4,16,1.0
4,17,4.0
4,18,1.0
```

Creating a Maven Project in Eclipse

This section shows you how to create a Maven project in Eclipse. To start Eclipse, change to the `eclipse` directory (using the `cd` command) and run the `./eclipse` command.

```
cd eclipse
./eclipse
```

The Eclipse IDE starts. Choose File ➤ New ➤ Other, as shown in Figure 11-6.

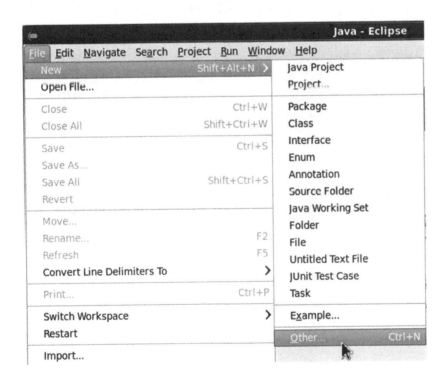

Figure 11-6. *Choosing File ➤ New ➤ Other in the Eclipse IDE*

In the New window, choose Maven ➤ Maven Project and click on Next, as shown in Figure 11-7.

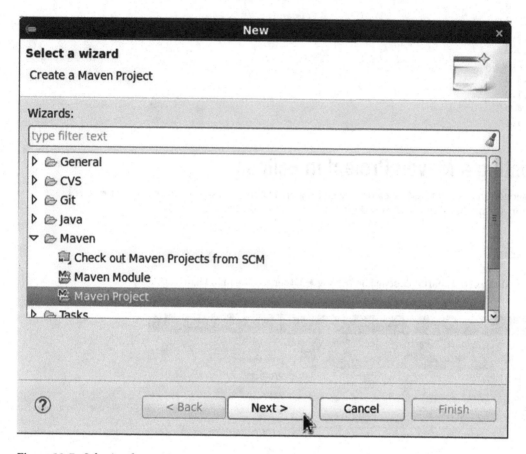

Figure 11-7. *Selecting the new Maven project*

In New Maven Project, select the Create a Simple Project checkbox and the Use Default Workspace Location checkbox if they are not already selected, as shown in Figure 11-8. Click on Next.

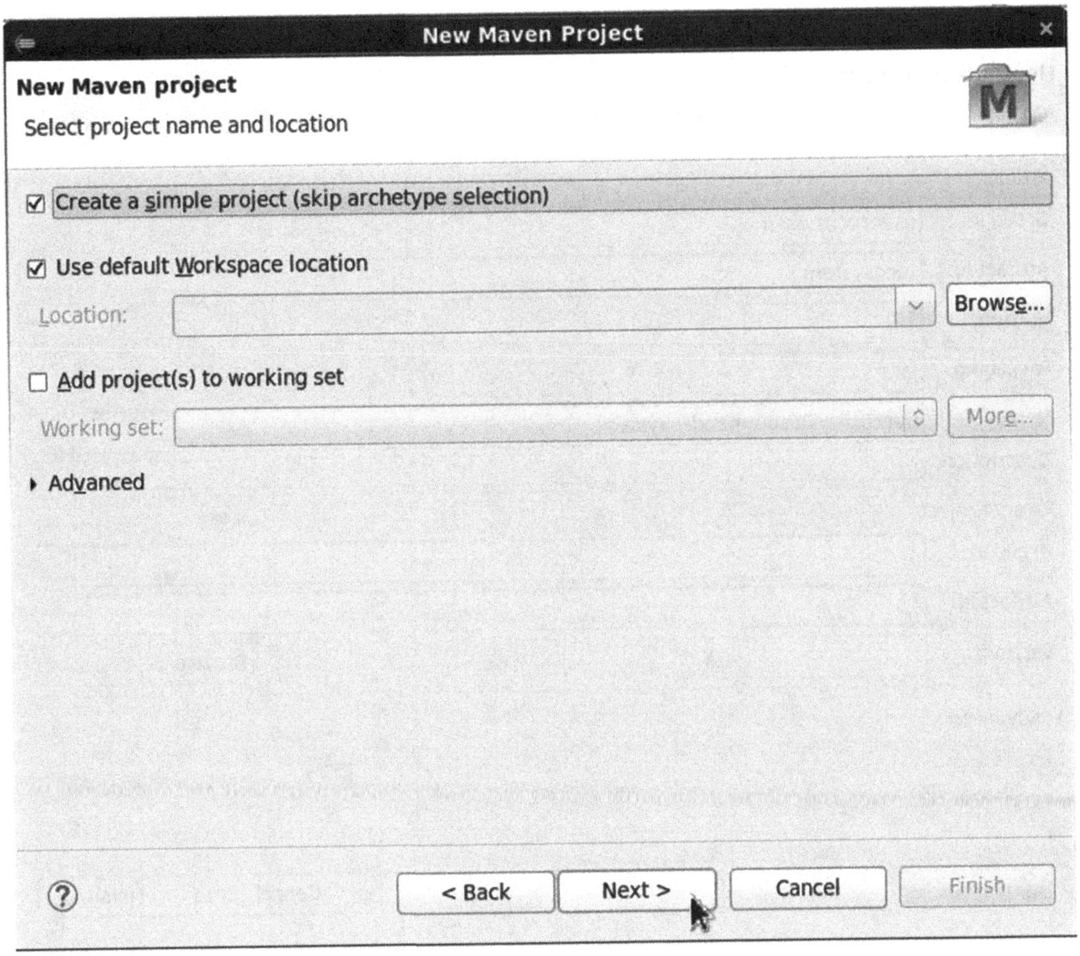

Figure 11-8. Selecting new Maven project name and location

In Configure Project, specify a group ID (user.recosystem), artifact ID (recosystem), version (1.0), packaging (jar), and name (UserBasedRecommenderSysem), as shown in Figure 11-9.

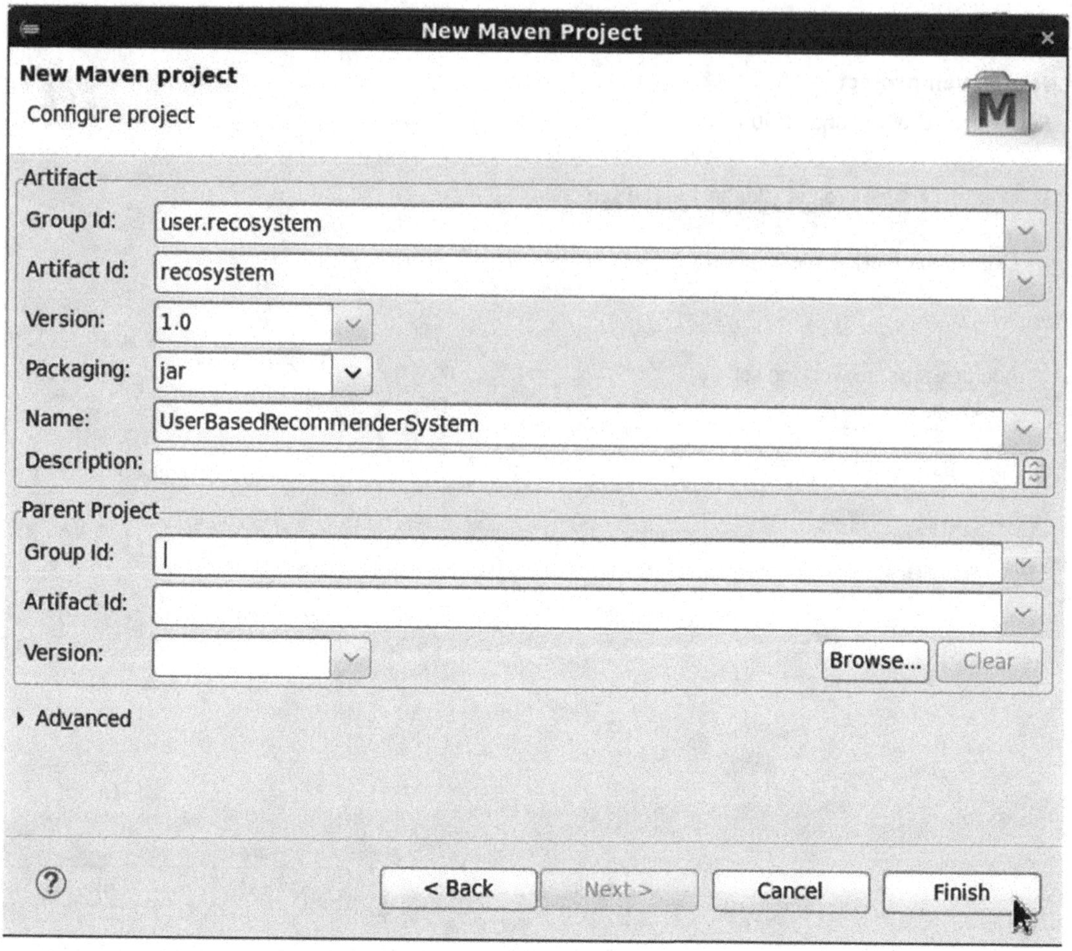

Figure 11-9. *Configuring a New Maven project*

To the pom.xml file, add the dependency for Mahout.

```xml
<project xmlns="http://maven.apache.org/POM/4.0.0" xmlns:xsi="http://www.w3.org/2001/
XMLSchema-instance"
        xsi:schemaLocation="http://maven.apache.org/POM/4.0.0 http://maven.apache.org/xsd/
        maven-4.0.0.xsd">
        <modelVersion>4.0.0</modelVersion>
        <groupId>user.recosystem</groupId>
        <artifactId>recosystem</artifactId>
        <version>1.0</version>
        <name>UserBasedRecommenderSystem</name>
        <description> </description>
        <dependencies>
                <dependency>
                        <groupId>org.apache.mahout</groupId>
                        <artifactId>mahout-core</artifactId>
```

```
            <version>0.9</version>
        </dependency>
    </dependencies>
</project>
```

The pom.xml file in the Maven project is shown in Eclipse, as shown in Figure 11-10.

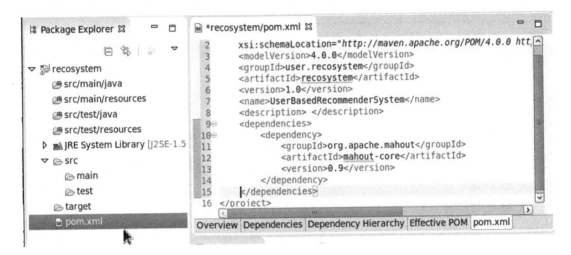

Figure 11-10. *The pom.xml file*

Next, add the two Java classes called UserRecommender and EvaluateUserRecommender for a recommender system and a recommender system evaluator, respectively. To add a Java class, choose Java ➤ Class in the New wizard and click on Next, as shown in Figure 11-11.

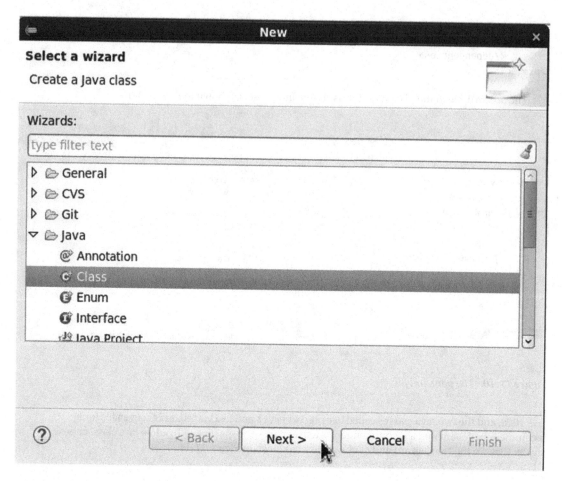

Figure 11-11. *Adding a new Java class*

In the New Java Class wizard, select the source folder as `/recosystem/src/main/java` if it's not already selected. Specify a package name (`recosystem`) and a classname (`UserRecommender`), as shown in Figure 11-12. Click on Finish.

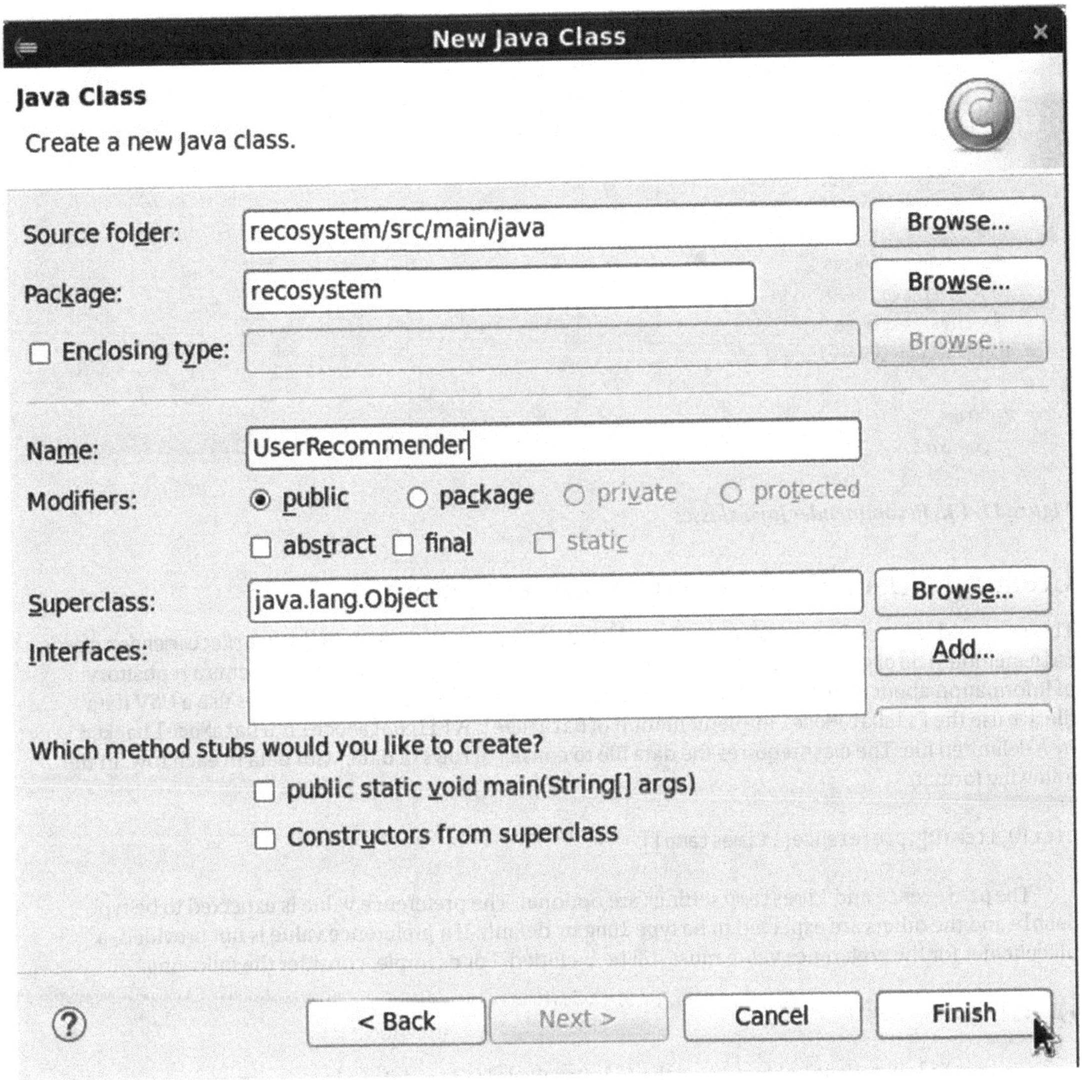

Figure 11-12. *Configuring a new Java class*

Similarly add another Java class (EvaluateUserRecommender). The two classes are shown in the Package Explorer, as shown in Figure 11-13.

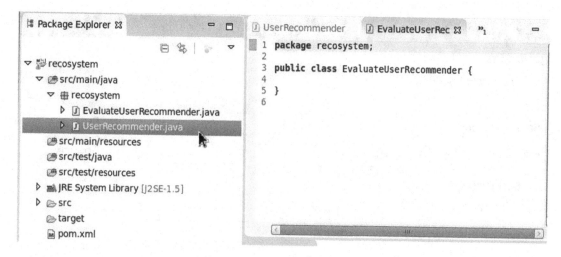

Figure 11-13. *Recommender Java classes*

Creating a User-Based Recommender System

This section shows you how to develop a user-based recommender system in the UserRecommender class's main method. The org.apache.mahout.cf.taste.model.DataModel interface represents a repository of information about the users and their associated preferences. Since these examples use a CSV data file, we use the FileDataModel implementation of DataModel. A FileDataModel is a DataModel backed by a delimited file. The class requires the data file to consist of rows of data, with data in each row, in the following format.

userID,itemID[,preference[,timestamp]]

The preference and timestamp settings are optional. The preference value is expected to be type double and the others are expected to be type long by default. If a preference value is not provided, a placeholder for the preference value must still be included. For example, consider the following.

1,2,,3452345

Create a FileDataModel object using the FileDataModel(File dataFile) constructor.

DataModel model = new FileDataModel(new File("/recosystem/ratings.csv"));

Similarity between items is represented with the org.apache.mahout.cf.taste.similarity. UserSimilarity interface. Several implementations of the interface are provided and each returns a value between –1.0 and 1.0, with 1.0 representing exact similarity. If preference values are available for all users, as in the ratings.csv file, the implementation to use is PearsonCorrelationSimilarity. Create a PearsonCorrelationSimilarity object using the PearsonCorrelationSimilarity(DataModel dataModel) constructor.

UserSimilarity similarity = new PearsonCorrelationSimilarity(model);

The org.apache.mahout.cf.taste.neighborhood.UserNeighborhood interface represents a neighborhood of users like a given user. The neighborhood is used to make recommendations to a user. Table 11-3 shows two implementations of the UserNeighborhood interface.

Table 11-3. *Implementation Classes for the UserNeighborhood Interface*

Class	Description
NearestNUserNeighborhood	The neighborhood of a given user is computed based on the nearness to other users. Nearness is based on UserSimilarity.
ThresholdUserNeighborhood	The neighborhood of a given user is computed based on a threshold for similarity with other users. Similarity is represented with UserSimilarity. A user must be at least the threshold similar to be included in the neighborhood.

This chapter uses the NearestNUserNeighborhood implementation. Create a NearestNUserNeighborhood object using the NearestNUserNeighborhood(int n,UserSimilarity userSimilarity, DataModel dataModel) constructor. The n in the constructor is for the neighborhood size and its maximum value is the number of users in the data model. Using a neighborhood size of 2, create a NearestNUserNeighborhood object.

```
UserNeighborhood neighborhood = new NearestNUserNeighborhood(2,
                              similarity, model);
```

Next, you need to create a recommender to make recommendations. A recommender is represented with the org.apache.mahout.cf.taste.recommender.Recommender interface with several implementations. Given a data model and a neighborhood, the recommender implementation to use is the GenericUserBasedRecommender.

Create a GenericUserBasedRecommender object using the GenericUserBasedRecommender(DataModel dataModel, UserNeighborhood neighborhood, UserSimilarity similarity) constructor.

```
Recommender recommender = new GenericUserBasedRecommender(model,neighborhood, similarity);
```

After a recommender has been created, you can make user recommendations using one of the methods listed in Table 11-4.

Table 11-4. *Overloaded recommend() Methods*

Method	Description
List<RecommendedItem> recommend(long userID,int howMany,IDRescorer rescorer)	The userID parameter specifies a user ID. The howMany parameter specifies the number of recommendations to make. The rescorer parameter is a rescoring function applied before recommendations are made.
List<RecommendedItem> recommend(long userID,int howMany)	Same as the preceding method. except that the rescorer parameter is not included.

Use the List<RecommendedItem> recommend(long userID,int howMany) method for user ID 2 to make three recommendations. A recommendation is represented with the RecommendedItem interface.

```
List<RecommendedItem> recommendations = recommender.recommend(2, 3);
```

Iterate over the list of recommendations using a for loop and output the recommendations.

```
for (RecommendedItem recommendation : recommendations) {
```

```
                    System.out.println(" recommendation: " + recommendation);
        }
```

The UserRecommender class is listed here:

```java
package recosystem;

import java.io.File;
import java.util.List;

import org.apache.mahout.cf.taste.impl.model.file.FileDataModel;
import org.apache.mahout.cf.taste.impl.neighborhood.ThresholdUserNeighborhood;
import org.apache.mahout.cf.taste.impl.neighborhood.NearestNUserNeighborhood;
import org.apache.mahout.cf.taste.impl.recommender.GenericUserBasedRecommender;
import org.apache.mahout.cf.taste.impl.recommender.RandomRecommender;
import org.apache.mahout.cf.taste.impl.similarity.EuclideanDistanceSimilarity;
import org.apache.mahout.cf.taste.impl.similarity.GenericUserSimilarity;
import org.apache.mahout.cf.taste.impl.similarity.PearsonCorrelationSimilarity;
import org.apache.mahout.cf.taste.model.DataModel;
import org.apache.mahout.cf.taste.neighborhood.UserNeighborhood;
import org.apache.mahout.cf.taste.recommender.RecommendedItem;
import org.apache.mahout.cf.taste.recommender.Recommender;
import org.apache.mahout.cf.taste.similarity.UserSimilarity;

class UserRecommender {

    public static void main(String[] args) throws Exception {

        DataModel model = new FileDataModel(new File("/recosystem/ratings.csv"));
        UserSimilarity similarity = new PearsonCorrelationSimilarity(model);

        UserNeighborhood neighborhood = new NearestNUserNeighborhood
                        (2, similarity, model);
        Recommender recommender = new GenericUserBasedRecommender(model,
                        neighborhood, similarity);

        List<RecommendedItem> recommendations = recommender.recommend(2, 3);

        for (RecommendedItem recommendation : recommendations) {
            System.out.println(" recommendation: " + recommendation);
        }
    }
}
```

Creating a Recommender Evaluator

A recommender evaluator evaluates the performance of a recommender. This section shows you how to develop a recommender evaluator using the EvaluateUserRecommender class. First, create a DataModel object as before.

```java
DataModel model = new FileDataModel(new File("/recosystem/ratings.csv"));
```

```
RecommenderEvaluator evaluator = new AverageAbsoluteDifferenceRecommenderEvaluator();
```

A recommender evaluator is represented with the
org.apache.mahout.cf.taste.eval.RecommenderEvaluator interface, which has the two implementations
explained in Table 11-5.

Table 11-5. Implementation Classes for RecommenderEvaluator Interface

Class	Description
RMSRecommenderEvaluator	Computes the "root mean squared" difference between the actual ratings and the predicted ratings for users. First, the difference between the predicted and the actual ratings for each user is evaluated. Subsequently, the difference for each user is squared. The mean of the squared differences is evaluated. The root of the mean is computed, which is the "root mean squared".
AverageAbsoluteDifferenceRecommenderEvaluator	Computes the average absolute difference between the predicted and the actual ratings. First, the difference between the predicted and the actual ratings for each user is evaluated, as in the preceding method. Subsequently, the mean of the differences is taken.

This example uses the AverageAbsoluteDifferenceRecommenderEvaluator evaluator to create a class
object.

```
RecommenderEvaluator evaluator = new AverageAbsoluteDifferenceRecommenderEvaluator();
```

Add an inner class (UserRecommenderBuilder) that implements the RecommenderBuilder interface,
which builds a recommender that makes recommendations that are subsequently evaluated. Implement
the buildRecommender(DataModel dataModel) method. It returns a recommender to be subsequently
evaluated. A recommender is built similarly to how a recommender is built in the UserRecommender class.

```
class UserRecommenderBuilder implements RecommenderBuilder {
            public Recommender buildRecommender(DataModel dataModel) {
                    UserSimilarity similarity = null;
                    try {
                            similarity = new PearsonCorrelationSimilarity(dataModel);
                    } catch (TasteException e) {
                            System.err.println(e.getMessage());
                            e.printStackTrace();
                    }
UserNeighborhood neighborhood = new ThresholdUserNeighborhood(0.1,similarity, dataModel);
UserBasedRecommender recommender = new GenericUserBasedRecommender(dataModel, neighborhood,
similarity);
return recommender;

            }
    }
```

Create an instance of the inner class UserRecommenderBuilder using an instance of the encapsulating class EvaluateUserRecommender.

```
RecommenderBuilder builder = new EvaluateUserRecommender().new UserRecommenderBuilder();
```

Using the RecommenderEvaluator instance, invoke the evaluate(RecommenderBuilder recommender Builder,DataModelBuilder dataModelBuilder,DataModel dataModel, double trainingPercentage, double evaluationPercentage) method. To evaluate, the sample data is split into training data and test data. The training data is most (80-90%) of the data. For example, use a trainingPercentage of .9. The evaluationPercentage is the percentage of users in the evaluation. To use all the users, set the evaluationPercentage to 1.0. The DataModelBuilder, which is used to build a DataModel, is specified as null since you already built a data model. Output the result of the evaluation, which is a score of type double that represents how close the predicted preferences are to real preferences. A lower score implies a better match and a score of 0 is an exact match.

```
double result = evaluator.evaluate(builder, null, model, 0.9, 1.0);
System.out.println(result);
```

The EvaluateUserRecommender is listed here:

```
package recosystem;
import java.io.File;
import java.util.List;

import org.apache.mahout.cf.taste.impl.model.file.FileDataModel;
import org.apache.mahout.cf.taste.impl.neighborhood.ThresholdUserNeighborhood;
import org.apache.mahout.cf.taste.impl.neighborhood.NearestNUserNeighborhood;
import org.apache.mahout.cf.taste.impl.recommender.GenericUserBasedRecommender;
import org.apache.mahout.cf.taste.impl.similarity.PearsonCorrelationSimilarity;
import org.apache.mahout.cf.taste.model.DataModel;
import org.apache.mahout.cf.taste.neighborhood.UserNeighborhood;
import org.apache.mahout.cf.taste.recommender.Recommender;
import org.apache.mahout.cf.taste.recommender.UserBasedRecommender;
import org.apache.mahout.cf.taste.similarity.UserSimilarity;
import org.apache.mahout.cf.taste.impl.eval.AverageAbsoluteDifferenceRecommenderEvaluator;
import org.apache.mahout.cf.taste.common.TasteException;
import org.apache.mahout.cf.taste.eval.RecommenderBuilder;
import org.apache.mahout.cf.taste.eval.RecommenderEvaluator;

class EvaluateUserRecommender {

        public static void main(String[] args) throws Exception {

                DataModel model = new FileDataModel(new File("/recosystem/ratings.csv"));
                RecommenderEvaluator evaluator = new
                AverageAbsoluteDifferenceRecommenderEvaluator();

                RecommenderBuilder builder = new EvaluateUserRecommender().new
                UserRecommenderBuilder();
                double result = evaluator.evaluate(builder, null, model, 0.9, 1.0);
                System.out.println(result);
        }
```

```
class UserRecommenderBuilder implements RecommenderBuilder {
        public Recommender buildRecommender(DataModel dataModel) {
                UserSimilarity similarity = null;
                try {
                        similarity = new PearsonCorrelationSimilarity(dataModel);
                } catch (TasteException e) {
                        System.err.println(e.getMessage());
                        e.printStackTrace();
                }
                UserNeighborhood neighborhood = new ThresholdUserNeighborhood
                                (0.1, similarity, dataModel);
                UserBasedRecommender recommender = new GenericUserBasedRecommender
                                (dataModel, neighborhood, similarity);
                return recommender;
                // UserNeighborhood neighborhood = new
                // ThresholdUserNeighborhood(0.1, similarity, model);
        }
    }
}
```

Running the Recommender

This section runs the recommender you developed to make the recommendations. Recall that you specified that the recommender class make three recommendations for User2. Right-click on the UserRecommender class and choose Run As ➤ Java Application, as shown in Figure 11-14.

Figure 11-14. *Running the UserRecommender application*

Three recommendations for User2 are listed. The recommendations are items 12, 13, and 14, as shown in Figure 11-15. The value assigned to each item's ID represents the strength of the preference. The most suitable recommendations have the highest values. For example, Item12 is most recommended.

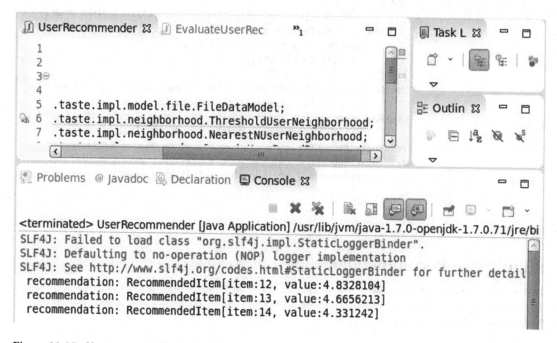

Figure 11-15. *User recommendations*

If you set the recommender to make only one recommendation, Item12 will be recommended in this case, as shown in Figure 11-16.

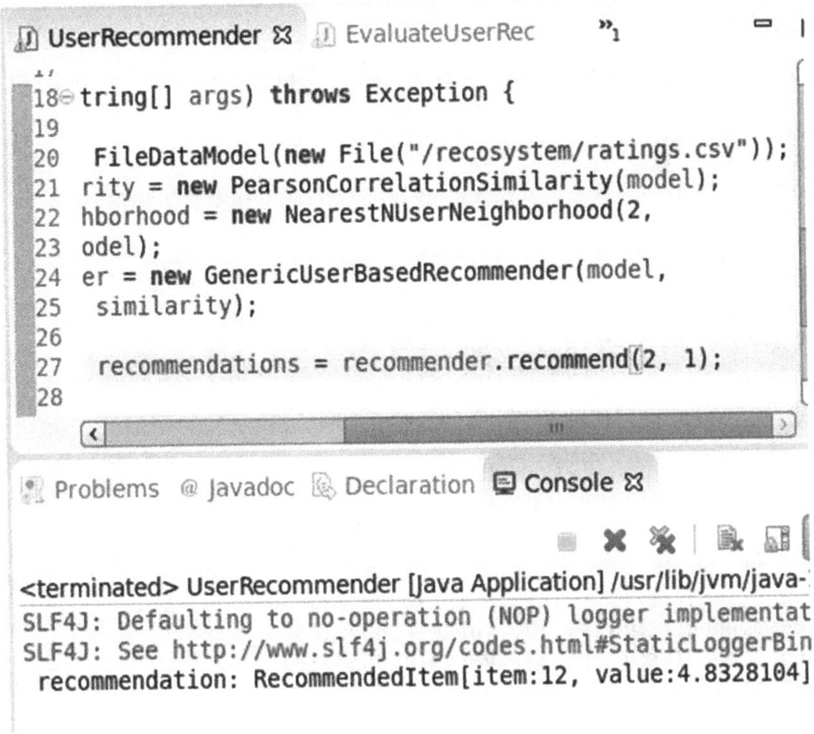

```
UserRecommender ⊠    EvaluateUserRec        »₁              —   |
18  tring[] args) throws Exception {
19
20    FileDataModel(new File("/recosystem/ratings.csv"));
21    rity = new PearsonCorrelationSimilarity(model);
22    hborhood = new NearestNUserNeighborhood(2,
23    odel);
24    er = new GenericUserBasedRecommender(model,
25      similarity);
26
27    recommendations = recommender.recommend(2, 1);
28
```

Problems @ Javadoc Declaration Console ⊠

```
<terminated> UserRecommender [Java Application] /usr/lib/jvm/java-
SLF4J: Defaulting to no-operation (NOP) logger implementat
SLF4J: See http://www.slf4j.org/codes.html#StaticLoggerBin
 recommendation: RecommendedItem[item:12, value:4.8328104]
```

Figure 11-16. Single recommendation for Item12

Choosing a Recommender Type

The recommendations can vary with the type of the recommender chosen. The most suitable recommender implementation, if all the ratings are available, is GenericUserBasedRecommender. If ratings are not available, use GenericBooleanPrefUserBasedRecommender. This example uses the GenericUserBasedRecommender recommender.

```
Recommender recommender = new GenericUserBasedRecommender(model,
                          neighborhood, similarity);
```

A RandomRecommender is also available to make random recommendations and preferences and is mostly used for novelty and benchmarking. For example, you could use a RandomRecommender instead of GenericUserBasedRecommender in the user-based recommender.

```
Recommender recommender = new RandomRecommender(model);
```

As a comparison, the recommendations with the GenericUserBasedRecommender are items 12, 13, and 14, with Item12 being the most preferred, as shown in Figure 11-17.

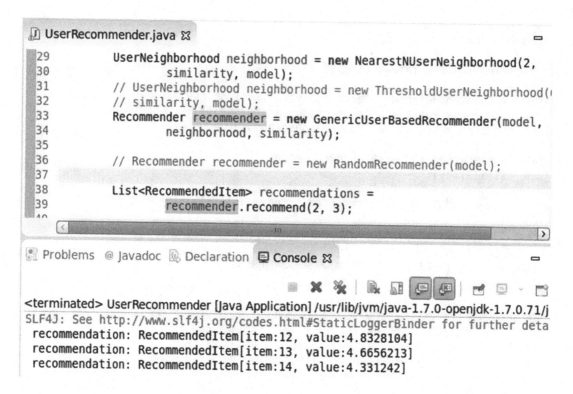

```
𝕁 UserRecommender.java ✕                                              ▭

29          UserNeighborhood neighborhood = new NearestNUserNeighborhood(2,
30                  similarity, model);
31          // UserNeighborhood neighborhood = new ThresholdUserNeighborhood(
32          // similarity, model);
33          Recommender recommender = new GenericUserBasedRecommender(model,
34                  neighborhood, similarity);
35
36          // Recommender recommender = new RandomRecommender(model);
37
38          List<RecommendedItem> recommendations =
39                  recommender.recommend(2, 3);
```

```
🖫 Problems   @ Javadoc   🗟 Declaration   🖳 Console ✕                    ▭

<terminated> UserRecommender [Java Application] /usr/lib/jvm/java-1.7.0-openjdk-1.7.0.71/j
SLF4J: See http://www.slf4j.org/codes.html#StaticLoggerBinder for further deta
 recommendation: RecommendedItem[item:12, value:4.8328104]
 recommendation: RecommendedItem[item:13, value:4.6656213]
 recommendation: RecommendedItem[item:14, value:4.331242]
```

Figure 11-17. *Recommendations with GenericUserBasedRecommender*

If the RandomRecommender is used, the recommendations are still items 12, 13, and 14, but the item with the highest preference is Item13, as shown in Figure 11-18. The recommendations happen to be the same as with the GenericUserBasedRecommender recommender, but they could be different.

```
🗋 UserRecommender.java ⊠                                              ▭
29          UserNeighborhood neighborhood = new NearestNUserNeighborhood(2,
30                  similarity, model);
31          // UserNeighborhood neighborhood = new ThresholdUserNeighborhood((
32          // similarity, model);
33          //Recommender recommender = new GenericUserBasedRecommender(model
34          //       neighborhood, similarity);
35
36          Recommender recommender = new RandomRecommender(model);
37
38          List<RecommendedItem> recommendations =
39                  recommender.recommend(2, 3);
```

```
🔖 Problems  @ Javadoc  🗟 Declaration  🖳 Console ⊠                       ▭
<terminated> UserRecommender [Java Application] /usr/lib/jvm/java-1.7.0-openjdk-1.7.0.71/j
 recommendation: RecommendedItem[item:12, value:3.3958733]
 recommendation: RecommendedItem[item:13, value:4.52554]
 recommendation: RecommendedItem[item:14, value:0.3753668]
```

Figure 11-18. Recommendations with RandomRecommender

Choosing a User Similarity Measure

The UserSimilarity implementation can also make a difference in how recommendations are made. The most suitable UserSimilarity if all ratings are available is PearsonCorrelationSimilarity, which was used here.

```
DataModel model = new FileDataModel(new File("/recosystem/ratings.csv"));
UserSimilarity similarity = new PearsonCorrelationSimilarity(model);
```

You can also use the EuclideanDistanceSimilarity implementation, which is based on the Euclidean distance between two users.

```
UserSimilarity similarity = new EuclideanDistanceSimilarity(model);
```

As a comparison, the recommendations by the PearsonCorrelationSimilarity similarity measure are items 12, 13, and 14, with Item12 being the most preferred, as shown in Figure 11-19.

```
recosystem/pom.xml        UserRecommender.java ⊠    EvaluateUserRecomm        ⊟
21
22        DataModel model = new FileDataModel(new File("/recosystem/ratings
23         UserSimilarity similarity = new PearsonCorrelationSimilarity(mod
24
25        //UserSimilarity similarity = new EuclideanDistanceSimilarity(mod
26
27        UserNeighborhood neighborhood = new NearestNUserNeighborhood(2,
28                similarity, model);
29        // UserNeighborhood neighborhood = new ThresholdUserNeighborhood(
30        // similarity, model);
31        Recommender recommender = new GenericUserBasedRecommender(model,
32                neighborhood, similarity);
```

```
  Problems   @ Javadoc   Declaration   Console ⊠                              ⊟

<terminated> UserRecommender [Java Application] /usr/lib/jvm/java-1.7.0-openjdk-1.7.0.71/j
 recommendation: RecommendedItem[item:12, value:4.8328104]
 recommendation: RecommendedItem[item:13, value:4.6656213]
 recommendation: RecommendedItem[item:14, value:4.331242]
```

Figure 11-19. *Recommendations with PearsonCorrelationSimilarity*

The recommendations by the EuclideanDistanceSimilarity similarity also happen to be items 12, 13, and 14, as shown in Figure 11-20. The preferences for each item are in the same order, but have slightly different values.

Figure 11-20. Recommendations with EuclideanDistanceSimilarity

Choosing a Neighborhood Type

The earlier example of running the recommender used the NearestNUserNeighborhood neighborhood type.

```
UserNeighborhood neighborhood = new NearestNUserNeighborhood
                           (2, similarity, model);
```

You can also use the ThresholdUserNeighborhood neighborhood type. Create a ThresholdUserNeighborhood object using a threshold of 0.1.

```
UserNeighborhood neighborhood = new ThresholdUserNeighborhood
                           (0.1, similarity, model);
```

The ThresholdUserNeighborhood recommender makes the same recommendations of items 12, 13, and 14, and the same item preferences, as shown in Figure 11-21.

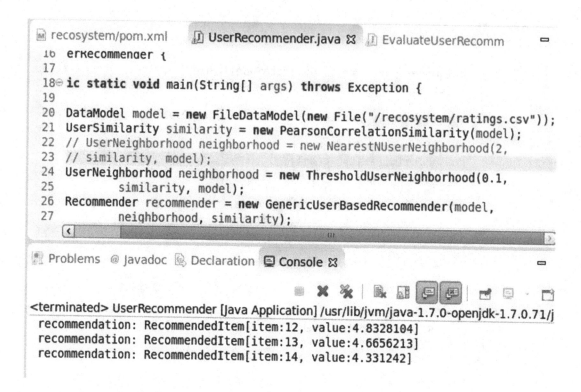

```
recosystem/pom.xml        UserRecommender.java ⊠    EvaluateUserRecomm    ▭
16  erkecommenaer {
17
18⊖ ic static void main(String[] args) throws Exception {
19
20  DataModel model = new FileDataModel(new File("/recosystem/ratings.csv"));
21  UserSimilarity similarity = new PearsonCorrelationSimilarity(model);
22  // UserNeighborhood neighborhood = new NearestNUserNeighborhood(2,
23  // similarity, model);
24  UserNeighborhood neighborhood = new ThresholdUserNeighborhood(0.1,
25           similarity, model);
26  Recommender recommender = new GenericUserBasedRecommender(model,
27           neighborhood, similarity);
```

```
Problems  @ Javadoc  Declaration  Console ⊠              ▭

<terminated> UserRecommender [Java Application] /usr/lib/jvm/java-1.7.0-openjdk-1.7.0.71/j
 recommendation: RecommendedItem[item:12, value:4.8328104]
 recommendation: RecommendedItem[item:13, value:4.6656213]
 recommendation: RecommendedItem[item:14, value:4.331242]
```

Figure 11-21. *Recommendations with the ThresholdUserNeighborhood neighborhood type*

Choosing a Neighborhood Size for NearestNUserNeighborhood

If the NearestNUserNeighborhood type is used, the neighborhood size can make a difference in the recommendations. For example, imagine you use a neighborhood size of 3 instead of 2:

```
UserNeighborhood neighborhood = new NearestNUserNeighborhood
                           (3, similarity, model);
```

The recommendations are still for items 12, 13, and 14, but the preference values and the order of preferences are different, as shown in Figure 11-22.

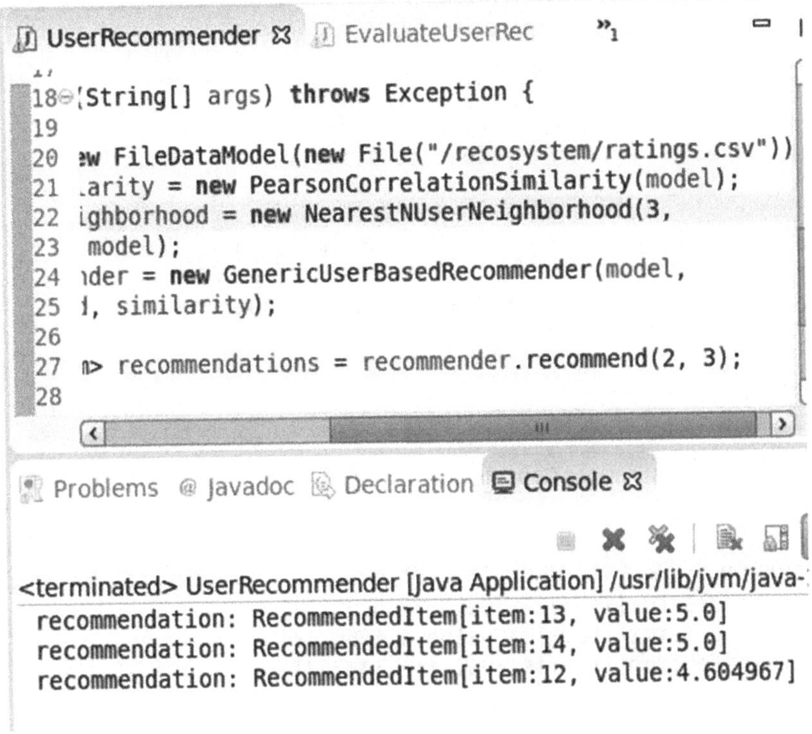

```
 UserRecommender ⊠   EvaluateUserRec      »₁         ▭   |

18⊖(String[] args) throws Exception {
19
20   ew FileDataModel(new File("/recosystem/ratings.csv"))
21   .arity = new PearsonCorrelationSimilarity(model);
22   ighborhood = new NearestNUserNeighborhood(3,
23   model);
24   ider = new GenericUserBasedRecommender(model,
25   i, similarity);
26
27   n> recommendations = recommender.recommend(2, 3);
28
```

 Problems @ Javadoc ⊠ Declaration ▣ Console ⊠

<terminated> UserRecommender [Java Application] /usr/lib/jvm/java-

```
recommendation: RecommendedItem[item:13, value:5.0]
recommendation: RecommendedItem[item:14, value:5.0]
recommendation: RecommendedItem[item:12, value:4.604967]
```

Figure 11-22. *Recommendations with a NearestNUserNeighborhood neighborhood size of 3*

Choosing a Threshold for ThresholdUserNeighborhood

If the ThresholdUserNeighborhood neighborhood is used, the threshold can make a difference in the recommendations. For example, consider a threshold of 0.2.

```
UserNeighborhood neighborhood = new ThresholdUserNeighborhood
                          (0.2, similarity, model);
```

Recommendations for items 12, 13, and 14 are again made, as shown in Figure 11-23.

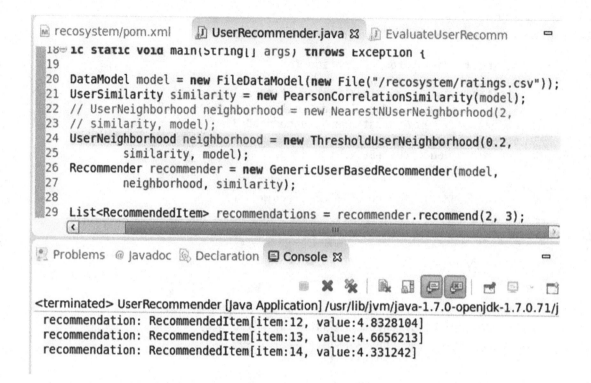

Figure 11-23. Recommendations with ThresholdUserNeighborhood set to 0.1

Now, lower the threshold to 0.05.

```
UserNeighborhood neighborhood = new ThresholdUserNeighborhood
                              (0.05, similarity, model);
```

The recommendations and preferences are the same, as shown in Figure 11-24.

```
recosystem/pom.xml        UserRecommender.java ☒      EvaluateUserRecomm          ▭

18○ ic static void main(String[] args) throws Exception {
19
20   DataModel model = new FileDataModel(new File("/recosystem/ratings.csv"));
21   UserSimilarity similarity = new PearsonCorrelationSimilarity(model);
22   // UserNeighborhood neighborhood = new NearestNUserNeighborhood(2,
23   // similarity, model);
24   UserNeighborhood neighborhood = new ThresholdUserNeighborhood(0.05,
25           similarity, model);
26   Recommender recommender = new GenericUserBasedRecommender(model,
27           neighborhood, similarity);
28
29   List<RecommendedItem> recommendations = recommender.recommend(2, 3);
```

```
  Problems  @ Javadoc   Declaration   Console ☒                                    ▭

                                        ▬  ✖  ✖  |  ▣  ▣  ▣  ▣  |  ▱  ▱  ▱  ▱

<terminated> UserRecommender [Java Application] /usr/lib/jvm/java-1.7.0-openjdk-1.7.0.71/j
  recommendation: RecommendedItem[item:12, value:4.8328104]
  recommendation: RecommendedItem[item:13, value:4.6656213]
  recommendation: RecommendedItem[item:14, value:4.331242]
```

Figure 11-24. *Recommendations with ThresholdUserNeighborhood set to 0.05*

Running the Evaluator

The quality of a recommender's recommendations is evaluated using a recommender evaluator, which is an implementation of RecommenderEvaluator. Earlier, you developed a AverageAbsoluteDifference RecommenderEvaluator-based evaluator class EvaluateUserRecommender using an 80/20 split between training data and test data. The evaluator returns a score with a minimum score of 0, which implies the best feasible evaluation. The lower the score returned by the evaluator, the better the recommendations. To run the EvaluateUserRecommender application, right-click on the EvaluateUserRecommender.java file in the Package Explorer and choose Run As ➤ Java Application, as shown in Figure 11-25.

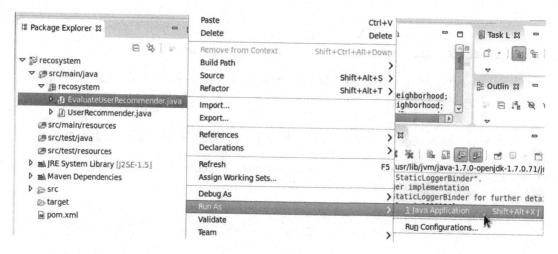

Figure 11-25. *Running the EvaluateUserRecommender application*

A score is returned based on how well the recommender recommends, as shown in Figure 11-26.

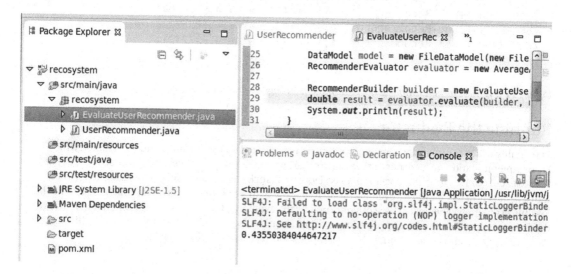

Figure 11-26. *Output from the EvaluateUserRecommender application*

The score returned could vary if the same application runs again. For example, in a second run of the application, the score is lower than the first run. A lower score implies a better recommender system, as shown in Figure 11-27.

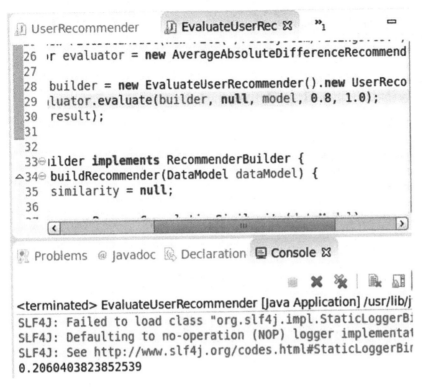

```
   UserRecommender        EvaluateUserRec ⊠      »1

26  ir evaluator = new AverageAbsoluteDifferenceRecommend
27
28  builder = new EvaluateUserRecommender().new UserReco
29  iluator.evaluate(builder, null, model, 0.8, 1.0);
30  result);
31
32
33⊖ilder implements RecommenderBuilder {
△34⊖ buildRecommender(DataModel dataModel) {
35  similarity = null;
36
```

```
  Problems  @ Javadoc  ⓖ Declaration  🖳 Console ⊠

<terminated> EvaluateUserRecommender [Java Application] /usr/lib/j
SLF4J: Failed to load class "org.slf4j.impl.StaticLoggerB:
SLF4J: Defaulting to no-operation (NOP) logger implementa1
SLF4J: See http://www.slf4j.org/codes.html#StaticLoggerBi
0.2060403823852539
```

Figure 11-27. Running the EvaluateUserRecommender application again to generate a lower score

A third run could produce an even different score. It is best to run the recommender evaluator a few times to evaluate the recommender, as shown in Figure 11-28.

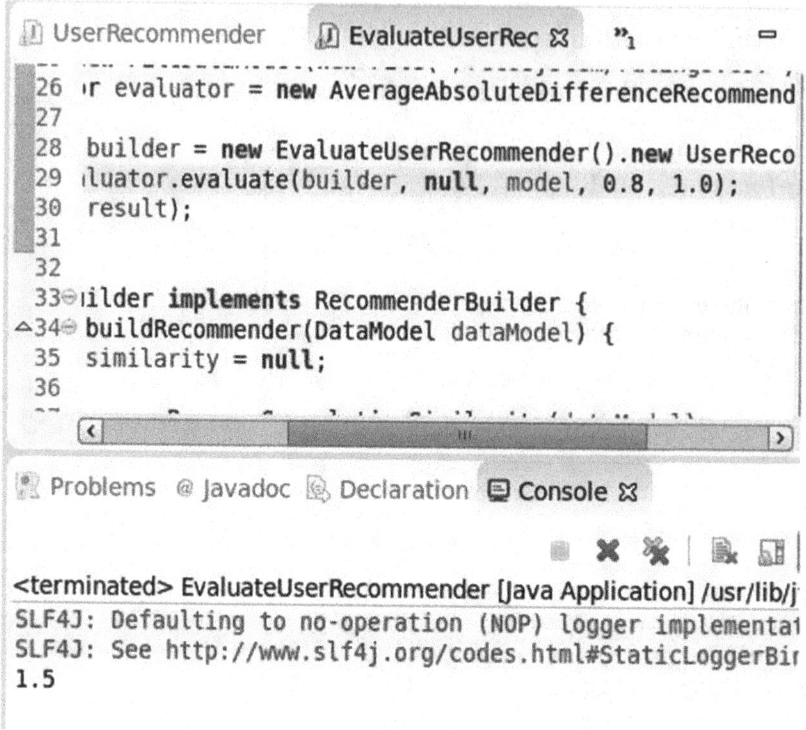

```
   UserRecommender        EvaluateUserRec 23      "1

26  'r evaluator = new AverageAbsoluteDifferenceRecommend
27
28  builder = new EvaluateUserRecommender().new UserReco
29  luator.evaluate(builder, null, model, 0.8, 1.0);
30  result);
31
32
33  ilder implements RecommenderBuilder {
34  buildRecommender(DataModel dataModel) {
35  similarity = null;
36
```

```
   Problems  @ Javadoc   Declaration   Console 23
```

```
<terminated> EvaluateUserRecommender [Java Application] /usr/lib/j
SLF4J: Defaulting to no-operation (NOP) logger implementa1
SLF4J: See http://www.slf4j.org/codes.html#StaticLoggerBir
1.5
```

Figure 11-28. *Running the EvaluateUserRecommender application a third time to generate a different score*

Choosing the Split Between Training Percentage and Test Percentage

It's best to use most of the sample data for training. Typically, 80-90% of the sample data is used for training. The percentage of training data you use can make a slight difference in the recommender's performance. For this example, use a training data percentage of 0.8, as was used in the earlier recommender example.

```
double result = evaluator.evaluate(builder, null, model, 0.8, 1.0);
System.out.println(result);
```

An evaluation score of about 0.40 is produced, as shown in Figure 11-29.

Figure 11-29. *Evaluation score using a training percentage of 80%*

Now run the evaluator with a training percentage of 0.9.

```
double result = evaluator.evaluate(builder, null, model, 0.9, 1.0);
System.out.println(result);
```

A slightly higher score of about 0.45 is returned, as shown in Figure 11-30. The score can vary slightly with each run.

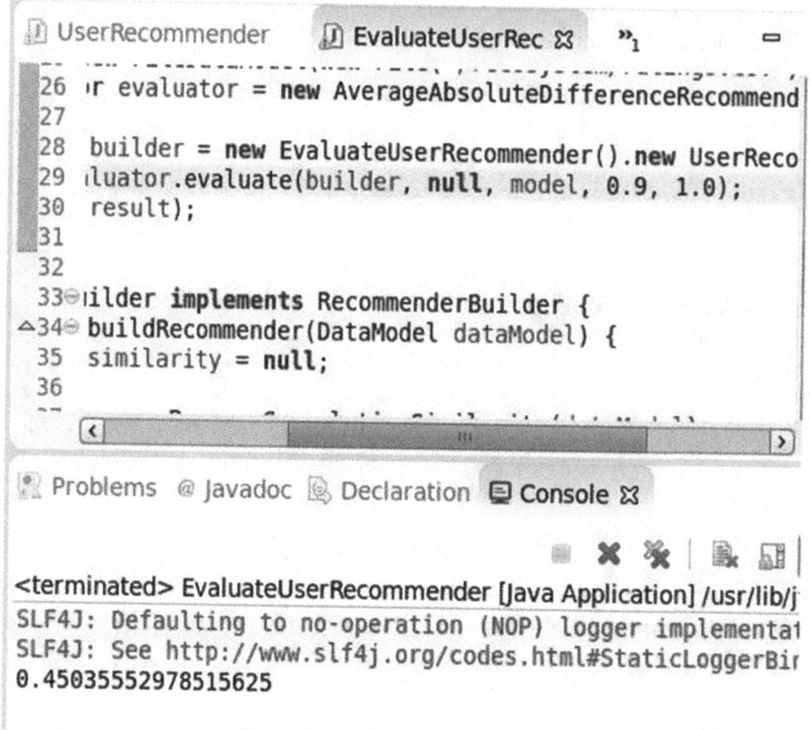

```
 UserRecommender       EvaluateUserRec ⊠    "₁          ▭

 26  ır evaluator = new AverageAbsoluteDifferenceRecommend
 27
 28  builder = new EvaluateUserRecommender().new UserReco
 29  luator.evaluate(builder, null, model, 0.9, 1.0);
 30  result);
 31
 32
 33 ⊖ıilder implements RecommenderBuilder {
△34 ⊖ buildRecommender(DataModel dataModel) {
 35  similarity = null;
 36

 ◀                      |||                              ▶
```

```
 Problems  @ Javadoc  Declaration  Console ⊠

                                    ▬ ✖ ✖  ▣ ▨

<terminated> EvaluateUserRecommender [Java Application] /usr/lib/j
SLF4J: Defaulting to no-operation (NOP) logger implementa1
SLF4J: See http://www.slf4j.org/codes.html#StaticLoggerBi1
0.45035552978515625
```

Figure 11-30. Evaluation score using a training percentage of 90%

Summary

This chapter introduced Apache Mahout. The examples ran sample scripts to model sample data using classification and clustering algorithms. The chapter also developed a user-based recommender system using the Mahout Java API. This chapter concludes the book on Apache Hadoop ecosystems. The Hadoop ecosystem has many more projects than can be discussed in a single book. Some NoSQL databases such as Couchbase and MongoDB, which are in the Hadoop ecosystem, are discussed in separate books; check out the Apress books *Pro Couchbase Development* and *Pro MongoDB Development* for more information.

Index

A

AllocateRequest, 27
Alter command, 250
ALTER TABLE statement, 227–228
AMRMProtocol, 72
Apache Avro
  binary data serialization, 303
  environment variables, 304–305
  fields, 305
  Hadoop tar file, 304
  in HDFS, 314
  heap space, 308
  Hive external table, 310, 314
  installation directory, 311
  SELECT statement, 313
  software, 303
  versions, 307–308
  wlslogavr, 312
  wlslog_avro table, 309
  wlslog.avsc file, 305–306
Apache Flume, 288
  architecture, 287
  configuring, 292–293, 295, 297
  environment variables, 289
  Hadoop configuration, 289–290
  HBase configuration, 291
  HBase table creation, 292
  HDFS directory, 291
  log file, 288
  memory, 287
  sink component, 287
Apache Hadoop, 210, 288
  ecosystem, 4
  filesystem, 5
  key/value pairs, 5
  large-scale computation models, 5
  map() function, 5
  MapReduce, 5
  medium-to-large files, 5

Apache HBase, 288
  altering a table, 250
  architecture, 233
  configuring Hive, 239
  data to table, 242–243
  deleting, table row, 251
  disabling and enabling, table, 253
  environment variables, 235–236
  exists command, 254–255
  GETs/PUTs, 233
  Hadoop configuration, 236–237
  Hive table, 255–257
  installation, 235
  list command, 244
  Oracle Linux, 234
  row of data, 244–245
  scalable database, 233
  software, 234
  start-hbase.sh, 240
  table column deletion, 252–253
  table dropping, 254
  tar file, 235
  truncating, 254
Apache Hive
  architecture, 209
  CLI shell, 209
  configuring, 213
  database creation, 216
  database to use, 217
  environment setting, 210–211
  external table, 229–231
  LOAD DATA statement, 221
  metadata, 210
  metastore, 209
Apache Kafka
  architecture, 339
  auto.create.topics.enable, 345
  consumer, 345
  Created topic, 344
  environment setting, 340–341

© Deepak Vohra 2016
D. Vohra, *Practical Hadoop Ecosystem*, DOI 10.1007/978-1-4842-2199-0

Get the eBook for only $5!

Why limit yourself?

Now you can take the weightless companion with you wherever you go and access your content on your PC, phone, tablet, or reader.

Since you've purchased this print book, we're happy to offer you the eBook in all 3 formats for just $5.

Convenient and fully searchable, the PDF version enables you to easily find and copy code—or perform examples by quickly toggling between instructions and applications. The MOBI format is ideal for your Kindle, while the ePUB can be utilized on a variety of mobile devices.

To learn more, go to www.apress.com/companion or contact support@apress.com.

Printed in the United States
By Bookmasters